EUROPE SINCE 1980

This book tells the dramatic story of the economic, social, political, and cultural transformation of Europe during the transition from the Cold War to the European Union. Ivan Berend charts, in particular, the overwhelming impact of the collapse of communism on every aspect of European life. Europe became safer and more united, and Central and Eastern Europe started on the difficult road to economic modernization. However, the western half of Europe also changed. European integration gained momentum. The single market and the common currency were introduced, and the Union enlarged from nine to twenty-seven countries. This period also saw a revolution in information and communication technology, the increasing impact of globalization, and the radical restructuring of the political system. The book explores the impact of all of these changes as well as the new challenges posed by the economic crisis of 2008–9 and asks which way now for Europe?

IVAN T. BEREND is Distinguished Professor of History at the University of California, Los Angeles, and member of the British Academy and six European Academies of Sciences. His numerous publications include *From the Soviet Bloc to the European Union* (2009), *An Economic History of Twentieth-Century Europe* (2006), and *History Derailed: Central and Eastern Europe in the "Long" Nineteenth Century* (2003).

THE WORLD
Since 1980

This new series is designed to examine politics, economics, and social change in important countries and regions over the past three decades. No prior background knowledge of a given country is required by readers. The books are written by leading social scientists.

Titles in the series

EUROPE
Since 1980

Ivan T. Berend

CAMBRIDGE
UNIVERSITY PRESS

CAMBRIDGE UNIVERSITY PRESS
Cambridge, New York, Melbourne, Madrid, Cape Town, Singapore,
São Paulo, Delhi, Dubai, Tokyo

Cambridge University Press
The Edinburgh Building, Cambridge CB2 8RU, UK

Published in the United States of America by Cambridge University Press, New York

www.cambridge.org
Information on this title: www.cambridge.org/9780521129176

© Ivan T. Berend 2010

First published 2010

Printed in the United Kingdom at the University Press, Cambridge

A catalogue record for this publication is available from the British Library

ISBN 978-0-521-11240-6 hardback
ISBN 978-0-521-12917-6 paperback

Contents

Illustrations

Credits: Photographs courtesy of the Photo Archive of the Hungarian News Agency unless otherwise stated.

Tables

Acknowledgements

I should like to express my gratitude and thanks to those who contributed to my work on this volume. First, I thank Michael Watson, Editor at Cambridge University Press, with whom I have worked harmoniously for years on the books I have previously published with Cambridge, and who initiated this exciting enterprise. As always, I am also grateful to the anonymous reviewers at Cambridge University Press who called my attention to important issues and helped my work with invaluable advice.

The University of California, Los Angeles, my intellectual home for two decades, also has to be mentioned here. Besides its intellectual environment, UCLA offers the limitless resources of the superb Charles E. Young Research Library, as well as generous research grants from the International Institute, which helped me to realize this project.

Finally, I am, as always, most indebted to my wife, Kati, who is the best reviewer, editor, advisor, and help at every stage of my work. She is the best partner for discussing and debating conceptual questions, performing practical library work, and for critical reading of drafts. She tolerated it when I transformed our evening hours and weekends into work hours and days – partly since that gave her time to work undisturbed on her own drawings and paintings.

Ivan T. Berend

Introduction

Why write a book called *Europe since 1980*? What is Europe? And why focus on 1980? Was 1980 a turning point in the history of the old continent?[1] This volume attempts to answer these questions, pointing to both global changes and unique European developments that were the main factors, as manifold as they were interrelated, in the dawning of a new historical period.

The first of these factors in order of importance, though not in chronological order, was *the collapse of communism and the Soviet Union, and consequently the division of Europe.* This had an overwhelming impact on every aspect of post-1990–1 Europe. Europe became a safer place and more united. A failed system disappeared and half of the continent emerged onto the road of a difficult but promising transformation. However, the western half of Europe also changed. The half-century-long rivalry between capitalism and socialism during the Cold War influenced Western society and politics. Besides the very visible arms race and the sometimes hysterical witch-hunting, the challenge of socialism inspired social awareness as well as a "social market" policy. This political competition had a long history, stemming from Chancellor Otto Bismarck's social insurance policy that he instituted to take the wind out of the sails of the rising social democratic movement in late-nineteenth-century Germany.

The decades following World War II were a period of breakthrough for social solidarity. While this development emerged partly as a legacy

---

[1] 1980 is a somewhat symbolic and arbitrary date for the turning point. In history, except for major revolutionary explosions, it is quite rare to connect major transformations to a single year. Europe began transforming economically, socially, culturally, and politically in the late 1970s, and it continued to do so throughout the 1980s.

of the Great Depression and war, the Cold War also played a role. While reformers in the East dreamed about "socialism with a human face," flexible Western capitalism institutionalized certain controls and checks on the social impacts of the market after World War II, and the system became more human than ever before. Of course, it is also true that deregulation and the impact of the so-called Anglo-Saxon model of capitalism gained ground from the 1980s on and reversed some of the previous developments.

The collapse of socialism and the triumph of Western democracies and the market system eliminated outside political pressure and competition. The capitalist market system became global and increasingly deregulated. Hazardous risk-taking and speculation gained ground. Whereas the regulated market system subordinated the economy to society, the deregulated market system subordinated society to the economy. This trend became dominant in the United States from the 1980s on. The attempts to privatize the American national parks and the social security system, which were undertaken by the Newt Gingrich-led Republican Congress and by the second Bush administration, respectively, were clear symbolic signals of this trend. The 2008–9 international financial crisis might be interpreted as an outcome of these changes as neo-liberal deregulation spread from America to Europe. Twenty years, however, are historically too short a period for a well-based evaluation of the consequences of the elimination of rivalry between competing systems.

All of these transformations and events were closely connected with the main international and European trends of the age, among them the technological revolution, or as it is more often called, *the revolution in information and communication technology*, a historical change comparable only to the British industrial revolution. As I will argue, the technological revolution played the central economic role in the collapse of communism because the Soviet Bloc countries were unable to follow in the technological transformation, making them terminally backward and vulnerable. In indirect ways, the technological revolution thus contributed to the reshaping of Europe. Besides radically transforming the economies of Europe, technological development also contributed to the change of demographic trends via medical and pharmaceutical technology, and also influenced the social fabric by causing a major restructuring of the occupational structure and class relations. Modern technology fundamentally changed everyday culture and entertainment as well.

Although strongly connected to technological transformation, *globalization* deserves a separate mention. This highly controversial and debated change emerged from the 1980s on as the outcome of a gradual quantitative development of world trade and financial transactions. It was also an outcome of corporate and managerial developments, and of the gradual rise to power of multi-functional and multinational companies. In this respect, globalization is the consequence of the development of market capitalism. This trend gained ground alongside rising industrial and financial capitalism in the late nineteenth century, which was a globalizing, though not fully globalized, system. Although its backlash in the interwar decades halted and reversed this trend, it reemerged after World War II and broke through from the 1980s on.

On the other hand, globalization is also a deliberate policy that gradually emerged after the postwar collapse of colonialism. The market and labor-seeking investments of multinational companies led to the foundation of subsidiaries throughout the world. The deregulated financial system penetrated the global economy, and venture capital funds replaced solid business activities and made enormous profits. The impact of globalization is far-reaching, influencing both winners and losers. Its economic consequences opened a new chapter in the advanced world, but they also did so in the transforming countries of the Eastern half of the continent, and in some of the former developing countries. It increased the flow of goods, capital, and labor in such a significant way that foreign direct investments transformed entire regions, partly by further enriching the advanced countries, but also by driving forward in an unheard-of way the process of catching up in some of the well-prepared less developed countries. Consequently, migration also became a central economic and socio-political issue.

The ideological impact of globalization also became global, resulting in a triumphant neo-liberal takeover and a conservative upsurge from the 1980s on, as well as the negation of the philosophical assumptions of the Enlightenment and the spreading of new postmodern cultural trends. The political party system was also radically restructured, including the rise of "catch-all" and populist parties.

The three decades around the turn of the twenty-first century, however, were a period of clashing and struggling trends. The spread of neo-liberal market fundamentalism generated powerful resistance, and the European Union successfully defended its Social Europe project, introducing a cohesion policy to counterbalance brute market forces and their polarizing impact by redistributing income and assisting backward regions.

Moreover, if the triumph of neo-liberal ideology and policy might be said to have originated in the dual crises of the 1960s and 1970s, the new major financial crisis of 2008–9 and its consequences might signal the end of neo-liberal dominance. The previous crisis caused the failure of Keynesian economics, but the 2008–9 crisis appears to have brought about the failure of neo-liberal economics and its Reaganite–Thatcherite realization. Has the circle closed? Will Europe return to a regulated market system?

Before the 1980s, it was commonplace in Europe to think that the state had to play an important role in the economy, and that it had to counterbalance the negative social impacts of the market. The unparalleled postwar European boom was the period of the big state, the mixed economy, and the building of the welfare state. After 1980, the state was disqualified as "being the problem, not the solution." The Cold War victory of the West inspired a triumphant ideological *Zeitgeist* of "de-statization." The 2008–9 financial crisis challenged this view. Nothing may illustrate that better than one of the spring editorials in the conservative publication *The Economist*. The journal, though it "stands firmly on the side of the liberal Anglo-Saxon model," registered the satisfaction of Europe that the idea that "their economies are sclerotic, over-regulated and too state dominated," which America and Britain consistently preached to them, became questionable after the global economic meltdown. "Rather than challenge *dirigisme*, the British and Americans are busy following it . . . Getting regulation right matters as much as freeing up markets; an efficient public sector may count as much as an efficient private one."[2] However, it is an open question whether this is a transitory change that will not last for long, or if it is the beginning of a new epoch with a new economic paradigm.

The interrelated trends of technological change, globalization, and the collapse of communism in the Eastern half of the continent opened a new chapter in the *European integration process*. The end of the de facto existence of "two Europes," and sharp worldwide competition in a strongly free-trade world system, led to a most impressive new development: the rise of the European Economic Community. The original Community of six countries was founded in 1957, expanded

[2] "A New Pecking Order," *The Economist*, May 9–15, 2009, 13.

in 1973 to include three new members, but then experienced an unparalleled and still open-ended enlargement process from the 1980s on that increased its numbers from nine to twenty-seven member countries, with seven candidates and potential candidates still waiting in line, most of them belonging to the peripheries of the continent. Such a feverish enlargement process sets new questions about the borders of Europe.

So, *what is Europe?* The traditional geographical content of the term is clear, but it is an insufficient answer to the question. When the European Community was established, the six founding countries were similar in an economic, social, and cultural sense. Since 1980, countries came forward to join that were mostly from the European peripheries: the Iberian Peninsula, the Balkans, and Eastern Europe. Economically they were much less developed, and had different historical, political, and cultural backgrounds. The half-millennium Ottoman rule in the Balkans, and its Greek Orthodox cultural characteristics, caused important differences. Many historians believe that the Greek-Orthodox borderline separates Europe into two differing worlds. Are the countries East of that dividing line able to fit into a homogenous European Union? Geography does not help to answer this question. Turkey's application and candidacy especially challenged the geographic concept because, except for a small edge at Istanbul, the bulk of the country, which includes 95 percent of its population and its capital city, are all geographically outside of Europe. Furthermore, several West European countries, *viz.*, Spain, France, and Italy, have traditionally had much closer connections with countries on the southern rim of the Mediterranean Sea than with the Balkans. Does the so-called "Mediterranean challenge" for the European Union reformulate the answer to the question on Europe, and suggest the inclusion of the entire Mediterranean Basin, North Africa, and the Middle East? Russia's location in Euro-Asia itself challenges the geographical definition. Some of the southern republics of the former Soviet Union, now independent states, are within traditional geographic Europe, but different in most other respects.

What is Europe? The old member countries of the European Union answered this question by rejecting a geographic interpretation. They considered historical factors, as well as economic, political, and cultural ties and interests. According to this view, Europe is a civilization project, based on the legacy of Judeo-Christian, Greco-Roman, Renaissance, and Reformation values. Industrial civilization originating in the British industrial revolution also offers a common base, together with civilized political arrangements embodied in the legacy of the Treaty of Westphalia. These legacies are called Western civilization. However, Europe has violated these values and principles thousands of times through vicious intolerance, inquisitions, bloody wars, ethnic cleansings, and genocides. The history of twentieth-century Europe tragically exhibited all the flaws of this civilization. As Tony Judt argues, while Europe creates "heritage sites" and memorial "chambers of historical horrors," it also wants to forget the twentieth century, as the subtitle to his volume suggests, in the hope that "all of *that* is now behind us."[3]

The 2003 draft constitution of the European Union speaks about "religious and humanistic traditions," and "overcoming old divisions," without even mentioning wars and ethnic cleansings. However, it is not enough to try to forget. "In spite of cooperation the Europeans will not achieve integration and a collective identity as long as their national images of memory diverge."[4]

The European project has still been based on those cherished and selected Western values originating in its heritage, even if it is still a work in progress. That set of values forms a common cultural base in spite of the multitude of cultures and languages, and different historical experiences. The European project is the outcome of being in a permanent state of change, accommodating several waves of external effects, among them a number of invading "barbarians," and during its entire history it has absorbed various ethnic and cultural influences.

Europe is a continent of the willing. Nation-states emerged 200 years ago because of the population's *will* to become one nation. Friedrich Meinecke, the leading German historian, concluded his study on the origins of the German nation-state by stating: "a nation is a community that *wishes* to be a nation."[5] This statement proved to be true throughout the nineteenth and twentieth centuries, including the end of the last century, when several new independent

---

[3] Tony Judt, *Reappraisals: Reflections on the Forgotten Twentieth Century* (New York: Penguin Press, 2008), 4.

[4] K. H. Jarausch and T. Lindenberger, quoting J. Fried, "Erinnerung und Vergessen," *Historische Zeitschrift* (2001), 273, in "Contours of a Critical History of Contemporary Europe: A Transnational Agenda," in K. H. Jarausch and T. Lindenberger (eds.), *Conflicted Memories: Europeanizing Contemporary Histories* (New York: Berghahn Books, 2007), 1.

[5] Friedrich Meinecke, *Weltbürgertum und Nationalstaat: Studien zur Genesis des deutschen Nationalstaates* (Munich: R. Oldenbourg, 1908), 9.

nation-states were established, some of them without historical predecessors. What happened to the nation-state would happen to Europe
as well. What the continent needs is the will to be a European nation.
Europe, according to this concept, belongs to those who want to
belong to Europe: "Europe is not the mere representation of a geographical or historical reality. Europe is better understood as the ema-
nation of the *will* of those who sense that they belong to it."[6]

The "widening" process of the European Union incorporated
countries with highly different economic and social levels. Nevertheless, the history of the Union is the history of an effort to homogenize
Europe. A successful cohesion policy assisted the elevation of several
backward regions to the level of the Western core. A parallel process
of a decisive "deepening" of economic integration also made great
progress towards establishing a single market and a common currency.
Further political integration also acquired major new incentives. The
European social model and the postwar welfare state, though they were
challenged and curbed several times, were ultimately preserved. The
new and permanently transforming European Union altered the face
of Europe. In the long run, it promises a much more homogenized
continent.

The question of Turkey, a strongly *willing* applicant of the European
Union, is central for the future of Europe. However, the people and
political elites of Europe are strongly divided about its acceptance.
Turkey introduced major reforms to adjust to European norms. For
half a century, it has been a solid part of the Western military alliance,
NATO. The Kemalist legacy of westernizing Turkey has been alive
for nearly a century. The country not only changed the alphabet of its
state language after World War I, but it also established a secular state
in an Islamic country. It was part of Europe for centuries, participating
in its wars and making alliances and trade connections. The destiny of
Turkey is probably to be a bridge between Europe and the neighboring
Islamic world.

According to opposing views, however, Turkey's non-European
cultural-political heritage, and the potential danger of the rise of its
fundamentalist Islamic opposition, combined with its huge population
and the backwardness of its economy, might undermine Europe's
economy and identity. This may endanger the development towards

---

[6] Robert Maclennan, "Foreword," in Guido Snel (ed.), *Alter Ego: Twenty Confronting Views
on the European Experience* (Amsterdam University Press, 2004), 9. Italics added.

a more homogenized and integrated unit, and the possibility of a European nation.

The debates are far from being concluded. Turkey, though a serious and legal candidate of the European Union, was not part of Europe in the period 1980–2010. Hence only the question of Turkey, and not the discussion of Turkey itself, belongs to the story of this volume.

With or without the Turkish question, the "European Project" has been a heatedly debated issue from the 1960s to the present. On the one hand, a powerful political and intellectual camp believes in, and works on, an ongoing "federalization process." Though it has a centuries-long history, national consciousness and identity, they argue, were artificially created, and so it is equally possible to build up a European identity. As one of its proponents argues, if there is an Indian nation, Europe can also emerge as a nation. Europe is indeed becoming more and more homogenous. Young people are spending more time in other European countries, and they are increasingly cosmopolitan, or European. The educational systems are more harmonized. History textbooks have dropped hostile, nationalist interpretations of the European past, and they use standardized images to illustrate dramatic events in the past. University diplomas have general European validity. European student exchanges, youth summer camps, and even transnational relationships and intermarriages forge closer ties. The European consumption model and way of life is becoming increasingly standardized. Transnational shopping has become an everyday experience in border zones. People are buying retirement homes in other countries, and two-thirds of the people spend vacations abroad. "Transnational links and hybrid identities could in the future form a new basis for European – rather than nation-state – integration."[7] Besides the single market and common currency, the way towards a federal future may be paved by common symbols, the European passport, and joint institutions such as an elected president, a common foreign policy, and a joint army. If some countries are not ready to go down the federalizing road, a two-tier structure seems to be an alternative for many, uniting those who are ready, while others remain in the second tier. In such a structure, the slowest-moving, hesitant, and "euro-skeptical" members would not determine the development of the European Union. A rapidly further integrating core, open to all other members to join, would reach the goal more easily.

[7] Karen Schönwälder, "Integration from Below? Migration and European Contemporary History," in Jarausch and Lindenberger (eds.), Conflicted Memories, 154–63, 160.

An equally, or even more powerful camp, however, rejects the federalization project, or has serious doubts about its reality. Europe never was a *Gemeinschaft*, it is "a conflictual space of existence rather than a chosen place to belong."[8] They maintain that the "illusion of Europe" cannot survive a continent-wide test, and a liberal order throughout Europe is much more important and realistic than federalizing part of the continent. While economic integration is serving a common European interest well, political integration – as several influential political groups maintain – is colliding head-on with national interests. Enlargement of the Union, argues the opposition, went too far and has to stop. The voting down of the European Constitution in France and the Netherlands was mostly rooted in these considerations. Several influential politicians and parties, and in some countries the majority of the population, worry about a further "deepening" of the integration towards a federal Europe. They speak about over-ambitious, utopian ideas that may even undermine Europe's achievements and lead to its disintegration, and which thus have to be dropped.

The description and analysis of these complex social, economic, political, and cultural transformations forms the content of this volume. An epilogue looks to the future. What happens if existing internal and international trends continue? Will Europe rise as a superpower? Will regional disparities wither away? Will the development of the "ever closer union" lead to the creation of a European nation and federal rearrangement, or will overexpansion and discord endanger the existence of the Union? Will the grim prophecies of decay and degradation turn out to be realities? Several alternatives are concealed in the future, and no one is able to answer these questions. But is it appropriate to forecast by extrapolating trends from the present? My answer to this question as a historian is negative. I think, however, that trying to look at various prospects may serve to give us a better understanding of the present and of the requirements of the future.

---

[8] Michael Geyer, "The Subject(s) of Europe," in Jarausch and Lindenberger (eds.), *Conflicted Memories*, 254–80, 274.

1

Europe Approaches the 1980s: The Dual Crises (1968–80)

World War II, the most shocking historical and demographic catastrophe in European history, undermined Europe's position in the world. About 40 million Europeans perished, and huge parts of the continent were left in ruins. At their postwar nadir, the combined Gross Domestic Product of Austria, Germany, Italy, Belgium, and France had declined to less than half its prewar level. Bombing and street fights fatally destroyed Berlin, Dresden, Hamburg, Leningrad, Warsaw, and Budapest. The population of the Soviet Union, Poland, and Yugoslavia was literally decimated, the European Jewry was nearly eliminated, and tens of millions of people were uprooted. Devastation, inflation, and starvation left Europe on its knees.

Moreover, the clouds of a rising new conflict darkened the horizon at the end of the war. A creeping Cold War, with conflict and confrontation between wartime allies, brought uncertainty and fear to the shocked continent. The Soviet Union occupied and soon sovietized the countries east of the River Elbe that it had liberated from Nazi German and local fascist rule. The Eastern half of the continent was isolated from the West by a Soviet-type economic system and social–political regime and formed separate Soviet-led economic and military arrangements. In terms of trade, travel, and communication, exchange between the two halves of Europe was limited to a minimum. Several people believed that Stalin wanted to enlarge his buffer zone by occupying additional parts of the continent. The Berlin crisis in the spring of 1948, when the Soviet Union blocked surface connection between the Western occupation zones of Germany to West Berlin, brought the possibility of armed conflict to within arm's length.

Postwar Europe was not one homogenous continent but separated into two hostile halves, East and West. In reality, there were not only two, but even three Europes. In the Mediterranean region – in Spain, Portugal, and Greece – the right-wing authoritarian regimes or military dictatorships left over from the interwar period were preserved and dominated. Some of these regimes were former allies of Hitler. These countries remained political pariahs in the democratic Western Europe, which excluded them. They followed an isolationist policy of self-sufficiency. However, the logic of the Cold War soon led to their incorporation into the Western system of alliances and institutions. Postwar European history comprises three different, though closely connected, histories.

The West emerged from its ruins on the road to democracy and economic prosperity. The United States played an important role in this, and had a strong influence on European lifestyle, consumption patterns, and new cultural trends. In a paradoxical way, the euphoric postwar prosperity and consumerism undermined itself after a quarter of a century and generated a major crisis beginning in the late 1960s and continuing through the 1970s and 1980s.

The Right and Left dictatorial regimes in the peripheries followed different roads. In the Mediterranean region, gradual erosion of the dictatorships undermined those regimes, eventually ending their isolation, and prepared the way for the ensuing collapse of the dictatorial regimes after the deaths of the dictators. The Eastern half of the continent ran amok trying to modernize and compete with the West in an arms race. Industrialization and social restructuring had major results, but oppression and authoritarian control of the population, and the repeated Soviet military interventions to suppress revolts, alienated great parts of the population and entire countries. In the end, and notwithstanding tremendous sacrifices, the Soviet Bloc simply reproduced backwardness and generated explosive dissatisfaction. Revolts and reforms weakened the system in some of the countries. The regimes gradually eroded and drifted at an increasing pace towards the collapse that happened only at the end of the 1980s.

Strangely enough, the three different postwar European roads and histories merged and turned in a similar direction: towards a major crisis in the late 1960s and early 1970s, and then radical and comprehensive change beginning in the 1980s.

The Western Phoenix Rising Again

After World War II, as it had done during the war, Western Europe badly needed American help to recover and secure itself both militarily and economically. The United States administration was ready to assist to curb the communist danger. In 1948 the Marshall Plan offered major aid for further European reconstruction, and in the following year most of the West European countries and the United States signed the agreement forming the North Atlantic Treaty Organization (NATO), the American-led military alliance that created a nuclear shield and security.

The *Pax Americana* made the United States the unchallenged world leader and the mentor of Western Europe. Against the communist challenge, the United States wanted to strengthen Western Europe by forming a United States of Europe, as Winston Churchill (in 1946) and Allen Dulles (in 1948) had suggested, and as the Marshall Aid program actually initiated.[1] The Marshall Plan, besides its main goal of assisting reconstruction, nurtured a new spirit and institutional framework for European cooperation. By April 1948, the sixteen-country Organization for European Economic Cooperation (OEEC) began operating. This organization determined how to use American aid, worked out the reconstruction program for the continent, and decided on trade liberalization and the formation of a payment union.

Under America's wing, the Netherlands, Belgium, Luxembourg, France, Germany, and Italy decided to unify their coal and steel economies under supranational governance and so formed the European Coal and Steel Community in 1952. The six countries soon wanted to go even further down the road to integration, and they established the European Economic Community of 160 million people in 1957. By 1968, they had abolished all tariffs and other trade restrictions and created a unified market. In ten years, trade among member countries increased four-fold and represented half of their foreign trade. Success attracted other countries as well: Britain, Ireland, and Denmark joined in 1973.

---

[1] Winston Churchill, "The Tragedy of Europe," [1946] *His Complete Speeches, 1897–1963*, vol. 7 [1974], in Brent F. Nelsen and Alexander C.-G. Stubb (eds.), *The European Union: Readings on the Theory and Practice of European Integration* (Boulder, CO: Lynne Rienner, 1998), 7–11; Allen Dulles, *The Marshall Plan* (Houndmills: Palgrave Macmillan, 1948).

With the assistance of the United States, the world's technology leader and its strongest economic power, European recovery went beyond mere success and in fact achieved the greatest prosperity Europe had ever enjoyed: Western Europe increased its national income by two-and-a-half times between 1950 and 1973. The most important "secret" of the economic boom was the possibility of using an *extensive* development policy, i.e., combining existing technology with huge labor input. In the given situation, Europe was able to build upon the newest and most advanced American technology, which was easily accessible by technology transfers facilitated by friendly American governments keen to strengthen their Western allies.

Labor input was made possible by restructuring the existing labor force away from less productive to more productive branches of the economy. The postwar quarter century became one of the most radical restructuring periods of the West European labor force. In Germany, the share of agricultural employment dropped from 23 to 8 percent, in France from 28 to 13 percent, and in Italy from 40 to 19 percent. In six countries, agricultural employment was halved. Meanwhile industrial employment increased from 38 to 42 percent, and most importantly, the service sector increased its employment from 35 to 45 percent between 1951 and 1971.[2] The structural changes in employment had a tremendous impact on economic performance. A telling example: a Spanish industrial worker produced five times more value in one hour than an agricultural laborer. In two decades, West European productivity levels jumped from 50 to 70 percent of the American level. Europe now stood on its own two feet.

Western Europe became not only stronger, but also more stable than ever before. The countries learned the lesson of the Great Depression and the war, sought to avoid poverty and want, and harmonized their social relations: the new feeling of social solidarity led to the building up of the postwar welfare states, which reinterpreted citizenship rights to include the rights of employment and social security. They achieved virtually full employment. Though there were important national differences in the form they took, high tax revenues allowed for the establishment of free social services, pensions, health care, schooling, and several family benefits in all of the West European countries during the postwar decades.

[2] Angus Maddison, *Monitoring the World Economy 1820–1992* (Paris: OECD, 1995).

Collapse of the Colonial Regime – Inward Orientation and Détente

After the war, a previously imperialist Europe lost its colonies and was forced to turn inwards. A trend of expansionism that had lasted more than 300 years suddenly ended. The war and the Japanese occupation of several European colonies weakened the colonial empires and generated an increasingly vigorous independence movement in Asia and Africa. The emergence of the Soviet superpower gave a lot of elbow room to the former colonial countries where they could find support and even supply of armaments. Therefore, between 1945 and the 1960s, most of the colonial empires collapsed. While some former colonial powers, such as Britain, peacefully accepted most of the changes, and the Dutch accepted Indonesian independence (1948), France tried to defend its Asian and African colonies with force, but was repeatedly defeated militarily in Indo-China (1954) and in Algeria (1962), and the former colonies became independent states. The Suez Canal incident in 1956 and the Belgian action in the Congo in 1960 were some of the last attempts to preserve the past. Some rearguard actions of colonialism such as the endless Portuguese colonial wars in Africa until 1974, and Britain's Falklands war in the 1980s, did not alter the fact that colonialism was *virtually* eliminated by the 1960s.[3] In 1963, the Treaty of Yaoundé between the European Community and former French Africa signaled the beginning of a new approach.

In a paradoxical way, and in contrast to perception, the collapse of colonialism made most of the former colonial empires stronger in the long-run. The old role of the colonies as sources of raw materials, food, and as markets for their European colonizers, which was so crucially important from the sixteenth to the nineteenth centuries, diminished. After the war, trade between non-industrialized agricultural countries and advanced, industrialized ones gradually lost its importance. A new division of labor replaced it within industries and between industrialized countries. Colonies became a burden after 1945, especially because of their strong and strengthening liberation movements, uprisings, wars, and increasing military expenditures.

---

[3] Martin Thomas, Bob Moore, L. J. Butler, *Crisis of Empire: Decolonization and Europe's Imperial States, 1918–1975* (New York: Oxford University Press, 2008).

An inwardly oriented and prosperous Europe was gradually liberated from the danger and burden of the Cold War as well. The political atmosphere and international relations for Europe radically changed as the world entered the 1960s and 1970s. The post-Stalin Soviet Union wanted to improve its standard of living at home. Consequently, it was ready to ease military burdens and tension. Meanwhile, a successful and spectacular Soviet space program caused panic in US military circles during the late 1950s. The newly elected President John Kennedy sent a letter to Moscow in February 1961 suggesting a personal meeting with Nikita Khrushchev in a neutral city. The failure of the badly prepared Bay of Pigs invasion of Fidel Castro's Cuba gave an additional incentive for normalizing relations.

The Kennedy–Khrushchev summit in Vienna in June 1961 ended without any agreement, but the first personal meeting between the top leaders was of groundbreaking importance. This became manifest in the following year. American actions continued against Cuba, and the Soviet answer was adventurous: in 1962, they deployed forty Soviet SS-4 missiles on nine sites in Cuba, ready for a first strike. The world reached the brink of a nuclear confrontation. Soviet and American warships sailed towards each other on the Atlantic Ocean. In the new situation, however, diplomacy triumphed. On October 28, Khrushchev ordered the dismantling and return of the rockets. The peaceful solution initiated the creation of the Moscow–Washington hotline in June 1963.

The superpowers went even further and signed an agreement in May 1972 to control the arms race. The Strategic Arms Limitation Talks (SALT) led to the SALT I agreement to freeze the number of strategic ballistic missile launchers at existing levels. In June 1979, the SALT II agreement curtailed the production of nuclear weapons, and banned new missile programs. The agreement that both parties honored broke the Cold War and replaced it with détente. The new international setting created a safe environment for Western Europe. Although the Cold War conflict returned briefly in 1979–81, Europe's dependence on the United States decreased considerably.

Enjoying the new international and European political environment, the advanced West European countries turned inwards and built more and more extensive connections with each other. This new inward orientation created a strong base for fast economic growth and social stability. Instead of conquering other continents, Western nations conquered the European common market. The value of their merchandise exports increased rapidly: nearly six-and-half times by 1973.[4] A dramatic increase in consumption followed. The West European countries became consumer societies during the postwar decades.

Housing was one of the most spectacular developments. German housing policy illustrated the West European trend well, with the building of 7.5 million dwellings and offering 22 million people the opportunity to move to new homes.[5] Household mechanization was also almost complete: washing machines, refrigerators, and TV sets became part of 60 to 80 percent of households in Western Europe. By the beginning of the 1980s, the number of private cars increased twenty-fold in Germany and forty-fold in Italy. In nine West European countries, there were 32 cars for every 100 people, i.e., roughly one car per family. Mass tourism crowned the hunger for consumption: in 1950, 25 million European people traveled to other countries; by 1970, 160 million did so. Consequently, an unparalleled demand-led economic upswing ensued and characterized the postwar quarter of a century. Food expenditure declined from one-half to one-third of family budgets, while expenditure for household equipment, health care, culture, and leisure increased from 23 to 44 percent between 1950 and 1973. A French historian stated, "In a quarter of a century, households changed from a struggle for survival to a search for personal fulfillment."[6] After the first miserable postwar years, a most prosperous quarter-century made Western Europe rich, as well as socially and politically stable.

Self-destructive Golden Age? Political Revolt and Mini-Revolutions in the West

At the end of the 1960s, however, a new political-social crisis shocked the Western world from out of the blue. It was more understandable in the United States. The brutal Vietnam War and the evaporation of American hopes for victory generated a passionate resistance and a generational revolt. University campuses like Berkeley and Columbia

---

[4] Angus Maddison, *The World Economy. A Millennial Perspective* (Paris: OECD, 2001), 127.

[5] Wolfram Weimer, *Deutsche Wirtschafts-geschichte: Von der Währungsreform bis zum Euro* (Hamburg: Hoffman und Campe, 1998), 144.

[6] François Caron, *An Economic History of Modern France* (New York: Columbia University Press, 1979), 211, 214–15.

became the scenes of virtual revolutions. The civil rights movement gained new impetus and took a violent turn. Burning ghettoes signaled the hot summer and fall of 1968.

Anti-Vietnam-War actions and revolts spread to Western Europe. "Vietnam became the touchstone for the morality of the free West, and for many at that time, the original sin." The author of that statement quoted Horst Mahler who recalled the following episode in an interview: "During a television report on Vietnam with horrifying images, Ulrike Meinhof jumped up, sobbing, and said that she would not put up with it, that this was debasing, and said: we have to do something; we cannot just sit back in our easy chairs."[7] The Vietnam War, and more generally speaking, decolonization and the rise of the Third World, had a strong influence on European intellectuals, and especially the youth. The 1966 resolution of the *Sozialistischer Deutscher Studentenbund* maintained that the Vietnam War was a "war of national and social liberation, a possible model for . . . colonial agricultural areas of Asia, Africa and Latin America . . . " Rudi Dutschke, one of the leaders of the German student revolt, stated that the continuous mobilization in 1965–6 against US intervention in Vietnam had created an anti-authoritarian psychological disposition among German students.[8]

What actually erupted in Europe was more of a general revolt against the status quo. Student riots shocked Paris and Berlin and spread like wild fire. The gates opened and dissatisfaction flooded Western Europe. Why did it emerge at the end of *les trente glorieuses*, "the glorious thirty years," as the French called the postwar decades? History often produces paradoxes. Just as the human immune system sometimes turns against the human body, great prosperities and rapid development sometimes prepare the best soil for the seeds of crisis and revolt. How did the glorious decades turn against themselves? Quite a few threads of the complex fabric of European society slackened and came undone. One of the most important elements was the *alienation of the young, postwar generation*. This itself was a complex process. The long war years undermined the traditionally strict hierarchical structure of

---

[7] Stefan Aust, "Terrorism in Germany: The Baader-Meinhof Phenomenon," *Bulletin of the Historical Institute*, Fall, 43 (2008), 45–7, 49.

[8] Giuliano Garavini, "The Colonies Strike Back: The Impact of the Third World on Western Europe, 1968–1975," *Contemporary European History*, 16, 3 (August 2007), 141–59. (Garavini quotes Massimo Teodori, *Storia delle nuove sinistre in Europa, 1956–1976* [Bologna: Il Mulino, 1976], 173.)

families. Sons and daughters addressed their parents differently. Compulsory forms of respect disappeared. Young people became much more liberated and independent than before. The new youth culture of the 1950s and 1960s separated them from their parents' generation. They dressed differently and quite uniformly. The blue jeans culture eliminated the visible signs of class differences. They followed different kinds of entertainment, and the Beatles culture, new dances, and the "swing" also became a "Chinese wall" between generations. The "Pill" liberated sexual behavior. The postwar generation developed its own characteristics, lifestyle, and value system.

The new generation was equally irritated by euphoric consumerism and the selfish, *nouveau riche* lifestyle of their parents. Oxford University students gathered in front of All Souls College, shouting, "You eat too well, gentlemen!" The new generation turned to idealistic moral values and sexual revolution, celebrated peace, liberty, and libertinism, lived a communal life, and rejected traditional, conservative values. Cultural changes generated their revolt against their parents' generation and it gained a crucial political content as well. They turned against their fathers' generation of Nazis, Fascists, and collaborators. They were fed up with the silence about the shame of war crimes, collaboration, and the postwar lies and myths about resistant nations. They were dissatisfied with their parents' efforts to *forget*, instead of to *reject*, the past. Moreover, they revolted against the preserved silent legacy of the shameful past, and the continued power of former Vichy officials, SS killers, and Nazi enthusiasts in business, legal, and political life. Their hatred of the past and their parents' officially celebrated values generated an idealistic dream to "live in the truth."

A parallel trend ignited an intellectual revolt as well. Postwar Western intellectuals, most of all in France and Italy, but also in Britain and other Western countries, were strongly Left leaning, including socialists and communists. They admired the Soviet Union's war efforts and the alternative values of the collective society. Marx and Gramsci were never as popular as during the postwar decades. The spread of the revolution to China and other countries, and even to other continents, mobilized their imagination about a transforming world. The war had taught them the value of activism and given them an incentive to influence history. The 1950s and 1960s shocked them, however: de-Stalinization unveiled the crimes of the Soviet regime. In addition, it was Soviet leaders, and not hostile enemies, who revealed the facts. Official publications appeared about the gulags. On the other hand, the very same de-Stalinizers, i.e., the post-Stalin Soviet leadership, launched ruthless military interventions against the Hungarian revolution of 1956 and the Czechoslovak Prague Spring in 1968.

The ideal collapsed. First, quite a few Left intellectuals turned to the "genuine Marx," and they idealized the versions of socialism manifested in Mao's "Cultural Revolution" and Pol Pot's Cambodian revolution, which were seemingly non-bureaucratic: not top down, but bottom up. New idols of "the great refusal" like Mao, Pol Pot, Fidel Castro, and Che Guevara emerged.[9] Disappointment followed almost immediately. The news about oppression, mass humiliation, killing, even genocide was the last straw. Their revolutionary enthusiasm not only disappeared but also turned inside out: fierce, neophyte conservatism replaced it. Several former Left intellectuals even turned against the Enlightenment, denying historical progress and even the possibility of understanding the historical truth. Relativism and nihilism characterized the newly emerging intellectual trends. These often turned against the institutions and goals of the epoch. The last period of postwar prosperity became the cradle of a new *Zeitgeist* that turned against the values of the postwar era.

The history of 1968 had a separate chapter in Eastern Europe. The heart of the matter here was the Prague Spring, a bold democratization effort by reform-communist intellectuals who took over the party leadership in Czechoslovakia, and the ruthless suppression of the peaceful reform movement by the Soviet-led Warsaw Pact military intervention. In the same year, the Polish students revolted as well and the reform-oriented Gomulka regime reacted in traditional Stalinist way by playing the anti-Semitic card and launching the police terror. Twelve years after the 1956 revolutions in Hungary and Poland, in 1968 the hope of reforms was dashed. This was the year when the dissident movement was born in Poland, Hungary, and Czechoslovakia. It did not directly endanger the regime but a moral virus gradually weakened it and led to the alienation of the young generations and in some cases a social-democratization of the intellectual base of the Communist Party.

Creeping Economic Crisis

Most paradoxically, the postwar prosperity in Europe undermined itself, and paved the way for a deep economic crisis. Virtually full

---

[9] Herbert Marcuse, *One Dimensional Man* (London: Routledge, 1964).

employment, the lack of a labor reserve that enters and leaves the labor market, as well as a shortage of labor that initiated the employment of guest workers and immigration, made the worker's position strong. Workers' attitudes changed. The unions became very strong and launched mass strikes for higher wages. The postwar social partnership between employees and employers ended, and class confrontation renewed. Workers' activities were also closely related to a generation change: "a new generation matured in the postwar prosperity, without memories of the Great Depression . . . the freedom from such constraints encouraged protest . . . "[10] Collective self-restraint disappeared. The Italian *Statuto dei Lavoratori* and the German *Arbeitsförderungsgesetz* gradually made wage levels and purchasing power independent of the labor market. A race between wages and prices initiated a wage-price spiral in Germany, France, Italy, and several other countries.

A contract in 1969 stipulated a 19 percent wage increase in Italian industry. In France, wages rose more quickly than GDP every year between 1968 and 1973. Social expenditure steeply increased in postwar Europe: by fourteen times in Italy, seven times in France, six times in Sweden, and four times in Western Europe as a whole. Public spending grew from 30 to 50 percent of GDP in Italy. The Western countries spent 40 to 50 percent of GDP on welfare expenditures.

Prices also soared and required the introduction of rigorous fiscal measures in June 1972 to regain control.[11] In Germany, the *rate* of wage increases doubled during the 1970s. Inflation emerged during the period of high prosperity and full employment, and became significant between 1968 and 1970. Clouds were gathering during the last boom years, and the long prosperity undermined itself.

As Andrea Boltho explains, "the success of the 1950s and 1960s had laid the preconditions for at least some of the failures of the 1970s."[12] High prosperity paved the way for its end in the form of over-investment and over-production. The gross capital stock per employee in France, Germany, the Netherlands, and Britain increased nearly three times between 1950 and 1973. As one chronicler noted: "Tremendous over-investment [took place] in the traditional industrial

[10] Michael J. Piore, and Charles F. Sabel, *The Second Industrial Divide: Possibilities for Prosperity* (New York: Basic Books, 1984), 167.
[11] OECD, *Structural Adjustment and Economic Performance* (Paris: OECD, 1987), 129.
[12] Andrea Boltho, *The European Economy: Growth and Crisis* (Oxford University Press, 1982), 28.

sectors of the modern consumption economy during the 1960s, causing massive overcapacity . . . the enormous investment in the secondary
and tertiary sectors, held out the prospect of a shortage of foodstuff,
raw materials and energy. The turning of the terms of trade in favour of
primary producers from the beginning of the 1970s came as a result of
this growing imbalance."[13] The economy became overheated: industrial output in the advanced West increased by 10 percent, and the
price of energy and raw materials increased by as much as 63 percent
between 1972 and 1973. The rate of inflation in Germany reached 7
percent that year.

A quarter-century of excessive growth and skyrocketing consumption led to the saturation of consumer goods markets. As part of this
trend, exports also became more difficult, and their growth slowed.
Mass production, a key factor for prosperity, became less and less
sustainable. Between 1965 and 1973, the aggregate manufacturing
profitability of the seven wealthiest countries of the world declined
by 25 percent.[14] The French economic historian François Caron
noted, "As early as the mid-1960s, it was evident that a slowdown
of growth did not bring about any appreciable slowdown in price
rises . . ."[15]

Because of its accumulating deficit, the United States first devalued
the dollar, which was the de facto international currency, and then,
in August 1971, the Nixon administration practically ended dollar
convertibility. This shocked the international monetary system. The
stable exchange rates, which had existed for a quarter-century, collapsed. Stability, the basis of mass production, dramatically weakened.
Keynesian stimulation of demand did not stop recession, but rather
provoked wage compensation and increased inflation.[16] Altogether,
the accumulated social, cultural, and economic factors generated a
deep crisis in the West.

Political crisis exploded first in France. In March 1968, riots began
at Nanterre University and continued in Paris. Events culminated in

---

[13] Herman Van der Wee, *Prosperity and Upheaval: The World Economy 1945–1980* (Berkeley:
University of California Press, 1986), 90.

[14] Robert Brenner, "Uneven Development and the Long Downturn: Advanced Capitalist
Economies from Boom to Stagnation, 1950–1988," *New Left Review*, Special Issue (May–
June, 1998), 138.

[15] Caron, *Modern France*, 322.

[16] Barry Eichengreen, "Institutions and Economic Growth: Europe after World War II," in
Nicholas Crafts and Gianni Toniolo (eds.), *Economic Growth in Europe Since 1945* (Cambridge
University Press, 1994 [1996]), 61.

May with general university strikes, occupations, and mass demonstrations by 1 million people. Street battles rattled the Latin Quarter, and
a special military headquarters was established for operations. President de Gaulle left to command from an air base. High schools also
joined the riot, but the most important development was the merger
of student riots with worker actions. Workers occupied about fifty factories, and 2 million of them went on strike and achieved substantial
wage increases. The concerted French actions and the Paris revolt –
celebrated in the Beatles' "Revolution" song – set off massive echoes
in several other countries, particularly in Italy and Germany.

Gudrun Ensslin and Andreas Baader set fire to a Frankfurt department store in protest, signaling the start of violent terror actions. Leftist groups founded the *Rote Armee Fraktion*, an urban guerilla force
in Germany. The Italian *autunno caldo* of 1969 – the "hot autumn"
that saw the occupation of the Fiat factory in Milan, the bombing of
the landmark monument of Vittorio Emanuele II in Rome, attacks
against banks, and the Piazza Fontana bombing that killed sixteen
people and wounded ninety – opened the *anni di piombo*, "the years
of bullets." Bombing, kidnapping, and the executions of kidnapped
politicians and business leaders flooded Italy and Germany between
1968 and 1977.

Terrorist methods frightened and alienated the population. Neo-
fascist actions, especially in Italy, deliberately attempted to increase
the fear and alienation. Far-right forces used the strategy of tension to
legitimize the eradication of the Left. The neo-fascist organizations
Golpe Borghese and *Ordine Nuovo* were responsible for two-thirds of
the violent actions, while the rest were perpetrated by *Brigate Rosse*
(Red Brigade) and similar left-wing organizations.

The kidnapping and execution of Hanns-Martin Schleyer by the
Baader-Meinhof group in Germany in 1977 was a clear symbolic
expression of hatred against both the corporate-bourgeois establishment and the Nazi past: Schleyer represented both by being the President of the West German Employer Federation and a former SS offi-
cer who served Hitler in occupied Prague. Similarly, the Italian Red
Brigades killed or wounded twenty-seven Fiat managers, signaling the
renewal of class warfare.

In the middle of the political turmoil, creeping economic instability suddenly became manifest and the seemingly endless postwar
prosperity in Europe came to a spectacular halt in the fall of 1973.
A political drama – namely, the October 1973 Yom Kippur War in

the Near East – followed by the boycott decision of the Organization of Petroleum Exporting Countries (OPEC), led crude oil prices to soar from $2.70 per barrel in 1973 to $9.76 by 1974. Another political drama, the Iranian Islamic revolution of 1979, generated a second "oil crisis" in 1979–80, and, taken as a whole, oil prices increased ten-fold.

From that time on, nothing worked as usual. Economic growth stopped, prices and unemployment sharply increased, and Keynesian demand-side economics – which held that economic crisis could be coped with by increasing demand and strengthening the purchasing power of the population through job creation and state investments – became unable to cure the stagnation and decline any longer. In fact, it generated even higher inflation. The Phillips curve, the classic "law" of economics describing the inverse relationship between inflation and unemployment, such that increasing inflation decreases unemployment and *vice versa*, stopped working as inflation and unemployment rose together. What followed was a sudden slowing down and then a decline accompanied by high inflation and unemployment. This odd pairing of stagnation *and* inflation led to the introduction of a new economic term: *stagflation*.

Finally, American interest rates, which increased sharply from 5.5 percent in 1977 to 13.4 percent by 1981, contributed to pushing the advanced industrial countries into a deep recession and made several less developed, indebted countries insolvent. The International Monetary Fund was unable to maintain the liquidity of the international banking system. Severe austerity measures became unavoidable and made the crisis manifest. A decade of instability followed the quarter-century of exceptional boom. Between the early 1970s and early 1980s slow growth, occasional setbacks, high unemployment, and frequently double-digit inflation replaced full employment and stability. Between 1950–73 and 1973–83, consumer prices in the leading Western economies more than doubled from an annual average increase of 4.2 percent to 9.4 percent. In the Mediterranean region, they more than quadrupled from 4 percent to 18.4 percent. World price levels had also more than doubled. Unemployment, averaging 2 to 4 percent in Western and Mediterranean Europe between 1950 and 1973, jumped to 12 percent and hit more than 7 million people.[17]

[17] Maddison, *Monitoring*, 84.

Based on ninety-four countries with 98 percent of the world population, the average annual rate of growth, i.e., the increase in produced
goods and services, dropped from 3.4 percent between 1950 and 1973
to −0.1 percent after 1973. Economic growth slowed significantly in
the sixteen most advanced countries of the world: after complete stagnation in the first three years after 1973, the average GDP in these
countries increased by only 20 percent in the entire decade after 1973.
Foreign trade almost stagnated and trade deficits accumulated in the
advanced countries because import prices increased 20 percent more
than export prices did.[18] The dominant economic powers were no
longer the engines of European economic prosperity.

The old leading sectors of the Belgian, British, and French
economies sank into crisis: the combined coal output of the three
countries decreased by 40 percent. By the early 1980s, the combined
textile production of Belgium, Britain, Germany, France, Italy, and
the Netherlands dropped to less than half of the production levels of
the 1960s.[19] At its lowest point, industrial output had declined by
13 percent.

"Structural Crisis" – Caused by Technological Changes

It turned out soon, however, that the real causes of the decline were
deeper than the transitory oil crisis. A similar phenomenon is familiar
in economics. Joseph Schumpeter, one of the greatest economists of
the twentieth century, described and analyzed it, calling it *structural
crisis*. "Industrial revolutions," he explained, "periodically reshape the
existing structure of industry by introducing new methods of production . . . new forms of organization . . . new trade routes and markets to sell in. While these things are being initiated we have brisk
expenditure and 'prosperity' predominates . . . and while those things
are being completed . . . we have the elimination of antiquated elements of the industrial structure and 'depression' predominates. Thus
there are prolonged periods of rising and falling prices, interest rates,
employment and so on, which phenomena constitute parts of the

[18] Angus Maddison, *Two Crises: Latin America and Asia 1929–38 and 1973–83* (Paris: OECD,
1985), 13.
[19] Wolfram Fischer, Jan A. van Houtte and Herman Kellenbenz, *Handbuch der europäische
Wirtschafts- und Sozialgeschichte vom Ersten Weltkrieg bis zum Gegenwart*, Vol. 6 (Stuttgart:
Franz Steiner, 1987), 117, 135.

mechanism of this process of recurrent rejuvenation of the productive apparatus."[20]

In this interpretation, the "whole set of technological changes" or industrial revolutions is what generates pressure for adjustment. Those firms and industrial branches that represent the old technologies and methods, and are unable to change, will disappear in time. Readjustment is difficult and requires a relatively longer period, especially because countries and companies are unable immediately to satisfy the demands for investments, credits, and new skills. This causes a period of economic turmoil and depression. The significant slowdown and destruction are, nevertheless, "creative" since they clear the way for new technologies and methods. New leading sectors emerge, based on new technologies and organizational principles, and the whole process brings about a restructuring of the economy. When most sectors of the economy have completed the transformation, a new wave of prosperity follows. This entire process is thus inherent in the market system and in free market competition. Extra-economic factors, such as wars and political upheavals, however, also contribute to this process.

The recession of the 1970s, which penetrated to the early 1980s, clearly exhibited the signs of a structural crisis. The old postwar leading sectors literally collapsed: in eight West European countries, employment in the iron and steel, textile, and shipbuilding industries dropped to 59, 61, and 37 percent, respectively, of their pre-recession levels.[21] The share of traditional industries – i.e., construction and building materials, iron and steel, traditional engineering, wood, paper, textile, and clothing – in the gross value added of total industry declined by 40 percent in Germany between 1970 and 1980. During the decade after 1973, exports slowed to roughly one-third and one-half of the growth rates of the previous decade.[22]

After decades of fluctuation-free rapid economic growth, these new developments were shocking. It was still difficult to realize that the period of high prosperity was over. It is worth quoting an OECD report from 1974: "There is little evidence of any general slowing down in the rate of growth . . . [It] is a strong presumption that the

---

[20] Joseph Schumpeter, *Capitalism, Socialism and Democracy* (London: Allen & Unwin, 1976), 67–8.

[21] OECD, *Structural Adjustment*, 236.

[22] Angus Maddison, *The World Economy in the 20th Century* (Paris: OECD, 1989).

gross domestic product of the OECD area may again double in the next decade and a half."[23] Even in 1977, a special OECD study, the McCracken Report, concluded that "the poor showing of recent years were likely to be only temporary and that a return to strong growth was possible . . . "[24] In reality, it was not. The stagflation of the mid-to-late-seventies was thus not an accidental event, but rather a characteristic long-term cyclical phenomenon. The market had shrunk dramatically.

The structural crisis of the world economy hit Western Europe especially hard because of its arrival at a turning point in its postwar development. During the later 1950s and 1960s, the region profited highly from its *extensive development model*, based on increased capital accumulation and restructuring and increasing the labor force by an average 1 percent per annum. The postwar boom generated the beginning of immigration to Europe which I will discuss in chapter 5. The demand for *Gastarbeitern* in the West European countries attracted Turkish, Portuguese, Italian, North African, and Yugoslav temporary workers. Europe, the continent of emigration, became a continent of immigration. The extensive development model would not be possible without the import of the existing stock of technological knowledge, mostly transferred from the United States. Fixed international exchange rates and regulations created a stable financial environment, and corporative social partnership and agreements between labor unions and employers made possible wage and price moderation. Keynesian regulated markets and state assistance played an important role.

However, the sources of extensive development and its institutional framework dried up and became inappropriate by the early to mid-1970s. The impacts of the Oil Crisis, the structural crisis, and the exhaustion of sources of extensive development combined and required difficult adjustment and a set of new institutions, because "the same institutions of coordinated capitalism that had worked to Europe's advantage in the age of extensive growth now posed obstacles to successful economic performance."[25] A strongly challenged Western Europe reached a turning point by 1980.

[23] OECD, *Economic Outlook*, No. 15, (Paris: OECD, 1974), 166.

[24] OECD, *Structural Adjustment*, 1987, 53.

[25] Barry Eichengreen, *The European Economy Since 1945: Coordinated Capitalism and Beyond* (Princeton University Press, 2007), 6–7.

The Crumble of the Dictatorial Regimes on the European Peripheries: Democratization of Mediterranean Europe

The Southern and Eastern peripheries of Europe followed different patterns than the West after the war. Leftover right-wing authoritarian dictatorships in the Mediterranean region and communist regimes in Central and Eastern Europe remained outside the orbit of postwar "European" trends. In different ways, they followed the road of modernization dictatorships: oppressive, isolated, and trying to be as self-sufficient as possible. However, both Right and Left dictatorial regimes had run into a dead-end. Their economic systems reproduced backwardness, and they began losing legitimacy. To solve their problems they had to build contact with the West, but these connections loosened the fabric of their politically controlled societies and required the modernization of their institutions. The demonstration effect of the successful Western alternative, with its freedom and new mass culture, conquered the young generations, intellectuals, and a growing layer of the society. A slow and gradual process of disintegration and dissolution began during the 1960s. All the dictatorial systems declined into a deep crisis, and they had to depart from their previous, separate roads and merge with that of the Western Europeans during the 1970s. The Mediterranean regimes collapsed in the 1970s. The bold modernization drive of Eastern communism sank into increasingly deep failure during the 1960s and 1970s. The whirlpool of crisis pulled them further and further down, though their collapse occurred only in the late 1980s.

Surprisingly enough for their contemporaries, the disintegration and reorientation of these societies became less and less confrontational, and instead shifted towards negotiation. Several factors helped this process. First of all, the international environment, and the decline of the polarized setting, and the strong involvement of the West in those processes. Inside these countries, the regimes gradually lost support. Their troubled past also offered important lessons. Common historical memories of wild and deadly national confrontations, bloody historical events, such as the Spanish and Greek civil wars, Portugal's endless and hopeless colonial wars, the tragic Polish war years and the series of anti-communist revolts, and the memory of the 1956 revolution in Hungary, pushed these societies towards negotiated solutions. Before 1980, the three different European roads thus started to merge and led to a joint and common European turning point that emerged from the crisis of the 1970s. In the end, the *entire* European continent entered a new epoch after the 1980s.

Spain, Portugal, and Greece were the disowned children of the European family until the 1970s. Bloody dictatorial regimes ruled these countries for decades. However, Cold War considerations shelved principles and political values and made all of the southern dictatorships allies of the West, leading to the building of economic ties. Unstable southern Europe had to be stabilized and economically revitalized. Strengthening Western influence, as well as establishing, consolidating, and developing the economies of backward Greece, Turkey, Spain, and Portugal, belonged to the logic and political requirements of the Cold War. Consequently, it was a major political agenda to incorporate this area into a strong and flourishing Europe.

It was, however, a difficult and often hidden goal. While Antonio Salazar and his regime were alive, while Francisco Franco was in power, and while the Greek military junta dictated politics in Greece, these countries were not officially *comme il faut* in Europe. Nevertheless, the United States and the West assisted the Iberian Peninsula and incorporated it into their network during the 1960s. In the case of backward Portugal, they institutionalized the incorporation: the country became a member of the European Free Trade Association (EFTA), initiated by Britain in 1960; it joined the IMF, the World Bank, and GATT; and in political-military terms, became a member of NATO.

The last one-and-half decades of Franco's dictatorship can illuminate this process and its importance. In 1959, with direct Western collaboration, the Franco regime gave up isolationism and self-sufficiency. A stabilization plan was prepared in 1961 with the close cooperation of the IMF, World Bank, OEEC, and the American government. Next year Spain even applied for membership in the European Common Market. The Community shelved the application since the Franco regime was still a political pariah. Without much ado, however, the European Community signed a Preferential Commercial Agreement with Spain in July 1970. The Agreement immediately reduced European tariffs by 60 percent for 88 percent of Spanish industrial exports to Europe, aiming eventually to establish completely free trade. Spain, now an "external" member of the European Community, had to make only insignificant concessions: a 25 percent tariff reduction for European goods by 1977. Western foreign investment flooded Spain: it increased twenty-seven-fold between 1960 and 1973 and covered 20 percent of Spanish industrial investments. Western tourists swamped the country, which increased the tourist-business income of Spain from $126 million to more than $3 billion by the 1970s.

Accordingly, a Spanish economic miracle emerged during the 1960s: economic growth reached 5.8 percent per annum, exports increased fourteen-fold, and Spain became an industrialized country.[26] Other Mediterranean countries performed similarly: Greece had 6.2 percent annual growth and Portugal 5.7 percent, both much higher than Western Europe's average. Thus a catching-up process began. Political-cultural factors were equally important. The oppressive state lost its ability to direct the fate of its citizens. A complex process of learning and a new way of socializing the new generation emerged. Universities, which had long obediently served Franco, began depoliticizing and in 1956 became the organizers of the first anti-Franco demonstration. They gradually turned to become the nests of political counter-culture. The Church, once a pillar of the regime, gradually distanced itself from it and became an institution of civil society.

When the dictators passed away in the 1970s, the soil was prepared for dramatic change. Salazar died in 1970, Franco in 1975, and the Greek junta of Papadopoulos lost power in 1974. The Mediterranean countries followed in the footsteps of postwar Italy and Germany. Democratization was fast and relatively smooth in the European environment and based on gradual internal transformation. Greece invited Konstantin Karamanlis, former conservative prime minister, to return from his exile in Paris, and the November 1974 elections restored democracy. In 1981, Andreas Papandreou, after having returned from emigration and formed his Pan-Hellenic Socialist Movement (PASOK), gained the majority and formed the government.

Spain's transformation after four decades of dictatorship, based on the economic prosperity of the late Franco period and close ties with the West, became exemplary. Franco, officially regent of Spain since 1947 and now seriously ill, prepared for the continuation of his regime by handpicking his successors. In 1969, Franco passed over the legitimate king and selected the king's son, Prince Juan Carlos

---

[26] Joseph Harrison, *The Spanish Economy in the Twentieth Century* (London: Croom Helm, 1985), 144–62.

de Borbón, as King of Spain, and Adolfo Suárez, the right-wing
politician in whom he had absolute confidence, as prime minister.
In 1974, 37-year-old Juan Carlos took over as head of state from the
ailing and soon dying Franco, and played the central role in democratic
transformation. The monarchy had a fundamental role in legitimizing
transformation during a period when the old legitimacy had already
collapsed, and the new one was only just in the making. The king
was also the central figure in the defeat of the attempted Francoist
military coup in 1981, and he rightly gained the nickname of *El
Pilota del Cambia*, the pilot of change. Suárez convinced the Francoist
parliament to give up power, became the first elected prime minister of
the country, and organized the Moncloa Pact between all the political
parties, conservative and communist alike, to accept and design a
post-Franco democracy.

In Spain and Greece, right-of-center political forces had the central role in transformation. They had better positions in the early
liberalization, while left-wing parties had to block the road against
the rise of other extreme elements. The two handpicked successors
of Franco orchestrated the destruction of Franco's regime and the
establishment of democracy in Spain. The transformation was institutionalized through free elections, a multi-party system, reestablished
democratic institutions, trade unions, and, in 1978, a new Western-
style constitution.

Portugal had a more painful transformation, because the successor
of Salazar, Marcello Caetano, kept the regime alive and continued the
devastating colonial wars in Guinea-Bissau, Angola, and Mozambique.
The regime was finally overthrown by the dissatisfied military. The
Movimento das Forças Armadas launched the "carnation revolution" in
April 1974. The far-left transition government rushed to national-
ize three-quarters of the Portuguese economy. A period of transitory
political chaos – the "Hot Summer" of 1975 with right-wing bombing, steeply rising wages, demonstrations, and uncertainty about the
future – accompanied the aftermath of the Oil Crisis. A devastating
decline of both industrial output and GDP followed, inflation soared,
and the trade deficit doubled. In 1974, the GDP per capita reached
roughly 56 percent of the level of the European Community. It took
seventeen years to reach that level again.

A flood of hundreds of thousands of colonial Portuguese citizens
made the situation even more difficult. Quite a lot of them had lived
in the colonies for several generations and even intermarried, but

now they flooded back to Portugal. The *Retornado*, a huge wave of about half a million refugees, led to a population increase of about 8 percent during 1973–5. Previous Portuguese emigration to Western Europe also sharply declined. Unemployment jumped to 14 percent. "In 1976–1977, it seemed that a total collapse of the Portuguese economy was imminent."[27]

In 1975, after a leftist coup attempt was crushed, free elections made Mário Soares, the moderate socialist, prime minister. Consolidation began. The Western world ran to assist the peaceful transformation and to incorporate Portugal into the Western camp, to push back the danger of communism. The European Investment Bank, the West German and American governments, the Swiss Central Bank, the European Council of Ministers, and the IMF opened a flood of aid and loans. Their amount reached $6 billion by 1979. Portugal became a privileged and assisted member of the Western community. Democracy was in the making, the achievements of the transformation soon became consolidated in the Mediterranean region, and the countries applied for membership in the European Community.

Economic and Political Crisis: Towards the Collapse in the East

The Eastern half of the continent, which was strictly isolated in the Soviet Bloc, attempted to create a parallel world market within the Council of Mutual Economic Aid (CMEA), and formed a Soviet-led military alliance, the Warsaw Pact. The Bloc countries followed their own road of bold modernization. In two decades, the traditional "agrarian half" of Europe became industrialized. The communist regimes ruthlessly destroyed the long unchanged traditional social hierarchies and launched a successful educational revolution. In spite of all these achievements, however, the Soviet Bloc declined as a result of one crisis after another from the mid-1950s to the 1980s. Poland turned against oppressive Stalinism and Soviet occupation in the summer and fall of 1956. The spontaneous Poznań workers uprising and its bloody suppression mobilized the reform-oriented wing of the Communist Party. The Party's Central Committee, ignoring Soviet

[27] Rodney J. Morrison, *Portugal: Revolutionary Change in an Open Economy* (Boston: Auburn House, 1981), 111.

warnings and threats, elected the independent-minded, and previously purged, Wladyslaw Gomulka as head of the Party. They stopped collectivization, made a historical compromise with the Catholic Church that partly pluralized the system, and introduced several freedoms, including traveling and publication. The peaceful Polish October was followed by Hungary's heroic 1956 revolution and fight for independence against the almighty Soviet Union and its powerful army. In two tumultuous weeks, the regime collapsed, a multi-party system was reintroduced, and the armed forces joined the insurgents in street fights in Budapest and defeated the Soviet troops trying to eliminate them. Only a second massive Soviet military invasion defeated the revolution, followed by bloody retribution. The next year, Milovan Djilas, a leading Yugoslav communist turned dissident, made a prophetic statement about the importance of 1956 in Hungary: "The wound which the Hungarian Revolution inflicted on Communism can never be completely healed . . . Yugoslav Communism, separating itself from Moscow, initiated the crisis of Soviet imperialism . . . Hungary means the beginning of the end of Communism generally."[28]

Hardly more than a decade later, the Prague Spring challenged the unchanged post-Stalinist structures by demanding openness and human rights. A group of disappointed reform communists took over the leadership of the Czechoslovak Communist Party. They wanted to replace "existing" socialism with the ideal Marxian dream of genuine democratic socialism "with a human face." As an unparalleled document from the 1968 Vysocany Party Congress stated, "The distorted model of socialism was applied in this country . . . socialist society must . . . de-monopolize politics and extend civic liberties and the self-determination of the individual as much as the nation . . . Socialism requires more, not less freedom, freedom of the press and of expression, of assembly, movement, travel . . . it requires more, not fewer human rights."[29]

This dramatic cry for change and courageous beginning of the realization of its ideals, followed by the Soviet-led Warsaw Pact military

---

[28] Milovan Djilas, "Hungary and Yugoslavia" [1957], in Béla Király *et al.* (eds.), *The First War Between Socialist States: The Hungarian Revolution of 1956 and Its Impact* (New York: Brooklyn College Press, 1984), 91–4, 92–3.

[29] Jiří Pelikan (ed.), *The Secret Vysocany Congress: Proceedings and Documents of the Extraordinary Fourteenth Congress of the Communist Party of Czechoslovakia, 22 August, 1968* (London: Allen Lane, 1971), 107, 111.

suppression of the Prague Spring in August 1968, became a turning point that led to the birth of dissident and opposition movements in several Bloc countries. The most important one emerged in Poland. After a student revolt in Warsaw and other major cities in 1968, strikes and confrontation with riot police, and the consequent arrests and retaliations, mobilized a group of young intellectuals, including Adam Michnik, Jacek Kuroń and others, to organize themselves. At the beginning, they aimed like the Czech reformers to return to the "real" Marx and ideal socialism. In September 1976, fourteen of them founded the Committee for the Defense of the Workers, later called the Committee for Social Self-Defense. The Committee's purpose was initially to help the families of workers who were arrested at the 1976 Ursus and Radom riots, but it later helped mobilize the entire society against the regime. That was the beginning of the merger of disappointed intellectuals and workers. Samizdat publications, and the "Flying University" lecture series in private homes, gradually transformed the movement to create a "parallel polis," a civil society independent from the regime.

Dissident movements were incomparably weaker in other countries. However, they also emerged in Hungary and Czechoslovakia. They were small in number: around 300 people in Hungary, and 200 people in Czechoslovakia signed the Charta 77 dissident declaration in 1977. However, Václav Havel became a symbol of courageous resistance and basic human values. Dissident writers and intellectuals raised their voices in Romania and Bulgaria as well. The influence of the dissidents and opposition groupings as a "moral virus" was much stronger than their numbers and influenced a significant part of the population and even Party intellectuals.

A series of spontaneous workers' uprisings in 1970, 1976, and 1980 revealed Poland to embody a permanent challenge to the system. When workers established their free and independent *Solidarność* (Solidarity) union in Gdansk in 1978, the dissident movement integrated into the workers' movement and assisted with making a deal with the government to legalize independent unions. Three million, and later 10 million, people soon joined the union, and Solidarity became stronger than the Communist Party and the government. The Catholic Church, the national symbol that had enjoyed strong independence since 1956, also joined Solidarity. As Timothy Garton Ash put it, when the newly elected Polish Pope, John Paul II, visited Poland in

1979, "Everyone saw that Poland is not a communist country – just a communist state."[30]

Euro-Communism and Reforms

Meanwhile, the unity of world communism also broke. After Yugoslavia courageously separated itself from the Soviet Union in 1948, China also turned against the Soviets in 1960, and soon two other countries, Albania and Romania, separated themselves from the Soviet Bloc, though only partially in the latter case. During the 1970s, West European communism gradually evaporated in response to the crisis of Eastern communism. The strongest Communist Party in Western Europe, the Italian, turned to *euro-communism* by accepting political pluralism, free elections, democracy, and a market economy. The Italian Communist Party, followed by the Spanish, shifted towards social democracy that was independent of the Soviet Union. Enrico Berlinguer, the head of the Italian Communist Party, stated in June 1976: "We are fighting for a socialist society that has its foundation . . . [in] individual and collective freedom and their guarantee, the principles of . . . [the] non-ideological nature of the State, and its democratic organization, the plurality of the political parties, and the possibility of altering government majorities . . . religious freedom, freedom of expression, of culture and arts and sciences."[31] West European communism melted away and the social-democratization of Western communism provided a strong incentive for the Eastern parties, especially the Hungarian one, to do likewise.

Some of the Central European communist regimes adopted major reforms to become more flexible and acceptable to the population. Poland made a compromise with the Church and allowed more freedom for the population. Hungary gave up communist indoctrination and replaced it by depoliticization. Czechoslovakia and Hungary in the mid-1960s tried to escape from the centrally planned non-market system that had proved inappropriate and inefficient. Extensive growth policy no longer worked. Stagnation and decline characterized Czechoslovakia between 1961 and 1963, and the Hungarian economy

---

[30] Timothy Garton Ash, *The Polish Revolution: Solidarity* (New York: Vintage Books, 1985), 29.

[31] Rudolf L. Tokes (ed.), *Eurocommunism and Détente* (New York University Press, 1978), 473.

in the early 1960s was characterized by severe imbalance. By that time, both countries' governments recognized the need for reforms and the replacement of the extensive growth model. Yugoslavia, after its split with the Soviet Union in 1948, began changing the Soviet model of a centrally planned economy. Yugoslavia, Czechoslovakia, and Hungary introduced reforms in 1965, 1967, and 1968 respectively, abolishing compulsory plan indicators, and introducing market prices and a profit motive into the economy. Market reform opened up the economy somewhat. In reforming countries, contact with the West became a determining factor. Yugoslavia, Poland, Hungary, and even non-reforming Romania developed extensive trade relations with the West, and at least half of their trade was with free market economies.

This reorientation failed, despite some partial results in Yugoslavia and Hungary. The Russian-led Warsaw Pact military invasion of Czechoslovakia in the summer of 1968 eliminated reforms in that country. Hungary, under strict Soviet control and assisted by a conservative domestic opposition, temporarily halted reforms in 1972–3. Other countries of the Soviet Bloc did not even attempt a new orientation in their economic strategy.

Liberalization of the system in some of the countries had important consequences. Freedom of travel in Poland and Hungary intensified cultural connections, while a successful American cultural Cold War using new Western mass culture to conquer the youth in the East, had a tremendous impact on the younger generations and intellectuals.[32] International developments influenced and strengthened this trend significantly. As part of the melting of Cold War tension and the détente, Willy Brandt's West German government made its own new opening towards the Soviet Bloc. Instead of isolating and launching propaganda wars against it, Brandt initiated a new *Ost Politik* of economic, political, and cultural connections. In 1970, he visited Poland, and his famous *Warschauer Kniefall*, honoring the victims of the Warsaw Ghetto who revolted against Nazi Germany and were massacred, established a new relationship, better economic connections, and cultural-political ties between Germany and the Soviet Bloc countries.

Even more importantly, the Helsinki Agreement of 1975 stabilized East-West relations and postwar arrangements. In fact, the Soviet

---

[32] Frances Stonor Saunders, *The Cultural Cold War: The CIA and the World of Art and Letters* (New York: New Press, 2000).

Union initiated the negotiations and sought to institutionalize the postwar status quo and the recognized balance of power. The West at first resisted, but then accepted the idea, and the Soviet Union had to make compromises to realize its goals of an official recognition of borders and of Soviet rule in Central and Eastern Europe. The Soviets accepted agreements on three groups of issues, or "baskets" as they were officially referred to: (1) security issues; (2) economic, scientific, and environmental concerns; and (3) cultural, human rights, and humanitarian problems, which represented the major Soviet compromise.

Without a doubt, Brezhnev achieved his goal of reconfirming the status quo in Eastern Europe and the existence of two Germanies. On the other hand, the ten principles guiding relations between participating countries affirmed the national sovereignty of signatory countries and non-interventionism. The agreement on the third group of issues provided the legal basis for safeguarding personal and social liberties, and it became a major factor in the political and moral undermining of state socialism. The oppression of opposition forces became more difficult and uncomfortable when it could be disclosed worldwide as a violation of the Helsinki Agreement. It also had more than symbolic meaning that the Czech opposition movement, Charta 77, based its manifesto on the Helsinki Agreement on social and cultural rights, which became law in state socialist countries. The communist alliance system also weakened because each country gained the legal basis for more independent foreign policy actions, and some, such as Hungary, immediately exploited it.

The Helsinki Agreement strengthened the connection of some of the communist countries with the West. Grants and visits, travel to Western countries, and the import of Western films and TV programs had a strong impact on the populations of those countries that enjoyed these opportunities. Poles and Hungarians, who were free to travel from the late fifties and early sixties, were definitely influenced. These contacts with the West generated further alienation from the regime and increased dissatisfaction. The demonstration effect of the Western alternative contributed to the disintegration of the regimes.

Reproduced Backwardness

Before 1980, the younger generations and some intellectuals had already become disillusioned and distanced themselves from state

socialism and the regime, particularly in Poland and Czechoslovakia. Others followed the euro-communist road and became social-
democratized, especially in Hungary. However, an orientation towards
reform was the exception, and not the main road taken by the
countries of Eastern Europe. An axis of non-reforming, post-Stalinist
countries – the Soviet Union, the German Democratic Republic,
post-1968 Czechoslovakia, Romania, Bulgaria, and Albania – continued to follow a rigidly isolationist and oppressive policy, preserving
their closed societies and their failed central planning.

The only way to at least temporarily legitimate themselves, and
to gain the support or even the passive acceptance of their population, was a renewed social policy and efforts to initiate consumerism.
The vast majority of these societies were traditionally poor. The adult
generations had suffered through the devastating Great Depression
and the even more distressing war, postwar starvation, and hyperinflation. It was relatively easy for paternalistic governments to satisfy their humble dreams. Through the 1960s and 1970s, people in
Central and Eastern Europe appreciated the newly established socialist welfare institutions and the modest consumer orientation of the
regime.

These attempts equally characterized reforming and non-reforming
countries. The Soviet Union, the German Democratic Republic, and
Czechoslovakia tried to satisfy the population with a modest consumer
orientation. The only real success for this policy, however, occurred in
reformist Hungary. On the other hand, all of the communist countries
introduced welfare institutions, free health care, guaranteed pensions,
and other social benefits such as child allowance and maternity leave.
All of these services gradually became citizen rights during the 1960s
and 1970s. One of these institutions, namely, free education at all
levels including higher education, generated an educational revolution in countries previously characterized by a high rate of illiteracy
and an extremely limited and elitist system of secondary and tertiary
education.

However, the Oil Crisis, and the world recession that followed and
turned into a structural crisis, challenged all these achievements, as
well as the hope of economic success through continued economic
growth, which had maintained the exceptionally rapid average annual
rate of 3.9 percent during the 1950s and into the mid-1970s. As in
the West, the solution had to be an economic renewal based on the
innovative new technology that had resulted from the information
and communication revolution. The communist countries of the East

were unable to develop a successful response to the challenge of a transforming world economy and instead declined to a deep and terminal economic crisis. From the mid-1970s on, they started to go down the road towards the collapse of the regime. The economic factors of the collapse that undermined all efforts to escape deserve special attention.

The rapid economic growth and industrialization of these countries became a heavy burden in the 1970s because its technological base and economic structure were obsolete. At the center of their industrialization policy was the rapid development of the coal, iron, and old fashioned engineering branches that had already declined in the West. Modern technology, and modern branches of industry, were lacking. For example, the telephone system, which gained extraordinary importance in the communication and computer revolution, was uniquely backward: in 1980, when the United States had 79 telephone lines per 100 inhabitants, and the Nordic countries and the European Union had 45 and 28 respectively, Central and Eastern Europe had, on average, only 7.4 lines. Moscow could not receive more than six long-distance calls simultaneously, and long-distance calls to other parts of the country had to go through Moscow.[33] The computer age had not yet arrived in Central and Eastern Europe. The ratio of personal computers to inhabitants reached only about 5 percent of the Western level in most of these countries.

The service revolution, which dramatically increased the division of labor and labor productivity in the West, also stopped at the borders of the region. While service employment in the West had increased by 1980 to roughly 60 percent of the active population, in Central and Eastern Europe two-thirds of the population were blue-collar workers and farmers. In the West, a worker produced $25–28 value in an hour, and about $10 per hour in the Mediterranean countries. In the East, however, workers in the 1970s produced only $5–6 value per hour.

In an age of industrialized innovation, the research and development (R&D) capacity of state socialist Eastern Europe remained backward. Although they built up huge research networks around their academies of sciences, they were basic-research oriented. The Soviet Union had a very advanced military R&D program, but it was hermetically isolated from the civilian economy and did not influence it.

---

[33] Michale Mastanduno, *Economic Containment: CoCom and the Politics of East-West Trade* (Ithaca: Cornell University Press, 1992), 1.

Of course, peripheral countries were never technology leaders, but rather followed the advanced countries by means of technology transfer. Cold War confrontation, however, blocked the possibility of importing technology. The American Congress initiated the ban on technology exports, and the Coordinating Committee for Multilateral Export Controls (CoCom) was established in November 1949, with all NATO members and allied countries joining. All telecommunication technology, biotechnology, computer technology and software, and all kinds of cutting-edge new technologies were on the list of controlled technologies, and their sales were banned. During the second half of the 1970s, the American government significantly strengthened export control and restrictions. Now they included all kinds of technology to prevent infrastructural development and "cultural preparedness" in the Soviet Bloc countries to exploit advanced technology.[34] The CoCom policy was thus not only a strategic embargo prohibiting the trade of products of direct military importance, it was also economic warfare against the Soviet Bloc, aiming to weaken its entire economy. The CoCom policy, the first peacetime export ban in history, successfully blocked technology transfer. Consequently, the countries of the region preserved obsolete economic branches and export sectors, and they were unable to adjust to the challenge of new technology.

Deep Economic Crisis

From the mid-1970s and through the 1980s, the deep economic crisis erupted and expanded, undermining all the temporary advantages for stability and increasing living standard, which the regime had derived from rapid growth. During the second half of the 1970s, the countries of the region, especially key countries like Poland, Hungary, Yugoslavia, and Romania, had relatively open economies and extensive trade with free market countries. As a clear expression of this opening up, Poland and Hungary joined international free trade and monetary institutions such as the General Agreement on Tariffs and Trade (GATT) (in 1967 and 1973, respectively) and in the eighties, they joined the IMF.

---

[34] *Ibid.*, 193–4.

In this situation, most of these countries suffered from a yearly 20 to 25 percent trade deficit. The prices of their imported goods increased much faster than the prices of their second rate, obsolete export items. Rapid growth rapidly increased the deficit, and they were thus forced to slow down significantly. The nearly 4 percent annual growth during the previous quarter century halved from the mid-1970s, and when the 1980s arrived, Poland's GDP declined in two consecutive years by 10 and then nearly 5 percent, while Yugoslavia's and Hungary's economies stagnated.[35] There was not enough income for the state to put into investments and social expenditure.

The political leadership, however, in its attempts to maintain political stability and popular acceptance, made every effort to keep full employment, wages, living standards, and social benefits unchanged. All of these countries gave up the previously adopted policy of economic independence from the West, and turned to the international credit market. It was easy to borrow at that time because the financial market was flooded with cheap "oil dollars," the large portion of the tremendous extra income of the oil-exporting countries that was exported as credits. The communist governments did not hesitate to bridge the trade deficit gap with loans. As a result, almost all of the countries of the region fell into a trap of indebtedness. In the Eastern half of the continent, the world economic depression in the 1970s consequently became even more severe and continued for longer.

The crisis in this region became complex due to the economic model they applied. As happened in the West, it became a crisis of the *extensive model of growth policy*. The dictatorial regimes suppressed wages and consumption for a long time, and the countries were able to accumulate and invest 20–25 percent of the GDP and create millions of new jobs. For quite a while, these agricultural countries have had unlimited labor resources that allowed a 6 percent annual increase of labor input. Imported technology from the more industrialized Bloc countries made possible the use of existing (though by international standards obsolete) technological stocks to generate rapid growth. The institutional system promoted an extensive forced growth policy that worked, at least for a while. "The centrally planned economies of Eastern Europe were able, initially at least, to perform tolerably well. The

---

[35] The World Bank, *World Tables 1984–90* (Washington, DC: The World Bank, 1990).

institutions of the command economy had several limitations . . . but they were best suited to the circumstances of catch-up growth."[36]

This situation changed, however, during the 1960s and 1970s. The sources of extensive growth policy were exhausted in the relatively better-developed Central European countries. Forced capital formation based on suppressed wage levels and living standards, and the exploitation of the peasantry, were no longer possible at the same levels, as the riots and revolutions clearly warned. The regimes had to pacify their populations. The best way to achieve this was by increased consumption and the revitalization of agriculture through higher prices for food products. Capital formation declined. Labor resources also dried up since the agricultural population dramatically decreased, and industry already employed half of the active population. The region was unable to respond to the challenge of the 1970s. Because of the two oil crises, Hungary suffered a loss equal to the severe destruction of the country during the six months when it became a battlefield in World War II. And Hungary was not alone. The downward spiral became unstoppable. The economic decline and the visible impotence of the communist leadership to find a way out had an extraordinary political impact on the region. The road was paved towards collapse.

[36] Eichengreen, *European Economy*, 5.

2

The End of "Two Europes" and European Integration

Major political and cultural-intellectual trends and events of historic proportions, most of which were surprising and unpredicted, have characterized Europe during the three decades since 1980. The outcome has been a dramatic transformation of the continent. I am going to discuss those elements of this political transfiguration that were of particular historical importance.

Unquestionably, the number one factor in bringing about these global changes was the *collapse of communism and the Soviet superpower*. The Cold War *division of Europe* and the world, which had determined its history since 1945, finally ended. The danger of war was eliminated. A closely related "side effect" of the end of communism was German reunification, a gigantic historical event in itself that nobody wanted to see outside Germany, but which no one was able to stop.

The announced *"new world order"* became a chaotic disorder. Europe rearranged itself and realized a new European order, though not without huge dramas, including the division of states along ethnic or religious lines, sometimes attended by civil wars, armed struggles, and terrorist methods in fighting for independence. These changes accompanied another equally historic change, a milestone in European history, which was the *transformation and elevation of the European Community*, both in terms of its expansion and its radically "deepened" integration. It took deep roots during the Cold War.[1] This development began the elevation of Europe as a superpower. A feverish

[1] Piers N. Ludlow (ed.), *European Integration and the Cold War: Ostpolitik–Westpolitik, 1965–1973* (London: Routledge, 2007).

enlargement process gained spectacular speed after 1980. The original six founder countries had accepted the first three newcomers, Britain, Ireland, and Denmark in 1973. Then, based on the transformation of the 1970s, three Mediterranean countries were accepted and joined the European Community: Greece in 1981, Spain and Portugal in 1986. German unification automatically generated the fourth enlargement: the incorporation of a former communist country, the German Democratic Republic, into the Community. The end of the Cold War provided an incentive for several countries to file their applications, among them all of the neutral countries of Europe that were unable to join before. National referenda voted down the Swiss and Norwegian accessions. The applications of Greco-Cyprus and Malta were somewhat postponed, but Sweden, Finland, and Austria joined in 1995.

Besides these advanced countries, however, the gates were also opened to former communist countries, even to former Soviet republics, which were now independent states. The new and major enlargement process began in the mid-1990s, and it was completed in the first decade of the twenty-first century with the incorporation of twelve new countries from the Baltic to the Balkans. In 2004, Malta, Cyprus, Poland, the Czech Republic, Slovakia, Hungary, Slovenia, Estonia, Latvia, and Lithuania joined the European Union, and Romania and Bulgaria followed suit in 2007. In a historically short period, the European Community of nine became the Community of twelve, fifteen, twenty-four, and finally twenty-seven. The transforming Central and Eastern European countries became part of the Union, i.e., in economic terms joined Western Europe's supply and production networks. The successive enlargement process, combined with a deliberate cohesion policy to assist backward regions and countries, generated and accelerated a catching-up process of the former peripheral countries of Europe.

In parallel with the ongoing enlargement process, however, the European Union made a new breakthrough by enacting the Single Market Act, clearing the road for the free movement of capital and labor, and launching the project for a common currency. Agreements on closing ranks and eliminating internal borders, as well as attempts to establish a common foreign policy and the nucleus of a common army, signaled the progress of further political integration. The political environment of Europe had changed immensely.

Collapse of Communism and the Soviet Union

Seen retrospectively, the crisis that emerged in the 1970s, though it seemed to be temporary, became unstoppable in the East and only deepened during the 1980s. The new decade started with a renewed Cold War. The reason this time was Afghanistan, outside Europe. In 1978, a military coup introduced communist command into the country, and rapid Sovietization began. This ignited a civil war, and the Soviet Union invaded Afghanistan in December 1979, in accordance with the Brezhnev doctrine. Nine years of bitter warfare followed against the Muslim *mujahedeen* forces, who were assisted by the United States, Saudi Arabia, and Pakistan. The cold political wave became icy when Polish communists, pushed by the Soviets, introduced martial law in December 1981 to eliminate the opposition movement.

In a new confrontation, President Reagan announced his intention in March 1983 to develop a new defense system that would destroy enemy missiles from space. In theory, it would make possible a first attack without fear of retaliation. "Star Wars," as the science fiction program was immediately nicknamed, was far from being an immediate danger, but the Soviet military establishment believed in its possibility and knew that they could not compete with it. In such a desperate economic situation, even the possibility of a further extreme arms race was unacceptable to the Soviet Union.

Meanwhile, the Soviet Bloc was unable to find a remedy for the sharply increased trade deficit and accumulated indebtedness. In the end, in contrast to the $6 billion in debt they had accumulated in 1970, the Soviet Bloc countries accumulated $110 billion in debt by 1989. This caused a repayment crisis. The $20 billion debt that Hungary owed was approximately two times greater than the value of the country's hard currency export income, but Poland's $42 billion debt was five times greater than its hard currency income. Debt servicing consumed 40 to 75 percent of the hard currency income of these countries combined. Meanwhile cheap credit disappeared and interest rates rose to between 14 and 16 percent. However, new credits were needed to repay the old ones, since the countries mostly consumed the money they borrowed to protect the "achievements" and stability of the regime. Only a small fragment of the credits was invested. In the case of Hungary, for example, only $4–5 billion out of $20 billion in credits found its way into investments.

Table 2.1. Comparative growth rates, GDP per capita[2]

Region	1950–73	1973–92
Western & Mediterranean Europe	4.8	2.0
Central & Eastern Europe	4.0	−0.8
Soviet Union (& successor states)	3.4	−1.4

The crisis grew deeper: Poland, Yugoslavia, and Bulgaria became insolvent and asked for rescheduling of their debt payments. Romania tried to escape from its indebtedness trap as Nicolae Ceaușescu, the paranoid "conducator" (leader), ordered repayment by cutting domestic consumption drastically. By 1985, electricity consumption had dropped to 20 percent of its 1979 levels. The stores were empty, and cities and homes darkened. Houses remained without heating in the winter. Romania, a broken and destroyed country, managed to repay her debts by 1989, a few weeks before a bloody uprising erupted, and the dictator was executed.[3]

Countries that had fixed prices under state socialism began to lose control over inflation. Hungarian consumer prices increased in the late 1980s by two-digit rates. In 1989, the rate of inflation in Poland reached 251 percent and in Yugoslavia 1,269 percent.[4] The countries of the region became unable to continue their previous growth policy. Between 1973 and 1989, they slowed to 1.2 percent growth per year.[5] During the second half of the 1980s, the Romanian and Yugoslav economies stagnated. The relative income level of the region significantly declined: in 1973, income levels in both Central and Eastern Europe and the Soviet Union stood at 49 percent of those in the West, but by 1989, they had fallen to 37 and 42 percent of the Western level, respectively.[6] While the West slowed to less than half of its previous growth rates, sharp decline replaced rapid growth in the East (Table 2.1).

---

[2] Angus Maddison, *Monitoring the World Economy 1820–1992* (Paris: OECD, 1995), 62.

[3] Ivan T. Berend, *Central and Eastern Europe 1944–1993: Detour from the Periphery to the Periphery* (Cambridge University Press, 1996), 230–2.

[4] European Bank for Reconstruction and Development, *Transition Report 2001* (London: EBRD, 2001), 61.

[5] Angus Maddison, *Explaining the Economic Performance of Nations* (Aldershot: Edward Elgar, 1995), 97.

[6] Angus Maddison, *Monitoring the World Economy 1820–1992* (Paris: OECD, 1995), 201.

The Collapse of Communism in Poland and Hungary – and the Domino Effect

Stagnation and then the downward spiral pushed the countries towards the abyss: economic crisis opened the floodgates of revolt. In August 1980, Gdansk became the center of the strike movement, and 156 factories joined. The newly established Inter-factory Strike Committee announced twenty-one demands. The government had to open negotiations, and an agreement was signed. The government accepted the *Solidarność* (Solidarity) trade union with Lech Wałęsa as its president as the authentic representative of the working class. Solidarity established its peasant wing, and by mid-1981 it had 10 million members. The Communist Party leadership resigned, and the government introduced a worker self-management system. Permanent strikes paralyzed the country. Coal exports, the most important export item of the country, declined by 60 percent. The opposition radicalized and became the decisive power in the country.

The Soviets presented the leadership of the country with a stark choice: either the Polish army suppressed the peaceful revolution, or the Soviet military would intervene to do so. The Party and government leadership were taken over by the military wing of the Party. General Wojtech Jaruzelski was elevated to head of the Party and government, and he introduced martial law on December 11–12. The entire Solidarity leadership was arrested and imprisoned. The regime hurriedly introduced economic reforms hoping to revitalize the economy behind the shield of military rule. It did not work. The population was hostile, and the West boycotted the military regime. A price–wage spiral deepened the misery. Since the military dictatorship of the party-state was only justifiable as a way of staving off the danger of Soviet intervention, when Gorbachev rejected the Brezhnev doctrine and initiated his perestroika in the mid-1980s, the military regime lost its last legitimization. The "Polish" Pope's second visit to Poland in 1983 strengthened the authority of the independent Catholic Church and Solidarity as the authentic representative of the people. Partial and then full amnesty followed in 1984 and 1986 respectively, and the situation came to a "political draw," as one of the most influential opposition leaders, Adam Michnik, put it.[7] When a

---

[7] Adam Michnik, *Takie czasy – rzecz o kompromisie* (London: Aneks, 1985).

new wave of strikes flooded the country in May 1988, the government had no other alternative but to come back to the negotiation table.

A compromise was born: the two parties agreed on power sharing. A pre-arranged, semi-free election was held in June 1989, in which all 100 seats of the newly established upper house, the Senate, were freely elected, but only 35 percent of the seats of the Sejm (Parliament). The posts of president, prime minister, and the ministers of the police and the military were guaranteed to the Communist Party. It looked like a good bargain for the Party, but it turned out to be a miscalculation. The elections led to a landslide victory for Solidarity, and the Communist Party did not get a single seat among the competitively elected representatives. It was a humiliating defeat, and the Party was unable to form a government. On August 24, 1989, President Jaruzelski appointed Solidarity's candidate, Tadeusz Mazowiecki, prime minister of Poland. In 1991, Jaruzelski resigned, and Lech Wałęsa became president of Poland. In October of the same year, an entirely free election led to the defeat of a badly broken Solidarity without any real winner: representatives of thirty fragmented parties occupied the seats of the Parliament. Communism, however, had peacefully collapsed in Poland.

Communism also collapsed in Hungary. Although a strong, organized mass opposition movement and strikes did not shock the regime from the streets, a strong "social-democratized" opposition wing emerged within the Party. The reform wing learned the lessons of the 1970s, when a conservative anti-reform policy partly destroyed the results of the previous reform process. In a telling episode, a group of economists and sociologists in 1986–7 worked out a radical new reform agenda, combining an economic reform program with guarantees of freedom of the press, information, and society. It was harshly attacked by the Party leadership. However, a sub-committee of the Party's Central Committee accepted the document that became the basis of a resolution demanding the reform of the political institutions.[8] In the second half of the 1980s, the reformers already wanted to radicalize the economic reforms and combine them with political reform. The process gained new impetus: Western-type taxation and banking systems were introduced.

In May 1988, an internal Party "revolt" forced the holding of an extraordinary Party conference, two years before the regular, planned

---

[8] Az MSzMP KB állásfoglalása, *Népszabadság*, July 14, 1987.

congress. It led to a landslide victory for the reform wing. János Kádár and most of his Politburo, who had resisted the radicalization of reforms, were removed, and one-third of the Central Committee was replaced. The reform wing gradually took over the Party and government leadership. A Historians' Committee was appointed to reevaluate the official version of postwar historical developments in Hungary, and its January 1989 report officially de-legitimized the Kádár regime, rejecting the official denunciation of the 1956 revolution as a "counter-revolution," and finding instead that it represented a "genuine peoples' uprising" of the abused and humiliated population against Stalinism, and a fight for independence against the Soviet Union.[9] In 1988, the government accepted a three-year privatization and marketization plan and started to implement it.

In February 1989, after the debate over the reevaluation of 1956 and before the Polish Round Table agreed to have semi-free elections, the Hungarian Party's Central Committee made a historic decision to hold free, multi-party elections in Hungary in the spring of 1990, just one year later (Figure 1). The reform-communist government effectively introduced a market economy by eliminating restrictive regulations and clearing the road for privatization and foreign direct investments (FDI). A series of Round Table talks with all the newly formed opposition parties and organizations reached agreements and prepared the road for transformation. The constitution was amended, abolishing the Soviet-type "people's republic" and its institutions, including the notorious "leading role of the Party." A Constitutional Court was established, and freedom of the press and human rights were declared – all before the collapse of the regime. The Communist Party also dissolved itself in October and was replaced by two parties: a small one, keeping the old name and representing a direct continuation of the Kádár era, and the majority reform wing, which reorganized itself as a European-type socialist party and was soon accepted by the Social Democratic International. The new party that led the transformation had the self-confidence to think that it could win free elections. This too turned out to be a miscalculation: at the free, multi-party elections in March 1990, the socialists got less than 10 percent of the votes, and a coalition of right-of-center opposition parties, led by the Hungarian Democratic Forum, had an absolute victory.

---

[9] Ivan T. Berend *et al.*, "Történelmi utunk. A Munkabizottság állásfoglalása," *Társadalmi Szemle*, 44, Special issue (March, 1989).

Figure 1. A huge crowd in front of the Hungarian parliament building listening to the announcement of the dramatic constitutional change and the establishment of a democratic republic in place of the "people's republic," Budapest, 1989.

It made for an emerging revolutionary situation in the entire region when virtually nobody was ready to defend the regime. A remarkable episode accelerated the collapse of the Soviet Bloc. In May 1989, the reform-communist Hungarian government announced the destruction of the old fortifications at the Austrian-Hungarian borders as a symbolic gesture. They had no importance for Hungarians who had passports and were free to travel. This symbolic step, however, opened the way for East Germans, who were not allowed to travel to the West: hundreds of thousands spent their vacations in Hungary and other neighboring countries. Now they could walk over to West Germany via Austria, and tens of thousands did so. Hungary did not keep its old agreement with East Germany to capture each other's citizens and send them back if they tried to leave illegally. Instead,

Figure 2. The fall of the Berlin Wall, November 1989. The wall was the symbol of the division of Europe and of the world; its collapse became the symbol of a new Europe.

the Hungarian government made an agreement in the early fall with Chancellor Kohl and officially allowed East Germans to leave. This situation generated huge mass demonstrations of hundreds of thousands in Berlin, Dresden, and all of the big East German cities, demonstrations which eventually swept away the hard-line government of Erich Honecker. The authorities opened the Berlin Wall, the symbol of a closed society and the separation of Europe, and the regime collapsed in November 1989 (Figure 2).

A domino effect followed, and in the six weeks before Christmas, state socialism collapsed in the other four countries of the region. It happened relatively peacefully in Czechoslovakia and Bulgaria. Romania experienced the only bloody revolution in the region because of the desperate resistance of its neo-Stalinist regime. In Yugoslavia, the regime also collapsed, but it took the federal state with it in a devastating civil war that ravaged the country between 1991 and 1995. Finally, in 1991, the regimes in Albania and the Soviet Union also collapsed. Gorbachev came too late, and his reform policy was too partial, to save the communist regime. No alternatives were offered in the Central and Eastern European situation, and the collapse of the status quo was definitive.

The Collapse of the Multinational Soviet State

The collapse of communism in the Soviet Union went hand in hand with the dissolution of the Empire. It occurred surprisingly smoothly because reform-communism had already conquered the Soviet party leadership in the second half of the 1980s. Some historical accidents contributed to it. After the partly paralyzed Leonid Brezhnev, the rigid anti-reform champion and military interventionist, died in November 1982, in the most grotesque way the Bolshevik Party decided to fill his empty chair with his close comrades and appointed two old and dying men, first Yuri Andropov and then Konstantin Chernenko. Neither of them survived much more than a year in office. In 1985, however, the Party selected Mikhail Gorbachev, a younger man who had emerged in the Party hierarchy. His first actions seemed to be nothing more than traditional and conservative campaigning against corruption, and advocacy for *uskarenie* (faster growth). However, Gorbachev very soon understood that major reforms were needed, and he announced the policy of *glasnost* (openness) and *perestroika* (restructuring) (Figure 3).

Gorbachev's new policy opened a new chapter in international policy as well. The Soviet acceptance of defeat in Afghanistan, and their withdrawal in 1988, signaled a new era. The Gorbachev regime also introduced a non-interventionist policy towards the Soviet Bloc countries. Gorbachev's Soviet Union accepted the collapse of communism in Poland, the strategically most important satellite country in the Bloc. The Brezhnev doctrine of military intervention to save socialism, if it was "endangered" in one of the state socialist countries, was

Figure 3. Mikhail Gorbachev, Soviet president whose *glasnost* and *perestroika* aimed to correct "real socialism," but ultimately led to its collapse.

quietly buried with its initiator. The gate was wide open for reform, the elimination of the state socialist regime, and the disintegration of the Soviet Bloc.

Mikhail Gorbachev also realized that the Soviet Union could not afford the arms race, and that it had to turn inwards to improve its economy and social-political situation. The Reykjavik summit between Gorbachev and Ronald Reagan in October 1986 became the most successful "failed" summit. On the one hand, it ended without an agreement, but on the other, it led to the Intermediate-Range Nuclear Forces Treaty, signed in Washington in December 1987. This treaty practically buried the Cold War.

In this renewed political environment, the Russian Republic of the Soviet Union elected a Congress in June 1990. The Congress declared Russian sovereignty, which was ratified by a referendum in March 1991. In June of that same year, at the first real elections in the history of Russia, Boris Yeltsin became president of the Russian Republic. At that time, however, nine out of the fifteen republics of the Soviet Union wanted the Soviet state to be kept together. The central government and President Gorbachev prepared a looser confederation.

The separation of the westernmost edge of the Soviet Empire, however, became the forerunner of dissolution. The western strip of the

Figure 4. The beginning of the end of the Soviet Union: Baltic demonstration in 1990, on the anniversary of the infamous Molotov-Ribbentrop Pact of 1940 that gave the three Baltic republics to the Soviet Union.

Soviet Union consisted of regions that were incorporated into Russia in the eighteenth century, but which then became independent after the Bolshevik Revolution. During and after World War II, however, Stalin reoccupied these countries. Now they were the first to reestablish independence. The three Baltic countries, Estonia, Latvia, and Lithuania, supported Gorbachev's perestroika and founded movements to accomplish it. In the agitated environment, they turned into national movements that organized massive demonstrations, which followed one after another during the late 1980s (Figure 4). Mass movements culminated in the August 1989 "Baltic Way," a human chain of 2 million people, stretched hand-in-hand across the three countries. In the spring of 1990, strengthened by the revolutionary events in Central Europe, all three countries declared independence. When the first among them, Lithuania, announced its separation in March 1990, Gorbachev sent tanks to crush them, but the mass demonstrations did not stop, and the Soviet Union recognized Baltic independence in September 1991.

A similar movement characterized the republic of Soviet Moldavia, where the Moldavian Supreme Soviet legalized the "Moldovan" (Romanian) language in the summer of 1989, and it officially revived the Latin alphabet alongside the Russian Cyrillic one. The republic even declared the formation of the Pridnestrovian Moldavian SSR in the fall of 1990, but independence was declared only in September 1991. However, the Russian and Ukrainian majority of the Transdniestria region, which totaled nearly 54 percent of the population, did not recognize the new, Romanian-led state, and wanted instead to establish a separate independent state on the eastern side of the Dniester River. The 14th division of the Russian Army, which was stationed there, assisted them and they defeated the Moldavian police and volunteer units, which were assisted by Romania. The separatist eastern region created the autonomous Dniester Republic in 1993. Resurfacing skirmishes caused roughly 1,000 deaths until a ceasefire was declared. A peace agreement was signed in 1997, followed by the withdrawal of Russian troops.

In a paradoxical way, the final straw that led to the dissolution of the Soviet Union was the bitter hard-liner coup in August 1991, in which Gorbachev was arrested in an attempt to return to a kind of neo-Stalinism that would suppress independence movements. However, the poorly organized coup failed, and Boris Yeltsin, the democratically elected president of the Russian Republic, mobilized the people against the coup, emerging as the hero of the day and taking over power. The Empire was dissolved, and fifteen independent states emerged, with Russia, Ukraine, and Kazakhstan as the largest. In December 1991, Russia, Ukraine, and Belarus signed the Belavezha Accord to establish the Commonwealth of Independent States. Gorbachev resigned.

While separation in the western half of the Empire was relatively peaceful, war exploded on the other edge of the former Soviet Union. According to the 1991 agreement, the only administrative units to have the right to declare independence were those that had the status of a republic in the Soviet Union. Accordingly, the declarations of independence by several small minority-national areas were rejected. This happened in the Caucasus, where the Chechen Republic of Ichkeria was declared in 1991. Two Chechen wars followed. The first war claimed the lives of about 40,000 people between 1994 and 1996, but it established de facto independence. The ceasefire in 1996, and a peace agreement the following year, consolidated the situation, but a second Chechen war erupted in 1999–2000. This time Russia easily reoccupied Grozny, the capital city, and reestablished Russian rule by establishing a pro-Russian Chechen regime. A regional constitution in

2003 granted autonomous rights. Assassinations and terrorist actions on both sides – even the declaration of a Chechen Emirate in 2007 – signaled continued unsolved problems and the continued efforts by Sunni Muslim Chechnya to gain independence.

Several unsolved minority problems generated conflicts and military confrontations in the Caucasus region, where roughly fifty different ethnicities are mixed. The Armenian population of Nagorno-Karabakh wanted to separate from newly independent Azerbaijan. The people of South Ossetia, which was not historically part of Georgia but had been incorporated into it in 1991, declared independence. Conflict characterized the entire post-communist period, and Russian peacekeeping forces stabilized the situation. When Georgia, in the summer of 2008, tried to reoccupy South Ossetia with its 50,000 inhabitants by murderous artillery and military attacks, the Russian army invaded, bombing and smashing Georgia. This military action also "liberated" the breakaway enclave of Abkhazia with its population of 200,000. In a few days, Russia recognized Ossetian and Abkhaz independence. Warfare is almost endemic in the Caucasus region.

Unification of Germany

The postwar division of Germany in the heart of the continent most visibly exhibited the division of Europe. Since 1961 the separation was dramatically and also symbolically embodied by the Berlin Wall. The division of Germany was always loudly condemned and stood at the center of Cold War rhetoric, but it was silently welcomed by most of Europe, East and West alike. Germany's role in the two world wars, and especially the enthusiastic popular support for – and unprecedented crimes of – the Hitler regime, made Germany a political pariah after the war.

President Franklin D. Roosevelt wanted to push back Germany to an agrarian-pastoral state by annihilating its industrial capacities. The Morgenthau plan to de-industrialize and dissolve Germany was not realized, however, because of the Cold War and the need for the rearmament of Germany. In his famous Zurich speech in 1946, Winston Churchill recommended the foundation of a federal Europe and the end of retribution. He spoke about a Europe where small states would have equal rights, and where "the *ancient states and principalities of Germany*, freely joined together in a federal system, might each take their *individual place* among the United States of Europe."[10]

In spite of loud accusations against the Soviet Union for establishing an independent East Germany, most West European countries were silently satisfied. As James Baker III, secretary of state in the first Bush administration, said in an interview in 1992: "The West rhetorically supported German unification for forty years... Now everyone knows that it was not a popular idea in France, and it was not a popular idea in the United Kingdom . . ."[11] The 1989 events, and the collapse of the Berlin Wall in November of that year, however, put unification automatically on the agenda. Chancellor Helmut Kohl wanted to realize it in a few months. However, "Thatcher made it unambiguously clear that for her reunification was not on the agenda... Instead, she spoke in favor of the maintenance... of a democratized GDR... Germany had to remain partitioned."[12] François Mitterrand, as secret archive documents made public, rushed to East Berlin in late December 1989 and "encouraged East German leaders at the time to preserve a separate state and resist unification pressure... [Mitterrand even promised] to deliver assistance from France and the European Community to help preserve the country."[13] Mitterrand's initiative was influenced by his short-lived ambitious plan, addressed in his televised New Year speech on December 31, 1989, stating that "I hope... to see emerge in the 1990s a European confederation [of all states] in a common and permanent organization for exchange, peace, and security."[14]

Unification, however, was an unstoppable process. Most East Germans wanted to be West Germans, whom they had envied for decades. One of their slogans illustrates the atmosphere: "Helmut [Kohl], take us by the hand, lead us to the economic wonderland." The Big Brother's prosperity and living standards were irresistible. In fact, 1.7 million East Germans, more than 10 percent of the population, did

---

[10] Winston Churchill, *His Complete Speeches, 1897–1963*, Vol. 7 [1974] in Brent F. Nelsen and Alexander C.-G. Stubb (eds.), *The European Union, Readings on the Theory and Practice of European Integration* (Boulder, CO: Lynne Rienner, 1998), 10 (italics added).

[11] National Security Archive, Cold War Interviews, www.gwu.edu/~nsarchiv/coldwar/ interviews/episode-23/baker3.html

[12] Klaus Larres, "Margaret Thatcher, the British Foreign Office, and German Unification," *Cercles: Revue Pluridisciplinaire du Monde Anglophone*, 5 (2002), 1–2.

[13] *International Herald Tribune*, May 4, 1996.

[14] Frédéric Bozo, "The Failure of a Grand Design: Mitterrand's European Confederation, 1989–1991," *Contemporary European History*, Special Issue, 17, 3 (August, 2008), 391–412.

Figure 5. Chancellor Helmut Kohl of Germany (left) and Prime Minister Gyula Horn of Hungary. Their agreement opened the Hungarian borders for East German citizens in the summer of 1989, which led to the collapse of East Germany.

not wait, but left for West Germany in the years immediately following the collapse (Figure 5).

The July 1990 currency unification between the two German states, the introduction of the West German institutional system in the East, and the 1:1 wage adjustment created a *fait accompli*. No one could block the road to the unification that was officially realized by October 3, 1990. The territory of the Federal Republic of Germany increased by 44 percent, its population grew by 26 percent, and the unified country became the strongest country in Europe, with 80 million inhabitants and an economy of global importance.

The fact and importance of unification was not challenged by the rapid mass disappointment of the East German population. The path to unification became a kind of *Gleichschaltung*, forcibly bringing the junior partner into line. Or, to use a metaphor: the big fish swallowing the small one. West German appointees took over most of the leading positions, including university jobs. Most of all, the East German economy collapsed immediately when the borders were opened for West German competition. Wage equalization annihilated their only potential comparative advantage: lower wages. By 1994, the *Treuhandanstalt*, or privatization agency, liquidated or began the process of liquidating nearly 4,000 East German companies. By 1992, 5 million jobs disappeared, hundreds of thousands had to retire early, and employment dropped to only 23 percent of the 1990 level. The former East German GDP declined by 42 percent, industrial output by 51 percent, and the value of exports by 54 percent in 1991, and then by a further 21 percent and 13 percent in 1992 and 1993 respectively.

After the postwar decades of prosperity, the West German political elite and government had absolute confidence that they could solve the difficult economic and social task of transformation, since they had sufficient financial and economic resources. Indeed, in six Central European transforming countries combined, the per capita foreign capital inflow amounted to $30 in 1993, but the former West Germany channeled $5,900 per capita to the former GDR, now the new "*Ländern.*" Consequently, however, economic growth slowed down significantly in the German Federal Republic: in the decade before unification, German GDP increased by 18 percent, but after the unification it rose by only 7.5 percent. That was much slower than in neighboring countries such as the Netherlands (21 percent growth) or Italy and France (10–11 percent growth). Even between 1995 and 2005, Germany's annual growth rate of 1.4 percent remained behind the euro-zone average of 2.1 percent.

However, after the monumental decline in the early years after unification, the economy of the new *Ländern* began consolidating: by 1994, it reached the pre-unification level of GDP.[15] Rebuilding the cities of the eastern states of the Federal Republic also exhibited spectacular results. Former East Berlin became a construction zone. Downtown Leipzig and Weimar exhibited similar trends. What did not change was the atmosphere in former East Germany, where the "*Ossi*" (Eastern) Germans considered themselves second-rate citizens, compared to the "*Wessi*" (Westerners). The younger generation was still ready to migrate westwards. The absorption of the shock of the unification would take generations.

New World Order?

From the mid-1980s, and especially after 1989–91, post-Cold War Europe was in a euphoric political state. Conflicts and dangers

---

[15] Productivity level, 29% of the West in 1990, elevated to 44% of it by 1995. Exports started increasing in 1994 by a modest 3%, but the following year already by 12%.

belonged to the past, the crisis of the 1970s to early 1980s was seemingly over, and the Eastern half of the continent nurtured exaggerated
expectations and hoped to be similar to the West in just a few years.
The early 1990s were characterized by inflated optimistic expectations. It was evident that a new world order was in the making, a har-
monious framework for a strong integrated Europe. What emerged,
however, was not the "New World Order" hurriedly announced by
the president of the only remaining superpower, the United States. At
the United Nations General Assembly meeting on October 1, 1990,
President George H. W. Bush spoke about a "whole world, whole
and free," where, instead of confrontation, a new order of "partnership based on consultation, cooperation and collective action" would
emerge. He spoke on several occasions about "shared commitment
among nations, large and small, shared responsibility for freedom and
justice."[16] In his speech to Congress on March 6, 1991, President Bush
stated, "Twice before in this century, an entire world was convulsed
by war. Twice this century, out of the horrors of war hope emerged
for enduring peace. Twice before, those hopes proved to be a distant
dream, beyond the grasp of man . . . Now, we can see a new world
coming into view. A world in which there is the very real prospect of
a new world order."[17]

In the post–Cold War world system, multilateralism was to govern
through "institutionalized patterns of cooperation among Western
democracies." "What we need to do now," said Lawrence Eagleburger
in November 1991 on behalf of the American administration, "is to
widen this circle to include many new members of the democratic
family."[18] Several calculations were made about the prospective "peace
dividend," i.e., the thousands of billions that would not be spent on
military expenditures after the Cold War arms race ended.

In reality, the high-minded term, the "New World Order," was
soon ridiculed as the "New World Disorder." Henry Kissinger once
rightly maintained that "the success of war is victory; the success
of peace is stability." Stability, however, was the first victim of the
post–Cold War "peace settlement." State borders, sacrosanct for half
a century, suddenly became subject to debate and changes. This was

---

[16] Ian Clark, *The Post-Cold War Order: The Spoils of Peace* (Oxford University Press, 2001), 181.
[17] G. H. W. Bush Presidential Library and Museum, 1991, "Address Before a Joint
Session of the Congress on the Cessation of the Persian Gulf Conflict," Bushli-
brary.tamu.edu/research/public_papers.php, 1991=03-06
[18] Quoted by Clark, *Post-Cold War*, 182.

sometimes achieved by peaceful agreements, as in Germany, the Baltic region of the Soviet Union, and in Czechoslovakia, and sometimes by military actions, as in the Balkans and the Caucasus region of the former Soviet Union.

Sharp conflicts and wars rattled the countries and regions neighboring Europe as well. Pressure to change borders in the neighboring Middle East came from several sides. That open wound, the Israeli–Arab conflict, the Palestinian question, Syria's aggressive role in Lebanon, as well as bloody Kurdish attempts to establish an independent Kurdistan provoked even bloodier Turkish and Iraqi responses. In this chaotic situation, Saddam Hussein miscalculated in his bid to change Iraq's artificial post-colonial borders by incorporating Kuwait by force. Instead of multilateralism and cooperation, an American-centered arrangement characterized the new global political order, supported by military posturing and pseudo-multilateralism.

The number one ally of Europe, and its protector since the war, the United States of America turned to more than questionable roads as the only superpower. A few weeks after the fall of the Berlin Wall, one of the first actions of the Bush administration was the invasion of Panama in December 1989. The American government removed the corrupt drug-trafficking dictator, Manuel Noriega, who had been on the CIA payroll for decades, but who had become unpredictable and disruptive to the United States' Latin American policy. The National Security Strategy Report to Congress in March 1990 stressed the need for military power targeting primarily the Middle East, where American interests were assumed to be threatened. It also argued for strengthening the defense industrial base.

The United States began acting as an unchallengeable superpower: a disturbing, uneasy reality for Europe. It was only a decade after President Bush announced the new principle of multilateralism that his son openly replaced it with the principle of American unilateralism. The world did not become a "whole democratic family," and history, in spite of Francis Fukuyama's 1989 prophecy, has not "ended" by melting into a uniform liberal democratic world system. Soon the "clash of civilizations" predicted by Fukuyama's teacher, Samuel Huntington, frightened the globe and started to emerge as a central question within Europe.

Geopolitical rivalry had not ended either. In an increasingly interconnected world system, new cutthroat racial and political conflicts emerged. Internationalization of the Western economies gained ground after the war, but the 1980s became the real watershed for its breakthrough. Globalization emerged as the new policy of the leading economic powers that replaced colonialism. This also had an objective economic basis in the new technological revolution, combined with a new development of companies that were both multi-functional and multinational. Advanced countries still sought to use the large market and cheap labor of the developing world, but no longer in a colonial framework. The multinational companies – which numbered 7,000 in 1973 and 64,000 by 2005 – established subsidiaries all over the world, and they supported a policy that eliminated trade barriers and strengthened competitiveness by outsourcing workplaces and establishing a new division of labor. Consequently, investments abroad increased four times in the last two decades of the twentieth century. Steeply increased world trade and financial transactions characterized the globalized world economy. The value of international trade stood at $1.7 trillion in 1973. It jumped three-and-a-half times, to $5.8 trillion, in the last quarter of the century. The value of exports from Western Europe jumped nearly nine times. The volume of financial transactions, however, was fifty times higher than the value of world trade. The world economy entered a new era and created both challenges and opportunities for Europe.[19]

In the changing international environment, what happened was the replacement of East–West rivalry by a rising global rivalry: a creeping Atlantic rivalry among postwar allies, dramatic Asian–Western competition, and a rising Islamic–Western conflict, which gradually became manifest during the decades after the end of the Cold War. These new economic–political trends strongly influenced politics and developed a new European self-confidence in the closing decades of the twentieth century. European–American relations became more equal, but were also characterized by more conflicts. Anti-Americanism also gained ground. As Alexander Stephan writes: "Europe believes that it offers an alternative model to the social and cultural overstretch of American postmodernism."[20] The 2008 financial crisis ignited a European attempt to reject American deregulationism and to return to Bretton Woods and regulated financial markets.

[19] Maddison, *World Economy*, 127, 362; OECD, *Structural Adjustment and Economic Performance* (Paris: OECD, 1987), 273.

[20] Alexander Stephan, "Cold War Alliances and the Emergence of Transatlantic Competition: An Introduction," in Alexander Stephan (ed.), *The Americanization of Europe: Culture, Diplomacy and Anti-Americanism after 1945* (New York: Berghahn Books, 2006), 1–22.

The content of anti-Americanism is puzzling, however. It has different variants, which are sometimes merged together. It is in part only an "uncomfortable awareness of a now unique and unchecked American might," the American "hyper-power," or *hyper-puissance*, as Hubert Védrin, French minister of foreign affairs put it.[21] As a reaction to arrogant American unilateralism, political anti-Americanism, or, more accurately, opposition to American government policy, became more widespread and open in the early twenty-first century than ever before. The euphoric reception in Berlin of Senator Barack Obama, the Democratic presidential candidate, by 200,000 people in the summer of 2008 clearly signaled the sharp difference between anti-American and anti-American-administration feelings.

Political trends often merged with or were based on cultural anti-Americanism. This had a longer history as a reaction to the dominance of American cultural products on the European markets, sometimes called "cultural colonization" ("mcdonaldization," "cocacolonization") by fast-food chains and Hollywood movies. However, this is paradoxical because "American" cultural trends meanwhile became quite international and European.[22] One may also speak about ideological anti-Americanism, or the rejection of the absolute supremacy of the neo-liberal, market fundamentalist, and neo-conservative ideologies that became dominant during the 1980s under Reagan. "Beginning with the Reagan administration, the United States took a sharp turn away from the path that it had followed in the post-World War II era ... This is a sharp departure from the path followed in Europe."[23]

An Ever Closer and Larger European Union

The integration process of Europe gained momentum after the foundation of the European Economic Community in 1957. The European Community made impressive progress in creating a free trade area by eliminating tariffs, import quotas, and other restrictions during the first decade of its existence. Soon the Community took the step of

[21] Richard J. Golsan, "From French Anti-Americanism and Americanization to the 'American Enemy'?" in Stephan (ed.), *Americanization of Europe*, 44–68, 63.

[22] Paul Hollander, *Anti-Americanism: Critiques at Home and Abroad, 1965–1990* (New York: Oxford University Press, 1992).

[23] Dean Baker, *The United States Since 1980* (Cambridge University Press, 2007), xi, xii.

Figure 6. Jacques Delors, visionary president of the Commission of the European Union and the main architect of its renewal from the mid-1980s.

forming a customs union with common tariffs around the Community's borders. Progress beyond the customs union was impossible, however. From the 1960s on, a more than decade long stagnation endangered the building of a united Europe.

However, in the new international and European environment, the 1980s marked a turning point, the period when the integration process gained new energy and reached a much higher level. The new European Commission under Jacques Delors' leadership took office in 1984 (Figure 6). The countries of the Community still struggled to cope with the recession and the new requirements of globalization. In addition, with the collapse of communism and the Soviet Union in 1989–91, one of the main motivations for integrating Western Europe into a strong and flourishing Union, the Cold War, also disappeared. Britain's Margaret Thatcher, an enthusiastic advocate of free trade and consequently the European common market, strictly opposed any

further integration beyond the intergovernmental level. Like President
de Gaulle in the sixties, Thatcher, in 1988, denounced the attempts
"to suppress nationhood and concentrate power . . . in Brussels . . . [in
the hands of] an appointed bureaucracy . . . Let Europe be a family of
nations . . . rather than let ourselves be distracted by utopian goals."[24]

British policy towards the European Union was, and remained,
controversial. The "sentiment about the past" haunted Britain. This
was more understandable in the time and case of Winston Churchill,
who painted the picture of a United States of Europe with a strong
stroke of the brush, but meanwhile excluded Britain from Europe and
established the long-lasting "misunderstandings about Britain's part in
this Europe." This ambivalence accompanied British policy during
the period from 1980. "Could Britain . . . truly accept," asked Hugo
Young rhetorically, "that her modern destiny was to be a European
country?" British ambivalence towards Europe characterized Tony
Blair's Labour government as well. Following in the footsteps of
Churchill and Thatcher, Blair, like his predecessors, remained "spec-
tator rather than actor in a continental drama from which Britain, the
island nation, chose to exclude herself."[25]

Stagnation or disintegration became a possibility, but just the opposite happened. The Community shifted into full gear to drive towards
a higher stage of integration from the late 1980s on. Jacques Delors,
the visionary president of the Commission of the Community, stated
in a speech in Bruges in 1989 – thus answering Thatcher, who had
spoken in the same place a year before – that there was more reason
to deepen integration than ever. His generation of European leaders still thought of political unification and federalization, and of the
indivisibility of European security. In the new world economy, Delors
stressed in his speech, "nations cannot act alone." The reality in the
new world system, he argued, is the "growing interdependence of our
economies, the internationalization of the financial world . . . [which
makes] full national sovereignty" a fiction. Europe has to consider
"worldwide geopolitical and economic trends . . . [It is] losing its place
as the economic and political center of the world . . . European market and common policies have supported national efforts to adapt to

[24] Margaret Thatcher's speech at the College of Europe in Bruges, September 20, 1988,
reprinted as "A Family of Nations," in Nelsen and Stubb (eds.), *The European Union*, 52,
54.

[25] Hugo Young, *This Blessed Plot: Britain and Europe from Churchill to Blair* (London: Macmillan,
1998), 1, 6, 147.

the new world economic order . . . Europe is once again a force to be reckoned with . . ."[26]

If globalization required a strong, more integrated Europe, further enlargement towards the East offered a huge advantage to the Union. Above all, the EU would stabilize the continent, and absorb 100 million new, hungry consumers, a rapidly growing market with much greater possibilities for exports and strengthening the economy of scale and competitiveness. Western Europe would be able to build up its economic backyard in low-wage countries near to its borders and might become a bigger global actor, with more influence in world trade and international organizations.[27]

Delors and the Commission set the agenda to complete the common market, i.e., the elimination of still existing obstacles to free trade and the free movement of labor, capital, and services, and thereby to reach the level of an economic union without internal frontiers. The Single European Act, the first major revision of the Treaty of Rome, was signed in Luxembourg in February 1986, and came into effect the following year. This set a deadline to realize the goals by 1992. The treaty also set the goal of further political cooperation between the member countries. Since the member countries had signed the Single Market Act, trade among them had already increased by an amazing twenty-three times. According to certain calculations, integration generated more than a 5 percent increase in the aggregate GDP of the six countries. To eliminate all the existing barriers, however, required detailed work lasting several years. Europe had to harmonize the innumerable different national regulations, which was a tremendous task, especially to make the movement of services free, including financial services. Although several goals were achieved by 1992, the "four freedoms" of undisturbed flow of goods, labor, capital, and services were not fully accomplished and required continuous regulatory work.

The declaration of the freedom of labor movement, for example, was not enough to eliminate several existing obstacles. Different

---

[26] Jacques Delors, "Address by Mr. Jacques Delors, Bruges, 17 October 1989," in Nelsen and Stubb (eds.), *European Union* 55–68, 58–9, 62.

[27] Barry Eichengreen compares the situation with the experience of postwar America: after World War II, the economic center of the United States shifted to the South, and America benefited from the South's lower level of unionization, more competitive wage level, more flexible labor market, and liberal land-use policy, which helped "greenfield" investments. "It is fair to ask whether the EU's expansion to the East could have a similar invigorating effect." Barry Eichengreen, *The European Economy since 1945: Coordinated Capitalism and Beyond* (Princeton University Press, 2007), 406.

wage levels and various national qualifications for skills and university diplomas created obstacles that required some harmonization of the educational systems of the member countries. Similarly, Community-wide regulation of pensions, welfare benefits, and the ability to open bank accounts abroad was needed. The declaration of free movement of capital could not eliminate the real obstacle presented by different national tax schemes, especially in the area of corporate taxes, differences in fiscal and monetary policies, and strict national licensing of banking and insurance companies, which all created different, unfair advantages for some and disadvantages for others. All these differences had to be leveled and the policies harmonized, but these processes required a long time.

In parallel with this ambitious agenda, a French–German and Benelux agreement in 1984–5 initiated a comprehensive treaty to eliminate all frontier control of the movement of people among them. Two agreements in 1985, and then one in June 1990, led to the acceptance of the Schengen Treaty signed by all the continental member countries of the Community, which shifted control from their national borders to the external borders of the Union.

The 1980s also marked the beginning of a breakthrough in monetary unification and the introduction of a common currency. This attempt also had a long history. The Hague Summit of the Community had announced the goal in 1969, and the Werner Report prepared the plan the next year. The breakthrough, however, happened only in the 1980s: the heads of states made the decision on a common currency at their Paris summit in 1988. The Delors Report of 1989 presented an exact plan and timetable for the introduction of the common currency. Strict norms about inflation and budgetary deficits regulated the prerequisites and forced financial discipline to accompany the introduction of the common currency. The European Union introduced the "euro" (€) in three consecutive steps between 1999 and 2002, when the new euro banknotes finally replaced national currencies (Figure 7). Although Britain, Denmark, and Sweden did not join, the common currency was soon also introduced in Greece, and then by the newly accepted Slovenia, Malta, Cyprus, and then Slovakia. Several other new member countries have a deadline for introduction of the euro somewhere in the 2010s.

The further integration process had its strong opposition and the project met with skepticism. When communism collapsed and the Cold War ended, even advocates and "enthusiasts" of the European

Figure 7. Euro banknotes.

cause lost their confidence in further measures to "deepen" integration, such as the introduction of the common currency. In his 1998
article, "Europe's Endangered Liberal Order," Timothy Garton Ash
flatly stated that, "[t]he end of the Cold War also ended a historical
constellation that was particularly favorable to a particular model of
West European integration." He argued: "our leaders set the wrong
priority after 1989." Monetary unification will soon lead to a crisis
and endangers the real European goals. "Liberal order, not unity, is the
right strategic goal for European policy in our time." In Maastricht,
the European Union – to use Garton Ash's metaphor – decorated and
upgraded the Western half of the European house while the Eastern
half – though no longer divided by a concrete wall – fell apart and
was burning in Sarajevo. "To consolidate Europe's liberal order and
to spread it across the whole continent is both more urgent and . . .
[a] more realistic goal for Europe at the beginning of the twenty-first
century than the vain pursuit of unification in a part of it." In the new
post-Cold War Europe, in an enlarged European Union, "a further
sharing of sovereignty [is] essential," while monetary union pushes
the European Union in another direction that "endanger[s] liberal
order."[28]

Tony Judt had similar views. The immediate postwar situation and
the Cold War "facilitated the construction of 'Europe,'" and the "illusion of Europe would not survive being put to a continent-wide test."
The European Union was tailored for the West in a particular way.
Incorporation of former communist countries was impossible since it

[28] Timothy Garton Ash, "Europe's Endangered Liberal Order," *Foreign Affairs*, 77, 2
(March/April, 1998), 51–65.

would be an "onerous burden" and "for the foreseeable future, it
would be an act of charity . . . for the European Union . . . therefore
be the better part of wisdom to stop promising otherwise." Judt under-
lines his conclusion in the preface to *A Grand Illusion? An Essay on
Europe*: "my essay thus concludes with a plea for the partial rein-
statement, or relegitimation, of nation states." He was convinced that
responding to the challenge of globalization, the traditional "old-
fashioned nation state is a better form in which to secure collective loyalties, protect the disadvantaged, enforce a fairer distribution
of resources, and compensate for disruptive transnational economic
patterns."[29]

The European Union, however, went further on its road. The common currency and a single European Central Bank became the most
important supranational institution of the otherwise mostly intergovernmental organization of the Union. The common currency offered
significant financial advantages, such as the elimination of conversion
costs and exchange rate fluctuations. It also played a role in price equalization, the unification of the financial markets, and efficient control of
inflation. The common currency, above all, significantly strengthened
Europe's global standing. In an astonishingly short period of time, the
euro became the second international reserve currency next to the
declining dollar, and within five to seven years of its introduction,
roughly one-quarter of international financial transactions were using
the European currency.

Based on the progress of integration, the meeting of the European
Council in March 2000 in Lisbon set a ten-year program for modernization of the economy and increased European competitiveness
to strengthen the Union's position in the globalized world economy.
The Union wanted to increase its employment rate to 70 percent, and
the employment of women to 60 percent. It also aimed to keep half
of its older workers in the labor force, and return to a faster annual
growth rate of 3 percent per annum. The Council declared the ambitious goal that the European Union "become the most competitive
and dynamic knowledge-based economy in the world." The program
set educational goals as well.[30] The Lisbon Treaty also addressed the

---

[29] Tony Judt, *A Grand Illusion? An Essay on Europe* (New York: Hill and Wang, 1996), viii, 27,
44, 91, 130.

[30] The targets included decreasing school drop-out rates to 10% of the students, and increasing
the share of students who complete upper secondary level studies to 85%. It also targeted an
increase in the teaching of mathematics and science to 15% of the curriculum, and increased
participation in lifelong learning to more than 12% of the 25 to 64 age group.

modernization of the European social model and protections by promoting social inclusion through education, training, and employment.[31] However, a mid-way evaluation clearly revealed that little progress has happened, and that Europe cannot achieve its goals by 2010.

A Common European Foreign Policy and Army?

The idea of a common European army was born after the war, though it was never realized. The European Union took the idea and stated in the Hague Platform in the summit in 1987 that the Union is not complete without security arrangements. In 1992, the Maastricht Treaty crowned the spectacular foregoing advances in integration by establishing the European Union and beginning the standardization of the system of law. This went hand in hand with the introduction of European citizenship. The treaty forcefully reintroduced the concept of a common foreign and security policy when it declared that the Union is "resolved to implement a common foreign and security policy, which might in time lead to a common defence." The Yugoslav crisis taught the Union the bitter lesson that "economic and political power alone does not work," and diplomacy "needs to be backed by credible military means . . . Building of effective military capabilities has been the main concern of this policy."[32] In the same year, Germany and France affirmed the goal of establishing a "Eurocorps" of 50,000 to 60,000 troops, the basis for a future European army, under the aegis of the Western European Union and NATO. The Union also appointed a common European anti-terrorism "tsar."

Common foreign policy and military ambitions occupied a central role in the newly planned European constitution. The Union formed a committee, headed by former French President Giscard d'Estaing, to prepare the document that contained the introduction of an elected, longer-term President and the establishment of a common foreign and security policy, thus taking the first steps towards the formation of a common army. Although the constitution was signed by twenty-seven states in 2004, the referendum failed in France and the Netherlands in 2005.

---

[31] European Council, *Presidency Conclusions of the Lisbon European Council on 24 March, 2000* (Brussels: European Commission, 2000), 1–36.
[32] European Union, Maastricht Treaty, www.eurotreaties.com/maastrichtext.html-18k–

The integration of military forces would offer the most rational solution for Europe. In 2007, the world spent $1,339 billion on military expenditures, equal to $202 per person. Expenditures have increased by nearly 50 percent since the late 1990s. The greatest investor in the armed forces was the United States, which spent $582.7 billion, or $1,756 per person, and 43.5 percent of total military expenditures worldwide. The United States increased its expenditures by 65 percent between 1998 and 2007. Japan, Russia, and China, though the latter increased its expenditures three-fold in the last decade, spent only 3 to 5 percent of the world's total. Western Europe occupies a very strong second place behind the United States in military investments by having spent $301 billion, or $614 per person, and 22.5 percent of the world's total in 2007. Additionally, a transforming Central and Eastern Europe increased its military expenditure by 162 percent, by far the fastest growth worldwide, and might be able to contribute to European armed forces.[33]

Despite Europe spending more than half the amount spent by America, its military power remained incomparably weaker. Duplication among twenty-seven different armed forces led to the waste of a great part of the investments. Spending was also extremely uneven: Spain spent $12.3 billion, while Britain spent $59.2 billion. Germany spent 30 percent less than France. However, Britain, France, and Germany *each* spent significantly more than Russia, and the West European countries together spent roughly nine times more than Russia.[34] More equalized spending and coordinated development by unification of the national armies would create a European military sufficient for defending the continent.

If diplomacy "needs to be backed by credible military means," as the above quoted Maastricht Treaty maintained, a united military force would create an appropriate political weight for a common European foreign policy. However, the harmonization of foreign policy itself failed during the entire three decades surrounding the turn of the century. The different countries of Europe have traditionally had diverse foreign policy interests. At least since World War II, and consistently from Churchill to Tony Blair, Britain followed an Atlantic

---

[33] *SIPRI Yearbook 2008: Armaments, Disarmament and International Security* (Stockholm International Peace Research Institute, 2008).

[34] Global Power Europe, www.globalpowereurope.eu/2007/10/european-military-spending-must-be-more.html.126k-)

orientation. On the other hand, France was strongly anti-Atlantic from de Gaulle to Chirac, and it was more inclined to cooperate with Russia, even Soviet Russia. Germany did not have an independent profile until unification and followed the American line.

The Yugoslav crisis immediately destroyed the very first attempts at policy harmonization: Germany unilaterally recognized Croatia's independence in December 1991. It collided head-on with the decision of the Council of Ministers and the plan to arrange a peace conference in The Hague. Roland Dumas, the French minister of foreign affairs, warned his German counterpart: "If you do that you will set Europe back twenty years." *Le Monde* drew a parallel with Hitler's step of creating an "independent" Croatia during World War II.[35]

Just over a decade later, the United States' war in Iraq drastically destroyed any possibility for a common standing. While Britain, Spain, Italy, and Poland enthusiastically joined President George W. Bush's war, several countries remained silent and passive. But the nucleus of the European Union, France and Germany, openly and vehemently opposed the war, as President Chirac and Chancellor Schröder clearly and strongly expressed in a joint press conference in Paris in January 2003. When left-of-center parties in Spain and Italy replaced right-of-center parties, these countries also joined the opposition camp.

The unilateral declaration of independence by Kosovo in February 2008 ignited a new crisis in European foreign policy. The foreign ministers of the European Union countries tried to harmonize the Union's answer, but failed again. Germany, France, Britain, and Italy – together with forty-six countries worldwide – rushed to recognize Kosovo's independence, while Alberto Navarro, Spain's minister of foreign affairs, spoke about a "breach of international law." Greece, Cyprus, Romania, Bulgaria, and Slovakia, all countries with minority problems, joined Spain and roughly 100 countries worldwide in rejecting the recognition.

European recognition of Kosovo's independence sharpened the conflict with Russia, an ardent opponent of independence. Sergei Lavrov, Russia's minister of foreign affairs, dramatically warned that this recognition might be the "end of Europe." American newspapers reported in February 2008 that, "Russian officials hinted last week

---

[35] Beverly Crawford, "Explaining Defection from International Cooperation: Germany's Unilateral Recognition of Croatia," *World Politics*, 48, 4 (1996), 482–521.

that if Kosovo declared independence it might retaliate by recognizing the independence claim of Abkhazia and South Ossetia – two Russian-supported provinces of Georgia. Russia's parliament repeated the threat Monday."[36]

Indeed, Russia made good on its warning after Georgia's irresponsible attack to reoccupy South Ossetia in August 2008. The Russian army launched a *Blitzkrieg*, crushed Georgia, and recognized the independence of the two regions. However, this step was more than retaliation for Kosovo. It was an answer to the American policy of enlarging NATO by inviting the three Baltic states, former Soviet republics, and America's plans to invite former Caucasian Soviet republics, including Georgia. American plan of missile placement in the Czech Republic and Poland also highly irritated Russia. For a few years after the collapse of the Soviet Union, a humiliated Russia followed a strict Western orientation. This gradually changed, however, as Russia regained strength. That became explicit during the Yugoslav, and especially the Kosovo, crisis.

The Georgian adventure and Russian response revitalized American Cold War rhetoric. European foreign policy, however, met a crucial challenge. How should the Union react to the Russian–Georgian conflict? What kind of policy is advisable in the long run, considering the unavoidable cohabitation with a rising Russia in Europe? Again, in 2008, Europe did not find a common foreign policy platform. Britain, due to its Atlantic policy tradition, entirely cooperated with the United States and urged harsh retaliation. Some of Russia's frightened Central and Eastern European neighbors joined that call, particularly Poland and the three Baltic countries, while Italy accused Georgia of provoking the crisis. Germany and France remained very cautious, partly because of their strong dependence on Russia for one-third of the oil and 40 percent of the gas consumption on the continent.[37] A divided Europe thus does not have a "European" answer to the Russian crisis.

The harmonization of European foreign policy has not achieved anything since 1980, and there seems to be a huge question whether it is possible at all. However, the European Union cannot establish

---

[36] *USA Today*, February 18, 2008.
[37] *International Herald Tribune*, August 29, 2008; Global Research, "Kosovo Independence: End of Europe: Top Political Analysts on Russian Foreign Minster Lavrov's Kosovo Warning," February 16, 2008, www.globalresearch.ca

itself as a major political power in the world without it. However, a major direct danger, and an institutional framework with a majority decision-making process, might unite the member countries more strongly and push them towards this goal.

Three Pillar Union or Two-Tier Union?

Alongside existing difficulties, the failure of the constitution was frightening in that it threatened to halt further political and military integration. The situation was ripe for a new and protracted stagnation. The lack of political integration weakened the position of Europe in crises, and hindered its ability to play a more decisive role in international affairs. Europe had bitter experiences of major dividedness in crucially important international questions such as the war in Iraq, the independence of Kosovo, and relations with Russia. In the absence of institutional structures to harmonize the national interests and standing of the various European nations, the continent became a second-rate player in international politics. Furthermore, the lack of political integration created obstacles to the accomplishment of full economic integration as well. Strengthening the supranational element in the Union's institutional structure was thus of central importance.

German and French initiatives sought a solution, and soon after the failure of the constitution, those efforts led to the Lisbon Treaty of 2007 to push forward political unification. The treaty's main initiatives were the strengthening of the European Parliament's role and the introduction of co-decision-making with the Council, based on the agreement of the two intergovernmental and supranational bodies. This change was a potential step towards coping with the "democratic deficit" that was manifest in the non-legislative role of the European Parliament, among other things. The treaty was going to introduce the most important elements of the failed constitution: the office of an elected president with a term of two-and-half years, a high representative for foreign affairs, and the introduction of the right for the Union to sign agreements, which was previously an exclusively national privilege. It also contained the first steps towards establishing a European army, the Eurocorps, of 50,000 to 60,000 troops which were pledged by France, Germany, Belgium, Spain, Luxembourg, and eight other countries that planned to join. The ratification of the substitute-constitution, the Lisbon Treaty, was planned by the end of

2008, but once again, the Union's boat was grounded when the Irish voted "no" in their referendum in June. New pressure and solutions were needed to persuade the European caravan to continue marching, and they succeeded.

Although unsolved questions are disappointing in the short run, the half-century history of the Union presents spectacular progress and promises. The European Union made impressive progress towards a multi-pillar structure. Until the 1990s, only the first pillar, economic integration, kept the Community together. Around the turn of the century, the Union made major efforts to build a second pillar: a common foreign and security policy. In 1999, the Amsterdam Treaty actually provided a successful third pillar: cooperation in justice and home affairs. An important step in that latter area was the cooperation agreement against cross-border crimes by seven member countries – and open for all the others – signed in Prüm, Germany, in May 2005. The signatories agreed on automatic, on-line information exchange, as well as on the exchange of DNA, fingerprints, car registration data, etc., to cooperate "in combating terrorism, cross-border crime and illegal migration."[38] A fourth pillar, "social Europe," is also in the making (discussed in chapter 5 below).

Integrationist enthusiasts are dissatisfied with the progress and argue that further advance has been made increasingly more difficult by the fact that there are twenty-seven member countries. As Jürgen Habermas, the leading philosopher-sociologist of Europe, stated, the "European Union is a convoy in which the slowest vehicle sets the pace for all." He recommended a Union-wide referendum on the new institutions, the position of the president, the minister of foreign affairs, and the Union's own financial basis. The referendum would be binding for those member states in which a majority voted one way or the other, and those with positive majority votes would create a fast-progressing core. This would mean a two-tier Union.[39] This idea of forming a fast-track core within the Union, open for all the other member countries to join, has surfaced and resurfaced from time to time. It was rejected, though it definitely represents one of the possible exits from deadlocks.

---

[38] *Convention between Belgium, Germany, Spain, France, Luxembourg, the Netherlands and Austria in Stepping up of Cross-Border Cooperation Particularly in Combating Terrorism, Cross-Border Crime and Illegal Migration* (Brussels: Council Secretariat, 7 July, 10900/05, 2005).

[39] Jürgen Habermas, "What Europe Needs Now," www.signandsight.com/features/1265.html

From the Community of Nine to the EU of Twenty-seven and towards the EU of Thirty-four

Meanwhile, the Community gradually enlarged. From the original six members, it became the Europe of nine when Britain, Ireland, and Denmark joined in 1973. This enlargement was, in many respects, "natural." Britain was invited to be one of the founding members, but refused to join. However, it changed its mind and applied for membership twice, but President Charles de Gaulle vetoed its application. Now, at last, British membership was arranged, and Ireland, a historical partner country, and Denmark, which was also closely connected historically, came along with it.

After 1980, however, enlargement exploded. In the half-decade from the early to mid-1980s, three countries entered as new members: Greece, Spain, and Portugal. In another six years, eight further countries knocked on the door: Turkey repeatedly applied in 1987, Austria in 1989, Cyprus and Malta in 1990, Sweden in 1991, Finland, Switzerland, and Norway in 1992. In the early 1990s, at least ten, but probably twelve, former communist countries of Central and Eastern Europe, including the Balkans and the successor states of the former Soviet Union, likewise became evident future candidates and were placed on the agenda. Enlargement continued at full speed in the 1990s. Three advanced countries – Sweden, Austria, and Finland – joined in 1995.[40] These neutral countries were unable to join during the Cold War and rushed to do so afterwards. They got the green light easily: they were rich countries, similar to the founding countries in income level, and had strongly established democracies. Their membership added a strong Nordic aspect to the Union, and a bridge, via Austria, towards the East. However, the Union delayed the acceptance of Cyprus and Malta, and national referendums in super-rich Norway and Switzerland voted down their governments' recommendation to join. Enlargement became a permanent process.

The collapse of communism automatically raised the question of further *enlargement towards the East* in the 1990s. This development played a central role in reshaping Europe by eliminating division. Because peace in the continent was the genuine idea behind European integration, the possible elimination of an East–West

---

[40] Desmond Dinan, *Ever Closer Union?* (Boulder, CO: Lynne Rienner, 2005); Ali El-Agraa, *The European Union: Economics and Politics* (Harlow: Prentice Hall, 2004).

separation and Eastern backwardness became an important consideration for the member countries of the Union. The central goal of the former Soviet Bloc countries, as their main slogan of 1989 expressed it, was "joining Europe." With accelerated expectations, they thought that joining meant an instant introduction of Western wealth and living standards.

In reality, it was a task for one to two generations. The obstacles were huge. The countries of the region had just emerged from a one-party, non-parliamentary regime, with bad human rights records and a weak or absent democratic legacy. Their economy worked as a non-market system, and was nearly entirely state-owned. The countries of the region were debt-ridden and economically bankrupt, their environmental record was tragic, and their infrastructure remained at least half a century behind that of Western Europe. On average, the per capita income level of the region reached only 32 percent of that in the European Union in 1995. The combined economic weight of the ten candidate countries, with roughly 100 million inhabitants, who lined up at the door to the Union, was roughly equal to that of Spain, and hardly more than one-third of Germany's.

The enlargement would increase the population of the Union by 20 percent, but the aggregate GDP by only 5 percent. None of the new members would be net contributors to the Union's budget. Moreover, they required huge amounts of assistance. Agriculture still represented an important part of their economies. Unlike in the West, agricultural population accounted for 22 percent of the active population in Central and Eastern Europe and produced about 9 percent of their GDP.

Nationalist and xenophobic atrocities rattled these countries in the early 1990s. The Central and Eastern European transformation, however, gradually consolidated. Institution-building made progress, macroeconomic stabilization succeeded, and formal democracy and a market economy took root. Most of the countries achieved economic growth and began recovering from their sharp decline. The worst part of navigating through dangerous whitewaters was probably over, and recovery and positive results prevailed throughout the region from the mid-1990s on. The boat of transformation, however, had still not reached quiet waters everywhere. Progress was uneven: while the Central European countries were advancing steadily, the Balkans and Russia remained painfully far behind. As a chronicler stated at the end of the 1990s: "Any traveler who . . . cross[ed] the border between Central Europe and Eastern Europe [the successor states of the Soviet Union, and the Balkans] cannot help but be struck by the enormous and ever growing contrast between these two groups of erstwhile communist states . . . [The collapse of communism] in Byzantine Europe . . . pushed these societies back to the nationalist rhetoric of earlier days."[41]

Nevertheless, the European Union-15 did not hesitate to prepare accession for these countries. Why did they rush to include a bunch of ill-prepared countries? Besides the central goal of creating a peaceful continent, the question of enlarging towards the East emerged at exactly the same time as the need for major restructuring of the European economy became unavoidable. This gave the advanced Western countries a stake in building a larger Union. Europe was the main player of the so-called first globalization in the late nineteenth century, and remained an important "globalizer" in the late twentieth century. Its position, nevertheless, was seriously endangered. Besides the United States, a strong and rising Asian economy represented a new challenge to Europe. After Japan and the "small tigers," a third wave elevated China and India into the group of key players.

While the United States traditionally had a Latin American "backyard," and the Asian economic center was also surrounded by subordinated and economically integrated countries, post-colonial Europe was not only fragmented into several medium- and small-sized nation-states, it also lacked a network of surrounding economies with cheap labor and resources. The opportunity, which opened up in 1989, for networking in the immediate neighborhood, offered a decrease in production costs and strengthened competitiveness on the world market; it presented a great advantage for restructuring the West European economy. Western Europe, in spite of its role in the international economy and globalization, could not appropriately respond to the challenge of sharpened competition during the 1970s to 1980s. Its postwar extensive growth model was exhausted, and its replacement by an innovation-based intensive growth model was badly needed. After 1989, Central and Eastern Europe offered a crucial opportunity for Western Europe to stabilize and fortify its position as one of the economic superpowers in the globalized world economy.

[41] Ilya Prizel, "The First Decade After the Collapse of Communism: Why Did Some Nations Succeed in their Political and Economic Transformation, While Others Failed?" *SAIS Review*, 19, 2 (1999), 1–15, 1, 9.

The Maastricht Treaty, or the Treaty of the European Union, opened the door for non-member countries in February 1992: "Any European State which respects the principles set out in Article 6 (1) may apply to become a Member of the Union." The European Council worked out proposals and approved the outlines. The main elements of the Europe Agreements introduced political dialogue, free trade, freedom of movement, economic, cultural, and financial cooperation, and appropriate institution-building for joint decision-making. They also introduced immediate economic assistance for countries associated with the Union.[42]

The Union signed preliminary agreements with Poland, Hungary, and Czechoslovakia in 1991. In May 1992, negotiations on a similar Europe Agreement began with Bulgaria and Romania, and somewhat later with Slovenia and the Baltic states. They took effect between 1994 and 1996. The agreements envisioned free trade within a decade. Export barriers were lowered within six years in an asymmetric way, with earlier reduction by the European Union than by the Eastern countries. However, the so-called "sensitive sectors" of textiles, steel, agricultural products, and coal – the only sectors of the economy where the Eastern region had comparative advantage, and which represented 40 percent of the exports of Poland, Hungary, and Czechoslovakia to the West until 1993 – remained subject to limitations.

The associated countries made capital movement and profit repatriations free, and they also committed to bringing their laws into line with Union legislation. In the summer of 1994, the Union's Commission clearly declared that the Europe Agreements' "goal for the period before accession should be the progressive integration of the political and economic systems, as well as the foreign and security policies of the associated countries and the Union . . . to create an increasingly unified area."[43]

The Union had already enthusiastically welcomed the Polish and Hungarian events of 1988–9, and at its Rhodes and then Madrid summits in December 1988 and June 1989, the Union expressed its readiness to assist the transition to democracy and to support

---

[42] European Union, Maastricht Treaty, www.eurotreaties.com/maastrichtext.html-18k-

[43] European Commission, *Europe Agreements and Beyond: A Strategy to Prepare the Countries of Central and Eastern Europe for Accession* (Brussels: Communication from the Commission to the Council, 1994).

economic reform in the two pioneering countries of transformation. After the Group-7 summit in Paris, the Union's Commission
coordinated the aid efforts of twenty-four OECD countries. The
main program of assistance to promote market reforms, "Poland and
Hungary: Aid for Restructuring their Economies" (PHARE), was
launched in December 1989. In 1990, ECU (European Currency
Units) 300 million was provided to the two countries, but another
200 million was added for other transforming countries. PHARE
assistance was increased and reached ECU 1 billion by 1992, and continued to provide roughly €1.5 billion per year during subsequent
years. Between 1990 and 1998, the OECD countries disbursed €5.6
billion to assist transformation. The Union had already made a series
of bilateral trade agreements with the rapidly and successfully reforming Hungary in 1988, before the regime collapsed in 1989. By 1993,
similar agreements were signed with all of the transforming countries.
Trade between Central and Eastern Europe and the Union increased
dramatically.

Although some basic principles existed before, the Copenhagen
Council summit in June 1993 defined the specific political and economic conditions for joining the Union. "Membership requires," the
Union declared, "that the candidate country has achieved stability of
institutions guaranteeing democracy, the rule of law, human rights and
respect for and protection of minorities, the existence of a functioning
market economy as well as the capacity to cope with competitive pressure and market forces within the Union . . . The associated countries
in central and eastern Europe that so desire shall become members
of the European Union . . . as soon as an associate country is able to
assure the obligations of membership by satisfying the economic and
political conditions required."[44]

At its Essen meeting in December 1994, the Council accepted a
White Paper, which served as a "road map" for adjusting to the single
market's pan-European regulatory regime. This outlined aspects of the
acquis communautaire, a huge body of laws and rules, which had been
developed and augmented over the years. When the *acquis* was presented to the Central and Eastern European applicants, it comprised
thirty-one chapters and 80,000 to 100,000 pages. A huge set of Union
laws and regulations had to be implemented and integrated into each

---

[44] European Council, *European Council in Copenhagen 21–23 June 1993*, www.consilium.
europa.eu/uedocs/cmsdata/docs/pressdata/eu/ec/72921.pdf, 12.

country's laws, including market legislation, intellectual property protection, veterinary and agricultural health inspections, and industrial
product testing. The supremacy of Union norms over existing national
ones required new institutional and administrative structures, and even
constitutional amendments.

The countries of the region submitted their applications beginning
in March 1994. Hungary was the first, followed in a month by Poland.
Latvia, Estonia, Lithuania, and Bulgaria applied in the fall and winter
of 1995, the Czech Republic and Slovenia in 1996. Negotiations
began with the five best-prepared countries in March 1998. Five
more countries joined in February 2000, when negotiations opened
with Slovakia, Latvia, Lithuania, Bulgaria, and Romania.

The European Union required the harmonization of the legal systems, as well as media and telecommunication, monetary, taxation,
and competition policies, but also the creation of institutional guarantees, i.e., the harmonization of national administrations. With the
Europeanization of the national administrations, a new element was
added to the requirements. An admittedly quite abstract model was
completed in 1999 that was based on the principles of professionalism
in civil services without direct political interference, and independence from political bodies. The candidate countries accomplished
civil service legislation between 1997 and 2002.

From 1998 on, the Commission regularly screened the fulfillment
of the *acquis* and administration reforms and made recommendations.
The Union virtually forced the candidate countries to adopt the European and international requirements and standards of legislation and
practice. The process of adjusting to the European Union was demanding and the candidate countries were in an unavoidably subordinated
position. The Commission and the Union, in spite of frequent com-
plaints from the candidate countries, forced the adjustment since the
gap between the advanced member countries and the candidates was
huge. Without legal and institutional reform and the reduction of
corruption and crime, the democratic political culture would not
develop to enable Central and Eastern Europe to integrate into a
well-functioning single market system. The reality was simple: if they
wanted to join the Union, they had to make adjustments, and it was
in their best national interests to do so.

In the summer of 1997, the Commission issued the program of
preparation for enlargement. In its budgetary and financial plan for
the years 2000–6, the EU guaranteed so-called pre-accession aid of

€500 million for agricultural transformation, and €1 billion per year in structural aid for modernizing the economy. These amounts were, of course, modest in comparison to needs.[45] Nevertheless, EU contributions to assist transformation became substantial. The experience of the first years of Union membership proved that even limited Common Agricultural Policy (CAP) payments doubled the income of the Polish farmers, and increased the income of the Czech, Hungarian, and Slovak farmers by 70, 30, and 30 percent respectively.

Since 1974, the European Union's cohesion policy had assisted backward regions, i.e., those that had an income level less than 75 percent of the EU average. All ten candidate countries qualified for aid from the structural and cohesion funds. Of the 268 regions of the European Union, 78 regions had a GDP level that was less than 75 percent of the EU average. Except for Prague and the central Hungary regions around Budapest, all the regions of the transition countries belonged to the "backward" category.[46] According to the "Agenda 2000" budgetary plans, the Union's expenditure for these goals reached ECU 275 billion between 2000 and 2006, of which 45 billion went to new members and associates. In 2006, approximately one-third of total expenditures from the Union's structural fund to assist backward regions went to new members.[47]

As Joseph Stiglitz stated, the European Union demonstrated a sense of responsibility and solidarity "by its assistance to Europe's post-communist countries . . . Europe's unprecedented generosity has paid off: the countries that have joined the EU have outperformed all the others, and not just because of access to Europe's markets. Even more important was the institutional infrastructure, including the abiding commitment to democracy and the vast array of laws and regulations . . ."[48] Indeed, the European Union generously assisted

---

[45] According to convincing calculations, to reach the *acquis* environmental standards alone would require about €100 billion investment in the region over ten years. Upgrading roads and railways to Western standards would involve investment of €50–90 billion over fifteen years. Jackie Gower and John Redmond (eds.), *Enlarging the European Union: The Way Forward* (Aldershot: Ashgate, 2000), 21, 83.

[46] *Regions: Statistical Yearbook 2005* (Eurostat, Luxembourg: EU Office of Publications, 2005), 41.

[47] Michael J. Baun, *A Wider Europe: The Process and Politics of European Enlargement* (Lanham: Rowman and Littlefield, 2000), 147–50. In 2000, Central and Eastern European countries received 3.4% of the Union's budgetary sources, but it gradually increased. In 2003, it had already reached nearly 12%, and by 2006, almost 19%.

[48] Joseph Stiglitz, "The EU's Global Mission," in *Project Syndicate*, www.project-syndicate.org/commentary/stiglitz85 (April 22, 2007), 2.

the Central and Eastern European transformation, with huge amounts of aid and subsidies. In 2000, the assistance represented less than 4 percent of the EU's budget, but almost one-fifth of it in 2006.[49]

However, this was not a self-sacrificing humanitarian action, but was self-serving as well. The incorporation of the huge market with its natural and human resources offered several advantages for Western Europe. They could increase economies of scale, exploit the low-wage and well-educated labor force, and rearrange their production networks with a new kind of division of labor. In the period around the turn of the century, two processes coincided: the "twin process of transformation in the East and structural adaptation in the West."[50]

The old member countries, while financing the transformation, also profited from trade and the ability to outsource labor-intensive jobs to the regions with low wages. In addition, 30 to 40 percent of the structural and cohesion fund assistance returned immediately to the advanced countries of the Union in the form of purchases by the assisted countries. The opening of the Eastern markets ignited an export boom for the West, which doubled or trebled its exports to the area within a decade. The EU became the main trading partner of the transforming countries and accumulated a huge trade surplus. At that stage, there were no losers from the enlargement process, only winners.

Furthermore, the negotiated agreements built in certain temporary safeguards to protect the old members from mass migration. In other words, the new members could not enjoy free movement of labor for five years, or, if needed by the old member countries, for seven years. In those transitory years, the new members would create more jobs and increase living standards domestically to mitigate the push effect of emigration. Nevertheless, Britain, Ireland, and Sweden opened their doors for workers from the new member countries immediately. Britain soon received 1 million immigrant workers from the newly joined countries. Four other EU members, Spain, Portugal, Greece,

---

[49] European Commission, *Communication to the Council and to the European Parliament on the Establishment of a New Financial Perspective for the Period 2000–2006* (Luxembourg: Office for Official Publications, 1998); *Bulletin of the European Union*, 3 (1999).

[50] Constanze Kurz and Volker Wittke, "Using Industrial Capacities as a Way of Integrating Central and Eastern European Economies," in John Zysman and Andrew Schwartz (eds.), *Enlarging Europe: The Industrial Foundation of a New Political Reality* (Berkeley: University of California Press, 1998), 63–95, 64.

and Finland lifted restrictions on May 1, 2006.[51] Economic integration was progressing faster than planned. Nevertheless, labor migration was limited from other countries, except Poland, Albania, and Moldova.

Besides practically guiding and commanding the entire transformation, the European Union also influenced the internal politics of the Central European governments. If some ultranationalist governments did not follow the line, which was the case with the Vladimír Mečiar government in Slovakia, they were swept away because the Union's expressed disagreement had a strong impact on a population that did not want to lose the opportunity to join Europe. If governments followed an anti-minority policy, as they did in Estonia and Latvia, that policy was reined back into line with EU standards. When the right-populist Viktor Orbán government in Hungary introduced a "Status Law" to give privileges to ethnic Hungarian citizens of Romania and Slovakia, creating unacceptable discrimination against the non-ethnic Hungarian citizens of those countries, the Union succeeded in having the law withdrawn. The ruling political trend was to cleave to the Union's prescriptions and demands. It is nevertheless paradoxical that the European Union was able to influence Central and Eastern European politics so much more directly before the accession than after it.

Preparation for Balkan Enlargement and Beyond

The accession process influenced potential future candidate countries, which had no chance of being included soon. From the late 1990s, official negotiations began with new countries, especially in the Balkans. Although they were far from being prepared for accession, the enlargement process and potential candidacy nevertheless influenced them strongly. This was partly the consequence of the demonstration effect: Serbia-Montenegro, Bosnia–Herzegovina, Macedonia, Croatia, and Albania watched the progress of their neighboring countries as they marched towards the European Union. They saw the possibility and the requirements, and these themselves influenced the political and economic trends in the countries. The Union, however, sought also to have a direct impact on the region. Stabilization of the area next to its southeastern borders – the traditional "powder keg" of

---

[51] *International Herald Tribune*, May 2, 2006.

Europe – was a central goal of the Union. The best guarantee of lasting peace and security in the Balkans was the transformation and prosperity of the region. To use Eugen Weber's witty phrase, a consumer society consumes revolts as well.

Consequently, after the Kosovo war, the Union decided to give priority to the western Balkan area, and it announced a special plan to launch a Stabilization and Accession Process for South East Europe in May 1999. As the Commission's report stated in 2002: "European Union leaders decided that a policy of emergency reconstruction, containment and stabilization was not, in itself, enough to bring lasting peace and stability to the Balkans: only the real prospect of integration into European structures would achieve that."[52]

The Union applied a gradual process of building institutionalized connections. As a first step, the Stabilization and Accession Agreements launched the Stabilization and Association Process, to be followed, pending good progress. Five countries were involved: Macedonia, Croatia, Serbia-Montenegro, Bosnia-Herzegovina, and Albania signed agreements during the first decade of the twenty-first century. Negotiations began with Croatia in October 2005, with Macedonia in December of the same year, with Albania in June 2006, and with Montenegro in October 2007. The Union, though it prepared agreements with Bosnia and Serbia, did not finalize and sign them. An agreement with Kosovo is also in preparation. Through trade liberalization agreements, the region was gradually adjusting to the free trade system of the Union. In 2004, the Union announced that these countries might achieve candidate status around 2010 and membership about 2020.

In November 2007, the European Commission adopted an "enlargement package," monitoring and assessing candidate and potential candidate countries. In the first category, the Commission listed Croatia, Macedonia, and Turkey, and it listed Albania, Bosnia-Herzegovina, Montenegro, Serbia, and Kosovo in the second. Besides appropriate domestic reforms to create a functioning market economy and democratic institutions, the European Union underlined the importance of fighting against corruption, the dangerous malignancy in all of those societies. As an equally general and central requirement, the Union stressed, "Regional cooperation in south-east Europe

---

[52] European Commission, *The Stabilization and Accession Process for South East Europe, First Annual Report* (Brussels: European Commission, 2002), 4.

is essential, regardless of the different stage of integration of the various countries . . . "[53] Due to the Union's initiative, the candidate and potential candidate countries established a Regional Cooperation Council. The Union also provided substantial financial support: within the framework of the Instrument for Pre-Accession Assistance, the Union's budget for 2007–13 offered €11.5 billion for the west Balkan countries.

The integration and adjustment process of the western Balkan countries began. The European Bank for Reconstruction and Development reported in 2000 that, "Albania has made progress towards opening negotiations on an EU Stabilization and Accession Agreement . . . Since October 1999, the EU has granted unilateral trade preferences to Albania . . . About 90 percent of all exports from Albania to the EU are now duty-free."[54] Investments in Bosnia-Herzegovina were five times higher in 2004 than at the end of the 1990s. Industrial output, which hit rock bottom in Bosnia-Herzegovina in 1995, began increasing from 2001. After hyperinflation of 73,000 percent, the currency, which was tied to the euro, became stable and inflation was curbed. For the first four years of the twenty-first century, GDP growth reached about 5 percent annually in this war-ridden country.[55]

The Union signed a Stabilization and Association Agreement with Macedonia in 2001, and the republic was elevated to candidate status in 2005. This situation revitalized the Macedonian economy. The acting chief economist of the European Bank reported in 2005 that "south-eastern Europe saw robust growth and record capital inflows in 2004–5, reflecting an underlying confidence in its future prospects."[56] Croatia's chance to be included in the next stage of the accession process emerged after the death of the extreme nationalist President Franjo Tudjman in December 1999 and the democratic elections which followed, and especially after the government signaled its readiness to cooperate with the Hague Tribunal to extradite war criminals.

---

[53] European Commission, *Regional Cooperation in South-east Europe: "Enlargement Package,"* ec.europa.eu/enlargement/press_corner/key-documents/reports_nov_2007_en.htm-61k-

[54] European Bank for Reconstruction and Development, *Transition Report 2000: Employment, Skills and Transition* (London: EBRD, 2000), 126.

[55] Lawrence Butler, "Peace Implementation in Bosnia and Herzegovina: Challenges and Results," *Südosteuropa Mitteilungen*, 4–5 (2005), 76.

[56] European Bank for Reconstruction and Development, *Transition Report Update 2005* (London: EBRD, 2005), vii.

Post-Milošević, Serbia also opened a new chapter of its transformation after 2000: reforms were introduced, and the country became an important recipient of investments. As the chief economist of the European Bank for Reconstruction and Development stated, "The progress in Serbia in particular has surprised many observers."[57] Economic progress became significant. The countries of the western Balkans reached 6.5 and 4.8 percent annual economic growth in 2004 and 2005 respectively. At the beginning of the twenty-first century, the ties between the Union and the western Balkans strengthened, and Croatia gradually emerged as a candidate in the next enlargement program. On the other hand, because Serbia did not collaborate with the Hague Tribunal, the doors to candidacy were closed for a while.[58] However, the 2008 elections in the country changed the situation and the pro-European government began fulfilling requirements for candidacy, including the arrest and extradition of one of the top war criminals, Radovan Karadžić. Whenever a country was accepted into the EU and a deadline for joining was set, increased foreign investment immediately followed. Romania, Bulgaria, and Croatia achieved record levels of investment in 2004 and 2005.[59] All the deadlines for acceptance are, of course, tentative. Their realization depends on the fulfillment of the Union's norms. Fulfilling the requirements will be a very long march for the west Balkan countries.

The Union's candidate countries from Central and Eastern Europe have gradually completed their "homework." The eight Central European countries closed the final chapters of the *acquis* in 2002, fulfilling the Union's requirements, and introduced 50,000 laws and regulations. The European Council consequently invited the Czech Republic, Estonia, Hungary, Latvia, Lithuania, Poland, Slovakia, and Slovenia to join the Union on May 1, 2004. Of course, these countries continued reforming, especially in terms of institution-building. A modern credit system, including mortgage credit, also took root.

Several of these countries joined the Union's Exchange Rate Mechanism as the first step towards introduction of the euro, but it will take several years until they can fulfill the requirements. By 2007, only

---

[57] European Bank for Reconstruction and Development, *Transition Report 2000*, 126.

[58] "The Cost of Non-Europe: Serbia's Future: Serbia Suffers Outside the European Union," *The Economist*, March 24, 2007, 60.

[59] Investments doubled in the new member countries and reached $16.3 and $25 billion in 2004 and 2005, respectively. Romania, Bulgaria, and Croatia received $12 billion in 2005. European Bank for Reconstruction and Development, *Transition Report Update 2005*, 35–6.

Slovenia, Malta, and Cyprus were able to introduce the euro, and Slovakia followed in 2009. The dramatic financial crisis of 2008–9, however, undermined the progress and certainly significantly postpones the realization of the optimistic plans.

The next wave of enlargement was planned and realized in January 2007 when Bulgaria and Romania were accepted to and joined the EU. These countries were not prepared. The European Union had never before accepted countries with such low income levels: Bulgaria's and Romania's per capita GDP was only $3,500 and $4,500, respectively, compared to the $9,240 of the eight previously joined Central European countries in 2004, and the Union average of more than $29,000. "And they are backward in many other ways. Infrastructure and public services are worse than in the rest of Eastern Europe; corruption is more entrenched, and the political culture more fragile."[60]

Further enlargements are still on the agenda. The number one candidate is Turkey, which had applied for membership already in 1959, and became an associate member in 1963. However, the accession process has stopped, partly because of the Turkish offensive against Cyprus and the foundation of the Turkish Cypriot Republic, and partly because of the 1980 military coup. Turkey applied for full membership in 1987, signed a customs union agreement in 1995, launched a series of domestic reforms, and became a recognized candidate for membership. Nevertheless, the member countries are split on this issue, and the outcome of the required referenda is extremely unclear.

Ukraine is also knocking at the Union's door, though the western and eastern parts of the country are seriously divided by ethnic differences and their respective Western and Eastern political orientations after the "Orange Revolution" in 2004 and 2005. However, several member countries, and the Union's leadership itself, realize the dangers of overexpansion. Ukraine, Armenia, Belarus, Georgia, and Moldova, which all expressed their hope to be members, are not on the enlargement agenda yet. Russia, which is attempting to regain its position as a great power through its rich oil and gas resources, its size, and its military-nuclear power, wants to stay outside the Union. The enlargement procedure has become the main guiding force for unification of the European continent.

---

[60] "Bulgaria and Romania – The New Kids on the Block," *The Economist*, January 6–10, 2007, 43.

The Bizarre Twin Process of Integration and Disintegration

In an integrating Europe, nation-states deliberately gave up important parts of their sovereignty, including their own border controls
and customs, their own national currencies, and independent monetary policies. Their national security became part of the international
system of NATO, and will probably be further curbed, as national
arrangements are incorporated into some common European military
organization. Therefore, at first glance, the growing wave of autonomy and independence movements is bizarre. As discussed above,
disintegration was a leading trend in the post-communist East. Most
of the transforming countries wanted to join the European Union, but
several peoples sought first to gain national independence, including
all the former Yugoslav republics, led by Slovenia and Croatia, and
then the various republics of the former Soviet Union, and last, but
not least, the Slovaks and the Czechs. The first item on their political
agenda was to conclude their unfinished nation-building.

Rising nationalism belonged to the chaotic first years of enthusiasm, hope, confusion, decline, and disappointment in Central and
Eastern Europe after the collapse of communism. All existing values collapsed in the region, and the old national agendas surfaced to
fill the gap. Besides, nation-building was still unfinished in that belt
of mixed populations that had been ruled by multi-ethnic, multinational empires for centuries. This situation led to an outcome that
was historically almost unparalleled: the eight independent states that
existed before 1989 were replaced by twenty-six independent states
during the 1990s. In the early twenty-first century, two more joined,
Montenegro and Kosovo. Not only the Balkans, but the entire Central and Eastern European region, became further "Balkanized." Late
twentieth-century separatism seems to be a unique historical config-
uration here.

This assessment, however, is only very partially true, especially if one
considers similar trends throughout the Western half of the continent.
Separation, or at least a certain distancing from the center through
autonomy and self-rule, similarly dominates the political agenda of
Spain because of the continuous efforts of the Basques and Catalo-
nians to be more or even totally independent from Spain. It likewise
characterizes the Belgian situation because of the de facto separation of
the Flemish and Walloons. Political movements and parties in northern

Italy started questioning the one-and-a-half-century-old Italian unification by setting the goal of independence, though they then reduced
it to autonomy. The Scottish independence movement challenges the
centuries-old political arrangement in the United Kingdom. Corsica
also aims for independence.

Instead of an isolated regional phenomenon, one can speak about a
widespread European trend. The bizarrely coexisting integration and
separation are, in reality, closely connected with each other. They
are two sides of the same coin. After World War I, the political
elite of Austria, whether of a Left or a Right political orientation,
was unable to imagine a reasonably independent Austrian state, and
instead wanted an *Anschluss*, joining Germany. The minority south
Slavic peoples of the Balkans sought stability and security in a Yugo-
Slav, or South Slavic, state. Establishing independent statehood at
the end of the twentieth century, and guaranteeing national security
and successful competition in the globalized world, would have also
been risky for 1.4 million Estonians, or 700,000 Montenegrins. All
the dangers, however, became negligible in the face of the prospect
for fast-track integration into the powerful European Union. Even
the smallest units may find an equal place in an integrated Europe.
The possibility of integration thus triggers separatism, by limiting or
even eliminating the potential dangers and negative consequences of
doing so.

In this fundamentally changed environment, various motivations
inspired national movements for autonomy or independence. One
of them was evidently old unsettled scores: earlier national humiliation as a minority, so that even the use of one's native language was
often banned and one's traditional culture suppressed. That was the
case in Franco's Spain for Basques and Catalans. National humiliation
repeatedly hit the Baltic region through recurring Russian and Soviet
occupations and their attempts to assimilate the Baltic peoples into
a "Soviet nation." The Dutch-speaking Flemish were long ruled by
French-speaking Walloons in the Belgian state. Czechoslovakia and
Yugoslavia were established as centralized states after World War I in
a strong effort to create Czechoslovak and Yugoslav nations, rejecting
Slovak and Croat demands for autonomy for decades.

With the fall of the Berlin Wall, all the "unchangeable" walls and
borders collapsed. Rearrangement became politically evident after the
acceptance of German reunification and the dissolution of the Soviet
Union, Yugoslavia, and Czechoslovakia. In an integrating Europe,

under the umbrella of the European Union, all the latent national questions surfaced and new ones even emerged. New attempts at separation were often motivated by economic factors. More than once, old national conflicts and new economic motivations merged. Slovenia, with its 2 million inhabitants, produced 20 percent of the Yugoslav national income and nearly one-third of the country's exports. Its economic level measured by per capita GDP was six times higher than in the poorest parts of Yugoslavia. Croatia was also much more developed and richer than Bosnia or Kosovo. Centralized or federal states – and Yugoslavia became federal in 1974 – redistributed incomes and tried leveling major economic disparities. The rich republics thought the time was ripe to stop financing the poorer ones.

In Spain, the advanced and industrialized Catalonia, with its separate language and culture and a history that was independent from Spain in earlier centuries, reached a GDP per capita that was 22 percent higher than the Spanish average. Central redistribution, however, diminished the Catalan advantage to 4.3 percent above the Spanish average. The richest autonomous regions of the Basque country, Catalonia and Navarre, represent 16 percent of the population, but they are responsible for one-third of industrial production and exports. These economic factors fueled separatist initiatives. In the case of the Basque and Catalan minorities of Spain, old grievances and economic motivations strengthened each other and fueled separatism. The same is true for Belgium. The northern Flemish part of the country represents 60 percent of the population, produces 81 percent of the country's exports, and has one-third the unemployment rate of the Walloon south.

Northern Italy's income level is traditionally twice as high as in the south. When unchangeable Cold War political arrangements collapsed in the early 1990s, several north Italian political organizations mushroomed and then merged in the *Lega Nord per l'Independenza della Padania*. "Padania," the League's made-up name for the northern parts of the country above the River Po, demanded independence. Umberto Bossi, the leader of the *Lega*, announced a deadline of one year for realization. In 1996, however, the Northern League dropped the program of independence and adopted the goal of a federal state, which controls its income and stops subsidizing the south. Separatism became an important issue in Italian politics. Major regional disparities in income certainly made separation attractive as a way of getting rid of the "burden" of less developed areas.

The pro-independence Scottish National Party, exploiting the opportunity provided by having gained autonomy and an independent parliament, declared its intention to hold a referendum on independence and elections before 2010. Scotland is not richer than England, but "Scottish oil" might be an economic motivation.

A further paradoxical phenomenon should also be noted: after long periods of centralized power and the oppression of minorities, sudden reform involving federalizing the state and granting autonomy to minorities often had a counterproductive impact and sharpened separatism, rather than diminishing it. This trend is somewhat similar to the one Alexis de Tocqueville recognized in his analysis of the outbreak of the French Revolution: "[I]t is not always when things are going from bad to worse that revolutions break out. On the contrary, it often happens that when a people, which has put up with an oppressive rule over a long period without protest, suddenly finds the government relaxing its pressure, it takes arms against it . . . The most perilous moment for a bad government is one when it seeks to mend its way."[61]

Croat–Serb conflict jolted Yugoslavia, a centralized state from its foundation, throughout its existence up to the 1970s. National conflicts led to the federal reorganization of the country with its new constitution in 1974. All the republics gained serious autonomy. After the death of Tito, rotating presidency was also introduced. It did not end, but rather strengthened, national movements and the drive for independence. The same happened in Czechoslovakia, where Czech and Slovak conflict exploded in the 1920s but the centralized state became federalized only in 1969. It actually paved the way for separation.

After the death of the dictator, Francisco Franco, who suppressed national movements with an iron hand, a democratizing Spain created seventeen autonomous communities within the Spanish state. The 1979 Statute of the Catalan Autonomous Community established autonomous institutions, as well as a Catalan parliament and government. After 1975, Basque home rule also established an independent parliament, police force, its own taxation, and government of the educational system. None of these curbed the drive for independence or full autonomy. The Basque Sovereignty Plan called for a referendum

---

[61] Alexis de Tocqueville, *The Old Regime and the French Revolution* (Gloucester: Peter Smith, 1978), 176–7.

on self-determination in 2002. Scottish autonomy generated a further drive for independence. An integrating Europe is getting to be a "Europe of regions," which might inspire separatist movements.

Fight for Independence via Terrorism

The politically motivated violence and terror attacks in Italy and France during the late 1960s and 1970s ended by the late seventies, but ethnically or religiously motivated mass killings continued throughout the decades from 1980. Terrorism and the struggle for independence are often combined and sometimes difficult to separate from each other. Moreover, what is seen as the struggle for independence for one group of people is often mere terrorism for another. The centers of violence became Spain and Britain. The *Euzkadi Ta Askatasuna* (ETA), the organization of the Basque Motherland and Liberty, continued its three-decades-long struggle for independence with repeated assassinations and bombings that had a death toll of between 800 and 900. ETA actually had an important role in ending the Franco dictatorship when they assassinated Franco's handpicked successor, Prime Minister Luis Carrero Blanco, in December 1973.

During the 1990s, however, their terrorist attacks targeted tourist amenities such as the Reus airport, as well as several coastal resorts in 1996. Terrorist actions were interrupted by ceasefires from time to time between 1998 and 1999. However, 2000 became one of the bloodiest years of the decade. Various concessions guaranteeing and increasing autonomy for the Basque country and other minority regions in post-Franco Spain did not stop the actions. During the three decades after the death of Franco in 1975, while terrorist actions continued, the non-violent political wing of ETA gradually grew stronger and gained parliamentary representation in the autonomous community. In May 2008, sensational news heralded a change: ETA, for the first time since its campaign began, announced a "permanent ceasefire" that will probably end Basque terrorism.

If this probability is borne out, it was strongly inspired by the Northern Irish development. Similarly to the violence of ETA, the Irish Republican Army (IRA) continued its struggle for independence after the foundation of the independent Irish Republic that left Northern Ireland part of Britain. A major terror campaign began in the 1970s with several bombings in London and Birmingham. After a ceasefire, the bombing of the Conservative Party's conference in Brighton in 1984, and the attacks on the City of London in the 1990s and London's Canary Wharf and a Manchester shopping center in 1996, signaled the continuation of endless warfare. The main obstacle for any kind of arrangement was the Catholic and Protestant Northern Irish divide. The Protestant Irish majority rejected independence under Catholic rule.

In spite of hopeless disagreements, the peace process slowly got under way with an agreement between the British and Irish governments in 1985. However, it took another decade before the next major breakthrough, which occurred in 1994 when a ceasefire was announced and official talks began. A mediated talk led to the Good Friday Agreement in April 1998. The leading Catholic and Protestant Northern Irish parties formed a shared autonomous government, and an agreement was reached on disarmament of the IRA. Although the realization of the agreement proved to be a bumpy road, with several stops and backtracking until real disarmament was accomplished, the formation of the autonomous government took over, and the British Army officially ended its "Operation Banner," i.e., its fight against the IRA, that had lasted for nearly forty years, and was withdrawn from Northern Ireland in 2006. Peace was established.

As the Basque and Irish struggles were seemingly concluded in the early twenty-first century, the Balkan war, as discussed before, also ended with the twentieth century. However, terrorist actions continued. The Kosovo Liberation Army continued their ethnic cleansing after NATO's intervention forced the Serbs to capitulate in 1999. Its very first act was to hunt out tens of thousands of Serbs and 80 percent of the Roma minority from Kosovo. They soon launched attacks to "liberate" Albanians in the western regions of the now independent Macedonia. An almost immediate Western intervention stopped military actions, and significant international peacekeeping forces stabilized the situation. Terrorist acts, which were aimed at avoiding a partitioning that would attach the Serb region to Serbia, continued against the small Serb minority in the northern part of Kosovo. Attacks against school buses, the burning of Serb houses, and the murder of more than 300 people, were all part of the continued fight that succeeded and led to the foundation of a Provisional Self-Government under the United Nations Administration and peacekeeping forces. In February 2008, Kosovo unilaterally declared independence, which was immediately recognized by the United States, Germany, and ultimately more than forty countries. The Kosovan struggle for self-determination and independence succeeded using terrorist methods. However, more than 100 countries, including Russia, Spain, India, and China, which were all struggling with difficult minority problems, did not follow in recognizing the one-sided declaration of independence. The impact of the Western decision to recognize Kosovo's independence is predictably unpredictable: various minorities in mixed ethnic areas from Transylvania to the Caucasus might be inspired and invigorated to follow Kosovo's example. It destabilized certain regions and countries, as the Georgian war in the late summer of 2008 illustrated.

In spite of the Muslim–Serb conflict in the Bosnian and Kosovo crises, and the large contingent of fundamentalist Muslim volunteers, no one considered the Yugoslav civil war to be a genuine Muslim–European confrontation. However, a historic turning point occurred on September 11, 2001 in New York and Washington when mostly Saudi Arabian fundamentalist Muslims committed a well-planned and coordinated suicide attack, using American civilian aircrafts as bombs, against the World Trade Center and the Pentagon. The Bush administration's strongly mistaken and irresponsible decision to launch war against Iraq, which had nothing to do with September 11, mobilized fundamentalist Muslim forces throughout the world.

Europe was not saved from their vicious revenge: various Muslim terrorist cells prepared retribution against European allies of the Bush administration. On March 11, 2004, three days before the national elections in Spain, Moroccan Muslim fundamentalists executed a devastating bomb attack against commuter trains during rush hours in Madrid, killing nearly 200 people. Somewhat more than a year later, on July 7, 2005, four suicide bombers launched similar attacks against crowded rush hour trains of the London underground and bus systems. Two weeks later another attempted bomb attack failed.

Two infamous assassinations in the Netherlands, one of the most traditionally tolerant countries of the world, signaled a different kind of fundamentalist warfare in Europe. The first victim was a Dutch politician, and then a filmmaker. In 2002, a day before the national elections, the rising and popular anti-immigration politician, Pim Fortuyn, was assassinated because of his strong and successful campaign against Muslim immigration. In November 2004, the even more symbolic ritual killing of Theo van Gogh shocked the entire Western world. He was first shot on the street, and when he fell from his bicycle, the assassin cut his throat and plunged two knives into his body.

The victim, director of *Submission*, a televised film on the oppression of Muslim women in immigrant families, outraged the Dutch Muslim community.

The two killings were more than just two ugly crimes for the Dutch population and for many Europeans, they symbolized the "clash of civilizations," or a declaration of war by fundamentalist European Muslim immigrants. Moreover, in the terrorist actions of the 2000s, home-grown, second generation immigrants, some of them well educated, had participated in actions, symbolizing the failure of integration. Immigration, a mass phenomenon, has gradually arisen as one of the most difficult social problems of Western Europe. The terrorist actions called attention to the social background of the phenomenon.

3

The New Cultural and Political Setting

The Rise of a New *Zeitgeist*

Ideological and cultural trends do not know state borders. In the second half of the twentieth century, the "Western world" – meaning Western Europe, North America, and Australia – were more closely connected than ever before. The United States of America, the recognized leader of the Western world, had special influence. The new ideological and cultural trends since the 1970s and 1980s were not narrowly European, nor merely American, but "Western."

The role of Western Europe was decisive, however. Neo-liberalism, one of the most important new ideological trends, was the child of both the Vienna School of Economics and the Chicago School of Economics. The newly emerging anti-Enlightenment philosophical trend, postmodernism, was strongly French, while neo-conservatism emerged in the United States. Decisive new political trends, such as the dramatic decline of the Left parties, were British and Italian-influenced, while traditional social democracy remained intact in Scandinavia. The rise of single-issue movements and leftover left-wing trends, such as the Green movement, was strongest in Germany. Feminism conquered Scandinavia and had strong roots in the United States as well. New populism emerged in Italy, while extreme right-wing populism was equally strong in France and Austria.

The "dual-crises" of the 1960s and 1970s, together with rising globalization and the transforming world order, generated a major about-face in the cultural-ideological environment of the Western world. The sudden change generated doubts about the policy, and harsh critiques erupted about the unintended negative side effects of postwar policies and institutions. A significant group of liberal, left-wing intellectuals became deeply disappointed and turned against their former ideas with neophyte vehemence. Genuine traditional conservatives, pushed aside after the war, reemerged and became influential again. In a situation of global competition, slowdown, and declining income, they challenged as "unaffordable" the belief in state interventionism and the achievement of social harmony by neo-corporatist intervention and redistributive welfare policy. According to the argument of its critics, the welfare state undermined the basic values of capitalism.

These doubts and critical views found their social base in a post-industrial society when the rising majority of white-collar employees and the middle class replaced the old class structure. During the period of postwar prosperity, the middle-class and white-collar layers of society significantly increased in number and influence. Now, they were frightened by the dual crises and demanded "law and order." At a Social Democratic Party congress, Helmut Schmidt spoke about a German *Ordnungs-hysterie*, hysteria for order.[1] In the globalized world economy, employment became uncertain, jobs outsourced, and investments shifted to low-wage countries.[2] In this new environment, huge groups of workers perceived their enemies in immigrant workers who occupied their jobs. Many of them turned towards the anti-immigration Right and shared new conservative ideas.

The entire concept of rationalism and the Enlightenment, which had dominated social thinking and actions since the eighteenth century, was vehemently questioned. Belief in historical progress and the power of human actions to influence and push it ahead – the basic idea of the Enlightenment and a popular concept of postwar Europe – lost ground and was replaced by skepticism about the possibility of understanding the world and historical truth. Disappointment generated relativism and nihilism. In this vacuum of values, old values gained ground: national ideas, religious beliefs, family values, and racist ideologies.

Left-leaning parties – communists, socialists, and left-liberals – lost their self-confidence and the belief in a politics they had regarded as successful before. Their identity crisis undermined their organizations.

---

[1] Quoted by Richard Wolin, "Introduction," in Jürgen Habermas, *The New Conservatism: Cultural Criticism and the Historians' Debate*, ed. Shierry Weber Nicholsen (Cambridge, MA: MIT Press, 1989), xxi.

[2] Terence Ball and Richard Bellamy (eds.), *The Cambridge History of Twentieth-Century Political Thought* (Cambridge University Press, 2003), 365.

The attraction of communism withered away, first because of the
Soviet policy of oppression and expansionism, demonstrated by the
1956 and 1968 interventions in Central Europe, and then because of
the deep disappointment in Mao's Cultural Revolution and the Cuban
revolution. Social democracy turned towards reorientation and the
search for a "Third Way," a "higher synthesis" of Left and Right, as the
Italian philosopher Norberto Bobbio characterized it.[3] The traditional
dichotomy is not absolute, argues Bobbio, and when Right or Left is
in a political *baisse* each of them is ready "to recycle itself as something
totally new, something which goes beyond the traditional distinction
(neither left nor right, or combining the positive values of both sides
to produce a modern, innovative movement)."[4] The Left became
fragmented, disorganized, and their mass parties lost the masses. On
the other hand, separate "single issue movements" emerged, such as
the feminist, green, anti-war, and anti-globalization movements.

This environment became the hotbed of a rising new political culture and ideology, a new *Zeitgeist* from the 1980s on. From that time,
neo-liberalism emerged, triumphantly rejecting Keynes and negat-
ing the role of the state. It merged with the rising neo-conservatism
or the new Right, as well as postmodern culture and ideology. The
cultural-ideological arena became the main battlefield.

Neo-liberalism, Neo-conservatism and Postmodernism on the Rise

Neo-liberal economics became the most powerful new ideological
trend. The return to a simplified classical liberal school in an extreme
way not only dethroned Keynesian economics, but also offered a
new comprehensive ideological political base, which was later often
called market fundamentalism. The prophets of this new *Zeitgeist* were
Ludwig von Mises and Friedrich Hayek of the Vienna School of
Economics, and Milton Friedman and other members of the neo-
liberal Chicago School of Economics. Hayek became the living bridge
between the two schools by moving from the Vienna to the Chicago
School. Hayek and Friedman launched an ideological war advocating

---

[3] Norberto Bobbio, *Left and Right: The Significance of a Political Distinction* (University of
Chicago Press, 1996), 7.
[4] *Ibid.*, Allan Cameron's "Introduction," viii.

deregulation, privatization, and unrestricted free markets as the only solutions in a free society in the grips of cutthroat global competition. Both Hayek and Friedman connected laissez-faire policy with social and political principles. They claim that undisturbed, self-regulating markets guarantee social and individual freedom and prosperity. Freedom of the individual and freedom of the market, they argue, are inseparable prerequisites of each other. State intervention, on the other hand, is *The Road to Serfdom*, as the title of Hayek's 1944 book proclaims.

For Friedman, state intervention is not the solution but the real cause of economic trouble because, he claims, it disturbs market automatism and undermines freedom. A self-regulated market has a strong corrective automatism. He advocates the privatization of various governmental functions to increase efficiency. Moreover, he argues, a self-regulated market is able to provide health care, pensions, and various kinds of insurance. Welfare institutions represent brutal intrusions upon personal freedom; it is like "sending a policeman to take the money from somebody's pocket." He recommended making radical tax cuts and introducing a flat tax rate of around 16 percent for everybody, reducing government expenditures drastically by privatizing nearly everything, as well as making families and individuals responsible for their own schooling, health care and pension schemes. He argued for "a free, competitive, private-market educational system" and for the use of vouchers for private schooling, health, and pension arrangements. Friedman also advocated "a high natural rate of unemployment" as a prerequisite of a dynamic and progressive economy.[5]

According to neo-liberal ideas, undisturbed and unregulated markets may solve all our economic *and* social problems. An advisor to Margaret Thatcher wrote in *The Guardian* in February 1985: "Ideas from Hayek and Friedman . . . were assimilated precisely because experience had already created a place for them by convincing people that neo-Keynesian economics, trade-union hegemony and the permissive society had failed."[6]

---

[5] Milton Friedman, *The Program for Monetary Stability* (New York: Fordham University Press, 1959); *Inflation: Causes and Consequences* (New York: Asia Publishing House, 1963); *The Optimum Quantity of Money and Other Essays* (Chicago: Aldine Publishing Co., 1969); *The Tax Limitation, Inflation and the Role of Governments* (Dallas: Fisher Institute, 1978).

[6] Alfred Sherman article in *The Guardian*, February 11, 1985, quoted by Ruth Levitas (ed.), in *The Ideology of the New Right* (Cambridge: Polity Press, 1986), 15.

Francis Fukuyama, the deputy director of policy planning staff at the American State Department who declared "the end of history" in his 1989 study, best expressed the *Zeitgeist* of the triumph of neo-liberal democracy. Liberal, free market democracy conquered the world, defeated all its rival ideologies, and became the "end point of mankind's ideological evolution" and the "final form of human government." While earlier forms of governments were characterized by grave defects and irrationalities, this system is "free from fundamental contradictions." If the reality exhibits imperfections and major faults, it is the consequence of "incomplete realization . . . rather than flaws in the principles themselves."[7] Three years later, in his book *The End of History and the Last Man*, Fukuyama mixed his original Hegelian approach with Nietzsche's concept of the "last man." Nietzsche attacked the French Revolution and its commitment to human equality and maintained that democracy is the victory of the slaves, producing the "last man," who gave up belief in his own superiority. Without the desire to be recognized, there is no excellence or achievements. Fukuyama used the questions of Nietzsche to suggest that free market liberal democracy offers efficiency and achievement. The engine of history, the desire for recognition requires sacrificing the ideal of equality.[8]

Around the same time, Norberto Bobbio, the Italian philosopher, with much less optimism warned about an emerging new world conflict. Communism had failed and proved to be unable to solve the problems its utopian agenda pledged to solve: poverty and the longing for justice. Would rich democracies be able to cope with these problems? In the West, two-thirds of the population are prosperous and in power, and they have nothing to fear from the poor one-third. Worldwide, however, this latter layer represents two-thirds to 90 percent of the population. Poverty was the basis for the communist project, but it remained after the collapse of communism as the central challenge in the world.[9]

Conservatives, however, were confident that neo-liberalism would solve all these problems. As they returned to old ideas, neo-liberalism's new twin ideology, *neo-conservatism*, arose. Neo-conservatives maintained that the postwar "values of modernity are irreparably

---

[7] Francis Fukuyama, "The End of History?" *The National Interest*, August 27, 1989, 27–46.

[8] Francis Fukuyama, *The End of History and the Last Man* (Harmondsworth, Penguin, 1992).

[9] Norberto Bobbio, "L'Utopia capovolta," *La Stampa*, 128, June 9, 1989.

corrupt," even "hostile," and offered a "total critique" of them.[10] Most of the neo-conservatives came from the left-leaning liberal camp, and some of them were disappointed former communists. "Neo-conservatism is the net into which the liberal can fall when he begins to fear his own liberalism."[11] That was definitely the case in France, while in Germany several of them were old conservatives whose star had reemerged again. They turned against the dominant values with typical neophyte passion. In their view, the system had become "ungovernable"; the postwar decades had resulted in the "inflation of expectations" about what could be expected from the state. The ideas of liberal intellectuals had undermined the basic principles and moral basis of capitalism; and postwar profane political culture had to be replaced by religion to reestablish social cohesion and the culture of obedience, service, duty, and faith.

The neo-conservatives also reinterpreted social justice. Egalitarian ideas became "destructive and counterproductive" in their interpretation. Rather, "inequality is the inevitable (and beneficial) outcome of individual freedom and initiative." "Human nature" explains inequality and serves as its legitimization. The balance between equality and freedom in the social state was broken, they claimed: it had been distorted towards an equality that undermined the self-assurance of private ownership and replaced it with the fear of ownership. In short, liberal democracy commits suicide.[12] In Britain, neo-conservative ideologues, such as Ferdinand Mount and Roger Scruton, rejected welfare intervention in the family because it "destroy[s] the father's role as authority," and they argued for the reestablishment of the traditional patriarchic family. In Britain in the early 1980s, they recommended controlling children's sexual lives and educating girls for family life. As a pressure group, they launched attacks against abortion by questioning, "when does life begin?"[13]

---

[10] Wolin, *New Conservatism*, xxiii.

[11] Jürgen Habermas, "Neoconservative Cultural Criticism in the United States and West Germany," in Jürgen Habermas, *The New Conservatism: Cultural Criticism and the Historians' Debate*, ed. Shierry Weber Nicholsen (Cambridge, MA: MIT Press, 1989), 22–47, 24.

[12] Walter Leisner, *Demokratie. Selbstzerstörung einer Staatsform* (Berlin: Duncker und Humblot, 1979), quoted by Iring Fetscher (ed.), *Neokonservative und "Neue Rechte." Der Angriff gegen Sozialstaat und liberale Demokratie in den Vereinigten Staaten, Westeuropa und der Budesrepublik* (Munich: Verlag C. H. Beck, 1983), 108.

[13] Levitas (ed.), *Ideology of the New Right*; Roger Scruton, *The Meaning of Conservativism* (London: Penguin, 1980); Ferdinand Mount, *The Subversive Family: An Alternative History of Love and Marriage* (London: Jonathan Cape, 1982).

Neo-conservatism merged with *postmodern arts and philosophy*. Postmodernism was partly a reaction to modernism in the arts, but according to its advocates, it was a new condition or a new reality of postindustrial society. Even the advocates of postmodernism "often found it hard to agree on how it should be applied and they also undermined their case by writing in an opaque and jargon-laden fashion."[14] This new art trend expresses heterogeneity and reflects unpredictability and controlled chaos. This is the art of relativism, the rejection of rationality, and the return to an eclectic pastiche of old styles. Postmodern architecture had nothing to do with the philosophy, but brought fresh change, and was in some ways a nostalgic eclecticism after the rigid and at that time already boring postwar functionalist, anti-decorative modernist architecture. "Those who use this 'post' want to set themselves apart from a past," explains Jürgen Habermas. Unlike the term "post-industrial," which expresses the reality that "industrial capitalism developed further," postmodernism is not continuous with, nor a development out of, its predecessor culture; rather, it is a total negation of it.[15]

However, the pinnacle of the new cultural trend is postmodern philosophy. This is a negation of the Enlightenment, its idealism, and its strong belief in progress and in the ability of human action to influence history. Postmodern philosophy, which − like neo-liberalism − is rooted in Nietzsche and Heidegger, gradually emerged in the postwar decades, and began to have a major impact from the 1980s on. French philosophical thinking in the last third of the twentieth century strongly questioned 200-year-old beliefs. In his first major groundbreaking work, *Madness and Civilization*,[16] Michel Foucault presented the scientific discovery that madness is a mental illness not as an objective scientific achievement, but as yet another interpretation of a phenomenon that has been interpreted and treated in very different ways since the Renaissance. His virtuoso analysis of changing interpretations of madness in history is ultimately a relativization of truth. Scientific truth, according to postmodern thinking, is mostly only the expression of ethical and political commitments. What appears as truth is nothing else but a particular representation identified with

---

[14] Tom Buchanan, *Europe's Troubled Peace, 1945–2000* (Oxford: Blackwell, 2006), 199.

[15] Jürgen Habermas, "Modern and Postmodern Architecture," in Habermas, *New Conservatism*, 13–21, 13–14.

[16] Michel Foucault, *Madness and Civilization. A History of Insanity in the Age of Reason* (New York: Pantheon Books [1961] 1965).

truth.[17] As Habermas expressed his view of his generation, "engaged in philosophical diagnosis of the times, Foucault has had the most lasting effect on the Zeitgeist."[18]

Deconstructionism; Relativization and Reinterpretation of History

Jacques Derrida went even further along the line of relativism and nihilism. He introduced his concept of deconstruction as a useful method, a technique of conceptual inquiry. Deconstructionism, however, metastasized as a new philosophy that rejected the possibility of knowing the truth and real history. What people know is only the perception of reality, but not reality itself. Derrida's point of departure was the imperfect representation of spoken words in writing that, over time, made the original meaning questionable. He took the "language game" concept from Ludwig Wittgenstein's *Philosophical Investigations*.[19] Wittgenstein taught that words and expressions are understandable only in a certain context of language, and may have different meanings in different contexts. He stated in various ways that the meanings of words depend on the uses to which they are put, the circumstances of their use, and even that "the meaning of a word is its use in the language." A statement might be a question; command and question are often confusable. Derrida drew upon the relativity of the meaning of words to relativize everything, stating the duality and interchangeability of possible and impossible, and of reality and perception. One cannot know the truth, deconstructionism maintains, consequently it is impossible rationally to decide, and therefore no decision is justifiable.[20]

Deconstructionism celebrated the demise of the Enlightenment and strengthened the neo-liberal economic philosophy through its denial of the possibility of understanding the truth and therefore making outside intervention seem irrational. These ideologies strongly dominated

---

[17] *Ibid.*

[18] Jürgen Habermas, "Taking Aim at the Heart of the Present: On Foucault's Lecture on Kant's What is Enlightenment?" in Habermas, *New Conservatism*, 173–9, 178.

[19] Ludwig Wittgenstein, *Philosophical Investigations* (Oxford: Blackwell, 1953).

[20] Jacques Derrida, *Writing and Difference* (University of Chicago Press [1967] 1978); Giovanna Borradori, *Philosophy in a Time of Terror: Dialogues with Jürgen Habermas and Jacques Derrida* (University of Chicago Press, 2003).

the last decades of the twentieth century. Besides Foucault and Derrida, a third French philosopher, Jean-François Lyotard, also played an
important role in building the new trend of ideology. He developed the
concept of the postmodern age as the product of post-industrial society. His point of departure was the computerization and technological
transformation that had had a major impact on knowledge. In the
postmodern age, he argued, grand- or meta-narratives have become
bankrupt. Values and beliefs have fragmented. Historical progress does
not exist, and science cannot lead to "knowability" of things. Reality consists of singular events and cannot be represented by rational
theory. Knowledge has lost its truth-value and became mercantilized,
i.e., its value is a trade-value, and lies in its "performativity." There are
multiple social realities; consequently, facts cannot justify any theory.
In the same way, Lyotard argued, political facts and events do not
justify any political philosophy or parties.[21]

The triumph of neo-conservative and postmodern political
culture – due to their anti-Enlightenment concept of history – had
a stong impact on historiography as well. The negation of the idea
that historical truth can be ascertained or understood, or even that
there is a truth of history to be ascertained or understood, led to the
relativization of history. The past is not discovered but *created* and represented as a text by the historian. History or historical documents are
just texts, language that represents nothing but itself. Personal experiences, biases, and interests, as well as the *Zeitgeist* of the age in which
the historian works, all influence history writing. Even "objective"
historical sources are products of their age and might be distorted. A
critical approach and doubts are always needed. "Telling the truth takes
a collective effort . . . knowledge seeking involves . . . struggle among
diverse groups of truth-seekers."[22] Postmodern historiography, however, rejects the possibility of discovering the truth. As C. Behan
McCullagh summarizes this approach, "the meaning of words and
sentences to which they are related is in the minds of those who read
them . . . so that it becomes impossible to define the meaning of sentences . . . Indeed, each sentence means something different to each

---

[21] Jean-François Lyotard, *The Postmodern Condition: A Report on Knowledge* (Manchester University Press, [1979] 1984).

[22] Joyce Appleby, Lynn Hunt, and Margaret Jacob, *Telling the Truth about History* (New York:
Norton, 1995), 309.

person who reads it, so it has no fixed meaning to be deemed credible or incredible."[23]

This absolute relativization revitalized alternative interpretations. A whole history literature was born to deny the Holocaust. David Irving, Robert Faurisson, Dietlieb Felderer, and others maintained that Auschwitz was a big lie. A group of German historians, Ernst Nolte, Klaus Hildebrand, Andreas Hillgruber, and others, reinterpreted Nazism in the 1980s. In Nolte's interpretation, Nazism was an "understandable response to Bolshevism. Anti-Jewish actions were self-defense generated by the alleged statement of Chaim Weizmann, President of the Jewish Agency, urging Jews to support democracy against Nazism. Auschwitz was just a part of a series of similar twentieth-century crimes, one among several, and only a delayed copy of the Soviet Gulag. The war was a defense against the Soviet danger that made the Germans potential or actual victims of Asian barbarism.[24] In Hillgruber's reinterpretation of Hitler's (Eastern front) war, it was "the desperate and self-sacrificing efforts of the German army in the East . . . to save the population of the German East from the Red Army's orgies of revenge, from mass rapes, arbitrary murder . . . [and] to keep the escape route to the West open."[25] A group of German historians, by reinterpreting history and relativizing Nazi crimes, sought to create an acceptable history and a positive past.

Another important expression of this ideological change was François Furet's reinterpretation of the French Revolution. In his highly influential 1978 book, *Interpreting the French Revolution*, Furet rejected the traditional interpretation that the revolution was a classic type of class struggle that destroyed feudalism. Instead it was the clash between different languages, discourses and symbols, it had nothing to do with class stuggle, it had political-cultural causes. What matters is not poverty or oppression, but politics and ideas. Capitalism was already under way and would have developed without violent revolution, the bourgeoisie was already part of the elite thus the struggle was a conflict of sub-elites.[26]

---

[23] C. Behan McCullagh, *The Logic of History. Putting Postmodernism in Perspective* (London: Routledge, 2004), 16.

[24] Ernst Nolte, "Die Vergangenheit, Die Nicht Vergehen Will," *Frankfurter Allgemeine Zeitung*, June 6, 1986.

[25] Andreas Hillgruber, *Zweierlei Untergang: Die Zerschlagung des Deutschen Reichs und das Ende des europäischen Judentums* (Berlin: Siedler, 1986), 24.

[26] François Furet, *Interpreting the French Revolution* (Cambridge University Press, [1978] 1981).

In the new intellectual-cultural political environment, a great part of Europe, including its entire Eastern half, departed from well-established postwar ideologies and principles. Liberal social-political and Keynesian regulated market principles were harshly attacked in the West. The ideological triumph of neo-liberalism and neo-conservatism, combined with the anti-Enlightenment cultural trends of postmodernism and deconstructionism, became influential in most parts of Europe in the 1980s. The cultural victory of these ideological trends paved the way for the conservative political revolution of Ronald Reagan and Margaret Thatcher. Domestic political party formations were partly rearranged along these lines.

Transforming the Party System

Together with the postwar economic model and social structure, the postwar political model also radically transformed from 1980 on. During the last quarter of the twentieth century the political party structure became very different from before. "Today most discussion on the state of political parties boils down to a single conclusion: 'the crisis,' 'the decline' or the 'obsolescence' of these organizations."[27] The most striking new development was the decline of the mass parties and the class- and/or ideology-based parties. Membership of political parties melted away: during the 1990s, it dropped to half that of the 1960s. In some countries such as Italy, Sweden, and Denmark, it dropped to one-quarter, and in Britain to one-fifth. The British Labour Party lost 1.5 million members. Alongside membership, turnout at elections also started to decline. In postwar Europe, an average of 88 percent of the electorate participated in elections. In Italy, Belgium, and Luxembourg, it was more than 90 percent. While 28 percent did not vote at the 1997 elections, 40 percent of British voters stayed away in 2001. The figure was 38 percent in Portugal at the 1999 and 2002 elections, and 37 percent in Ireland at the 2002 elections. Analysts spoke about less and less identification of the population with political parties, "growing anti-political feelings," "political apathy," and "disillusionment with democracy."[28] What emerged was a crisis of political

---

[27] G. Bettin Lattes and Ettore Recchi (eds.), *Comparing European Societies* (Bologna: Monduzzi Editore, 2005), 229.
[28] *Ibid.*, 244–7.

representation and even of representative democracy. The nationwide mass parties with huge partisan support were "agents" of existing social interests, often class interests – working class versus bourgeoisie, urban versus rural, church versus state – because of the class polarization of European societies. Therefore political parties formed around the main conflict lines.[29]

From the late 1970s on, and during the 1980s, social and international relations radically changed the political stage and its actors: the rural and blue-collar working population drastically decreased, and white-collar workers and the middle class became the majority. The lower classes became dominated by immigrants. Globalization and neo-liberal economics, together with the major development of European integration, shifted a great deal of traditional decision-making power from national parliaments to international corporations, uncontrolled market forces, the European Central Bank, and Brussels. Welfare institutions became endangered. State sovereignty became limited. The power of the mass media and the increasing role of the judiciary, including the European Court of Justice, contributed to weakening the old power structures. In the new post-1980 situation, postwar party formations collapsed and were replaced by new types of party structures.

However, the transformation of the party political system was not only exhibited in the disappearance of some parties and the transformation of others. There was a fundamental change in the political representation and character of these parties. Around the turn of the century, the new parties had become state (or "statal") parties, with flexible ideologies and issue-based positions. They aim to represent national interests and aspirations. This is a kind of "top-down" representation, on behalf of the state and nation, the opposite of the previous "bottom-up" representation of social groups. It also means that these parties are considered to stand in for "The People." Consequently they are "catch-all" parties, which try to convince the majority of the population that they best represent the general national interests.[30]

---

[29] Michael Saward, "Making Representation: Modes and Strategies of Political Parties," *European Review*, 16, 3 (July 2008), 271–86; Zsolt Enyedi, "The Social and Attitudinal Basis of Political Parties: Cleavage Politics Revised," *European Review*, 16, 3 (July 2008), 287–304, 289.

[30] Saward, "Making Representation."

Disappearing Parties and New Single-Issue Parties

Some of the old parties disappeared, as did almost all of the West and East European communist parties. Where they remained in political arenas such as Russia, the Czech Republic, and Italy, they were only fragments of the former communist parties, leftovers from the old party regimes that recruited a mostly elderly constituency. Some of them were shifted towards the middle, others towards populism. These parties are weakened day by day by unstoppable demographic trends. By far the strongest communist party is the Russian party, established after the collapse of the Soviet Union. During the troubled 1990s, the party gained 22 to 24 percent of the votes at parliamentary elections. At the presidential elections in 1996, Gennady Zhuganov, the Communist Party leader, got 32 percent of the vote, only 3 percent less than the incumbent President Boris Yeltsin. By 2003, however, paralleling the improving situation of the country, the party lost half of its electorate and started to become marginalized. The Czech Communist Party, the only one in Central Europe that kept its name, remained an important player in transformation politics, gaining nearly 19 and 13 percent of the votes at parliamentary elections in 2002 and 2006, and remaining the third largest party in the republic. The Italian Communist Party, the strongest in Western Europe in the postwar decades with 1.8 million members, dissolved and has been replaced by several smaller groups such as the Communist Refoundation Party. However, the real successor became the *Democratici di Sinistra*, the Democratic Party of the Left, which remained the second largest parliamentary party with 600,000 members and almost 18 percent of the votes even in 2006.

Some typical Cold War parties also disappeared, such as the Italian Christian Democratic Party that dominated postwar Italy, and which did not hesitate to use any method in the fight against communism, including collaborating with the Mafia. Major corruption scandals contributed to the destruction of the old party structure in some countries, especially in Italy. Because of economic and social changes, the previously strong agrarian parties were also severely weakened. Some of them, however, reoriented themselves towards new electorates. The Danish *Venstre*, for example, became an anti-social democratic party. The social democratic parties also radically transformed by dropping their class character and shifting towards the middle of the political spectrum as all-national parties, sometimes with neo-liberal economic policies. In several cases, such as in Austria, Germany, Sweden, and somewhat later in Britain, they attracted a new social base of public-service employees, instead of working-class voters.

Besides the disappearance of old party affiliations, growing absenteeism at elections, and the rise of "catch-all" parties, "the last twenty years show the electoral growth of new political formations (the greens, and the populist parties of the extreme right)."[31] Several new parties gained ground in the new European environment, several of them being "single-issue" parties. The *green parties'* point of departure was that none of the political parties were concerned about ecological problems, even though a human-caused ecological crisis endangered the globe. Environmentalist critique was also connected with anti-capitalist and left-libertarian ideas. The green parties became parliamentary and government parties. The German Green party, the strongest such party in Europe, was founded in 1980 by the idealistic and revolutionary generation of 1968, and it was elevated to political importance when it gained parliamentary representation in 1983. The party, led by Joschka Fischer, was in power between 1998 and 2005 in coalition with the Social Democratic Party. Most of the green parties were founded in the 1980s and 1990s. Several of them achieved national importance and parliamentary representation. Moreover, in Ireland, the Czech Republic, and Bulgaria, they participated in coalition governments. In the spring of 2008, when the European Federation of Green Parties held their 8th Council meeting in Ljubljana, thirty-five green parties existed in Europe. Their star declined after they reached their best electorial results between the late 1980s and the mid-1990s. In some countries, however, especially in Germany, the party became a solid part of the political establishment.

Feminist movements had a century-long history. Around the end of the twentieth century, they became powerful in the fight for equal rights and against economic and political gender discrimination. Their strength is due to their strong social orientation, detailed analyses of the "feminization of poverty," and their focus on the gender aspect of several social issues. However, Eric Hobsbawm called these single-issue movements "the not very important continuum of the left" that emerged because of the crisis of the traditional political Left.[32]

---

[31] Bettin Lattes and Recchi (eds.), *European Societies*, 237.

[32] Eric Hobsbawm, *On the Edge of the New Century* (conversation with Antonio Polito) (New York: The New Press, 2000).

Rising Populism and the Right

In the new social-political situation one of the most important new phenomena was the spectacular rise of *populism*.[33] During the post-war decades, populism was a strictly Right or even radical right-wing movement. Post-1980 populism has been more diverse and better embedded in the new social-political environment. It represents a different answer to the same unanswered questions that undermined the old political structures and party formations. Populists exploit the crisis of liberal democracy and present themselves as defenders of national sovereignty, if needed, against the European Union. Populist rhetoric presents the party as the only true representative of the people. On behalf of the majority they reject the "corrupt political elite." They offer a defense against the "dangerous others," such as special interest groups, including multinational companies and those in support of globalization, as well as minority groups and immigrants that, in their view, endanger national homogeneity. Populists reject the neo-liberal challenge of welfare institutions. In Central and Eastern Europe, the concept of "dangerous others" had a long tradition and an extremely strong reappearance, as populist parties exploited dissatisfaction with the negative side effects of transformation and adjustment to the European Union.

Populist parties represent a new style in politics. Their organization is centralized, and they are strongly based on the principle of charismatic leadership, of having a leader who has a direct link to the people. They are "non-ideological" but "serve the people" and prefer "straight talk," the language of common sense. Populism became important in the turn-of-the-century European political arena. Populist parties and movements are not exclusively radical right, but also center-right, and even left-wing. One of the most successful center-right populist parties is Silvio Berlusconi's *Forza Italia* (Figure 8). Several traditional center-right parties such as the French Gaullist party – which was called the Union of Democrats for the Republic (UDR) after 1968, but has been renamed a few times, and is now called the Rally for the Republic (RPR) under Nicolas Sarkozy – also embodies typical populist characteristics. Representing this trend on the Left are the German Party of Democratic Socialism, merged into Oskar Lafontaine's *Die Linke*,

[33] Andrej Zaslove, "Here to Stay? Populism as a New Party Type," *European Review*, 16, 3 (July 2008), 318–32.

Figure 8. Silvio Berlusconi, the most successful European populist politician, has been prime minister of Italy several times.

the fourth largest party and parliamentary faction in Germany; the Italian anti-globalist *girotondi* movement; and some of the former Eastern European communist parties.

However, most of the populist parties are right-wing, anti-immigration, and xenophobic. They became important in European politics at the end of the century. The common policy base of these heterogenous party formations was anti-immigrationism, euroskepticism, and anti-Americanism. They often use rhetoric that is rabidly anti-multinational and anti-bank capital. All of these characteristics are part of their overwhelmingly *nationalist* policy and program directed at national homogeneity and cultural identity. They conquered the lower middle-class and working-class layers who wanted efficient safeguards against wage and welfare competition and who became ardent anti-immigrationists. They also attracted people who became disappointed with the performance of democracy.

In some West European countries such as Switzerland, France, and Austria, populist parties were already part of the political system before 1980, but in most cases they emerged and had their first political victories during the 1980s. The *Schweizerische Volkspartei* (Swiss People's Party), founded as a peasant party in 1929, became a typical right-wing populist party in the 1980s. It occupied a significant place in the Nationalrat, focusing on a strongly anti-Islamic asylum and immigration policy, and opposing the building of minarets in the country. The *Fremskrittspartiet* (Progress Party) in Norway received more than 12 percent of the votes at local elections in 1987, and 13 percent at the national elections in 1989. The *Fremskridtspartiet* of Denmark reached its maximum votes in 1981, with nearly 9 percent of the total.

The *Freiheitliche Partei Österreichs* (Freedom Party of Austria), founded in the 1950s, gained political importance in the 1980s when Jörg Haider became the head of the Carinthian party organization, and the party shifted to the far right with a strong xenophobic program that attracted mostly manual laborers, who form more than one-third of the party's constituency. The party got between 10 and 27 percent of the vote in elections during the 1980s and 1990s. In the 1991 regional elections, they had a huge victory in various local elections.[34] In 2008, the two right-wing parties, *Freiheitliche Partei* and *Liste Jörg Haider*, gained 13 percent compared to previous elections and together received nearly 29 percent of the votes, the largest victory of that political trend to date.

The *Front National* in France, founded in 1972, reached the peak of its success at both the national and presidential elections under the leadership of Jean-Marie Le Pen in the 1990s. About one-quarter of the party's constituency is manual laborers, who form its strongest base, and it has more widespread support in southern France, where the especially large immigrant population generates strong xenophobic reactions. In the presidential elections of 2002, Le Pen received nearly 17 percent of the votes, compared to the incumbent President Jacques Chirac's 19 percent and Lionel Jospin's 16 percent in the first round. Populist parties became successful in Germany where the *Republikaner Partei* received 12 percent of the votes in Baden-Württemberg in 1992. The Belgian *Vlaams Blok* of Flemish nationalists was founded in 1978, but after the usual 2 percent of votes during the 1980s, it got nearly 18 percent in Antwerp in 1988, and 20 percent at the European parliamentary elections in 1989. The regional-populist *Lega Nord* received 9 percent of the vote and became the fourth largest party in Italy in 1992, but in local elections in Mantua it received the relative majority of 34 percent. The neo-fascist *Alleanza Nazionale* of Gianfranco Fini was originally strongly rooted in the south, and it retained

---

[34] In 1991 in Vienna (nearly 23%), and in 1993 in Carinthia, Graz, Salzburg, and Tyrol (33, 20, 20, and 16% respectively).

this association even when it achieved its maximum popularity at the national elections of 1994 with nearly 14 percent of the vote.[35] In the mid-1990s, the West European radical right-wing probably reached its peak and then began losing ground. However, they are still strongly represented in the political palette of the continent.

Right-wing populist parties gained special ground – as discussed later – in Central and Eastern Europe. The hardships resulting from the process of transformation, the disillusionment after the exaggerated expectations of 1989–90, the all-round corruption that penetrated politics, and the social shock of transformation paved the way for the political success of populist demagoguery.

European "Party Families"

In parallel with the restructuring of the political arena of Europe, and as a consequence of the European integration process and the development of the institutions of the European Union, four major *political "party-families"* were founded to coordinate national social-democratic, conservative, populist, and green party activities on a pan-European scale. "These groups are similar to the party factions in the domestic parliaments . . . [P]arty federations bring together the leading party figures . . . to draft manifestoes . . . and coordinate policy positions . . ."[36] The social democratic party family has a century-long tradition of European cooperation in the framework of the Second International. This is the best-organized and most effective alliance that tries to regulate its member parties if they offend socialist principles. For example, the "family" membership of the Slovak *Smer – Sociálna Demokracia*, established in 1999 by Robert Fico, was suspended by the social democratic party family when it formed a coalition with right-wing, xenophobic-nationalist parties after the 2006 elections.

The other party families consisted of parties with rather different characters. British Conservatives and German Christian Democrats, for example, had little in common. Several populist-nationalist parties were inwardly oriented and somewhat anti-European parties *par excellence*, opposing the Union's intervention and mandatory rules in

[35] Hans-Georg Betz, *Radical Right-Wing Populism in Western Europe* (Houndmills: Palgrave Macmillan, 1994).

[36] David S. Bell and Christopher Lord (eds.), *Transnational Parties in the European Union* (Aldershot: Ashgate, 1998), 86.

favor of national sovereignty. However, they had little in common otherwise. The possibility of their cooperation was *ab ovo* limited. Do these party families constitute embryonic all-European parties or only insignificant alliances? The answer to this question will be determined by the further political integration of the European Union.

Shift to the Right and the Thatcher Phenomenon

After the tumultuous 1960s and 1970s, the historical transformation of the 1980s and 1990s brought some surprising about-faces. The left-wing mini-revolutions of the 1960s immediately generated a right turn in West European politics. In France, a few weeks after the revolutionary May of 1968, the June 23–30 parliamentary elections led to an absolute victory for the Right, first of all for the Gaullist Union of the Defense of the Republic (UDR), which gained 293 out of 487 seats, while the Left garnered a total of 67 seats. This was the first election in French history in which a party gained an absolute majority.[37]

When Europe entered the 1980s, conservative governments were in the driver's seat. Italy was still in shock over the unbelievable 1978 kidnapping and execution of Prime Minister Aldo Moro, who was ready to make a historic compromise and include the social-democratized euro-Communist Party in the government. The country remained firmly under the rule of the Christian Democratic Party controlled by Giulio Andreotti, nicknamed "*divo (divine) Giulio*," the Party's Jolly Joker. From the late 1950s until the early 1990s, Andreotti occupied the central place in Italian politics seven times: as minister of defense, minister of the interior, minister of foreign affairs, but most of all as prime minister. He and his party had secret connections with the Mafia, as a Mafia informant, Tommaso Buscetta, confessed. In October 1990, Andreotti acknowledged before the parliament the existence of the secret and illegal anti-communist NATO organization, Operazione Gladio. In 2002, at the age of eighty-three, Andreotti was sentenced to twenty-four years in prison because of his close Mafia connections and his use of the Mafia against assumed enemies,

---

[37] The following year, in June 1969, at the presidential election after the resignation of Charles de Gaulle, the Gaullist candidate Georges Pompidou received more than 58% of the votes at the second round.

Figure 9. Margaret Thatcher contributed most to the victory of neo-liberalism in Europe.

including the alleged murder of Mino Pecorelly, a journalist who wrote about Andreotti's Mafia connections. Andreotti was later acquitted, but his party had disappeared from the political arena in the 1990s.

In Germany, the Günter Guillaume affair – the scandal in which Willy Brandt's personal assistant, a successfully planted East German spy, was arrested in April 1974 – led to the resignation of the charismatic social democratic leader. Although Helmut Schmidt, a member of his cabinet, replaced him, a no-confidence vote removed the Social Democratic Party from power, and the Christian Democrats took over. Helmut Kohl became chancellor in 1982 and remained in power to preside over German unification. The Red Army Faction was already history: in May 1975, its leaders were sentenced at the Stuttgart trial, and Ulrike Meinhof was found dead in her prison cell in May 1976. The same thing happened to Baader, Ensslin, and Raspe in October 1977.

The most spectacular political change happened in Britain. The "Winter of Discontent" belatedly hit the island in 1978–9. Public services collapsed and strikes paralyzed the economy. A no-confidence vote removed the Labour government and the general elections put Margaret Thatcher, leader of the Conservative Party, in 10 Downing Street (Figure 9). Thatcher started her government work in 1970 as secretary of state for education and science, where she abolished free milk for 7–11-year-old school children. When she took over the government, the economy was in a desperate situation. Unemployment reached 2 and soon 3 million. Inflation rose to 18 percent, and manufacturing output declined by 30 percent. Thatcher started the restoration of order with an iron hand. Her populist style, optimism, and toughness in action impressed the Britons. Thatcher resisted making any compromise on the home front. She defeated the one-year-long miners' strike, and in 1982, the National Union of Mine Workers gave in. Thatcher closed all but fifteen of the pits. She was successful at reinvigorating the economy and became the embodiment of neo-liberal economics.

In 1982, during her first years in power, an adventurous Argentine military junta decided to "liberate" the Malvinas or Falkland Islands from British rule. Thatcher acted with the same vigor, sent in the navy, and emerged triumphant. National euphoria flooded Britain and paved the way for Conservative rule for more than a decade. Helmut Norpoth explained Thatcher's popularity with the following statement: "War and economics have few rivals when it comes to making or breaking governments."[38] In 1983, Thatcher's Conservative Party had a landslide victory, gaining almost twice as many seats in Parliament as its Labour Party opponents.

Market fundamentalism effectively influenced politics and public opinion. Prime Minister Margaret Thatcher and President Ronald Reagan, who were elected to office at almost the same time and dominated the 1980s, fully accepted these ideas, based their policies on them, and became the most influential propagators of this ideology. It was successful because of the breakdown of Keynesian economics, which was unable to cope with the challenge of recession-*cum*-inflation in the 1970s. The bankruptcy of the regimes that applied state interventionism in Latin America, India, and the Soviet Bloc delegitimized interventionism in general.

On the other hand, the advanced and rich core countries, especially the United States, which turned to laissez-faire policies, adjusted relatively quickly to the new technological and communication revolution, and managed to develop new high-tech industries and to generate a new prosperity from the mid-1980s onward. It was interpreted by the advocates of laissez-faire as the triumph of neo-liberalism.

---

[38] Helmut Norpoth, "Guns and Butter and Government Popularity in Britain," *The American Political Science Review*, 81, 3 (September, 1987), 949–59.

Augusto Pinochet's Chile, which fully adopted Milton Friedman's prescriptions, also became a prosperous model country for Latin America.

Strengthened by cooperation and friendly personal relations with President Reagan, Thatcher began privatizing the state-owned sector in 1983, selling off the state-owned oil industry, British Telecom, and several factories piece by piece, and privatizing various services performed by the 200 hospitals of the National Health Service. In a few years, she single-handedly liquidated the mixed – private and state-owned – British economy, the trademark regime of postwar Western Europe.

Lady Thatcher launched a crusade against the further integration and interventionism of the European Union: she revolted against a common agricultural policy because Britain gained little back from its contribution to the common budget. She succeeded in arranging an annual rebate of 66 percent of the difference between Britain's contribution and what it received in return. In her speech in Bruges in 1988, she harshly opposed any further integration based on, as she put it, "the dictates of some abstract intellectual concept," as well as interventions and control "by an appointed bureaucracy" aiming at the realization of "Utopian goals."[39]

Margaret Thatcher delivered, and she emerged victorious in the elections of 1979, 1983, and 1987, governing three consecutive terms, a first in British history. She went so far as to attempt replacing income tax with the unpopular neo-liberal ideal of indirect taxation. Her uniform "Poll Tax" of 1989 required the payment of the same amount of rates per individual, regardless of income, though people without wages received an 80 percent reduction. Two hundred thousand people demonstrated against it in Trafalgar Square in London. Her party became divided and one wing revolted. Sir Geoffrey Howe, who ranked second in her government, resigned because of Thatcher's European Union policy, and Michael Heseltine, another key member of her government, challenged Thatcher for the Conservative Party leadership. Since she did not perform well in the first round, Thatcher resigned. Her policy, however, influenced the Western world and beyond.

---

[39] Margaret Thatcher's speech at the College of Europe in Bruges, September 20, 1988, reprinted as "A Family of Nations," in Brent F. Nelsen and Alexander C.-G. Stubb (eds.), *The European Union: Readings on the Theory and Practice of European Integration* (Boulder, CO: Lynne Rienner, 1998), 51–2, 54.

Social Democratic Shift to the Center

Conservative ideologies strongly penetrated the disorganized political Left during the 1980s and 1990s. The old Left, with its industrial working-class base, declined visibly. The objective basis for that change was the radical structural transformation of the Western economies and societies in the last decades of the century. The previously dominant blue-collar working class strongly decreased in numbers in the de-industrialized West, and in the age of the service revolution, white-collar employees reached roughly two-thirds to three-quarters of the working population. Except in the Nordic countries, the middle class, or at least huge social groups with middle-class consciousness, turned their backs on old-style social democratic policy, social solidarity, and on the Left in general. The riots and killings of the late 1960s and the 1970s frightened and alienated them even more. They wanted law and order and to continue their comfortable consumer lifestyle with further increases in their standards of living, long vacations abroad, and better cars and kitchens. Free trade and European integration seemingly served their interests, and they welcomed the conservative parties' policy to adjust to the globalization challenge. However, people only partly accepted the neo-liberal ideology, and they defended their welfare privileges when needed. The European conservative Right either did not question welfare institutions at all, or did so only very cautiously.

Through the 1970s, it was only Western Europe that exhibited similar economic, social, and political trends, and that followed the road towards integration, but what Samuel Huntington called "the third wave of democratization" in the 1980s moved the Mediterranean countries into the same group.[40] In 1982, the Spanish Socialist Party of Filipe Gonzales achieved electoral victory and led the country's smooth transformation until 1996. Gonzales and the Socialist Party guided the privatization of Franco's strongly state-owned economy from 1984 on, but combined it with increased public spending and job creation, shaping the social safety net for smooth transformation. Welfare expenditure increased by 40 percent between 1975 and 1982, and then by another nearly 58 percent between 1982 and 1989. In other words, Spain successfully combined neo-liberal and

---

[40] Samuel P. Huntington, *The Third Wave: Democratization in the Late Twentieth Century* (Norman: University of Oklahoma Press, 1991).

Keynesian economic policies. Negotiated wages through the neo-corporatist cooperation of government, employers, and employees copied the postwar Western social partnerships. The socialists skill-fully created the spirit of national reconciliation.

Socialist and social democratic parties in the Mediterranean countries led most of the peaceful and successful transformations. They were also successful in France. In 1981, France elected François Mitterrand, who remained president until 1995. Mitterrand had a very mixed political background. He was a decorated official in the collaborator Vichy government, but then joined the resistance movement. In 1946, he launched a vicious anti-communist campaign to win a seat in parliament. He served in several governments as overseas minister, minister of the interior, and minister of justice. The Socialist Party rejected him when he initially wanted to join, but he was accepted in 1971. Moreover, he was the one who signed an agreement in 1972 with the communist party chiefs, Georges Marchais and Robert Fabre, to form the Union of the Left.

After running for the presidency but losing several times, Mitterrand at last defeated the incumbent president, Giscard d'Estaing, in 1981, and he began his presidency in coalition with the Communist Party in 1982. This coalition went against mainstream politics in Europe and began realizing the program of the Union of the Left with widespread nationalization, including of the banking system, the introduction of a 39-hour working week and a 56-day vacation system, and the raising of both the minimum wage and taxes on the wealthy. However, the next year Mitterrand made a 180-degree turn towards neo-liberalism, split with the communists who left the government, privatized all the state-owned firms, and opened private radio and TV channels. Left-wing socialism evaporated in France.

After the long Conservative rule in Britain, the renewed Labour Party had a landslide electoral victory in 1997. The leader of the party, Tony Blair, became prime minister and remained at Downing Street for ten years, followed by one of his close aides, Gordon Brown (Figure 10). The Labour victory clearly signaled the changes in the European socialist movement. In 1983, 1987 and 1992, the traditionally left-wing Labour Party led first by Michael Foot and then by Neil Kinnock lost three consecutive elections. The Oxford-educated Blair recognized the melting away of the long-established blue-collar base of the party and shifted it to the middle. As its leader from 1994 on, he transformed the party by eliminating the Marxist "common

Figure 10. Jacques Chirac (left) of France and Tony Blair of Britain, two leading and long-lasting European politicians.

ownership of the means of production" formula from the party pro-gram. Stressing its democratic socialist character, the Labour Party became a middle-class party, somewhat sensitive to social needs. Blair combined neo-liberal and welfare policy, and he significantly increased spending on health care and education.

This was not at all his invention, however. Willy Brandt had turned the German Social Democrats into a party of the entire society and not just of the working class. Filipe Gonzales made the same change in Spain in the 1980s, and President Bill Clinton shifted the Democratic

Party to the center in the United States in the early 1990s. In the new social environment, winning elections with leftist programs in advanced countries became impossible. "New Labour" and the new social democrats became successful by departing from their traditional principles.

The New Political Setting in the East

Against the odds, Central and Eastern Europe introduced well-established multi-party parliamentary systems during the 1990s and early 2000s. These countries separated executive and legislative power, and – at least formally – the courts became independent. Western-type modern legislation was enacted, including property, criminal, and civil rights codes. Privatization of the economy began, and, in most of the cases, functioning formal democracies were established and parliamentary rotations worked, as noted by the European Union's watchdog organization. Nevertheless, as throughout the modern history of these countries, form and content remained sharply different. Clientelism and corruption penetrated the political institutions, especially in Russia and the Balkans. In the summer of 2008, the European Union warned Bulgaria that if it did not fight successfully against corruption, the Union would suspend payments from its regional and cohesion funds (Figure 11).

The political shift towards the middle and the Right was even more dramatic on the Eastern half of the continent, where former communist countries adopted neo-liberal policies and neo-conservative ideologies, which together with a revival of religiosity and old-fashioned passionate xenophobic nationalism, filled the ideological vacuum after the collapse of communism. With few exceptions, the socialist parties of the region that repeatedly won elections – in Hungary, socialists formed and dominated three out of five governments between 1990 and 2009 – followed the same neo-liberal policy, and they competed with right-wing parties to gain support by populist measures. After the collapse of state socialism at the end of the 1980s, a peaceful revolution transformed the region, liberating it from nearly half a century of communism, but also from the fascist and authoritarian legacy of earlier periods. With the introduction of multi-party systems and free elections – in some of these cases, for the first time ever – the historic march towards democracy began. However, the first elections

Figure 11. Chancellor Angela Merkel with Central European prime ministers.

were special in the given circumstances. Only Hungary experienced elections in a well-structured political arena with several parties, representing the interests of various social-political groupings that competed with each other. In March 1990, the first free election led to the formation of a right-of-center coalition of populist-nationalist, conservative, peasant, and Christian democratic political forces that won 60 percent of the seats in parliament. The Hungarian Socialist Party, the former reform-communist party that led the reform-revolution or "refolution," as Timothy Garton Ash called it, and had a track record of fast and peaceful transformation, gained less than 10 percent of the votes. Former dissident forces, the only open opposition to the communist regime, remained in opposition in the new era as well.

Electoral Victories of a Monolithic Opposition and Re-elected Communists in the Balkans

A second type of election outcome characterized Poland and Czechoslovakia. Here the victory of a monolithic opposition replaced the monolithic communist rule. Solidarity took over Poland in 1989. The Czech Civic Forum Party, formed by the Charta 77 opposition, gained 67 percent of the seats in parliament. However, the united former oppositions, which now governed in both countries, were united only against the communist regime. After their landslide victory, their fragmentation and split started immediately. Poland's first entirely free election in 1991 ended with the defeat of a broken Solidarity, the admired and heroic leader of the opposition against the communist regime. The former absolute winner of the 1989 elections now gained a total of only 5 percent of the votes. However, no clear winner emerged from the thirty parties that competed, and five parties had to form a coalition to govern. In 1993, the third parliamentary elections led to the total elimination of any Solidarity- or Church-based political parties. The former reform-communists, now the Democratic Left Alliance, won 64 percent of the seats. Former opposition groupings and their parties disappeared in the Czech and Slovak republics as well. The structuring and restructuring of the party system, the formation of new parties and new mergers characterized the entire decade in these countries.

A third type of election dominated the entire Balkans. In these still mostly rural countries, no real opposition movement had ever existed. The communist regimes started industrialization and modernized these countries which therefore exhibited definite achievements. The former communist parties renamed themselves socialist and had no real competition. They gained absolute majorities in the first free elections. The Bulgarian Socialist Party, the former Communist Party, got 53 percent of the seats; the Romanian National Salvation Front of former communists got 67 percent of the votes, and their presidential candidate, Ion Iliescu, 85 percent. The Serbian Socialists – also former communists – captured 194 out of 250 seats, and their presidential candidate, the former secretary general of the Communist Party, Slobodan Milošević, was elected by 65 percent of the voters. The same happened in Albania, where the former communists got 65 percent of the votes, and the successor of Enver Hoxha, the communist hard-liner party chief, Ramiz Alia, had a landslide victory. Signaling the paradoxical situation, he was soon not only removed, but also arrested. Nationalist advocates of independence, regardless of their political orientation, gained easy majorities in former Yugoslav republics of Bosnia-Herzegovina, Croatia, and Slovenia.

Nationalist Upheaval and the Yugoslav Tragedy

Exploding nationalism characterized the political landscape in several countries of the region. In the ideological vacuum that remained after state socialism, people turned towards the traditional values and behavioral patterns of the region. The most evident reorientation was towards religion and nationalism. Both penetrated the countries in the early 1990s. Ugly xenophobia became an everyday phenomenon: Roma people were beaten and chased from the Czech Republic; Roma villages were burned in Romania; and Roma workers were dismissed, causing an unheard of 50 to 80 percent unemployment in Roma communities. Anti-Semitism was revitalized in countries such as Poland and Romania, which were practically without existing Jewish communities. Militant and noisy anti-Semitism polluted the political and social atmosphere in Hungary. Old reflexes of territorial revisionism gained ground in Hungary, Albania, and Bulgaria. In Romania and Slovakia nationalist forces organized anti-Hungarian campaigns. Although these phenomena calmed down somewhat after the mid-1990s, they resurfaced from time to time.

Nationalist upheaval exhibited the most widespread explosion of all in the multi-ethnic, multinational states of the region: Yugoslavia, the Soviet Union, and Czechoslovakia. In Yugoslavia this took the form of a bloody civil war, a Serb versus Croat, Serb-Croat versus Bosnian, and Serb versus Kosovar conflict that killed 200,000 people and uprooted a million (Figures 12 and 13). Yugoslavia was never a homogenized quasi-nation-state. Deadly conflicts and murderous civil war had characterized the first thirty years of its existence. The unfinished struggle renewed in the early 1990s. Nationalist upheaval consumed Yugoslavia after the death of Tito, the ironhanded unifier. Serb nationalists at the Academy of Sciences and Arts spoke about the Serbs as victims. The richer republics such as Slovenia and Croatia sought to get rid of the burden of the more backward eastern republics. Nationalism generated nationalism, and the first free elections in 1990 ended with an unchallenged victory of nationalist parties that ran under the banner of independence. In June 1991, the Croat parliament voted for independence, and a day later a Slovene referendum declared the same. Serbia, led by the ardent nationalist Slobodan Milošević, rejected the dissolution of the federal state and ordered the army to suppress separatism. He withdrew from the Slovene war, but in the same month a Serbian guerilla army attacked Croatia, which had rejected its Serb minority's request for autonomy.

Figure 12. Civil war in Yugoslavia in the early 1990s: Serb soldiers in the trenches.

Figure 13. Serb demonstration in Belgrade protesting the announcement of Kosovo's independence.

Serb nationalists reintroduced the old doctrine of "Greater Serbia": the unity of all Serbs living outside Serbia, who actually represented 40 percent of the total Serb population. The war spread and became deadliest in Bosnia–Herzegovina, where the Serb military and paramilitary forces launched ruthless campaigns. The international vocabulary was enriched by the expression "ethnic cleansing," a translation of the

Serbian *rascistiti teren* (or territorial cleansing), used by Serb nationalists in Bosnia and Kosovo. Slobodan Milošević reinvented himself as
Serb nationalist, and Serbia ran amok in pursuit of the Greater Serbian cause after the dissolution of Yugoslavia. Terrorist and genocidal
actions were committed on both sides during and after the Yugoslav
civil war. In the new crisis of the late 1980s, all of the nationalities –
Croat, Slovene, and Bosnian Muslim nationalists – sought to establish
independent nation-states. If Yugoslavia dissolved, the Serb nationalists wanted to unite all the Serbs, and they fought for Serb unification against the Croats and Bosnians. The Serb population in
Bosnia and Croatia – one-third and 12-percent minorities respectively in those newly independent states – wanted the same right to
self-determination as the Slovenes, Croats, and Bosnian Muslims, and
they also wanted to join Serbia.

The war concluded in 1995, when Serbia, while militarily successful in the first few years of the war, was defeated and internationally
condemned. Serbs undoubtedly committed the greatest number of
war crimes, rapes, and murders in the Yugoslav civil war. The brutal Srebrenica mass murder of several thousand Muslim men, and
the Kosovo rape campaign to chase the Kosovar Muslims out of the
province, belonged to the most brutal and inhuman war crimes committed in postwar Europe. The Dayton Agreement, imposed by the
United States, divided Bosnia into autonomous regions: Republika
Srpska and the Croat-Bosnian (Muslim) Federations that together
form the independent Bosnia-Herzegovina. The West accepted the
dissolution of Yugoslavia, but forced the unity of the divided Bosnia-
Herzegovina. The seeds of future conflicts were sown. The devastating
war set back the west Balkans for more than a decade, and it blocked
their road to the European Union.

However, the conflict did not end even with Dayton. The last
chapter of the drama, the Kosovo crisis, reached its climax at the end
of the 1990s. Kosovo exhibited a different history of belated nation-
building. The Serb versus Albanian conflict and violence began in
the early twentieth century, during the Balkan wars. During that
time, the province gradually developed an Albanian majority. When
Yugoslavia was established after World War I, the 1921 census registered 45 percent Serbs, 24 percent Croats, and 3.7 percent Albanians in the country. Though the numbers are highly tentative, 50
to 60 percent of the population of Kosovo was Albanian, and their
share increased after World War II to 75 percent, and then to nearly

90 percent by the 1990s. It was partly the result of immigration from the south, but mostly because of the extremely high Albanian birth rate and population growth: from 500,000 in 1900 to 800,000 in 1950, and to 2.4 million by 2003. Serb population growth was very slow and even became stagnant, and then, as in Europe generally, it began declining below reproduction level. Moreover, Serb emigration from the region became almost continuous. During World War II, collaborating fascist local authorities expelled 100,000 Serbs, and between 1961 and 1989, the non-Albanian population drastically decreased due to ongoing, quiet atrocities against Serbs, especially after the 1981 riot that aimed at achieving an ethnically pure Kosovo. According to the biased 1986 Memorandum of the nationalist Serb Academy of Science and Arts, Kosovars expelled 200,000 Serbs from the province from the late 1960s to the late 1980s.[41]

Kosovo gained limited autonomy in 1963, and became an autonomous province in 1974, and, in fact, it became a virtually autonomous Yugoslav republic. The 1981 Pristina revolt resulted in permanent tension and local skirmishes. The extreme nationalist Yugoslav government of Slobodan Milošević used police terror, imprisonments, and the revoking of the autonomous status of the province to defeat the rising demand for self-determination. Kosovo was surprisingly quiet during the Yugoslav civil war in the first half of the 1990s. In 1995, however, the Kosovo Liberation Army was established and launched violent terror attacks against the Serb minority, and then mounted an insurgency to push out Serbs. The Milošević regime responded with a ruthless counter-offensive. Burning houses, killing, and rape were all among the methods employed in the offensive that chased 300,000 Kosovars from the province in 1998. NATO responded by mounting an air offensive against Serbia. The heavy bombing of Kosovo and even Belgrade forced Serbia to capitulate. The war ended. The United Nations deployed peacekeeping forces and Kosovo was put under UN protection (Figure 14).

After their success at home, the Kosovo Liberation Army escalated the war, seeking to "liberate" the Albanian minority of western Macedonia as well. International pressure and peacekeeping forces were able to stop the Kosovo Liberation Army's attacks and to

---

[41] Dušan T. Bataković, *Kosovo i Metohia, istorija i ideologija* (Belgrade: Hriscanska Misao, 1998); Mile Bjelajac, "Migrations of Ethnic Albanians in Kosovo 1938–1950," *Balcanica*, 38 (2007), 219–30.

Figure 14. United Nations peacekeeping forces try to stabilize the situation in Kosovo after NATO intervention.

stabilize the situation. The dissolution of the former Yugoslavia resumed at the beginning of the twenty-first century, with the emergence of an independent Kosovo and a peacefully separated and independent Montenegro.

Russian Collapse and Recuperation under Authoritarian Rule

The successor states of the former Soviet Union also had a bumpy road to travel. The former Soviet Empire introduced free elections and a multi-party system, but authoritarian regimes were slow to change because of the criminalization of the state and economy. Boris Yeltsin remained in power until 1999 and presided over the humiliating collapse of the economy. While GDP dropped by half, a small group of "oligarchs" robbed the state either by means of their political connections, or bribery, or both, which made it possible to privatize state companies for themselves. A few hundred people became multi-millionaires overnight. Privatization was corrupt everywhere in the region but nowhere so much as in Russia.

Transparency International's Worldwide Corruption Perception Index put Russia, so far as its level of corruption was concerned, in 143rd place, *worse* than countries such as Ethiopia, Libya, Pakistan, and Burundi, even in 2007.[42]

In the first years of transformation, companies did not pay wages for several months. Even in 1993–4, 60 percent of the workforce was not paid fully on time, and 32 percent of the population fell below the poverty level. A deep demographic crisis shocked Russia, dramatically shortening life and increasing the death rate in proportions that were unparalleled in late twentieth-century Europe. Male life expectancy declined by nearly ten years to 58.6 years, and infant mortality was 4.5 times higher than in the West. Between 1989 and 2005, Russia lost nearly 3 million people. The Baltic countries shared this experience: male life expectancy declined from 65.3 to 60.8 in Latvia, from 65.7 to 61.7 in Estonia, and from 66.9 to 63.5 in Lithuania between 1989 and 1995. Female life expectancy also declined by one to two years. The mortality rate did not drop to pre-crisis levels until 2001.[43]

Russia held formally democratic elections and introduced democratic institutions, but the reality was, and has remained, that the country is governed by an "authoritarian democracy." Under the presidency of Vladimir Putin and his former KGB network, the government strictly controlled the media and cut short the freedom of the press. The imprisonment and even murder of members of the opposition, including journalists who unveiled political or economic crimes, were frequent events (Figure 15). The mafia, organized in the Gulags, took over and criminalized the economy and politics. Turn of the century Russia was still in a hopeless situation.

However, during the Putin era between 2000 and 2008, the country doubled its GDP, mostly because of the oil price explosion. Russia, the world's number one exporter of oil and gas combined, profited hugely from the multiplying prices and became able to improve the economy and the living standard of the population. Putin ended his second term with an 80 percent popularity rating. "Any politician would envy his association with stability, prosperity, security, restored imperial power and vigorous state authority."[44]

---

[42] Transparency International, Worldwide Corruption Perception Index, www.transparency. org/policy.research/surveys_indices/cpi-19k–
[43] UNICEF, *Social Monitor* (Florence: Innocenti Research Centre, 2003).
[44] Simon Sebag Montefiore, "In Russia, Power has no Heirs," *New York Times*, January 12, 2009, A23.

Figure 15. Chancellor Gerhard Schröder (left) and President Vladimir Putin: the delicate balance between Europe and Russia.

Putin's name, however, is also associated with authoritarian mockery of democratic forms. As a characteristic event, President Putin respected the law and left office when his second term expired. However, his protégé successor initiated a law in early 2009 that changed the length of the president's term of office from four to six years, and the law was rubber-stamped by the parliament. This allows for the former president, now Prime Minister Putin, to run for office again and to serve for another two terms, or twelve years, i.e. to be president virtually for life. Formally, everything operates according to the law, but in reality, it is not the rule of law, but the rule of persons, arranged by covert but transparent manipulation.

This situation is quite widespread in most of the former Soviet republics, which are now independent states. In Kazakhstan, the post-Soviet democratic constitution was changed to legalize President Nursultan Nazarbayev's lifelong presidential power. In Turkmenistan, President Saparmurat Niyazov, "Turkmenbashi," father of all Turkmens – as he called himself – officially became president for life. In Azerbaijan, a hereditary presidency was introduced: after the death of President Heydar Aliyev, his son, Ilham, followed him into the presidency in 2003.[45]

___

[45] *Ibid.*

Right-Wing Populism

Since 2004, a new wave of right-wing populism has flooded several countries, from Poland, Slovakia, and Romania, to Hungary. It easily gained ground in the troubled and nervous social environment. With extreme demagogy, it offered defense against Europeanization and globalization, and reinterpreted the national project. Nationalism usually played an important role in nineteenth- and twentieth-century Central and Eastern Europe. It was easy to mobilize dissatisfied people against the "enemies," but also against the "establishment," against "robber banks," multinational companies, the "corrupt elite," and against governments that cut welfare expenditures. Large parts of the population had not yet recovered from the shock of transformation, especially those who became losers in the transformation. Populist parties were renewed, and they exploited old territorial conflicts and anti-minority sentiments.

The Hungarian populist party, Fidesz, launched a campaign on behalf of the Transylvanian Hungarians, and it mobilized the Budapest mob which committed violent acts in 2006 against the government under wartime Hungarian Fascist Arrow Cross flags. The newly formed, frighteningly black-uniformed, *Magyar Gárda* militia began using fascist symbols. Ján Slota, the Slovak nationalist-populist politician – in coalition with Robert Fico's and Vladimir Mečiar's populist-nationalist parties – spoke about "Mongoloid Hungarians" and about the Slovak army flattening Budapest. The Polish Law and Justice Party of the Kaczyński brothers advocated a better redistribution of wealth and increased support for farmers, promised the elimination of corruption and crime, and required greater weight for Poland in the European Union, blaming Germany for wartime destruction.[46]

All of the populists are strongly "Euro-skeptic," blaming the European Union's requirements for the social pain their countries' populations had endured, and arguing for the defense of national independence. Populist parties often revolted against representative democracy as a self-serving system of corrupt politicians, and they demanded referenda to "defend" people's constitutional rights to free education and health care. Populists apply the well-worn method of using half-truths in arguments that end in false conclusions. The new

---

[46] Marian L. Tupy, "The Rise of Populist Parties in Central Europe: Big Government, Corruption, and the Threat of Liberalism" (Washington: CATO Institute, November 8, 2006), www.cfr.org/publication/11847/cato_institute.html

political environment was advantageous for populist politics because huge swathes of society did not feel that political parties represented their interests. Widespread de-politicization followed the alienation of people from representative parliamentary systems. The process of de-industrialization, job losses, and wage decline had marginalized trade unions. In Hungary, their membership declined to one-quarter of the employed population. Populist propaganda painted government parties which wanted to introduce painful cuts as enemies of the people, not as rival parties in a multi-party democracy. They repeatedly represented a change of government to be akin to a regime change.

Populist parties gained new strength from returning economic troubles. Transformation is not a smooth, linear process. In spite of basic economic consolidation, economic crises or slowdowns revisited the countries of the region from time to time. Each generated political dissatisfactions and an opportunity for populist forces to exploit them. A short list of these economic tumults clearly illustrates the numerous opportunities to stand up for the "people's interests." Consequently, in some countries, the government changed twelve times in the first twelve years. Let me list the series of economic difficulties: economic decline returned to Romania in 1997, 1998, and 1999, when GDP decreased by 6.1, 5.4, and 3.2 percent, respectively. Severe GDP decline also characterized Bulgaria in 1996 and 1997 (nearly 11 and 7 percent, respectively). The Czech Republic experienced similar GDP decline in three consecutive years between 1997 and 1999. Poland slowed down significantly in the early twenty-first century to 1.2 percent and 1.4 percent annual growth in two consecutive years. In 1997, hyperinflation (1,082 percent) returned to Bulgaria, while Romanian inflation reached 154 percent that year.[47] Albania sank into chaos in 1996–7 with the collapse of pyramid investment schemes, which had borrowed from the public at up to 300 percent monthly interest, and then "collapsed," draining virtually the entire domestic savings of the population. General unrest led to a virtual civil war in the country, and international forces reestablished order.[48] One of the most successful transformation countries, Hungary, suffered a huge budgetary crisis and major slowdown when previous growth rates halved in 2006–8.

---

[47] European Bank for Reconstruction and Development, *Transition Report, 2001: Energy in Transition* (London: EBRD, 2001), 59, 61.

[48] Marta Muço and Luljeta Minxhozi, "Albania. An Overview Ten Years After," in Domenico Nuti and Milicia Uvalic (eds.), *Post-Communist Transition to a Market Economy: Lessons and Challenges* (Ravenna: Longo Editore, 2003), 181–202, 197–8.

In the first quarter of 2009, 3.9 percent decline occurred, and the forecast for the year was 6 percent decline. Since 2006, Central European
growth has actually slowed down, and in 2008–9, sharply declined
in the entire region. The so-called "small Baltic tigers," Latvia and
Estonia, offer the best example. Latvian growth increased from 2002
to 2006, when it achieved a 12 percent annual growth rate. By 2008,
this development had stopped. The country's industrial output has
decreased by more than 6 percent. The inflation rate reached 17 percent. Crisis thus hit the Baltic economic miracle countries as well. Slovakia's growth rate slowed down. The crisis of 2008–9 was connected
with the Europe-wide recession that slowed down export opportunities and foreign investment activities. Hungary is especially dependent
on exports, since it accounts for 40 percent of its GDP. The 2008–9
international financial crisis hit the region particularly hard and ended
rapid previous growth, especially because 80 to 87 percent of the
banking system of the transforming countries is in foreign hands and
the mother institutions stopped giving credit abroad.

These crises and the strict requirements of the European Union
offered good opportunities for populist parties to mobilize the masses,
and sometimes even the violent mob, as in the case of Hungary in the
fall of 2006. Attila Ágh called the turmoil that continued until 2008,
a post-accession or "membership shock," the "losers' riots." The
anti-reform populist opposition party, Fidesz, ruthlessly exploited the
"reform fatigue of the Hungarian population."[49]

Nearly two-thirds of disappointed and de-politicized Bulgarians do
not know any party that represents their interests, and 84 percent do
not want to have any party connections.[50] Corruption and organized
crime are considered to be the central issues and generated the need
for strong hands, i.e., a "law and order regime." This offered an
excellent ground for populists. The GERD party of Sofia's mayor,
Boiko Borisov, and Volen Siderov's xenophobic and Europe-critical
Ataka Party filled the political vacuum.[51]

Populist parties have ruled Romania since 1989. As Anneli Ute
Gabanyi expressed in the title of her study, populism is an instrument

---

[49] Attila Ágh, "Hungarian Politics in the Early 21st Century: Reforms and Post-EU Accession
Crisis," *Südosteuropa Mitteilungen*, 48, 2 (2008), 68–81.

[50] Local elections attracted only 40% of the voters, but the 2007 European Parliament elections
only 28%.

[51] Sonja Schüler, "Zur politischen Kultur im heutigen Bulgarien," *Südosteuropa Mitteilungen*,
48, 2 (2008), 38–55.

for securing power. Indeed, in post-1989 Romania, populism was the instrument to gain and secure power, first, by the left-wing populist National Salvation Front that preached a "third way" policy. In the early twenty-first century, right-wing populist parties mushroomed: the Great Romania Party of Corneliu Vadim Tudor, the New Generation Party of Gigi Becali, and the anti-elitist "folk" party of Traian Băsescu. The latter actually gained the presidency on this wave of populism.[52]

The populist wave that flooded Central and Eastern Europe in the first decade of the twenty-first century is clearly expressed in Poland by the excessive populist rule of the twin-brothers, Lech and Jarosław Kaczyński, and by Slovakia with its important populist forces of Ján Slota's extreme right-wing, xenophobic Slovak National Party, and Vladimir Mečiar's Movement for Democratic Slovakia. Populism is both an instant political danger and a roadblock to economic rationalization that cannot be achieved without social pain. Populist parties may cause serious losses and the slowing down of integration to Europe.

During the first two decades of transformation, however, all of the parties and governments, regardless of their name and political orientation, had to follow a path determined partly by the past of their countries, and mostly by the pressure of the great powers and the European Union. After being accepted as a member of the European Union, populist parties, paradoxically, gained more ground for maneuvering, and the Union had less power to control them.

The Main Factors of the Changing Cultural Environment: Suburbanization

In the quarter-century following World War II, the culture of everyday life was revolutionized in Western Europe by the increased wealth of the middle class and the mechanization of households, as well as by almost universal car ownership, increased vacation time, and exploding mass tourism. The "pill" radically changed sexual behaviour in the younger generation, and the Beatles and blue-jeans changed their cultural and clothing habits. All the significant changes in everyday

---

[52] Anneli Ute Gabanyi, "Rumänien: Populismus als Instrument der Machtsicherung," *Südosteuropa Mitteilungen*, 48, 2 (2008), 56–67.

life that emerged during the 1960s and 1970s continued to char-
acterize the decades around the turn of the century. However, the
emerging new *Zeitgeist*, the conservative intellectual and political culture of the 1980s and 1990s, exhibited its own new features and also
penetrated everyday culture and arts, thus further altering post-1980
everyday life. The transformation was also connected to a significantly changing physical and social environment, including the new
settlement structure, urbanization and suburbanization, with all of its
influence on lifestyle. The gradually changing family structure and
further increased leisure time also had major impacts. New technology probably played the most significant role by radically transforming
communication, behavior, attitudes, leisure time, and entertainment
habits.

New trends in urban development gained an increased importance
in Europe around the turn of the twenty-first century. The Western
half of the continent was already urbanized in the nineteenth century,
but the process continued, and gained new incentive as a result of
globalization. Expanding service sectors and high-tech industries led
to a strong spatial concentration to exploit the advantage of proximity.
Agglomeration economy gained ground and served urban networks.
Some European countries became *entirely* urbanized for the first time
in history. More than 97 percent of the population in Belgium lived
in cities, in Iceland 93 percent, in Britain 90 percent, in Germany 88
percent, in Denmark 86 percent, and in Sweden 83 percent. Within
the European Union as a whole, 75 percent of the population became
urban inhabitants. Most of Central and Eastern Europe, the former
rural-agrarian half of the continent, also became highly urbanized:
two-thirds to three-quarters of their population live in urban settlements. The gradual but permanent process of urbanization offered a
new, modern urban environment and lifestyle, as well as more educational and cultural opportunities for Europeans.

Europe does not have super cities such as Tokyo with 35 million inhabitants, nor even cities like New York, Shanghai, or Mexico
City with 15 to 20 million people. Europe has only one "global
city," London.[53] Nevertheless, huge agglomerations also emerged
around the Paris, Essen, and Moscow areas, with roughly 10 million
inhabitants in each. Between 4 and 5 million people jammed into

---

[53] Saskia Sassen introduced this term in her *The Global City: New York* (Princeton University
Press, 1991).

agglomerations around Madrid, Brussels, Manchester, and Berlin. Among the 300 "1-million-resident" cities of the world, 13 percent are in Europe, and thirty-six European agglomerations concentrate more than 1 million people. Among these huge urban agglomerations, some secondary "semi-global" centers play important European and even global roles: Zurich is a global financial center, and Paris and Brussels have major all-European roles. Moreover, the Vienna–Prague–Budapest–Warsaw city-network has a broad Central European role.[54]

In the European Union, somewhat surprisingly at first glance, only one-quarter of the urban population lives in big cities with over 250,000 inhabitants, and another quarter lives in middle-sized towns of 50,000 to 250,000 residents. These figures, however, signal a new phenomenon in urbanization: namely, that the smaller administrative urban units are not independent small or middle-sized cities, but suburbs of big cities. A new urban development characterized European urbanization between 1970 and 1980, with "a break in the traditional model of European urban form, or compact city," and the emergence of a new urban system, sometimes called a "*rurban*" or rural-urban development.[55] As opposed to the 1960s and 1970s, when small town development dominated, these small urban units are either amalgamating into large urban regions, or declining back into the rural environment. In the title of its dramatic 2006 report on the phenomenon, the European Environmental Agency named this new trend "urban sprawl."[56] The previously compact type of European city began following the American model of suburbanization: the physical expansion of cities with huge, less densely populated residential areas built up with semi-detached or detached family houses that made the physical distinction between city and countryside rather difficult. The archetype and most extreme illustration of this city model is Los Angeles.

Sprawling urban settlements or "losangelized" European cities increased the built-up areas by 20 percent, though the population of the settlements enlarged by only 9 percent between 1980 and

[54] György Enyedi, *Városi világ – városfejlődés a globalizáció korában* (Pécs: Pécsi Tudományegyetem Közgazdaság-tudományi Kara, 2003).

[55] Bettin Lattes and Recchi (eds.), *European Societies*, 289.

[56] European Commission, *Urban Sprawl in Europe: The Ignored Challenge*, European Environmental Agency Report No. 10 (Luxembourg: Office for Official Publications of the European Community, 2006).

2000. With its sparsely populated settlements, urban Europe occupies one-quarter of the territory of the European Union. The suburban chains consist of independent administrative units, small townships with between 1,000 to 50,000 inhabitants. Half of the European Union's population lives in this category of settlements. This phenomenon characterizes all the countries. The most extreme examples are in Belgium, the Netherlands, northern France, northwest Germany, northern Italy, and coastal Spain and Portugal. While urbanization in the European Union increased by 5.4 percent in the 1990s, the Madrid agglomeration grew by 50 percent in one decade. The number of the city's inhabitants increased by 240,000, but the number of new houses increased by more than half-a-million, and Guadalajara and Toledo became part of the enlarged Madrid region. Coastal urbanization in Spain, Portugal, and Ireland increased 30 percent faster than that of inland areas. In 2000, a 13-kilometer long strip along Portugal's Atlantic seashore concentrated 50 percent of the country's urban settlements. In coastal Spain, 50 percent of the land area was built up in loose, elegant settlements. New urban developments sometimes cross state borders and international waters, as in the case of Germany and Poland, and experts are forecasting the appearance of combined Malmö-Copenhagen and London–Paris–Brussels agglomerations. These urban regions are not only enlarged settlements but exhibit new urban structures as well. Instead of the traditional one city center, they have multiple centers.

Within the process of continued urbanization, a new and rapidly growing suburbanization offers a new, rich environment: gardens, fresh air, and far fewer poor people around. The communication revolution provides most of the advantages of city life, while gigantic shopping malls, mechanized households in gated communities, and car ownership eliminate most of the disadvantages of living at a distance from city centers, effectively establishing a new lifestyle for half of the urban population. However, the first signs of true "losangelesization," i.e., the creation of permanent traffic-jams and wasted hours on the motorways, are also among the first negative consequences of suburbanization.

In the transformation of Central and Eastern Europe, de-urbanization went hand in hand with suburbanization. At the same time that Hungary's total population declined by 1.1 percent, urban population decreased by 2.5 percent. Budapest had 2.02 million inhabitants in 1990, but only 1.72 million by 2003. Similar trends emerged in the Czech Republic where the entire population declined by 0.7 percent, but the populations of Prague and Plzen fell by 3.7 and 4.5 percent, respectively. Tallinn, in Estonia facing the Gulf of Finland, though it was elevated to the rank of capital city, decreased in population by 16 percent between 1989 and 2003. However, as around Prague, and in parallel with de-urbanization, a "booming suburban area was mushrooming: the number of completed houses and apartments per 1,000 inhabitants was three times higher than the national average."[57] While the population of Budapest declined by 4.4 percent, the population of the forty-four settlements comprising the Budapest agglomeration increased by 4 percent during the first half of the 1990s. The same trend was reproduced in thirty-two metropolitan areas in Hungary: their population dropped by 2.9 percent, but the number of inhabitants in their suburbs increased by 2.3 percent.[58]

The meaning of "suburbs" also altered radically. During the entire twentieth century, suburbs in Central and Eastern Europe meant a mixture of industrial zones, poor working-class residential "dormitory" towns, with commuting residents who worked in various industrial zones of the city. These suburbs were also semi-village areas, where residents kept pigs and goats and grew vegetables for the family. During the transformation period, the Western type of middle-class suburban developments in certain areas accompanied the de-industrialization and de-agrarianization of most of the suburbs. A new suburban area developed at a distance of 10–15 kilometers from Tallinn, and one-third of its population, half of them in single-family houses, live in buildings completed in 2005.

Although Central and Eastern European urban development is following the new Western trend, the two halves of the European continent are in different stages of urbanization. In the West, the communication and service revolution generated the new urban trends. The industrial mass production sectors disappeared from big urban settlements, and knowledge-based sectors, research and development institutions, services, including financial services, and cultural industries became dominant urban agglomerations. Central and Eastern Europe is still one phase behind. Modern industrial mass production, which

---

[57] Ronald Van Kempen, Marcel Vermeulen, and Ad Baan, *Urban Issues and Urban Policies in the New EU Countries* (Aldershot: Ashgate, 2005), 18.

[58] János Ladányi and Iván Szelényi, "Class, Ethnicity and Urban Restructuring in Postcommunist Hungary," in György Enyedi (ed.), *Social Change and Urban Restructuring in Central Europe* (Budapest: Akadémiai Kiadó, 1998), 67–86, 68–9.

was an earlier factor in Western urbanization, is primarily responsible for urban development there.[59] However, the European integration process confused the clear chronological stages of urban development in Central and Eastern Europe, and it has combined the earlier (industrial mass production) and contemporary (knowledge-based industries and services) incentives for urbanization.

Some analysts called the new urban development trends "neo-liberal urbanization": a deregulated process where settlement development became an "elite playing field." Instead of traditional city planning, individual urban projects became dominant, concentrating the business interests of the cities, and neglecting social requirements. The former "centralist, formalized, bureaucratized, hierarchical, top-down planning approaches decentralized [into] more horizontal, informal, flexibilized, bottom-up planning . . . [that goes] hand in hand with increasing inequality in access to decision making."[60] To put the same point in more ordinary terms: "urban growth is the result of family and individual choices rather than professional practices, and lies increasingly beyond the scope of architects or town planners."[61]

These characteristics of an unplanned and barely controlled urban construction policy became even more explicit in Central and Eastern Europe. They considered decentralization as part of democratization. Several independent communities were established within the big cities. Warsaw consisted of seventeen independent communities guaranteed by the new constitution. The Act on Municipalities and the Act on Local Self-Government in Czechoslovakia and Hungary, respectively, created fifty-seven autonomous local districts in Prague, seventeen in Bratislava, and twenty-three in Budapest. These units became the basis of urban planning. This situation led to fragmented and unplanned building activities.

Urban development at the turn of the century renewed the trend towards creating "dual cities," with poor inner parts and rich suburbs and exhibiting huge social disparities. Social polarization led to growing socio-spatial segregation. This phenomenon was also literally "colored" by ethnic diversity. Immigrants, especially illegal immigrants, settle in big cities and try to make a living doing

[59] G. Enyedi, *Városi világ*, 12, 14.

[60] Erik Swyngedouw, Frank Moulaert, and Arantxa Rodriguez, *The Global Restructuring and Social Polarization in European Cities* (Oxford University Press, 2003), 33, www.ru.ul/socgeo/colloquium/antipode.pdf.

[61] Bettin Lattes and Recchi (eds.), *European Societies*, 312.

low-wage seasonal work, construction, and household employment. Their numbers are permanently increasing. Between 1997
and 2003, about 125,000–230,000 illegal immigrants settled in the
Netherlands.[62] During the 1990s, migratory totals were balanced in
most of the big cities of Europe: in 2000, 283,000 people moved
out from London, and 294,000 moved in; in the same year, 123,000
persons left Berlin, and exactly the same number of people moved
in to the city.[63] A great part of the departing people belongs to the
middle class, and an increasing part of the incoming population are
immigrants.

In a few less-developed transforming countries, slums concentrate significant parts of the increased urban population. One of the
most striking figures comes from Moldova, where income levels have
declined since independence through the early twenty-first century,
and 31 percent of the urban population lives in slums. In war-ridden
Bosnia-Herzegovina and troubled Romania, nearly one-fifth of town-
dwellers live in slums, while in Macedonia the number is 8 percent.

In 1999, the European Union's Commission published a concept
paper called the "European Spatial Development Perspective," which
recommended reversing suburbanization by *revitalizing inner cities*, creating modern dense communities that are less dependent on transportation. The European Union invested huge amounts of money
into rebuilding inner cities, with required local matching money. One
of the worst slum areas, the Józsefváros district of the Pest side of
Budapest, became modernized, as well as parts of the east Hungarian
town, Nyíregyháza. A modern waterfront residential area enriched
Bratislava. Indeed, inner city reconstruction gained impetus in several countries, including the Eastern transforming countries, but in
most cases as business centers. Old apartment houses were remodeled
as office buildings. Banks, office buildings, inner city shopping malls,
and shopping areas occupied most of the city centers. Warsaw's skyline
was radically transformed during the 1990s and early 2000s by several
new and dominant high-rises. The Blue Tower (29 floors), the FIM
Tower (26 floors), the Millennium Plaza (28 floors), the Eurocen-
trum (22 floors), the Warsaw Financial Center (32 floors), the Warsaw
Trade Tower (43 floors), the Intercontinental Hotel (43 floors), and

[62] Arjen Leerkes, Godfried Engbersen, and Marion Van San, "Shadow Places: Patterns of
Spatial Concentration and Incorporation of Irregular Immigrants in the Netherlands,"
Urban Studies, 44, 8 (2007), 1491–516.
[63] Bettin Lattes and Recchi (eds.), *European Societies*, 299.

the 60,000 square meter Promenada Shopping Center may all be mentioned. In the first decade of transformation, 1,196,200 square meters of modern office space and 400,000 square meters of retail space were added. In central Budapest, the architectural environment was changed with vast shopping malls, such as the WestEnd City Center (named in English), the Asia Center, and the Mammut Centers I and II, among others, and new luxury hotels and dozens of modern office buildings.

Comparing the transformation of Prague, Budapest, and Warsaw, one analyst describes a process of de-industrialization and "transformation towards the postindustrial model," from the late 1980s on.[64] Their downtowns became centers for banking, multinational companies, and various service branches. Prague's historic downtown area lost nearly one-quarter of its population between 1991 and 2004 because the "originally strong residential function has been turning into . . . predominantly administrative and business functions."[65] During those years, 70 percent of the new and modernized office spaces were jammed into the city center. During the 1990s, about three-quarters of all floor-space in the historical core of Prague had been put to non-residential use, driving out residential functions.[66] In its controversial way, urban transformation became an important and visible factor of turn-of-the-century European modernization and everyday life.

Transforming Families

Continued significant *changes to the basic unit of society, the family*, during the last decades of the century, also strongly influenced everyday life. Rossella Palomba speaks of "a break with the past and an extreme fragility of current family lifestyles . . . [the] disappearance of standard family forms, and the fragility of new forms of family life, and the relationship within the family." Marriage rates drastically decreased, people were getting married several years later

---

[64] Luděk Sýkora, "Commercial Property Development in Budapest, Prague and Warsaw," in G. Enyedi (ed.), *Social Change*, 109–36, 111.

[65] Boris Burcin and Tomáš Kučera, "Socio-Demographic Consequences of the Renewal of Prague's Historical Center," in György Enyedi and Zoltán Kovács (eds.), *Social Changes and Social Sustainability in Historical Urban Centers. The Case of Central Europe* (Pécs: Center for Regional Studies, 2006), 174–88, 178–9.

[66] Sýkora, "Commercial Property," 124.

in life, or not at all. In Germany, every third marriage ends in divorce, but every second marriage fails in the big cities. "The long-term family project," Palomba added, "transformed and became short-term amusement connection."[67] Cohabitation became a widespread phenomenon. In Denmark and Sweden, seven in ten women in their early twenties cohabitate.[68] One-third of women do not have children at all. Significant numbers of children are born into unmarried families. The *Badische Zeitung* reported in December 1999 that in Freiburg, only 12 percent of children belong to married families, the others to non-married or single parent families.[69] All these, Palomba and Moors conclude, represent the "end of the family," at least in the form it had existed before.[70] Family is becoming more and more a loose "partnership of individuals. Members of the family have gained greater independence and the right to live their own lives."[71]

Similar change characterized the presence of elderly parents in the family. The three-generation family had already disappeared from Europe – except some Balkan countries and Russia – by the end of the nineteenth century, and the entire phenomenon vanished by the mid-twentieth century, though some remnants survived. Until the mid decades of the century, widowed parents often lived together with their married children, and many unmarried children lived with their aging parents. This custom radically changed after the 1970s and 1980s: in the 1960s, 42 percent of elderly people in Britain lived together with their children. By the 1980s, this had dropped to 14 percent, but it dropped to 11 percent in the Netherlands. In some more traditional societies, the percentage of elderly parents in families is still higher. In Ireland and Italy in the late 1980s, the number was 43 percent and 35 percent, respectively.[72] Michael Mitterauer concludes: "With an

---

[67] Rossella Palomba, "Value Preferences and Attitudes on Population," in Rossella Palomba and Hein Moors (eds.), *Population, Family, and Welfare: A Comparative Survey of European Attitudes*, Vol. 2 (Oxford: Clarendon Press, 1998), 51–71.

[68] Joe Bailey (ed.), *Social Europe*, Second edition (London: Longman, 1998), 58.

[69] Wolfgang Reinhard, *Lebensformen Europas: Eine historische Kulturanthropologie* (Munich: C. H. Beck, 2004), 225.

[70] Rossella Palomba and Hein Moors, "The Image of the family," in Palomba and Moors (eds.), *Population, Family, and Welfare*, 72–93, 73.

[71] Michael Mitterauer and Reinhard Sieder, *The European Family. Patriarchy to Partnership from the Middle Ages to the Present* (Oxford: Blackwell, 1982), 88.

[72] Colin Crouch, *Social Change in Western Europe* (New York: Oxford University Press, 1999), 226. It pays to note that rising unemployment among young people reversed this trend in France: in 1975, 28% of 24-year-old males lived together with their parents, but by 1990, 37%. *Ibid.*, 228.

eye solely on statistics, the development of the European family could be cynically portrayed as converging to a single-person household. Indeed, in many European metropolises this type already accounts for more than 50 percent of the total number of households."[73]

A further major factor changing everyday life was a consequence of considerably increased leisure time. Daily and annual hours worked per employed person greatly shortened in turn-of-the-century Europe. It was the consequence of a gradually curbed working day, longer paid vacations, and increased paid sick days. Two-day weekends, a vacation of 25 to 30 days a year and an average of 15 to 25 days at home on sick pay in cases of illness became virtually universal in Europe. During the 1980s and 1990s, the total hours worked in fourteen West European countries declined by 6 percent, and the hours worked per person decreased by 12 percent.[74]

The Impact of the Communication Revolution; Americanized Mass Culture and Consumption as Entertainment

Among the historical changes that influenced everyday culture, the *communication revolution* deserves special attention. Communication and information technology exploded in the three decades around the turn of the century. Few factors influenced people's lifestyle more than this. Since 1980, the most remarkable new development came in the form of telecommunications infrastructure. Radio, TV, and telephone became everyday household items after World War II. Between 1950 and the mid-1970s, radio and TV licenses increased in Europe from 52 to 117 million, and from 348,000 to 30 million, respectively. Surprisingly, however, the number of radio sets in households during the 1980s and 1990s more than quadrupled, and households with TV sets nearly quadrupled.

More importantly, the most modern communication technology gradually conquered Europe. In 2003, 31 million households had digital TV. By 2007, the number stood at 89 million, i.e, half of the

---

[73] Michael Mitterauer, "A 'European Family' in the Nineteenth and Twentieth Centuries?" in Hartmut Kaelble (ed.), *The European Way: European Societies during the Nineteenth and Twentieth Centuries* (New York: Berghahn Books, 2004), 140–60, 151.

[74] Angus Maddison, *Monitoring the World Economy 1820–1992* (Paris: OECD, 1995), 347.

households and the same percentage of penetration as in the United States – striking progress in such a short period of time. Broadcasting became deregulated after the late 1970s, and hundreds of private radio and TV stations appeared in Europe. The Netherlands and Italy were among the pioneers; France followed only later. Smaller European countries used cable first, but by 1990, one-quarter of German households were connected by cable. In the late 1990s, the digitalization of cable systems suddenly made available hundreds of channels. New genres – games, reality TV, talk shows – enriched TV culture. Around the turn of the century, however, a great deal of the broadcasting was of low quality. In the early period of TV broadcasting, a deliberate goal was the popularization of "high culture" through adaptations of plays and novels. Educational programs occupied a distinctive part of broadcasting time and advertising either did not exist, or was strictly limited by regulations and shown only between programs but not during them, as was the case subsequently in Scandinavia. When multiple and private channels became dominant, advertising became crucially important. In 1970, only 12 percent of total advertising expenditure was spent on TV ads in Europe, but by 1990, more than 50 percent. It generated a race to the bottom to broadcast programs that attracted the greatest number of people.

Another factor in the decline of quality was the far-reaching Hollywoodization of TV programs and film theaters. Traditional postwar European *art movies*, mostly Italian and French, lost ground and mostly collapsed because of competition from the American *film industry*. Distribution and film theaters were also taken over by American companies, and Hollywood action movies produced with the latest technology now attract many more Europeans than domestic films.

In 2000, Hollywood sometimes produced films for more than $500 million, while a French or Italian film was produced for $5 million and $2 million, respectively. Cutting-edge technical effects, expensive animation, and acting by world-famous stars, not to mention extreme, well-presented brutality, made American movies extremely attractive, especially for the younger generations. The best illustration of what some critics call "cultural colonization" via Hollywood films is that, in 1960, only 35 percent of box office revenues came from American films, but at the turn of the century, it jumped to 80 to 90 percent in continental Europe. In 2000, although the countries of the European

Union produced significantly more feature films than the United States – 595 compared to 460 – only 15 percent of the films distributed in Europe were domestic, 8 percent were films from other European countries, and 73 percent of them were American.

European TV broadcasting has the same characteristic. In 1982, the American *Columbo* series was the most popular TV show in Italy, and it attracted twice as many viewers as the best Italian series. The same was true in communist Hungary. American series and feature films flooded European TVs: in 1994, American film broadcasting occupied more than 28,000 hours on German TVs, while French, British, and Italian occupied less than 4,000 hours, combined. In France, nearly 14,000 hours of American films were broadcast, more than four times the broadcasting of German, British, and Italian films.

Since most European countries questioned and condemned the Americanization of film and TV, their national film and TV industries, as well as the European Union itself, made efforts to create a more balanced program. In the five years between 1996 and 2001, combined domestic fiction broadcasting in Germany, Britain, France, Spain, and Italy increased from 4,120 to 5,883 hours. In 2007, the European Commission launched the "Media International" initiative against the domination of Hollywood. The Commission is providing €755 million over seven years to support European movies, with 55 percent of that money going to distribution.

With regard to technological developments that transformed culture, the number of telephone lines deserves special interest in the *age of computerization*. The number of fixed lines had already increased by five times between 1950 and 1979, but until the 1980s Europe still remained far behind the United States: in 1979, every hundred European families used thirty telephone lines; by 2005, the number had increased to fifty-three lines, while in the United States it was sixty lines. The Central and Eastern European countries remained far behind, with ten to fifteen lines per hundred families until the collapse of communism.

Around the turn of the century, the mobile phone revolution radically changed the situation. The number of fixed lines barely increased in the European Union-12. Indeed, the number decreased in several countries. On the other hand, on average, every person (99/100) had a mobile phone by 2005, and in several Western countries, each 100 people had 130 to 150 mobile phones. In recent years, mobile phones have come to serve as photo cameras and small computers as well.

At the beginning of the 1980s, telephone lines, and later direct cables and wireless connections, helped the spread of computers, the key instrument of modern communication: in 2001, 50 percent of households had access to computers in Western Europe; by 2005, the number was already 65 percent. By that later date, practically every second person used a computer, and 55 percent of households, i.e., every fourth person, had Internet connections.[75] Less than one-sixth of the world population used the Internet in 2005, but more than 37 percent of Europe's population did, representing 29 percent of Internet users worldwide. In 2007, 54 percent of the population of the European Union-27 had Internet connections.[76] As happened with TV, saturation will certainly be complete within two decades.

Computers and the Internet themselves generated major cultural changes. They created a new public space and made interactivity possible. Huge numbers of private, individual websites, and blogs offering open entries and commentaries, generated a widespread discourse on news, politics, and cultural issues. The Internet opened forums for expressing and exchanging views to an international public. According to some calculations, 112 million blogs were already created in 2007. The new generation of mobile phones made it possible to write, comment, and send photos via mobile phone. Electronic communication forums, unlike any previous ones, are not hierarchically organized and are not limited to national territories. Computer communication eliminates the difference between interpersonal and mass communication, and between public and private. Besides texts, audio and video communication also became possible. As Donald Sassoon writes: "The World Wide Web has enhanced the common elements of international culture, but because the producers have multiplied and will go on multiplying, what is produced is likely to have even less coherence than the culture of the past."[77]

---

[75] Based on OECD, *Factbook: Economic, Environmental and Social Statistics* (Paris: OECD, 2007); The Economist, *World in Figures, 2008* (London: Profile Books, 2008).

[76] In the Netherlands, this percentage reached 83%, in Sweden and Denmark 79 and 78% respectively, while in Greece, Romania, and Bulgaria only 25, 22, and 19% respectively. In the entire Union-27, 93% of companies with more than ten employees had Internet access. In the least advanced Bulgaria and Romania, this share was 67%.

[77] Donald Sassoon, *The Culture of the Europeans from 1800 to the Present* (London: HarperCollins, 2006), 1378–9. I am drawing on this book in the following pages on cultural changes.

Computers are replacing traditional mail and telephone by widespread e-mailing and video telephoning. Shopping habits have also been changed by the rapid spread of electronic shopping. In Denmark, Ireland, Britain, and Finland, 15 to 20 percent of companies' income from sales originates from electronic trade, while in Italy, Romania, and Bulgaria only 1 to 2 percent, and the Union-wide average is 11 percent.[78]

The Internet is rapidly replacing printed journals and enriching entertainment. Electronic games radically transformed the entertainment of the younger generation. Teenagers spend several hours a day in front of the screen playing newer and newer games and living in totally artificial environments. Although this is considered controversial, the younger generation's technological knowledge and ability to integrate the new technology of the electronic revolution into their lives, and its ability to keep up with its rapid development, became major factors in the development of a new kind of literacy of the computer age.

With very few exceptions, Western Europe reaches the level equivalent to the highest average international standard represented by Japan and the United States.[79] The Information and Communication Technology Index[80] clearly reflects Europe's progress: Iceland, Sweden, Denmark, and the Netherlands had already surpassed the United States by 2005, while Luxembourg, Finland, Switzerland, and Norway are relatively near the American level, followed by Britain, Germany, and France. Except for the latter two European countries, all the others surpassed Japan.[81]

Lifestyles also transformed in the richer urbanized and technologized environment. Consumerism had already conquered Western Europe during the decades of postwar prosperity. America, the ally and protector of Western Europe, and the world's first consumer society, emerged as an ideal and model. As Victoria de Grazia documents in her major work, *Irresistible Empire: America's Advance Through*

---

[78] András Kezán, "E-kereskedelem az Európai Unióban," *Európai Tükör*, 13, 4 (April 12–14, 2008), 161. In 2007, 50% of the population of Germany, Holland, Sweden, and Britain did some electronic shopping, but the Union's average is 30%, because in Bulgaria and Romania that share is only 3%.

[79] OECD, *Factbook 2007*, 157.

[80] This is an aggregate index of the usage of information and communication technology, per capita, relating to fixed lines and mobile phones, personal computers and Internet use.

[81] The Economist, *World in Figures, 2008*, 62–3.

Twentieth-Century Europe, the American consumer culture, though it also catalyzed discontents, pushed aside obstacles, and resulted in a New Europe by the 1970s.[82] The rock 'n' roll and sexual liberation of the "Americanism from below" of the 1960s was crowned by the 1970s and 1980s with consumption mania as a realm of freedom.

This trend did not stop at the River Elbe but gradually penetrated the Eastern half of the continent. It started before the collapse of communism, but during the transition of the 1990s, "the consumer society had to be recognized as 'our only future' [in the East]." As a symbol and vehicle of the Americanization of consumer culture, McDonald's opened its first restaurant at the corner of Pushkin Place in Moscow three months after the collapse of the Berlin Wall. Where market reform had begun earlier, as in Budapest, McDonald's had already opened in the 1980s. Fast-food chains soon covered the former communist world. Shopping malls and supermarket culture conquered the entire European continent. By the 1990s, 80 percent of Europe's population did their everyday shopping in supermarkets and malls.[83] Consumption became "*Lebensform der Moderne*," a modern form of life in Germany, when shopping became free time entertainment, so called "recreation shopping."[84] High- and even medium-income level European countries spend most of their income on durables, entertainment, and on maintaining the health that makes possible "entertainment shopping." According to the so-called Engel Law, the higher the income, the lower the spending on basics. The population of low-income countries spends 55 to 60 percent on food and drink, while some African countries spend around 70 percent of their income on staples.

Before World War I, even an average citizen of Switzerland spent 60 percent of his income on food. During the 1980s, however, the traditionally rich West European countries spent only 15 percent of their income on food and drink, while the new member countries of the European Community, such as the Mediterranean countries and Ireland, spent 25 percent. The same was true for more well-to-do communist countries such as Slovenia and Hungary. On the other hand, Lithuania, Romania, and Bulgaria spent between 50 and 60 percent. As lifestyles became richer, the percentage of spending on

---

[82] Victoria de Grazia, *Irresistible Empire: America's Advance Through Twentieth-Century Europe* (Cambridge, MA: The Belknap Press, 2005).
[83] *Ibid.*, 11, 466, 471, 476.   [84] Reinhard, *Lebensformen*, 468–9.

food and drink decreased further. By 2008, the population of Western European spent 12 to 16 percent, the Central European countries about 25 percent, Russia and most of the Balkan countries roughly 34 to 40 percent, and Ukraine and Belarus 50 to 53 percent.

Consequently, except for the low-income countries of the continent, more people have moved to larger and more comfortable houses, fitted out with the most modern equipment. Eating out was no longer the privilege of a small upper layer of society, but became more frequent in general. Foreign cuisine and a huge variety of ethnic food became available in cities, together with consumer goods from other European countries. Consumption of these kinds of products lost its extraordinary, luxurious, and individualistic character. People were spending to go to resort locations and, frequently, even going abroad to entertain themselves during their increased leisure time. Expenditure for recreation and culture reached between 6 and 8 percent of GDP in virtually all European countries.[85]

Traveling and, in the case of the younger generation, even staying abroad for an extended period became common around the turn of the century. This was in sharp contrast with the immediate postwar years when 75 percent of Germans had no personal experience of foreign countries and most of those who did had it from wartime experience. In 1990, 75 percent of the younger generation in European Union countries had visited another country. "One-third of these young people had not only traveled to other European countries but also had more intensive experiences there during stays of three months or more . . . Traveling and living abroad became common . . . became a component of the European standard of living and lifestyle."[86] In 1995, 60 percent of arrivals in hotels and at borders – one way that statisticians measure world tourism – were by Europeans, the highest share of the world. Between 1998 and 2005, West European tourism increased annually by 1 percent on average; tourism from Germany, Spain, and the post-communist countries increased yearly by 4 to 5 percent. According to the forecast of the World Tourism Organization, even taking into account rapidly increasing Indian and Chinese tourism, Europe's share will remain near half of world tourism in 2020.[87]

[85] Sassoon, *Culture of the Europeans*, 1220, 1147–1208.
[86] Hartmut Kaelble, "Social Peculiarities of Nineteenth and Twentieth Century Europe," in Kaelble (ed.), *The European Way*, 276–317, 300–2.
[87] *Tourism 2020 Vision* (Madrid: World Tourism Organization, 2001).

Democratization of Culture or the Death of "High Culture"?

In many intellectual circles of Europe, electronic culture generated daily debates, criticism, and gloomy forecasts about the death of traditional culture. In his monumental cultural history of modern Europe, Donald Sassoon lists similar forecasts from ancient times on. "Socrates warned that the introduction of the written text will create forgetfulness... because [people] will not use their memories... In 1859, Baudelaire blamed photography for the impoverishment of the *'génie artistique français'* ... Paul Valéry ... wondered whether 'very soon oral and sound culture will not replace the written text'. Walter Benjamin... suggested that 'in the era of mechanical reproduction' the days of the museum objects... were numbered."[88]

Triumphant Mass Culture

Together with electronic culture, the popularization and simplification of high culture, or the triumph of popular culture, is often considered to sound the death-knell of traditional European culture. While mandatory communist "socialist realism" required the arts to be easily intelligible and understandable for everybody, Western Europe, in a paradoxical way, experienced a somewhat similar trend in the arts under the banners of "democratization" and "accessible arts," "culture for everybody" and "civil right to culture." It was not the consequence of central state intervention, but mostly of an increased market orientation. For example, the German audiovisual industry changed from "high culture" to popular entertainment systems during the 1990s.

Besides highly commercialized TV broadcasting, music culture also became big business. Pop superstars and pop music created a huge industry: in 1990s Britain, the music industry employed 115,000 people and became larger than the shipbuilding industry, one of the most traditional industries in the country. The musicians' union has more members than the miners' union. In the Merseyside region, Beatles country, 1,000 bands compete for the attention of 1.5 million

---

[88] Sassoon, *Culture of the Europeans*, 1372–3.

people. In London, 377 separate bands perform live popular music. In Sweden, 100,000 musicians play in bands.[89]

Critics also consider some new art trends as anti-art. The new *conceptual art* wants to present an "idea" instead of aesthetic values, and rejects craftsmanship by exhibiting objects, as represented by the Young British Artists after 1988 and the Saatchi Gallery in the 1990s. Damien Hirst's shark in formaldehyde, titled "The Physical Impossibility of Death in the Mind of Someone Living," became a model piece of this art trend in 1991. Martin Creed's highly lamented Turner Prize winner, "The Lights Going On and Off," was an art piece exactly as its title described: in an empty room, lights went on and off. Tracey Emin's "My Bed," with its stained sheets, worn panties, and empty bottles lying around, and the embroidered names of all her sexual partners, "everyone I have ever slept with" between 1963 and 1995, was praised by some for sharing her most personal space with all of its "embarrassing glory," but denounced by others as scandalous.

Installation art presented any kind of materials, sound, video, and performance, often in an interactive way with the participation of the audience. *Performance art* destroyed any borderline between arts and life. The Belgrade-born, Amsterdam-based Marina Abramovic's "Seedbed" performance in a gallery, with her lying naked under glass while masturbating and talking with the audience by microphone, belonged to *body art*, exploring the artist's own body in public.

Épater le bourgeois? The revolutionary avant-garde already did this on a high artistic level a hundred years ago. Rejecting taboos? Narcissistic reality-TV series, with shouting, crying, fighting couples, discussing their sexual and other most intimate problems in public, exhibit this every day. There will always be experts who explain the philosophical message and an interested public who likes it. In the end, it is a question of personal taste.

Cultural Adjustment of the East

Central and Eastern Europe, still under communist rule in the 1980s, preserved some basic elements of Stalinist anti-modernism. Since technological change was also mostly missing, new cultural trends only partially penetrated the region. Strict command and socialist realism

---

[89] *Ibid.*, 1343, 1354.

was no longer compulsory in Yugoslavia, Poland, and Hungary, and abstraction and other elements of modernism appeared. The dominant culture, however, was traditional. "The citizens of eastern and central Europe, when communism prevailed, did not have as many consumer goods as those in the West, but they had plenty of culture."[90] As the 1988 UNESCO report reflected, annual attendance at performing arts was as high as 600 to 660 per 1,000 people in Hungary, Romania, and Poland – three times more than in Italy or the Netherlands. Theaters, the media (including TV), and publications followed a paternalistic educational mission. Moreover, a profit motive did not exist, since cultural products were highly subsidized and accessible. People had read the reprinted classics of world literature, and seen numerous theater performances of the classics. In the Soviet Union, 300 publishing houses supplied the population and reading was common. After the regime change, especially in Russia, this traditional culture nearly collapsed. Instead of the 1.8 billion books they published in 1988, they published only 422 million in 1996. Subsidies disappeared, and prices of cultural products reflected market prices: in Hungary between the mid-1980s and 2001, book prices increased by two-and-half times in real terms. Pornography flooded the market, and the media closely followed Western trends. Modern arts and electronic culture, however, rapidly penetrated the region. Cultural change was quite dramatic and contributed to a cultural shock that characterized the entire transformation period of Central and Eastern Europe.

"End of Culture," or Democratization of Culture?

The "end of culture," destroyed by modernism, has been announced many times in history. It happened with the first impressionist exhibition in France, and Arnold Schönberg's piano performance in Vienna in 1908. Many saw the end of painting when the Russian Kazimir Malevich exhibited his simplified Suprematist *White Square on White Background* in 1918. Dada deliberately mocked and dethroned art during World War I with meaningless texts and performances. German expressionism in the early twentieth century generated scandals.

---

[90] *Ibid.*, 1250.

There has never been enough reason to announce the death of culture. The popularization of culture, contradictory as that notion is, spread culture on a previously unknown scale. High culture was always elite culture, the monopoly of a small layer of the traditional class societies in Europe. The building of Euro Disney near Paris, and the remaking of classic French movies by the Hollywood film industry, naturally irritated France's intellectual circles, while "The influx of U.S. cultural products in Sweden has been seen as a threat to Swedish culture . . . [bringing] commercialism, shallowness, and sentimentality."[91] The spread of popular culture that conquered the lower layers of the European societies, however, ignited an "Americanization from below . . . the reconfiguration of social boundaries . . . popular culture was used by the underprivileged to legitimate their values . . ."[92]

The democratization of culture, according to certain interpretations, contributed to the democratization of society because it contributed to the elimination of class differences. Furthermore, popular culture is the engine to "cosmopolitanize the nation-state from within." It has built up a transnational youth culture and consecutive younger generations transnationalize the European nation-states.[93] Popular culture may also serve as the antechamber to higher culture.

Turn-of-the-century European culture is extremely complex, offering endless variations on new and old art trends, new and old types of cultural entertainment, education, and popular and high culture alike. It is a personal choice and decision what to select. A significantly enlarged middle class and essentially increased educational level amplified the audience for every kind of arts, including traditional high culture. Donald Sassoon reports the flourishing theater life in London. The figures are impressive: in one month, January 2003, theaters opened thirty-eight new productions. A new theater, opened in a disused factory building, performed twenty-five new productions in only a few weeks in the spring of 2003. The London National Theatre complex of three theaters held 1,000 performances in 2003–4, selling

---

[91] Dag Blanck, "Television, Education, and the Vietnam War: Sweden and the United States During the Postwar Era," in Alexander Stephan (ed.), *The Americanization of Europe: Culture, Diplomacy, and Anti-Americanism after 1945* (New York: Berghahn Books, 2006), 91–114, 98.

[92] Konstantina E. Botsiou, "The Interface Between Politics and Culture in Greece," in Stephan (ed.), *The Americanization of Europe*, 277–306, 297.

[93] Rob Kroes, "Imaginary Americas in Europe's Public Space," in Stephan (ed.), *The Americanization of Europe*, 337–60, 355.

731,000 seats, filling some of them with 100,000 first-time visitors. "[T]he theatre, as did the cinema, survived the onslaught of television, renewing itself, specializing, offering the audience something they could not get from the screen in the box at home."[94]

In Germany in 1996–7, 809 theaters with more than a quarter of a million seats gained state subsidies to remain able to perform and be accessible. Ticket sales cover about one-fifth of the theaters' budgets. In 1994–5, 305,000 pop concerts were performed in the European Union-15, as well as 85,000 classical music concerts. In the same year, classical records represented 9–14 percent of total record sales in eight European countries, roughly three times higher than in the United States. The number of exhibition visits in the three biggest London museums in 2004 neared 15 million. New museums were opened, including Tate Modern in London in 2000 in the remodeled building of a former power station. The Louvre was expanded to almost twice its former size, and Musée d'Orsay was opened in a former railway station in 1986. Mass tourism gave a new impetus for exhibitions and museum visits. In four months in 1997, 770,000 people visited the Technical and Industrial Museum in Mannheim, Germany. In the late 1980s, hardly more than a decade after the death of the dictator, Franco, Spain became the fourth largest publisher of books, exporting nearly half of its production to Europe.

While modern trends in fine art are often controversial, turn-of-the-century "deconstructionist" architecture – not connected to the philosophical trend – is broadly admired. Bold modern buildings in traditional downtown areas changed urban skylines. In traditional, sometimes centuries-old inner cities, landmark pieces of new architecture signaled a new age. One of the most symbolic signs of the new architectural age is the 1988 glass pyramid in the central courtyard of the Musée du Louvre, one of the classic buildings of Paris, originating from the twelfth to thirteenth centuries. The landmark Reichstag building in Berlin which is more than a century old and the new home of the German Bundestag or parliament, was crowned by a huge glass dome in 1995. In the center of London, a monumental, egg-shaped iron and glass City Hall changed the architectural environment in 2002 (Figure 16).

From the late 1980s, pioneering architects introduced a radical freedom of imagination (Figure 17). Their buildings present unpredictable

---

[94] Sassoon, *Culture of the Europeans*, 1247.

Figure 16. Twenty-first-century urban architecture: London.

forms, a kind of well-organized chaos. The first pioneer of this new architecture, the Swiss-born Bernard Tschumi's entry for the Parc de la Villette in Paris in 1982, introduced a new non-geometrical style without direct visual logic. The best-known and celebrated architects who deconstructed traditional architecture and denied geometry are Daniel Libeskind and Frank Gehry. Libeskind's Jewish Museum in Berlin is an architectural *trouvaille*: its crushed Star of David shape and its labyrinth – where the visitor is hopelessly lost – symbolize the Holocaust. His Imperial War Museum building near Manchester, as well as Gehry's Guggenheim Museum in Bilbao, Vitra Design Museum in Weil-am-Rhein in Germany, and "dancing houses" in Prague, are trademark buildings of this new architectural trend. Strikingly new buildings in several European cities signal the opening of a new age of architecture. This trend, as with many other forms of modern art, would be unimaginable without the most modern technology. The planning and design of these kinds of buildings would be impossible without computer modeling.

One of the most often heard arguments about the negative consequences of modern popular culture is the decline of reading. It is unquestionable that in several European countries, a huge part of the

Figure 17. Twenty-first-century urban architecture: Berlin, Potsdamer Platz.

population does not read. The share of the population in Italy and France that did not read in the 1980s was 40 and 53 percent, respectively, and these figures represent a quite general European trend. However, reading is more "normal" nowadays than in the "good old days." It is amazing how many books are regularly published and sold in some countries. In 1991–4, Italy and Bulgaria published more than 500 books per year per 100 inhabitants: five times more books than people. Portugal, Spain, Poland, and Romania published between 220 and 270 books per 100 inhabitants. Just counting book titles (not copies), Finland and the Netherlands published 220–250 new titles per 100,000 inhabitants in 1991–4; Norway, Sweden, Belgium, and Britain published about 140–150. Public libraries are flourishing throughout Europe.[95] Traditional high culture and a great variety of cultural entertainment are equally present in Europe, offering a choice of alternative possibilities.

---

[95] In Ukraine, Finland, and Bulgaria there were roughly 700 books per 1,000 inhabitants in public libraries in 1991–4; in Sweden, Hungary, and Norway about 500.

4

The Economic Response to Globalization; Recovery and Growth; the Integration of Eastern and Western Europe

The New International Economic Environment: Technological Revolution

During the last decades of the twentieth century, a new chapter opened in world economic history: the robust *new technological revolution*, led by information and communication technologies. This was combined with a near-total internationalization of the world economy, or *globalization*. Internationalization had a long history in Europe, going back to the late nineteenth century and more directly to its reemergence after World War II after the backlash in the interwar decades. However, the transition from the 1970s to the 1980s became the real watershed for its breakthrough. Globalization emerged as a new policy that replaced colonialism for the leading economic powers, but it also had an objective economic base in the new technological and corporative-managerial revolution.

The communication and technological revolution that conquered the advanced world after 1980 like the British industrial revolution had 200 years before, has a history that is several decades long. Its beginning goes back to World War II, when the first mainframe computer, the British "Colossus," started decoding German military communications at the beginning of 1944. The other most visible invention of the time, which had monstrous worldwide reverberations, was the atomic bomb, or, better put, the path-breaking use of nuclear energy.

The revolution in electronics had advanced by leaps and bounds after World War II. The watershed was the invention of the transistor in the Bell Laboratory. The real importance of the transistor, however, became clear when Jack Kilby produced the first silicon integrated circuit in 1958. "Mass production of chips with thousands of transistor circuits reduced the price drastically . . . Since the mid-1960's the chip has become increasingly an internal part of the 20th century civilization . . . The chip made possible reliable computers, personal computers, lap computers, and calculators. It also made possible digital watches, increased efficiency in automobiles, control robots, and . . . communications. The chip has made possible cellular telephones, satellite communications . . . electronic mail . . . home banking and many other new technologies."[1]

The transistor and the chip created the real foundation of the computer revolution. The first stored-program computer, EDVAC, was commissioned in late 1944. IBM's Defense Department produced the Defense Calculator in 1953 and a commercial version in 1954. In 1971, Intel worked out the first microcomputer. The first real personal computer appeared in San Francisco in 1974.[2] In 1969, interconnected computers created the first networks for military use, followed by the first civilian networks: the DARPA Internet and BITNET.

Although it was the outcome of a continuous process, the technological revolution began a new chapter after 1980, especially because of its decisive impact on everyday life. Around the turn of the century, Europe entered the age of a new civilization. In 1986, the US National Science Foundation created a network, founded by the Irishman Dennis Jennings, followed by commercial networks. In 1991, the World Wide Web, a revolutionary system that introduced a new age of communication, was invented in the European particle physics laboratory (CERN) in Geneva (Figure 18). The electronics revolution gained greater and greater momentum in the last third of the century. The most important impetus was the new age of telephony: glass fiber optics using digital transmission modernized the international telephone network, and soon the analog cellular phone service emerged and quickly led to its second generation and the digital cellular revolution of the 1980s. The endless waves of the technological revolution produced the Compact Audio Disc (CD) in 1982, and the Digital Compact Cassette (DCC) and Digital Video Disc (DVD) in the 1990s. From the 1980s, the new technological age flourished.

---

[1] Edward N. Singer, *20th Century Revolution in Technology* (Commack, NY: Nova Science Publisher, 1998), 76, 77.
[2] *Ibid.*, 93–106.

Figure 18. Tim Berners-Lee, inventor of the World Wide Web, a key element of the "communication revolution."

The Globalized World Economy and the EU's Response to the Challenge

This was the time when advanced countries, exploiting the achievements of the communication revolution, established subsidiaries all over the world and supported a policy eliminating trade barriers, strengthening competitiveness by outsourcing workplaces, and establishing a new division of labor. Multinational companies became dominant in the world economy by monopolizing most of the industrialized innovations, as well as 75 percent of the world trade in manufactured goods. The dramatic expansion of their activities has resulted in the foundation of hundreds of thousands of subsidiaries throughout the globe: by 2005, 866,000 affiliates were in operation abroad, one-quarter of them in developing countries.

Consequently, the stock of Foreign Direct Investments (FDI) abroad increased to $2.5 trillion by 2004. Although developing countries received 42 percent of such investments that year, in a surprising new development, advanced countries also began investing into each other. In 2004, the outward and inward direct investments stocks of the OECD countries, i.e., the advanced world, were $8.4 and $6.7 trillion, respectively, meaning that the developed world invested only 20 percent more capital abroad than it invested within the OECD countries.[3] Globalization allowed rich, highly developed countries to outsource labor-intensive and polluting sectors, as well as production of old products with a declining life cycle, to less developed countries. They also invested to conquer new markets, and cut the cost of production by producing their products in low-wage countries that have a well-educated labor force. Outsourcing production allowed the advanced countries to concentrate on service and high-tech industries, as well as on research and development. Adjustment to globalization was the way out of the economic crisis of the 1970s and early 1980s and the opening of a new paradigm of economic development for the West.

Steeply increased world trade within the framework of postwar and new international agreements characterized the globalized world economy. The Tokyo Round in 1979, and then the Uruguay Round in 1986, which led to the foundation of the World Trade Organization (WTO), had a great impact. During the two decades between 1984 and 2004, the number of bilateral and regional trade agreements increased six-fold. International trade increased three-and-a-half times from $1.7 trillion in 1973 to $5.8 trillion at the end of the century. In 1970, nearly 9 percent of the world's gross products were exported, but, by 2001, already more than 16 percent.

Cross-border transactions of bonds and equities, which reached only 10 percent of the aggregate GDP of the most advanced G-7 countries in 1980, rose to 140 percent of their GDP by the end of the century. Daily financial transactions amounted to $15 billion in 1973 but increased to $1.3 trillion by 1995. This amount was fifty times higher than the value of world trade. The world economy entered a new era.[4]

Europe was challenged by the technology superpowers, the United States and newly emerged Japan, which were both far ahead in the technology race. To cope with this challenge became the historical task for Europe after 1980. This was the main reason that, when the Cold War ended and the potential Soviet threat evaporated, taking with them the main impetus for Western integration, European integration did not reach a dead-end. On the contrary, it gained a new and even

---

[3] In 2005, only by 13%. In 2003–5, 30 countries received 99% of total FDI, mainly the industrialized ones, and China got nearly $60 billion, roughly one-quarter of the foreign direct investments in developing countries.

[4] Angus Maddison, *World Economy: A Millennial Perspective* (Paris: OECD, 2001), 127, 362; OECD, *Structural Adjustment and Economic Performance* (Paris: OECD, 1987), 273.

stronger rationale and impetus. From 1980 on, globalization became the new and strongest stimulus to further West European integration.

Giuliano Garavini notes another aspect of the forces accelerating European integration: the impact of the post-colonial Third World on Europe. He stresses that the European revolutionary movements of the 1960s–1970s, which were influenced by the Vietnam War, as well as the new attempts at modernization in the post-colonial Third World, were characterized by a rejection of past nationalism that became an ideological component of the students' movements. Nevertheless, a few activists of the seventies joined the extreme nationalist Right in the 1990s.

This had its impact on the European Community in that its "momentous 1969 . . . summit in The Hague was deeply influenced by the 1968 revolution . . . [which consequently] strengthened efforts to build a political and cultural Europe to react to the scant legitimacy of nation-states . . . The Third World had a profound impact on Western Europe in the period ranging from the advent of the global youth movements of 1968 to the end of détente in 1975."[5]

The end of the Cold War division of Europe created a more favorable political environment for further globalization, opening up large new markets and resources in the significantly enlarged laissez-faire system. "This is probably the time in which European integration tried most openly to perform as the engine of world economic co-operation . . . [As Jürgen Habermas stated] the European Community aimed at becoming the developing world's most understanding partner."[6]

Inspired by the transformation of the world system, the European Community, thirty years after the Treaty of Rome, introduced its first major revision with the Single European Act implemented in the summer of 1987. Instead of a united Western Europe as a defense against war, the Act declared that the Community protects the common interests of its member countries by creating a common market with the free movement of goods, people, services, and capital. The realization of these ambitious goals was assisted by 282 detailed measures. "As regards research and technical development," Article 130F of the agreement established the objective "to strengthen the

[5] Giuliano Garavini, "The Colonies Strike Back: The Impact of the Third World on Western Europe, 1968–1975," *Contemporary European History* (August 2007), 303–4.
[6] *Ibid.*, 305–8.

scientific and technological basis of European industry and to encourage it to become more competitive at international level." Jacques Delors summed up as follows: "History is accelerating and we should make it with her."[7]

The integration process shifted into high gear: following final negotiations in December 1991, the Maastricht Treaty, signed in February 1992, led to the establishment of the European Union, and within the next decade, this was served by a common currency and a central bank. Development of a common foreign policy, citizenship, and a European constitution sped the integration process during the 1990s towards the goal of an "ever closer union." In this environment, even before the total collapse of the Soviet Bloc, Jacques Delors, the president of the Commission of the Community, launched a further major process in a speech in Bruges in October 1989: "The Twelve [member countries] cannot control history but they are now in a position to influence it once again. They did not want Europe to be cut in two at Yalta and made a hostage in the Cold War. They did not, nor do they close the door to other European countries . . . The present upheavals in Eastern Europe are changing the nature of our problems. It is now merely a matter of when and how all the countries of Europe will benefit from . . . the advantages of a single market."[8]

In this international environment, a window of opportunity opened for the former Soviet Bloc countries to join the new world system of a "liberal peace settlement." It helped the countries' democratic transformation and stabilization, as well as their introduction of functioning market economies and rapid economic growth. The path they had to follow was strictly pointed out. Meanwhile it also opened a new window of opportunity for Western Europe to give a better answer to the challenge of globalization.

Europe's Competitors: the United States and Asia

The world economy has been significantly transformed and a three-pillar system emerged during the decades of globalization. In the

---

[7] European Union, Activities of the European Union. Summaries of Legislation, europa.eu/scadplus/treaties/singleact_eu.htm–31K–

[8] Jacques Delors, "Address by Mr. Jacques Delors, Bruges, 17 October 1989," in Brent F. Nelsen and Alexander Stubb (eds.), *The European Union: Readings on the Theory and Practice of European Integration* (Boulder, CO: Lynne Rienner, 1998), 59.

twentieth century, especially during the Cold War decades, the United States became the world economic leader, a superpower with equal measures of economic, political, and military strength, the unquestionable leader of the Western world.

The *United States*, the cradle of the new communication and technological revolution, and the first post-industrial society, was a towering economic power. The United States' GDP increased nearly two-and-half times in the first postwar quarter-of-a-century, and then three-and-half times again during the three decades from the mid-1970s to 2005, and reached $12,398 billion. On a per capita level, it was $41,640. After the war, American GDP represented nearly 37 percent of the world's total, but half a century later it reached 46 percent of the world's economic output. By 2004, 76 percent of American exports were high-tech and medium-high-tech products. The United States achieved the most advanced occupational structure, reflecting the post-industrial age: agriculture employs 2 percent of the active population and industry 21 percent, while services concentrate 77 percent of them.

Asia, however, rapidly emerged as a strong rival. After the war, Japan performed the first Asian economic miracle: its GDP increased nearly eight times up to 1973, and then more than three-and-half times again, reaching $4,534 billion by 2005. Japan's income level per person increased from 35 to 75 percent of the United States's level, and the country became one of the world's technological and economic leaders, which gradually generated a uniquely rapid development in neighboring South Korea, Taiwan, Hong Kong, and Singapore by outsourcing less sophisticated production sectors, those that were closed in Japan. The four "small tigers" mentioned above emerged with spectacular speed: their GDP per capita increased by four to seven times between 1970 and 2000. They also approached the American income level significantly.[9]

Asian success spread further in the region: sixteen East Asian countries, led by Japan, emerged as dominant world economic factors: together they increased their aggregate GDP by more than fourteen times in the second half of the twentieth century. Southeast Asia occupied an eminent role in modern technology sectors: nearly 37 percent

---

[9] GDP per capita increased by 7.5 times in South Korea, 5.4 times in Taiwan, 4.7 times in Singapore, and 3.7 times in Hong Kong. In the last third of the twentieth century, Singapore's income level increased from 13 to 79% of the USA's, Taiwan's from 20 to 59%, and Hong Kong's from 38 to 76%.

of its exports were high-tech products, a much higher share than in the most advanced countries, and in addition, more than 32 percent was medium-high-tech.

From the 1980s on, China, India, and Vietnam joined the Asian miracle-development with 7 to 10 percent annual economic growth. China, after the death of Chairman Mao in 1976, turned to a unique road of reform: starting with agriculture, it established the first "special economic zone" in Shenzhen, a laboratory for a capitalist economy that had significant Japanese participation. For one-and-half decades, however, China did not privatize the state-owned economy. In 1993, a second stage of reform eliminated central planning and sharply decreased the state-owned sector of the economy by privatizing a great part of it. Employment in state-owned industry declined from 76 million to 28 million between 1992 and 2004. China built up the institutions and legal system of a market economy, and introduced a strictly regulated capitalist market system and an export-led economy. In 1999, it knocked on the door of the World Trade Organization, and entered into the international free trade system.[10] One-party dictatorial political rule was preserved during the entire transformation. Although formally a communist regime with strict control over the population, in reality the Chinese system became a typical Asian modernization dictatorship, which was not very different from the non-communist Asian authoritative regimes of previous decades.

China became the second largest economy in the world, with $3.42 trillion GDP in exchange rate terms, but $7 trillion in purchasing power parity (ppp).[11] On a per capita basis, Chinese GDP is still only $7,800 ppp because the country concentrates 20 percent of the world's population. China has the most rapidly growing economy: since 1990, the annual growth was 10 percent, and the GDP since 1978 has increased ten times. During the 1990s, the country's GDP

---

[10] Loren Brandt and Thomas G. Rawski (eds.), *China's Great Economic Transformation* (Cambridge University Press, 2008), 127.

[11] Official exchange rates do not reflect the differences of price levels in two countries. The purchasing power parity calculation is equalizing the purchasing power of two currencies and comparing the two countries' GDP on a one-price level. Price equalization uses the method of a fixed basket of goods and services to determine the real exchange rate. More simple indexes such as the Big Mac index calculate the real exchange rate based on the price of a Big Mac in two countries. If the Big Mac is $4 in one country and 800 forint in the other, then the ppp exchange rate is 1:200 between the dollar and the Hungarian forint. The ppp-based GDP reflects the difference of the income level between two countries more realistically.

doubled in a single decade. In the early twenty-first century, China accounts for 75 percent of the world's toy production, 58 percent of its cloth, and 29 percent of its mobile phone output. As the world's third largest trading nation after the United States and Germany, China influences the world market more than the United States.

Unlike most developing countries, China climbed the technology ladder rapidly and reached an impressive level of participation in the high-tech and medium–high-tech sectors: in 2004, 55 percent of China's exports contained such products. Medium–low and low technology products, on the other hand, represented only 13 and 32 percent of Chinese exports. China is a combination of a dynamic advanced country and a developing one. Its agricultural population is still significant at 49 percent of the total, and a large part of it still lived in poverty in 2005. Coming from twenty-first century Shanghai and Beijing, a traveler would arrive at medieval-looking villages. The industrial and service employments are 22 and 29 percent, respectively. Urbanization and the restructuring of the labor force is extremely fast, and the country's economic position is strengthening every year. The successful transformation also dramatically decreased poverty. Mostly because of Chinese and Indian progress, poverty in East Asia and the Pacific dropped from 58 percent in 1981 to 15 percent by 2001.

India, the other rising Asian giant with 1.1 billion inhabitants, is rapidly developing: between 1995 and 2005, its annual growth rate reached 6.3 percent. The country and whole subcontinent has a more modern economic structure: agriculture produces only 19 percent of the GDP, and services produced nearly 54 percent in 2005. On the other hand, while India has a well-educated middle class, as large as the entire population of the United States, 39 percent of the adult population remains illiterate.

In 1950, Asia produced less than one-fifth of the world's GDP, by 1973, nearly one-quarter, and 37 percent of it already at the turn of the century. Counting in purchasing power parity, China is the second biggest economy after the United States, Japan the third, and India the fourth. The aggregate $16,589 billion GDP (ppp) of the three Asian giants is 25 percent bigger than the United States' economy.

From the early twenty-first century on, Brazil, which has enormous potential enriched by the discovery of huge oil reserves and nearly 200 million inhabitants, appears to be joining the group of the spectacularly rising developing countries. Its economic growth, which was moderate around the turn of the century with an annual 2.2 percent rate, shifted up to between 5 and 6 percent after 2005. China, India, and Brazil are joining the club of the globalization winners.

Several countries and entire continents, however, became losers: economic polarization became sharper than ever before in the critical period of the last quarter of the century. During these decades, per capita GDP increased in the advanced Western world by an annual rate of roughly 2 percent. Latin America achieved less than half that growth rate, while absolute stagnation characterized Africa. Eastern Europe, including the former Soviet Union, suffered a serious decline of −1.1 percent per annum.

The world financial crisis of 2008 slowed down significantly the spectacular growth of China and other rapidly emerging developing countries, but hit harder the weaker and less successful transformation and developing economies. The positions of countries and continents changed, and in some regions, a huge number of so-called developing countries declined into hopeless poverty and dependence on international aid. On the other hand, the emerging developing giants – which really deserve this name – significantly strengthened their position in the international economic arena. The World Trade Organization's meeting in the summer of 2008 clearly reflected their strength: a united China and India successfully resisted American pressure and realized their own interests.

Western Europe: Adjusting to the New Economic Requirements

After 1980, Western Europe entered a radically transformed era of economic globalization with a miraculously recovered and strengthened economy: its aggregate GDP increased roughly three times after the war and reached $4.134 trillion by 1973. It had to adjust to sharp global competition by creating new requirements and adopting new technology based on European innovation and world-class productivity levels. The challenge was tremendous, and the shock of 1973–80 was frightening. At the same time as Japan's prosperity was continuing to grow, and China had just switched into high gear, Europe had to cope with the demanding task of restructuring. Success was not initially evident at all, but the impressive development of the European Union offered a solid basis from which it could enter the ring with the same chance as its rivals.

From the 1980s, as will be discussed in this chapter, Europe emerged as the strong third pillar of the global system. By 2004, Europe became the most globalized region, and Belgium the most globalized country, of the world. According to the Swiss KOF globalization index, which assesses the economic, social, and political aspects of 122 countries, the first sixteen of the most globalized countries are European, with a score of between 80 and 92 on a scale of 100. Among the first twenty countries, only four – among which are the United States and Canada – are non-European.

Adjusting to the new requirements, however, was a difficult task. The crisis of the late 1970s–early 1980s hit Europe hard. The sectors of the economy that suffered the most were those that developed the fastest during the postwar prosperity. The iron and steel industry, the shipbuilding industry, and others were heavily downsized, and some, such as Swedish shipbuilding, temporarily almost closed. The Belgian mining industry declined by half, construction by one-third. In ten West European countries, employment in the three ailing industrial sectors dramatically decreased between 1974 and 1985: in the iron and steel industry to 58 percent, in textiles to 62 percent, and in shipbuilding to 28 percent.[12]

How was the sharp decline of the old sectors to be counterbalanced? Replacing them with new industries representing the latest word in technological development was not a simple task. The West European core, as an OECD analysis found in 1987, was suffering from structural rigidities, and could not keep up with modern technology. Because of slow adjustment, Europe's position in intensive research and development branches significantly worsened after 1973.[13] The slow structural-technological adjustment was clearly expressed by Europe's losing ground to international competition in technology-intensive products. Around the mid-1980s, European companies had only a 9 percent world market share in computer and data processing products, 10 percent in software, 13 percent in satellites and launchers, and 29 percent in data transmission services.[14]

The lack or slow rise of modern high-tech sectors and the crisis of several old sectors curbed economic growth, which slowed severely in the European Union-12: from 4.8 percent annual growth between

---

[12] Based on OECD, *Structural Adjustment*, 236. Unweighted average of Austria, the three Benelux countries, Britain, France, Germany, Italy, Norway, and Sweden.
[13] *Ibid.*   [14] *Ibid.*, 213.

1960 and 1973, to 0.5 percent during the first half of the 1980s.[15] Exports, one of the prime movers of rapid growth, dropped during the early 1980s by 12 and 5 percent in Germany and the Netherlands. Unemployment increased ten times in Germany and then remained high during the entire 1980s, at between 5 and 12 percent. In some countries, such as Spain, it reached 20 percent.[16] Countries lost control of inflation, which reached an average of nearly 10 percent per year in Western Europe and nearly 20 percent in Mediterranean Europe.

Counterbalancing the harsh impact of the recession and the collapse of some traditional branches of the economy, European governments sought to slow down the decline by subsidizing ailing industries. Alexandre Lamfalussy, the founding president of the European Monetary Institute, called them "defensive investments," which was an old response to a new challenge. The British government increased its aid to steel, mining, and shipbuilding from less than 8 percent of total industrial assistance before 1973 to one-quarter of the total by 1982–3. German federal aid to industry more than doubled during the decade after 1973, while aid to shipbuilding and the steel industry rose from 23 to 50 percent of total federal industrial subsidies.[17]

State assistance reached its zenith during the early 1980s. Between 1970 and 1983, government aid to industry increased from 0–2 percent to 3–6 percent of industrial value added in various West European countries. Dutch assistance doubled, Danish government contributions increased four-fold, and Swedish aid by fourteen times.[18]

Between 1981 and 1986, state aid for the manufacturing sector in ten European Community countries reached 42,161 billion ECU[19] annually. During the second half of the decade, aid decreased to 25 billion for fifteen countries. State aid dropped from 3 percent of GDP

---

[15] Instead of nearly 5% annual growth in Germany before 1973, growth rates dropped to 1.6% between 1974 and 1983. In the Netherlands growth declined from 5 to 1.4% per annum in the same period.

[16] The unemployment rate was nearly 14 and 13% in the Netherlands and Britain.

[17] OECD, *Structural Adjustment*, 231. The same two industries received one-quarter of government aid in France in the same decade. Danish shipbuilding received more than 51% of industrial subsidies.

[18] *Ibid.*, 229–31.

[19] The "ECU" or European Currency Unit was introduced as an artificial internal accounting "currency" of the European Community, composed from a basket of member countries' currencies. In 1999, when the common currency, the euro, was introduced the exchange rate was €1=1 ECU.

in 1981 to 1 percent by 2000.[20] Most countries provided *ad hoc* aid until the turn of the century, but Britain, Sweden, and Denmark stopped giving this kind of assistance entirely. European governments also increased their tariffs and restrictions to defend their domestic markets. The European Economic Community raised restrictions on imports. Before, restrictions influenced 11 percent of imported industrial goods, but now it increased to 15 percent of its total imports of manufactured goods. Import restrictions on goods from Japan and the newly industrialized countries of Asia increased from 15 percent to as much as 30 percent by the early 1980s.[21]

To keep the economy above the water, the European countries also increased their export assistance. In the 1970s, this assistance reached between 1 to 5 percent of the value of capital goods exports, but increased to 10 and even to 28 percent by 1981–3.[22]

Deregulation and the End of the Mixed Economy

Adjusting to the new situation, Europe turned towards the neo-liberal, American-type laissez-faire system. Although it did not influence the popular welfare policy, the change eliminated most state interventions and regulations of the financial market, as well as those of the mixed (mostly private but partly state-owned) economy that characterized the period of postwar prosperity.

The main economic trends are not national or even regional, but international. This is especially true after 1980, when the world economy became more interconnected than ever before. When discussing this process, I have to present the transformation from a regulated to an unregulated market system not as an exclusively European process, but as a "Western" phenomenon that actually emerged first in the United States, followed closely by Britain and the West European countries. The deregulation process began in 1971, when President Nixon stopped the free exchange of the dollar and abolished the Bretton Woods system, which had dominated the entire postwar period. The collapse of Bretton Woods meant the end of a fixed

---

[20] *Tableau de bord des aides d'état, Commission of the European Union* (Brussels: EU, 2002). Italy and Ireland subsidized industry by more than 5% of their GDPs but also decreased it back to hardly more than 1%.

[21] OECD, *Structural Adjustment*, 229.   [22] *Ibid.*, 230–1.

international exchange rate policy and of control of international money movements. The advanced countries entered into vast international financial transactions. Their foreign assets and liabilities have increased five times since 1980, and they doubled in the single decade between 1998 and 2008.

The United States, the world's leading economic power, went further along this road and deregulated its banking system.[23] Britain followed the same path during the 1980s, and gradually the Western half of the continent followed. *The Economist*, looking back from 2008, evaluated these steps in the most positive way: because of "financial deregulation . . . freer markets produced a superior outcome. Unencumbered capital would flow to its most productive use, boosting economic growth . . . "[24] Indeed, deregulation increased flexibility for relocating resources from crisis-ridden areas to emerging sectors of the economy. America's growing advantage in coping with the crisis of the 1970s and early 1980s lay not simply in its technology, but in its flexible financial system that provided incentives and helped employ the new technology.

The entire banking and financing industry changed radically. The separation of commercial and investment banking, a regulation introduced during the Great Depression, was abolished. Banks increased their liabilities (loans) far beyond their assets (deposits). Their capital was far from sufficient to repay deposits if some financial panic pushed people or institutions to withdraw them. Insurance companies also performed banking activities, and the most flexible financial institutions, the hedge funds, began playing a crucially important role in investment activities. Their activities clearly illustrate the deregulated financial markets. Among the big hedge funds, the "billion dollar members" of the "club," 120 have their headquarters in New York, 65 in London. In 2007, 370 new hedge funds were established in Europe that are investing globally. For example, 160 hedge funds invested in Russia and Central and Eastern Europe. The more than $2.68 trillion hedge fund business (in the summer of 2008) financed most of the start-up companies and assisted technological development since 1980. On the other hand, however, they attracted huge amounts of

---

[23] Paul Krugman, *The Return of Depression Economics and the Crisis of 2008* (Harmondsworth: Penguin, 2008).

[24] "When Fortune Frowned," *The Economist*, October 11–17, 2008, 10. I used this study (pp. 3–16) in discussing the transformation of the international financial markets in the next pages as well.

capital by offering spectacular profits. Hedge funds performed lucra-
tive investments for their investors for a 20 to 40 percent performance
fee, deducted from the capital gain. However, if the investment failed,
the fund did not share the loss, it was the investors' trouncing. This
rule transformed the hedge funds' investment activities into reckless
gambling. The fund managers, who were strongly interested in the
gain, but did not suffer as a result of the losses, continued wild spec-
ulations. When the German government initiated the regulation of
the hedge funds before the financial crisis, the British government
and the American administration blocked any regulatory measures.
Compared to the five years before 2008, when hedge funds gained 47
percent profit from investing in Central and Eastern Europe, their loss
amounted to 57 percent in 2008.

Bond markets that were national became international: countries
issued bonds and sold them to other countries to manipulate interests. One of the flexible financial innovations allowed by an unregulated market was the *securitization* of credits, which entirely transformed commercial lending. Creditors (mortgage loans, credit card
loans, student loans, corporate loans, car loans, etc.) performed this
transaction by pooling their assets, issuing securities, and selling their
existing loans to an investor in this form. The borrowers gradually
pay the fully amortized securities back in the specified term. Selling
these assets became legal in the 1970s in the United States, first in the
mortgage business, but from 1985–6 they were used in non-mortgage
businesses, such as car loans and credit card loans. From 1990, it spread
to the insurance business as well. Britain followed soon after, and during the Reagan–Thatcher 1980s, this became part of the Anglo-Saxon
deregulated financial system.

Securitizing credits increased money circulation; the company that
issued the loan did not have to wait until the borrowers repaid it, sometimes in three to thirty years, but sold it, received cash, increased its liquidity, and could issue new credits and gain new profits. Besides, they
could report the transaction as new earnings that attracted investors
and steeply increased CEOs' bonuses. On the other hand, investors
such as hedge funds were ready to buy to diversify their portfolios.
Deregulation opened the door for easier access to credit, including
the less- and the least-creditworthy consumers. The lending companies transferred the risk to other companies. Between 1995 and 2005,
these transactions increased in the United States by 19 percent per
year. By 2005, the amount of securitized credits was $8.06 trillion.

About one-third of it was mortgage credits, 40 percent corporate credits, and one-fifth credit card loans. American household debt, which accounted for 80 percent of the disposable income of borrowers in 1986, reached 140 percent by 2007. However, the indebtedness of British households was even greater. Deregulated financial markets offered the advantage of more flexible and risky financial activities, which mostly earned higher profits and resulted in cheap credit for the economy.

One of the most innovative new characteristics of the financial market was the *derivatives* business. Traders – first of all commercial and investment banks and insurance companies – bought and sold future contracts, future commodity trade, and future options on shares, bonds, currencies, and interest rates. These transactions aimed to avoid risk by selling or buying at an assumed (forecasted) price to eliminate future changes in exchange or interest rates or commodity prices. In Germany, the leading banks established a Derivate Forum in 2004 to provide risk ratings. Banks ended their traditional practice of assessing the creditworthiness of their clients because of this trading practice. The derivatives business thus served risk management, but it was itself at the same time a major risk, involving speculation about future prices, exchange rates, and interest rate movements. In other words, this business became gambling, based on assumed future price movements. It might offer huge profits as well as huge losses, based on real price and rate formations. According to the Bank for International Settlements, the world's derivatives trade reached $600 trillion in 2007, increased from $75 trillion in 1997. To evaluate these astronomical figures, it pays to note that the 1997 figure was already two-and-half times the world's global GDP. It thus became impossible for any single company, or even a single nation, to handle the potentially huge losses.

In the title of its 1994 article, *Fortune* magazine offered a good starting point for understanding the attitude of financial institutions towards the new business methods: "Learning to Live with Derivatives. They're here, they're weird, and they're not going away. These beasties bite, but companies that tame them have a competitive edge."[25]

Deregulation and the flexible financial market worked and helped to cope with the crisis of the early 1980s. Neo-liberal ideologues and economists, as well as governments under their influence, celebrated

---

[25] *Fortune* magazine, July 25, 1994, money.cnn.com/magazines/fortune . . . /1994/ . . . 25 . . . index.htm

the success. They did not worry about possible negative consequences, since they blindly believed in the self-correcting mechanism of the unregulated market. The warning they often made was just the opposite: not to interfere, not to destroy the market mechanism that would correct itself if needed and solve all the emerging problems.

In reality, however, the question was not *whether*, but *when* the negative effects would become dominant. Since the 1980s, local crises have actually accompanied the transformation of international financing in Mexico, Asia, Russia, as well as the bursting of stock market and housing market bubbles. George Soros, one of the main winners in, and experts on, the unregulated financial markets, actually warned of the danger in 1998: "market fundamentalism . . . put financial capital into the driver's seat . . . Market forces, if they are given complete authority . . . produce chaos and could ultimately lead to the downfall of the global capitalist system."[26] Indeed, global crisis and the collapse of financial systems, on a scale unheard of since the Great Depression, arrived in 2006–8 in the United States, and spread to Europe and throughout the world in 2008–9.

During the 1980s, the burgeoning neo-liberal ideology, besides spreading deregulation, seriously questioned both of the two peculiar postwar institutions that distinguished the European model: the mixed economy and the welfare system. The *mixed economy*, established by major wartime and postwar nationalizations, created a 20 to 25 percent state-owned sector in the West European economies. The state sector, which worked in a market environment and acted accordingly, played a strategic role in modernization and economic growth during the postwar decades. However, neo-liberals attacked the state-owned sector as a parasite and inappropriate in the new global environment. Privatization became a universal agenda. The first steps were taken by Margaret Thatcher: several services covered by the Ministry of Defence and the National Health Service (in its 2,000 hospitals) were contracted out to private companies in Britain. By 1985, the government had privatized nearly a dozen major state companies: among them, the North Sea Oil licenses and part of the stock of British Petroleum, followed by major assets of British Aerospace, Associated British Ports, British Gas, and British Telecom. Altogether, they transferred more than £5 billion value and 400,000 jobs from state to private ownership.

---

[26] George Soros, *The Crisis of Global Capitalism: Open Society Endangered* (New York: PublicAffairs, 1998), xx, xxvii.

In Mitterrand's France, after the unique nationalization wave of the early 1980s, when 53 percent of the assets of French companies were put into public hands, the July and August 1986 privatization bills placed thirteen major companies in private hands in nine months. In another nine months all the nationalized companies were reprivatized. In post-Franco Spain, where a huge part of the economy was state-owned, a privatization wave began in 1984, and 350 industrial firms and 92 banks, and then the Instituto Nacional de Industria, the huge holding company with 700 industrial and banking interests, were taken over by private firms in two years. Italy also privatized a dozen major firms in the traditional state sector, including Alitalia, Autostrada, Banca di Roma, and Elsag.[27] Europe eliminated one of the main characteristics of its postwar economic model: the mixed economy. The blind neo-liberal belief in a self-regulating market and the withdrawal of regulations and the state helped prosperity in the short-run, but meanwhile paved the way towards the 2008–9 financial crisis.

Research and Development

Although the first reaction of the West European countries to the new challenge was to defend "sunset industries" or declining branches, a new recognition emerged after the mid-1980s. Governments started assisting "sunrise industries," those high-tech branches that are based on new technology, and which were rapidly gaining ground overseas. France and Britain assisted so-called strategic sectors to assure competitive advantage. Germany gave tax relief for electronics.

The most important method of assisting structural changes, however, was to assist research and development (R&D), especially in advanced high-tech sectors such as aerospace, nuclear energy, electronics, pharmaceuticals, telecommunications, and electrical engineering (Figure 19). Government funding of these sectors was 96, 91, and 67 percent in Britain, France, and Germany, respectively, while the share of government funding of R&D in general reached only 32, 24, and 14 percent of total R&D investments in these countries, respectively. France, with government control over banking, was able to push the

---

[27] J.-J. Santini (ed.), *Les privatisations à l'étranger: Royaume-Uni, RFA, Italie, Espagne, Japon* (Paris: La Documentation Française, 1986).

Figure 19. The Super Proton Synchrotron, the second largest machine at the accelerator complex of CERN, the European Organization for Nuclear Research, which was established by eleven European governments in Geneva.

private sector to implement pre-planned structural adjustment following government guidelines. Consequently, the country was rather successful in the nuclear and telecom industries.[28]

Britain initiated the LINK program to strengthen links between universities and industry. In the case of joint research, the government financed half of the costs of programs, while industry had to provide matching funds. Norway established the Foundation of Scientific and Industrial Research (SINTEF) at the Norwegian Institute of Technology. Government and industry jointly funded this national center.[29] Meanwhile, the advanced Western countries made important steps towards a collaborative solution: during the first half of the 1980s, nearly one thousand intra- and inter-area production agreements were made in the OECD. More than one-quarter of them served integrated R&D programs, 17 percent served technology transfer, and 28 and 16 percent served marketing and production integration, respectively.[30] In the mid-1990s, 1.6 million people were employed in the R&D sector.

[28] *Ibid.*, 218, 225.   [29] *Ibid.*, 112.   [30] *Ibid.*, 255.

Collaboration among the advanced Western countries was closely connected with the new character of division of labor. Advanced countries turned towards each other. Half of German investment was channeled into developing countries in the 1960s and 1970s, but less than 20 percent around 2000. Consequently, the share of other West European countries increased from 14 percent before the 1980s, to 50 percent by the early twenty-first century. Trade between West European countries gained a huge incentive, and it jumped from 30 percent of the trade of these countries in the 1960s, to 60 percent by the 1990s. Specialization developed within industries, rather than between them. As a typical consequence of this new, emerging trend, intra-industry trade became the most important and dominant trade transaction: intra-industry trade increased from 51 to 72 percent of the total combined value of German, British, and Belgian trade.[31]

In the mid-1980s, the European Community initiated several programs to assist with catching up the United States and Japan technologically. They launched Esprit (European Strategic Programme for Research and Development in Information Technology) in 1984. It provided €750 million[32] for four years that had to be matched by the participating companies. RACE (Research in Advanced Communications for Europe) was started in 1985 with €21 million, but followed by programs funded with €460 million and €489 million between 1990 and 1994. The BRITE/EURAM (Basic Research in Industrial Technologies in Europe/European Research in Advanced Materials) program ran from 1985 to 1992 with a total of €1,210 billion in funding. The European Community invested €63,245 million between 1984 and 2006 in research and technological development projects.[33]

European Community spending was limited, reaching only 5 percent of the member countries' R&D expenditures. It definitely gave an incentive and pushed Europe towards a new orientation, however. By 2004, total expenditure on R&D reached 3.2 and 2.66 percent of the Japanese and American GDP, respectively. Compared to these leading countries, Sweden and Finland surpassed the Japanese level with 3.95 and 3.48 percent, respectively. Denmark, Switzerland, and Germany were nearer the American level with between 2.5 and 2.6 percent,

---

[31] *Ibid.*, 273.

[32] Originally they used the "ECU" but here the amounts are presented in euros.

[33] European Commission, *Towards a European Research Area: Science, Technology and Innovation, Key Figures* (Official Publications of the European Communities, Luxembourg, 2002), 20.

but the European Union-15 weighted average remained behind with 1.9 percent.

The number of patents granted also mirrors the difference: West European countries together granted 35,329 patents a year between 2002 and 2004, far less than the nearly 110,000 Japanese and 85,000 American patents. Regarding the number of employed researchers, the EU-15 had only six per thousand people employed, behind both Japan (10.4) and the United States (9.6). It pays to note, however, that Finland and Sweden are by far the best globally, with 17.3 and 11.0.[34] The Innovation Index[35] reflects the leading role of the United States and Japan, but among the twenty best-performing countries in 2005, thirteen were West European.

Building Modern Infrastructure: The Energy and Transportation Sectors

The new technological regime was, as is always the case, closely connected with new infrastructure. The energy sector deserves special attention in this respect. The consumption and generation of electricity increased and changed massively. In the roughly quarter century before 2005, electricity output increased globally by more than three times, and it increased by nearly two-and-a-half times in Western Europe and the transforming Central and Eastern European countries.[36] However, the structure of electricity generation radically changed. Globally, coal was responsible for the same share of electricity generation: 40 percent in both 1971 and 2005. Within the European Union-27, coal's role declined to 31 percent. Their oil dependence, however, remained strong at 20 percent, much higher than the world's total 7 percent. The most remarkable positive change, however, was the increased role of renewable sources and nuclear power, which worldwide produced 32 percent of energy, but 45 percent in Europe.[37]

In some European countries, nuclear power stations produce the majority of electricity output: in Lithuania, 80 percent; in France, 78 percent; and in Slovakia, Belgium, and Sweden, 57, 55 and 50 percent,

---

[34] OECD, *Factbook: Economic, Environmental and Social Statistics* (Paris: OECD, 2007), 149.

[35] Measuring the adoption of new technology, the interaction between business and the scientific sector, granted patents, and higher educational enrollments.

[36] OECD, *Factbook* 2007, 109.   [37] *Ibid.*, 108–9.

respectively.[38] The 1960s and 1970s were a period of extensive nuclear power plant construction, and the majority of the world's 400 nuclear power stations were built in 30 countries during this period, with a combined capacity of 351 gigawatts. After the 1980s, however, this trend almost entirely stopped in Europe. Two frightening accidents, the Three Mile Island (1979) and Chernobyl (1986) catastrophes, led to strong environmentalist resistance against nuclear power stations. After Chernobyl, two-thirds of the nuclear power station construction that had been ordered during the 1970s was canceled. In Denmark in 1985, and in Austria in 1997, parliamentary decisions banned new construction. Belgium, Germany, the Netherlands, Spain, and Sweden joined the ranks. Moreover, Belgium decided to close seven reactors between 2015 and 2025. Ireland and Greece decided not to have nuclear plants at all. In 2000, the German "Nuclear Exit Law" decided to close nineteen nuclear stations by 2020. They did shut down one station in 1997, but postponed closing the second in 2003.

The anti-nuclear stand, however, started to change. Europe seemingly returned to nuclear power generation in the early twenty-first century because of skyrocketing oil prices. France had decided already in 1974, after the first oil shock, to be energy self-sufficient. In 2008, a new nuclear plant was opened, and building a second one is on the agenda. Britain decided to build a new generation of nuclear plants in January 2008, and the deadline for the first is 2020.

During the entire period since 1980, the use of new renewable energy sources such as hydro, geothermal, solar, wind, tide, wave, biomass, biogas, and waste gained ground. In the entire OECD group, while the total energy supply increased by 1.5 percent per annum between 1971 and 2005, renewable supply increased by 2.2 percent in a year. Nevertheless, its role is limited, on average about 6 percent of total energy sources, and in some countries such as Britain, Ireland, and Luxembourg, it remains only 1 to 2 percent. In a very few European countries with special natural assets, renewable energy sources have a significant role: Iceland and Norway lead the way with, respectively, 74 and 44 percent of their total supply in 2005 coming from renewable sources. A few other countries follow with 13 to 28 percent of renewable energy in their total supply.[39]

---

[38] David Charter and Rory Watson, "Europe Agrees to Embrace Nuclear Option in Battle to Save the Planet," *The Times*, March 10, 2007, 41.

[39] *OECD Factbook, 2007*, 110–11. These countries are Sweden (28%), Finland (23%), Austria (22%), Switzerland (18%), Denmark (16%), and Portugal (13%).

The automobile revolution that, in real terms, arrived in Europe after World War II, continued during the entire second half of the century, including the period since 1980. The number of cars more than doubled between 1973 and 2005, and, on average, there are 529 cars for every 1,000 inhabitants.[40]

These decades became a period of extensive *freeway construction* as well: by the mid-1970s, the freeway network linking seventeen West European countries stretched 22,000 kilometers; by 1987, it had expanded to 37,000 kilometers, and by 2005 to more than 57,000 kilometers. From the 1990s, countries that had short freeway networks, or did not have them at all, such as Finland, Greece, Ireland, and Portugal, had extensive construction, and their network grew by 6 percent per year. The European Union issued guidelines for the development of the trans-European transport network in 1996. Even in France and the Scandinavian countries the length of motorways increased by 3 to 6 percent per annum. If one adds in five of the transforming countries from the East, including Russia, where motorways hardly existed before, the length of the European freeway network neared 89,000 kilometers by 2005. Germany has the world's third largest road network, and Switzerland has the highest freeway density.[41]

New technology radically transformed the old infrastructural sectors as well. Germany, typical for most of Western Europe, accomplished the *electrification and dieselization of the railroads* by the end of the 1980s: 41 percent of the railroads were electrified, and all other lines used diesel engines.

From the 1980s, a new chapter was opened in European railroads. In 1981, the Paris–Lyons line was opened for the Train à Grande Vitesse (TGV), the high-speed train (Figure 20). In 2001, high-speed trains on the Paris–Marseilles line reached 400 kilometers per hour, and on TGV's Paris–Strasbourg line, the record was 553 kilometers per hour. High-speed networks rapidly increased, and in February 2008, news agencies reported that the new French Alstom train, the Automotrice à Grande Vitesse (AGV), powered by motors under each carriage and without a separate engine car, runs at 360 kilometers per hour. Italy and Germany have already ordered the new AGV trains.

---

[40] *Eurostat Yearbook, 1998–99* (Luxembourg: EU, 2000); *OECD Factbook*, 2007, 237. In 1950, there were only 22 cars per 1,000 people.

[41] George W. Hoffman, *Europe in the 1990s: A Geographic Analysis*, sixth edition (New York: John Wiley & Sons, 1990), 173; OECD *Factbook*, 2007, 235.

Figure 20. French bullet trains reach speeds of 400 to 500 kilometers per hour on the renewed European railroad system.

Railroad modernization created a renewed rail system in Germany as well. In 1991, the country rebuilt its railroad network for the fast Intercity-Express (ICE) service. The new trains run at 250–80 kilometers per hour. Britain's High Speed Trains started service in the 1980s, as well. The Class 220 runs at 200 kilometers per hour. Spain began rebuilding its entire network, completing more than 1,000 kilometers of modern rail lines, which increased to 1,621 kilometers by the end of 2008. The Madrid–Valencia line was opened in 1999 and trains run at 220 kilometers per hour.

Europe renewed its railroad transportation to compete with air transportation. Moreover, it is becoming more pan-European as well. Railroads had already connected the countries of the continent since the second half of the nineteenth century, but trains in twenty-first-century Europe do not have to stop for customs at national borders. Eurail and Eurostar passes guarantee unlimited travel over twenty countries of the continent for periods from two weeks to three months.

Landmark achievements signal a much better integrated European transportation network. The railroad development that is most symbolic of an integrating Europe is the Channel Tunnel opened between

France and Britain. It was the realization of an old idea[42] that was implemented by an agreement that was signed and ratified in 1987. In 1994, the two heads of state passed through the tunnel, and regular service between Paris and London opened that year. A rail-ferry "Freeway" agreement was also signed by Germany and Sweden that established fast transportation between Rostock and Trelleborg, spanning the sea and the physical separation of the European countries.

European integration had a major impact on air transportation. Civil aviation became a major form of mass transportation in post-war Europe, but only a little more than 100,000 million passenger-kilometers were flown by national airlines in 1974. Three decades later, there were already eight times more. In 2006, 738 million passengers traveled by air in the European Union-27.[43]

One of the milestones of European integration was the Airbus initiative: the French, German, and British cooperation, with subsequent Spanish participation, to create a European aviation company that was competitive with the American air industry (Figure 21). The original three countries had already signed the first agreement in 1967, but Airbus Industrie was formed only at the end of 1970. By the end of the decade, eighty-one Airbus aircraft were in service. The breakthrough was the launch of the A380 project in 2002 to produce a double-decker, four-engine, 555-seat giant plane, which had its first flight in 2005. The European Airbus company employs 57,000 employees and has branches on sixteen sites in Toulouse, Hamburg, Bristol, Nantes, Bremen, and Cadiz, with subsidiaries in the United States, Japan, and China. In 2007, nearly 5,000 Airbus planes were in service, all delivered between 1990 and 2007. The European company has delivered more planes since 2000 than Boeing.

The European Union took the initiative to create a more connected and integrated trans-European transport system. The idea emerged in the 1980s, in connection with the single market program. In 1994, the Council meeting in Essen agreed on a Trans-European Transport Network project, and it selected fourteen priority projects to accomplish

---

[42] The idea of a tunnel under the English Channel was born in 1802, and a plan was even prepared in 1856. In 1882, works began in Kent and Calais but stopped almost immediately.

[43] Brian R. Mitchell, *International Historical Statistics: Europe 1750–1993*, fourth edition (London: Macmillan, 1998), 724–7; *Basic Statistics of the Community* (Brussels: Statistical Office of the European Community, 1977), 103; based on *Eurostat Yearbooks*.

Figure 21. The Airbus, a successful product of EU industrial cooperation.

by 2010. In 2003, a High Level Group was appointed to amend the plan in connection with enlargement of the EU eastward.[44] In 2006, the Commission established an Executive Agency to implement and manage the program.

The central goal was to connect all of the member countries into a more homogenized European network in the most efficient way possible, eliminating transportation bottlenecks around big cities, border crossings, and especially in mountainous regions. One of the projects was a high-capacity railroad via the Pyrenees; another a high-speed train between Verona and the Brenner Pass connecting Italy to Western Europe, and a third joining Western Europe to Eastern Europe via high-speed railroads from Stuttgart to Vienna and the East.

Another central idea was to combine rail, water, and air transportation better by connecting ports and international airports by high-speed trains. The Union's projects concentrated on missing links, and planned to build 4,800 kilometers of road, 12,500 kilometers of

---

[44] The original fourteen priority projects were increased to thirty projects, eighteen of them for high-speed, high-capacity railroads, two for inland water transportation and the others for roads.

railroad lines, and to upgrade existing roads, waterways, and lines.[45] The program's Galileo project involved the launching of thirty satellites for an autonomous radio navigation system. Financing this ambitious program is a combination of national and Union expenditures, with a 10 to 20 percent Union contribution. For the priority projects, the Union plans to spend €225 billion by 2020, but it will increase to €600 billion.[46]

Other major steps towards integration were the White Paper of the European Commission on Transportation Policy in September 2001, and the program for the "Air Traffic Freeway System for Europe," or the "Single European Sky." The foundation of EUROCONTROL, a non-national but joint institution, offered a way of controlling the upper air space above 7.5 kilometers, separating the short-haul airport traffic and the high altitude long-haul traffic, with connections and junctions between them.

The Service Revolution

The modern economic formation, which was characterized by the extraordinary spread of various kinds of services, was also clearly expressed in radical structural changes that took place in the economy. Occupational structure clearly expressed the dramatic decline of the agricultural population, the decrease in industrial employment, and the enormous increase in service employment. At the end of 2006, twelve Western member countries of the European Union employed, on average, slightly more than 4 percent of their active population in agriculture and almost 29 percent in industry. All of these countries experienced a service revolution: this sector employed roughly one-third of the active population after the war, half of them in the early- to mid-1970s, and roughly 70 percent in 2005. This share reached three-quarters of the active population in quite a few countries, including Belgium, Denmark, France, Norway, Sweden, Switzerland, and Britain. The service sector produced roughly half of

---

[45] The plan contains the upgrading of 3,500 kilometers of road, 12,300 kilometers of railroad, and 1,740 kilometers of inland waterways by 2020.

[46] www.dft.gov.uk/stellent/groups/dft_about/documents/pdf/dft_about_pdf_503849.pdf–12k Between 2000 and 2006 the Union spent €600 million per year, but the new budget between 2007 and 2013 provides €8 billion.

total value added in the 1970s, but it became the leading sector of the Western economies around the turn of the twenty-first century, producing nearly three-quarters of total value added.[47]

The structural changes in occupation, and the considerably increased contribution of services to the GDP, also reflected increased productivity in agriculture and industry, which produced more value with far fewer employees and thus freed a greater part of the labor force for work in other sectors of the economy. On the other hand, these changes also clearly placed at center stage the service revolution brought on by a more sophisticated division of labor and the separation of several important functions from production. In various works, Alfred Chandler has described the emergence in the United States at the beginning of the twentieth century of something that was revolutionary at the time: multi-functional and multi-division companies that merged mining, manufacturing, research, transportation, and services within the framework of a single company.[48]

During the last decades of the twentieth century, several functions were separated from manufacturing: research, design, accounting, transportation, and various other activities were taken over by specialized service companies serving several firms and increasing efficiency. In industrial agglomerations like Silicon Valley, several service companies settled to serve dozens of high-tech companies. In agriculture, specialized companies provide almost every function of cultivation: pesticide is spread from airplanes by specialized firms, newly harvested grain is dried by specialized companies, delivered by trucking firms, etc. In short, several functions that were parts of agricultural or industrial production became independent services, provided by specialized service companies.

As an OECD report phrased it: "Technological progress is transforming the nature of the relationship between manufacturing industry and the service sector, as a result of which they are becoming increasingly complementary. Indeed, it is one of the major causes

---

[47] Based on OECD, *Science, Technology and Industry Outlook* (Paris: OECD, 2000), 63.

[48] Alfred Chandler described and analyzed this development in his major works such as *The Visible Hand: The Managerial Revolution in American Business* (Cambridge, MA: The Belknap Press, 1977); *Scale and Scope: The Dynamics of Industrial Capitalism* (Cambridge, MA: Harvard University Press, 1990); and, with Franco Amatori and Takashi Hikino (eds.), *Big Business and the Wealth of Nations* (Cambridge University Press [1997] 1999).

of the growing service content of manufactured goods, sometimes referred to as the 'dematerialization of products'; at the same time it promotes the 'industrialization' of services."[49]

Rising Productivity, Structural Renewal: High-Tech Industries – Consolidation of the Economy

Structural changes resulting from the huge difference in the value of the output coming from different sectors further contributed to the increase in labor productivity. The most advanced countries increased their labor productivity level, i.e., the value produced by one worker in one hour, by several times during the second half of the twentieth century: in Japan, it increased by more than ten times, in the United States by nearly three times, and in Western Europe by more than five times. Ireland, one of the formerly backward European countries, increased productivity by more than seven times after the 1980s, thereby catching up with the most advanced countries in rather spectacular fashion.[50]

According to the calculations of the Groningen Growth and Development Center, the European Union-15 equaled the productivity level of the United States in 1995 and fell behind by only 1 percent in 2000, but, by 2004, the gap had increased to 8 percent. In the newest information and communication technology industries, European Union productivity increased by 11 percent per annum between 1990 and 1995, and by 14 percent between 1995 and 2000, but it still remained behind the American productivity growth rate of 15 and 24 percent during the two periods, respectively. By 2000, seven West European countries surpassed the productivity level of the United States, but European productivity growth slowed during the first decade of the twenty-first century, while American productivity gained new impetus.[51]

---

[49] OECD, *Structural Adjustment*, 256.   [50] Maddison, *World Economy*, 2001, 351.

[51] Robert Inklaar, Mary O'Mahony, and Marcel Timmer, *ICT and Europe's Productivity Performance, Research Memorandum GD-68* (Groningen: Groningen Growth and Development Center, December 2003); Bart van Ark, Robert Inklaar, and Robert H. Guckin, "ICT and Productivity in Europe and the United States: Where do the Differences Come From?" *CESifo Economic Studies*, 49, 3 (2003), 295–318. Norway surpassed the US level by more than 30%, France and Denmark by more than 20% in 2000.

After the stagflation of the troubled 1970s and early 1980s, Western Europe made great progress in adjusting to the requirements of the new technological regime and the globalized world economy. Europe was unable to continue the postwar development model of extensive growth that used existing American technology and just increased labor input. The countries of the European Union had to turn towards their own innovation base and establish competitive modern high-tech sectors. The investments in information and communication technology (ICT) doubled between 1980 and 2005, and in some countries, it nearly quadrupled. Sweden, Finland, and Britain exhibited especially impressive performances in this area. During the 1980s, the United States had a huge advantage, which increased in 1992 with 24 percent of total investment in ICT, as compared to the European Union-15 countries that, on average, invested only 13 percent in cutting edge technology, hardly more than half of the American investment share. By 2003, the average European investment increased to 17 percent, but Sweden and Finland (each nearly 27 percent) and Britain (22 percent) approached the 27–29 percent American share.[52]

Accordingly, modern high-tech sectors emerged only gradually in Europe. Their share of manufacturing output increased in Finland from 3.6 to 5 percent and in France from 12 to 13 percent, as well as increasing somewhat in Belgium and Germany. More successful was the adjustment in technological modernization and the renewal of traditionally strong medium-high-tech industries. The country leading this trend was Germany. The output of medium-high-tech branches – motor vehicles, engineering, and chemicals – increased from 32 to 41 percent of total industrial output in Germany, and to about one-third of the industrial output in several other West European countries.[53] Through renewed technology, product differentiation, and specialization, they were able to lower the cost of production and to conquer markets that were less saturated and less competitive. These medium-level R&D-intensive sectors significantly increased their exports.[54]

[52] OECD, *Factbook*, 2007, 155. Investment rates in general recovered from a severe decline – from a 5.6% annual increase before 1973, to an annual decrease of 0.6% between 1973 and 1980 – and again reached a 5.7% increase per year in the second half of the 1980s.

[53] OECD, *Structural Adjustment*, 254. During the 1980s, the share of medium-high-tech industries increased from 29 to 34% in France, from 29 to 32% in Italy, from 20 to 25% in Holland, and from 30 to 37% in Belgium.

[54] *Ibid.*, 215.

As a clear sign of structural adjustment, the output of the ICT
sector made good progress in Europe. The income share of this sector
tripled in Europe between 1980 and 1996. In 1980, it stood at only
one-third of the US level, but by 1996 it had reached one-half of the
US level, signaling that capital stock in the most modern technology
branches was accumulating in Europe. This had an important impact
on output growth: during the first half of the 1990s, ICT contributed
less than a third to growth, but during the second half of the decade, it
contributed one-half. At the turn of the century, Europe lagged only
about five years behind the United States in the diffusion of modern
technology. The output of the ICT sector in Western Europe reached
more than 4 percent of GDP. Only Ireland, at nearly 8 percent, and
Sweden and Finland, at nearly 6 percent each, were near the American
level of almost 7 percent of GDP. In another clear sign of modern
structural changes, even though job creation was weak and slow during
the 1990s, 75 percent of net job creation during the second half of the
decade occurred in high-tech sectors whose workforce was at least 40
percent constituted of individuals with tertiary education.

By 2004, high-tech exports from the European Union-15 nearly
matched the Japanese level: 23 percent of total exports, compared
to 24 percent for the Japanese. This remained behind the United
States, for whom high-tech exports comprised 33 percent of the total.
Regarding medium-high-tech exports, Europe's share increased to 47
percent, while only 44 percent of total exports from the United States
were in this category. Although somewhat later than the United States,
Europe closely followed modern technological and structural changes
around the turn of the century.[55]

Western Europe was consequently able to counterbalance the
decline of the old sectors with a rapid increase in the modern sectors,
i.e., it was able to cope with the structural crisis. As a clear sign of
it, consumer price inflation, which reached roughly 10 to 14 percent
in Western Europe, dropped to 3–5 percent in the second half of the
1980s and after. The surprisingly reversed movement in oil prices on
the world market played an important role in this: from $36 a barrel
in 1981, oil prices dropped to $11 a barrel by early 1986. The second
half of the 1980s represented a consolidation of the Western European economy. Private consumption also almost recovered, though it

---

[55] European Commission, *European Economy* (Brussels: European Commission, 2000), 37,
    108–9, 115, 117.

increased by only 3–4 percent annually, instead of the 4–5 percent it had increased per year before 1973. After a series of years of negative figures, fixed capital formation regained the pre-oil shock dynamism of 6–8 percent increases annually. In the late 1980s, industrial production in Germany increased by 4–6 percent per annum, and it increased in Western Europe as a whole by 2–4 percent. The increase in GDP also returned to a solid 2.5–3.5 percent annual growth rate.[56] Around the turn of the century, however, growth slowed down again; a new oil crisis temporarily skyrocketed prices to $150 per barrel in the summer of 2008. However, that year became the scene of a major international financial crisis that started in the United States and spread throughout the world. Oil prices again declined drastically, but credits, the fuel of modern economy, stopped at least transitorily. Neo-liberal countries not only bailed out the banking sector, but – following the British lead – partly or fully nationalized their leading banks. Further slowing down and even stagnation was unavoidable.

Fast Track from the Periphery to the Core: Ireland and Mediterranean Europe

Structural crisis – the decline of the old branches of the economy and the rise of new technology-based branches – on the Southern and Eastern European periphery had a somewhat different outcome than it did for the core. As in the late nineteenth century and the interwar decades, the crisis was more destructive and prolonged. The peripheral countries lacked the ability to establish new technology sectors and to adjust to the new requirements. Consequently, they suffered more because their export goods became obsolete and their value declined, especially when compared to the prices for imports. The prices and markets for their exports goods, which were less processed and much less sophisticated than those of the core countries, declined drastically. They did not have sufficient resources for research and development; they lacked the know-how and financing to follow closely the new technological–industrial revolution and to build up new leading export sectors. In other words, they suffered all the negative consequences of the structural crisis, but they were unable to catch in their sails the stormy wind of technological change

---

[56] United Nations, *Economic Survey of Europe* (New York: UN, 1991).

that was developing in the advanced countries. Paraphrasing Joseph Schumpeter's term on capitalist economy and structural crisis, "creative destruction," the *peripheral structural crisis* was destruction without creation.

In the last quarter of the century, however, we have to differentiate within Europe between the Southern periphery and Ireland, and the Central and Eastern European peripheries. Southern Europe and Ireland did not share in the pain of the peripheral structural crisis and began emerging from it. The first impact of the Oil Crisis and the changing world economy was shocking in Spain. Oil, mostly imported, represented nearly three-quarters of the energy consumption of the country. Expenditure for oil imports dramatically increased from 13 percent of total import expenditures in 1973 to more than 42 percent of the total. This amount was equal to two-thirds of the total value of Spanish exports. As Joseph Harrison writes: "By the end of 1974, the oil crisis put an end to 15 years' economic progress. In the following year, the rate of growth of GNP fell from 5.4 percent to 1.1 percent. Over the period 1976–8, growth rates recovered a little, averaging 2.8 percent a year. Nevertheless, these figures represented only one-third of the growth level of the 'miracle' years and one-half of the prevailing rate in the European Economic Community countries."[57] After the period of rapid expansion, investments decreased by 2–4 percent annually during the second half of the 1970s. The number of the unemployed jumped from 0.4 million (less than 3 percent) to 2.2 million (more than 17 percent) between 1974 and 1982. Sudden and high inflation in the late 1970s exaggerated the rate of price increases to 37 percent per annum.

In spite of the dramatic economic turnover, Spain did not sink into a peripheral structural crisis. In November 1975, the ailing dictator Franco died, and Spain emerged onto the road of democratic transformation in the late 1970s. A hidden ally of the West during the Cold War years, Spain became a partner of the West and soon a part of it. With significant help from the West, the country began controlling the situation and solving the challenges of the structural crisis. Direct foreign investments played a central role in the recovery. Foreign capital inflow doubled to $1,204 million, and the multinational companies began establishing new modern sectors, which built up

[57] Joseph Harrison, *The Spanish Economy in the Twentieth Century* (London: Croom Helm, 1985), 175.

the country's competitive export capacities. The Suárez government made new steps towards the European Community. By 1978, nearly half of all Spanish exports, and 72 percent of its industrial exports, went to the Community. The number of foreign tourists increased by one-third, but income from tourism more than doubled. The October 1977 *Pactos de la Moncloa* between the government and the left-wing opposition parties led to the introduction of a wage ceiling of 22 percent, which helped cope with inflation. Meanwhile the devaluation of the peseta by 20 percent increased export competitiveness. Due to the *Plan Energético Nacional*, Spain enlarged its nuclear energy capacities.[58]

From several points of view, Portugal's history exhibited a lot of similarity. The recession of 1973–5 probably hit even harder because it coincided with a political revolution and the collapse of Portugal's colonial empire.[59] Transitory political chaos, steeply rising wages, demonstrations, nationalizations, and uncertainty about the future accompanied the aftermath of the left-wing revolution that took place during the oil crisis. Inflation soared, following the price of imported wheat, sugar, and oil, which doubled, trebled, and quadrupled, respectively. Price increases remained roughly 25 percent per annum during the 1970s. The dramatic decline, however, was soon halted. The Western world ran to assist a peaceful transformation and to incorporate Portugal into the Western camp. Between 1975 and 1986, Portugal became a privileged and assisted member of the Western community. As founding member of the British-led EFTA, Portugal became an external member of the European Community in 1973, and it received a separate schedule to eliminate its tariffs before 1985.

Portuguese industrial products entered the Community market without duties, and they represented half of the country's exports. Portugal applied for full membership in 1977, but it had to wait until its economy was consolidated. At the time of application, the country's per capita GDP was about half the Community's level, and 70 percent of its exports consisted of food and raw materials. Enjoying all the advantages of the free European market, Portugal became an equal

---

[58] *Ibid.*

[59] The *retornados*, a huge wave of approximately half a million refugees from the former colonies, led to a population increase of about 8% during 1973–5. In addition, previous emigration to Western Europe, which had reached 120,000 persons annually, also sharply declined. Unemployment, consequently, jumped from 6 to 14%.

member in 1986.[60] Modern structural changes followed. During the
decade following 1988, modern sectors such as electrical engineering,
motor vehicles, and others increased their share of total value added in
manufacturing from 18 to 29 percent, while traditional engineering,
food, tobacco, and metal production declined from 35 to 21 percent.[61]

Ireland, too, was hit hard by the economic crisis that began in
1973.[62] However, the country did not suffer a major decline because
of the positive effects of joining the European Community that very
same year. Massive foreign capital inflow exceeded net national savings
by the early 1980s. Multinational companies entered the country and
played the leading role in creating modern, export-oriented sectors:
by 1980, fifty-five large foreign firms produced almost one-fifth of
the industrial output, but they delivered nearly two-thirds of Irish
industrial exports. The latter, which had earlier accounted for only 6
percent of Irish exports, jumped to 60 percent of the country's total
exports by 1980. The rate of export growth was the second fastest
in the world behind Japan.[63] Irish exports were geographically reoriented: the British market, which had absorbed three-quarters of Irish
exports before, now received only one-third of them. The continental
European Community countries became the most important market
for Ireland. The export performance of Ireland was based on the
marked structural changes in manufacturing. The output of modern
sectors, such as medical equipment and precision and optical instruments, electrical machinery, communication equipment, and chemicals, increased from 30 to 48 percent of total value added between
1988 and 1998. In the same period, the traditional sectors of engineering, food, tobacco, and metal production declined from 49 to 34
percent.[64]

Because of massive foreign investments, multinational participation, and the advantages of the European Common Market, Southern
Europe and Ireland, which were previously part of the relatively backward periphery of Europe, increased their economic development.

---

[60] Rodney Morrison, *Portugal: Revolutionary Change in an Open Economy* (Boston: Auburn
House, 1981).

[61] European Council, *Strategies for Educational Reform: From Concept to Realization* (Strasbourg:
Council of Europe Publishing, 2000), 195.

[62] Retail sales declined by 10% during the 1970s. Foreign trade deficit increased since terms
of trade fell by 26% between 1973 and 1981. Real income, which increased at an average
annual growth rate of 4.4% during the sixties, dropped to 1% between 1973 and 1981.

[63] L. M. Cullen, *An Economic History of Ireland Since 1960* (London: Batsford, 1987), 187–90.

[64] European Council, *Strategies*, 195.

During the 1980s, they regained their vitality and export-led growth. For most of the decade, their exports increased by 8 to 10 percent per annum. While West European exports, in constant prices, more than doubled between 1973 and 1992, Spanish exports jumped by more than three times. Although inflation remained high and consumer prices increased annually by 15 to 20 percent, private consumption and capital formation still grew quickly, industrial growth reached 2 to 3 percent, and the GDP reached 3 to 4 percent per annum.[65]

Integration into the EEC and increased trade with the Community stimulated economic restructuring. Massive foreign investments contributed to narrowing the technological gap, especially because multinational companies used Ireland during the second half of the 1980s as a platform for access to the European single market, which was planned for 1992. Investments in electronics and other high-tech sectors played a determining role in structural modernization and rapid growth. During the 1990s, Ireland had an average of nearly 7 percent annual growth. An impressive process of catching up followed: in 1973, Ireland reached only 59 percent of the average EEC income level; in the early twenty-first century, it surpassed the average by 15 percent.[66] Spain continued to catch up with the Western core and emerged from its former peripheral position: in place of its 1973 per capita GDP of 75 percent of the EEC, it reached 84 percent of the EU level by 2005.[67]

The most outstanding heroes of economic development during the last quarter of the century in Europe were Ireland and Spain, but one should add *Finland* to this list as well. This country was at the same economic level as Ireland, Spain, and Hungary a century ago, but had rapid economic growth after World War II. When the Soviet Union collapsed, Finland's income level reached 88 percent of Western Europe's. In a few years, severe economic crisis curbed Finnish development and required a radical restructuring of the country's export and

---

[65] Irish and Spanish labor productivity, less than two-thirds of the British in 1973, had reached 90% of the British level by 1992.

[66] Economic Commission for Europe, *Economic Survey of Europe 2000 No. 1* (New York and Geneva: United Nations, 2000), 170; OECD, *Factbook*, 2007, 29. Regarding the United States, Ireland enjoyed only 50% of the American income level even in 1990, but by 2005, it had risen to 80% of it. Calculating on purchasing power parity, i.e., adjusting to the difference between price levels, Ireland cut the distance even more and reached 92% of the American income level.

[67] EEC *Economic Survey of Europe 2000*, 166; *World in Figures, 2008*, 28–9. Portugal's level remained far behind, and by 2005, reached 54% of the Union's level.

Table 4.1. Leaders of catching up (GDP per capita 1973–2005)[68]

Year	Ireland	1973=100	Finland	1973=100	Spain	1973=100	euro-zone	1973=100
1973	7,023	100	10,768	100	8,739	100	19,192	100
2005	49,220	700	37,150	345	26,090	299	32,130	167

production structure, which had previously adjusted to the require-ments of the Soviet market, which played the most important role in Finnish exports until 1991.

After the collapse of the Soviet Union, Finland had to deliver to the Western markets and develop competitive new industries. This required a painful transformation, accompanied by a sudden decline in GDP. Between 1989 and 1993, the per capita GDP of the coun-try dropped by 14 percent. During the second half of the decade, however, Finland became one of the technology leaders of Europe in certain high-tech industries, and the country surpassed the Swedish income level by the late 1990s. At the end of the century, accord-ing to the World Economic Forum's Growth Competitiveness and Current Competitiveness index,[69] Finland was number one, ahead of the United States, Canada, Germany, the Netherlands, and Switzer-land. In other words, Finland, because of a gradual improvement of its economy, and a spectacular restructuring in the 1990s, became one of the economic leaders of Europe with a higher than average income level. While the euro-zone increased its per capita GDP since 1973 by 67 percent, Spain trebled its income, Finland increased it by three-and-half times, and Ireland seven times (Table 4.1).

The Expanded Crisis in the East

Like in other peripheral regions, such as Latin America, the crisis of the 1970s–80s was extremely severe in Central and Eastern Europe. The failure to adjust to the technological revolution led to a rapid deterioration in the terms of trade, i.e., the ratio of export to import prices. The Central and East European countries suffered growing

---

[68] Based on Angus Maddison, *Monitoring the World Economy 1820–1992* (Paris: OECD, 1995); and *World in Figures, 2008*.

[69] This index evaluates technological level, macroeconomic parameters, the efficiency of public institutions, and the microeconomic environment.

trade deficits, and countries that were heavily dependent on imported energy suffered a 26 to 32 percent decline in their terms of trade by 1985. In other words, these countries had to boost exports by at least one-quarter, and sometimes by one-third, in exchange for the same amount of imports. One should also not forget that the growing gap between rising import prices and lagging export prices already characterized the entire state socialist period: Hungary, for example, had a terms of trade loss of 50 percent between 1938 and 1989.

Between 1970 and 1989, the net amount of debt in the region increased from $6 billion to $110 billion. The $20 billion debt that Hungary owed was approximately two times greater than the value of the country's hard currency export income, but Poland's $42 billion debt was five times larger. Debt service consumed 40 to 75 percent of the combined hard currency income of these countries. Meanwhile cheap credits disappeared, and interest rates rose to between 14 and 16 percent. New credits, however, were needed to repay the old ones. The credits were mostly consumed to keep the regimes' "achievements" intact, and only a small fraction of them was invested. For example, out of the $20 billion in debt that was incurred, Hungary invested only $4–5 billion.

The crisis grew deeper: Poland, Yugoslavia, and Bulgaria became insolvent and requested a rescheduling of their debt payments. Nicolae Ceauşescu, the "conductor" (leader) of Romania, tried to escape from the country's indebtedness trap by ordering drastic cuts in domestic consumption. That effort ruined the country and led to a bloody revolution.[70]

Growth policy had to be changed, and the economy slowed significantly, from an annual 3.9 percent increase in GDP between 1950 and 1973, to 1.2 percent between 1973 and 1989.[71] Between 1978 and 1983, the Polish GDP declined by more than 10 percent. During the second half of the 1980s, the Romanian and Yugoslav economies stagnated, with 0.7 percent and 0.5 percent growth, respectively. Several Central and Eastern European countries that had fixed prices under state socialism began to lose control over inflation. Hungarian consumer prices increased by 16 and 17 percent in 1988 and

---

[70] Ivan T. Berend, *Central and Eastern Europe 1944–1993: Detour from the Periphery to the Periphery* (Cambridge University Press, 1996), 230–2.

[71] Angus Maddison, *Explaining the Economic Performance of Nations* (Aldershot: Edward Elgar, 1995), 97.

Table 4.2. Comparative GDP growth rates per capita[72]

Region	1950–73	1973–92
Western & Mediterranean Europe	4.8	2.0
Central & Eastern Europe	4.0	−0.8
Soviet Union (& successor states)	3.4	−1.4

1989, respectively. In 1989, the rate of inflation in Poland reached 251 percent. Yugoslavia fell into a period of hyperinflation that reached 1,269 percent annually.[73]

Central and Eastern Europe, as well as the successor states of the Soviet Union, could not follow the Western and Mediterranean trend of technological and structural change, combined with the gradual transformation from an extensive to an intensive growth model. The slow but permanent post-crisis recuperation and growth of Western Europe after the mid-1980s did not happen in the East. The income level of the region's countries declined significantly in the one-and-half decades before 1989, from nearly one-half to slightly more than one-third of Western Europe's.[74]

Needless to say, this one-and-a-half-decade-long economic crisis did not end with the collapse of the regime in 1989. In fact, it became even more serious. The traditional escape routes, which relied on a self-sufficient regional integration system operating with trade-in-kind agreements,[75] were not available any longer. For the first time since World War I, the countries of the region were forced to enter the world market and to compete with advanced industrialized countries that were already in the process of adjusting to the new technological regime. Furthermore, they had also to compete in their own domestic market, which was now open to foreign competition. Accordingly, the peripheral crisis became much deeper during the early 1990s (Table 4.2).

In sharp contrast to their previous rapid growth rates, economic growth in the countries of Central and Eastern Europe during the last

---

[72] Maddison, *Monitoring*, 62.

[73] European Bank for Reconstruction and Development, *Transition Report 2001: Energy in Transition* (London: EBRD, 2001), 61.

[74] Maddison, *Monitoring*, 201.

[75] These kinds of agreements characterized the region in the 1930s under the Hitler-led *Grossraumwirtschaft*, and within the safe and uncompetitive Comecon market of the Soviet Bloc during the state socialist period.

third of the century generally slowed and in most cases was replaced by stagnation and even decline. Although economic growth returned after 1992–3, decline characterized some countries even during the last three years of the 1990s.[76]

Transformation and Decline

Nevertheless, the countries of the region transformed their economic, legal, institutional, and ownership systems during the troubled 1990s. After the failure of state socialism, the marketization and privatization of the economy was the only promising road to follow on the march towards Europe, and in Central and Eastern Europe there was therefore a shift away from planned to market economies. Transformation, however, caused a partially unavoidable "transformational crisis." Self-sufficient economic regimes were non-competitive and technologically backward, and they lacked market motivation and modern managerial systems. The countries also had to reorient their trade from the Soviet Bloc to the free market, and they were unable to sell the same products on the new markets. Decline was unavoidable.

Unfortunately, the economic policy that was pursued during the first part of the transition period was also mistaken in many respects. The sudden jump from a centrally planned to a laissez-faire economy, from an entirely state-owned to an entirely privatized economy, from a system where the state was almighty to a system where the state withdrew from the economy, caused additional shocks. A smoother transition would have been achieved by gradualism. A government-regulated market, instead of a self-regulating one, as well as allowing – at least temporarily – a mixed economy with a small state-owned sector that was restructured and efficient, instead of simply selling state-owned firms at any price, would have allowed for a more natural transition from a planned to a market economy.

This approach, however, was immediately rejected. The international financial institutions and the Western governments required the implementation of the Washington Consensus policy package.[77]

---

[76] This was the case in the Czech Republic (−1.0, −2.2, −0.2), Romania (−6.1, −5.4, −3.2), the Russian Federation (0.9, −4.9, −3.2), Ukraine (−3.0, −1.7, −0.4), and Moldova (1.6, −8.6, −4.4).

[77] The Washington Consensus was a transformation plan originally prepared by the Washington-based international financial institutions and the American government for

"The suggested measures," as interpreted in 2001, "were a natural outgrowth of the neo-liberal policy framework that already held sway in the developed world."[78] The neo-liberal package with all of its economic and political content uniformly determined the policy of the governments of the Central and Eastern European countries, and indeed most of the new political elite enthusiastically accepted and realised it. The countries were forced to throw open the doors to their markets from one day to the next and to liberalize trade and prices. Consequently, entire sectors of their economies collapsed, industrial output sharply declined, and mass unemployment pushed millions into poverty. The unemployment rate reached 12 to 20 percent in the early 1990s, and remained high during the entire decade. Even during the last years of the century, unemployment in Hungary, Poland, and Russia was still 10 to 13 percent. In Macedonia, Bosnia-Herzegovina, and rump Yugoslavia, unemployment reached the tragic proportions of 47, 40, and 27 percent, respectively.

Inflation, which reached hyperinflationary levels in some countries in the early 1990s, remained high even in 1998–9, ranging between 9 and 250 percent in the various countries.[79] Consequently, living standards sharply declined, especially for the more vulnerable layers of society. People in relative poverty, i.e., those with incomes less than 35 to 45 percent of the average wage in those countries, increased dramatically to one-quarter, and even one-half, of the population.[80]

Latin America in 1988–9, and then used unchanged for Central and Eastern Europe as well. The set of policy measures contained ten main elements: fiscal discipline with a deficit not greater than 2% of GDP; public expenditures redirected from politically sensitive areas to fields with high economic returns; tax reform, broadening the tax base, and cutting marginal tax rates; financial liberalization with market-determined interest rates; unified, "competitive" exchange rates; trade liberalization with restrictions eliminated, and low tariffs (of about 10%); elimination of barriers to foreign direct investment; privatization of state enterprises; deregulation to free the economy; and finally, secure property rights. John Williamson, "The Washington Consensus Revisited," in Louis Emmerij (ed.), *Economic and Social Development into the XXI Century* (Washington, DC: Inter-American Development Bank, 1997), 48–61, 60–1.

[78] Ben Fine, Costas Lapavitsas, and Jonathan Pincus (eds.), *Development Policy in the Twenty-first Century: Beyond the Post-Washington Consensus* (London: Routledge, 2001), x.

[79] The inflation rate was 10 and 9% in Hungary and Poland; 50 to 55% in Yugoslavia, Macedonia, and Romania; between 40 to 85% in Russia, and 200 to 250% in Belarus.

[80] UNICEF, *Central and Eastern Europe in Transition: Public Policy and Social Conditions: Crisis in Mortality, Health and Nutrition*, Economies in Transition Studies, Regional Monitoring Report, No. 2 (Florence: UNICEF Regional Office, August 1994), 2. In Bulgaria from 14 to 54% of the population was in relative poverty, in the Czech Republic from 4 to 25%, in Poland from 25 to 44%, and in Romania from 34 to 52% during the early 1990s.

However, a group of at least six Central and Eastern European countries – Albania, the Czech Republic, Hungary, Poland, Slovakia, and Slovenia – basically recovered the ground they lost in the early decline and by 2000 once again reached or approached their 1989 levels of per capita GDP. Bulgaria, Romania, and Croatia only recovered roughly three-quarters of their 1989 GDP levels; the Baltic countries two-thirds of them, while the Commonwealth of Independent States (the former Soviet Union) stood in 1999 at barely more than half of their 1990 levels.[81] The gap between Central and Eastern Europe and the West increased in that single decade from a nearly 1:2 ratio in 1973, and roughly 1:3 in 1989, to an unprecedented disparity of 1:4 in 1999.[82] The entire former Soviet Bloc needed twenty years to reach the 1989 income level. Industrial performance lagged even further behind. Industry only recovered in Hungary and Poland, reaching 1989 levels in 1997–8, while the Czech Republic, Slovakia, and Slovenia had only recovered 75–80 percent of their 1989 levels by 1999.[83] In some of the countries, industrial output was still declining at the end of the 1990s.[84] In a clear sign of a failure to adjust technologically, labor productivity stagnated between 1973 and 1992, reaching less than one-third of Western Europe's level. In Russia, labor productivity even declined by 14 percent and stood at roughly one-fifth of the Western level.

After the disastrous collapse, Russia went into a kind of free fall during the decade of the Yeltsin presidency. The proudly announced shock treatment led to 2,000 percent inflation in 1992 that decreased to 1,000 percent by 1993. Budget deficits reached 20 percent, and the GDP declined by 50 percent. Privatization, which was corrupt everywhere, amounted in Russia to the open robbery of the state by the elite of the political and managerial *nomenklatura*. Privatized firms were mostly bought by insiders or corrupt-criminal robber barons, the "oligarchs" who amassed wealth in the billions in a matter of days. The National Bank continued to extend credits to bankrupt companies, and modern banking did not emerge at all. Appropriate legislation to develop the requisite legal environment for a market economy was mostly missing, and political connections determined economic activities.

---

[81] European Bank for Reconstruction and Development, *Transition Report Update* (London: EBRD, 1999), 6.; United Nations, *Economic Survey of Europe*, 2000, 225.

[82] United Nations, *Economic Survey of Europe*, 2000, 175.

[83] United Nations, *Economic Survey of Europe* (New York: UN, 1998), 146–8.

[84] United Nations, *Economic Survey of Europe*, 2000, 70. The decline in Moldova was 15–20%, in Bulgaria 13–14%, in Romania 17 and 9% in 1998 and 1999 respectively.

Transformation and Recuperation – with Huge Foreign Investments

Technological and structural adjustments were the central elements of the transformation, the end and the essence of it. However, only a few countries began making those adjustments, and very little or nothing was done in two-thirds of the region's economies until the early twenty-first century. Reforms and systemic change have no doubt already triggered structural adjustments. Basic private initiative, business-like behavior, and an entrepreneurial attitude have been revitalized in part of those societies, and domestic capital accumulation has increased in some of the countries. This latter factor has become the prime mover of economic growth, and a major factor in economic restructuring, throughout the region.

The most spectacular result of privatization and domestic accumulation has been the foundation of millions of new small enterprises. Deregulation eliminated all communist restrictions on private business, and small, mostly family businesses began to emerge in the very first years. Additionally, the so-called "small privatization" sold off the former state-owned retail chains, gas stations, repair shop networks, and restaurants that previously belonged to nationwide, centralized state-owned companies. They were reorganized, and the units were sold piecemeal at auction. These investments generated the most important structural change to date: the rise of the previously neglected and undeveloped service sectors in Central and Eastern Europe.

"Big privatization," i.e., the sale of large enterprises such as steel mills, chemical factories, and huge engineering companies, turned out to be extremely difficult. Most of the companies on sale were bankrupt and technologically obsolete. The population did not have enough money to buy them. Practically, the only way to sell them was to attract foreign investors who were ready to reorganize and modernize them. In some countries, mostly the former Yugoslav republics where workers' self-management governed the economic units, insider privatization became dominant. The community of employees became owners but were unable to invest.

In Romania, the government looked for a "third way" and resisted privatizing the so-called strategic sectors, i.e., the energy and investment good industries such as iron and steel, and engineering, which represented more than half the economy. Russia likewise designated

1,000 giant companies as "strategic enterprises," keeping them in state ownership. In the early 2000s, some companies that had been privatized were re-nationalized again, especially in the key oil sector. Slovenia decided to reorganize and modernize state-owned factories before selling them and only very partial privatization occurred until 2000. On the other hand, Czechoslovakia improvised a "voucher privatization" by distributing shares of reorganized joint-stock state-owned companies among the adult population. It was celebrated in the West as overnight privatization, but it turned out to be a failure. People did not want to keep a few shares of industrial firms, but rather dreamed about remodeling their kitchen or buying a car, and so they sold their shares, which ended up being bought by banks, which were actually state-owned institutions. Thus, the circle was closed, and real privatization had to be undertaken a few years later.

Privatization was a long process, and, in most cases, only 70 to 80 percent of the economy became privately owned by the end of the century. Agricultural land was re-privatized by de-collectivization. It was an extremely painful process involving a tremendous decline in output, sometimes by 50 percent. Many genuine landowners were elderly or urban inhabitants and they did not return to the land. Small machinery was missing, and the huge machine parks of the former collective farms became useless. Horse-driven plows and primitive cultivation methods returned. An overambitious liberalization, which eliminated protective tariffs and subsidies, crippled the new peasant farms. In most cases, it took one-and-half decades for agriculture to return to its 1989 level.

In most cases, the key elements of adjustment – the adoption of revolutionary new communication technologies, establishing high- or at least medium-high-tech industries, and the building up of a competitive, highly productive export sector – have been achieved only very partially. This process became possible only through a massive influx of foreign capital and investments. The Western countries pledged only limited financial aid from the very beginning of the transformation. Most of the countries of the region received between $300 and $600 million, with only two or three countries receiving more than $1–1.5 billion in aid per year. On a per capita basis, this aid did not surpass $40 to $100, except in Bosnia, Serbia, Macedonia, and Albania, where it reached between $120 and $175.[85]

---

[85] The Economist, *World in Figures, 2007* (London: Profile Books, 2007), 44–5.

In November 1989, the same month the Berlin Wall collapsed, the European Community's Commission hosted a meeting of representatives from twenty-four advanced industrial nations and pledged $6.5 billion in economic aid for the two countries that destroyed state socialism first: Poland and Hungary. Four days later, President Bush signed a bill authorizing nearly $1 billion in aid for Poland and Hungary. The rush to support transformation culminated in a pledge by the twenty-four countries to disburse $27 billion between 1989 and 1991 to assist economic stabilization and restructuring in Poland, Hungary, and Czechoslovakia. Moreover, they pledged $62.5 billion over a five-year period for the transformation of the entire Central and Eastern European region.[86] In the summer of 1991, the European Commission revealed that only 11 percent of the amount committed was actually sent.[87]

Global foreign direct investment (FDI) dramatically increased around the turn of the century: from $60 billion in 1985 to $800 billion by 2000. A small segment of the total amount of international private investment was channeled into Central and Eastern Europe. Capital inflow took several forms. By far the most important was FDI, which represented 55 percent of the total capital inflow during the transformation period. The second most important form that investment took was portfolio inflows (through bonds and equity investment in the region's stock markets) and international securities issuances. The international bank lending that started in the mid-1990s, mostly to private companies, and reached an average of $5 to $15 billion annually, also played an important role.[88] Between 1993 and 2002, 26 percent of capital inflow took the form of loans, and 19 percent came in the form of portfolio investments.[89]

FDI was not only the largest, but also the most important form of capital inflow. It had a decisive impact on the transfer of advanced

[86] G-24, *Coordinated Economic Assistance* (Brussels, June 13, 1991); *Scoreboard of Assistance Commitments to the CEEC 1990–1994* (Brussels, February 8, 1995).

[87] Krzysztof J. Ners and Ingrid Buxell, *Assistance to Transition Survey 1995* (Warsaw: PECAT, 1995), 34. In reality, only $11 billion was disbursed to six countries of the region during the first four years of transformation. Counting Polish debt reduction, the disbursed amount totaled $19.1 billion.

[88] European Bank for Reconstruction and Development, *Transition Report 2000: Employment, Skills and Transition* (London: EBRD, 2000), 84–6.

[89] Ivan Teodorović, Željko Lovrinčević, Davor Mikulić, Mustafa Nušinović, and Stjepan Zdunić (eds.), *The Croatian Economic Development: Transition Towards the Market Economy* (Zagreb: Institute of Economics, 2005), 84, 86.

technology and management, and consequently on the restructuring of the economy, export growth, and increases in productivity. A few thousand multinational companies, which formed virtual international business empires, monopolized cutting-edge technology. Several of them took over a significant part of the region's economy. During the first one-and-a-half decades of transformation, Central Europe and the Baltic countries received roughly $162 billion in foreign direct investment, and the Balkans received another $42 billion. On a per capita basis, FDI surpassed $2,300 and $830 in the two above-mentioned regions, respectively. In the middle of the first decade of the twenty-first century, FDI inflows reached an average of 2.6 and 4.8 percent of GDP in Central Europe and the Baltic countries, respectively.[90]

Behind these average amounts of investment, however, lay huge disparities. The main winners were the Czech Republic, Hungary, and Poland. These three countries received more than $135 billion of the total $204 billion – or $258 billion, counting the successor states of the former Soviet Union – investment in the entire region. From 1997 on, reinvestments of profits represented one-quarter of FDI, but in Hungary this share reached half of the total FDI between 1998 and 2000, and then two-thirds between 2001 and 2005.[91]

Capital inflow in this form remained substantial in the four leading countries. The combined capital stock of FDI in the Czech Republic, Slovenia, Hungary, and Poland increased from less than $82 billion, to more than $222 billion, between 2000 and 2005.[92] For the first time in the transformation period, the increase in FDI was also high in the Balkans during these years: between 2000 and 2005, capital stock rose in value from $15,128 million to $56,562 million, i.e., by 374 percent, compared to a 270 percent increase in Central Europe.[93] Foreign capital inflow to Russia and the other successor states of the Soviet Union was not significant compared to Central and Eastern Europe, totaling only $54 billion, most of which went into raw material extraction. The real difference, however, was not the

---

[90] It pays to note that capital inflow to Central and Eastern Europe significantly surpassed FDI inflow to the three Mediterranean countries – Spain, Portugal, and Greece – in the decade after their acceptance by the European Union, when the inflow reached only about 1 to 3% of their GDP.

[91] *Report of the Ministry of Economy and Transportation* (Budapest: Ministry of Economy, July 12, 2006); The Economist, *World in Figures, 2007,* 64; European Bank for Reconstruction and Development, *Transition Report Update 2005* (London: EBRD, 2005), 19.

[92] UNCTAD, *World Investment Report* (New York: United Nations, 2006).

[93] *Ibid.*

amount of capital inflow, but the fact that a tremendous amount of illegal capital flight from Russia accompanied the entire transformation period.

Political and macroeconomic instability and uncertainty, a lack of appropriate control, and an extremely high level of corruption made it possible to smuggle out a huge part of export income by under-invoicing export earning, making fake advance import payments, and through illegal bank transfers. Exact measurement of illegal transactions is always difficult, and there are many opportunities for making mistakes when attempting to do so, but there are also well-established methods for evaluating capital flight. The various available research results from government, local, and foreign studies all basically agree that $15–20 billion annually of Russian and foreign funds, including IMF loans, landed in private accounts established by Russians in several foreign countries. During the decades of transformation, about $150–300 billion left the country illegally.[94] The most elegant and expensive resorts of the world were filled by Russian *nouveau riche*, who also sent their children to the Swiss boarding schools, which had earlier been preferred by the British upper classes, for exorbitant prices. The minister of finance, Alexei Kudrin, proudly stated in 2008: "This would have been a significant event in the past, but this time $20 billion left the country in two months and the country did not even feel it."[95] The criminalization of the Russian economy in the post-communist transformation left the country's economy in tragically bad shape until the turn of the century, and led to the rise of a small group of extremely rich people, while a large layer of society declined into deep poverty.

Because of excessive foreign investments in Central Europe, the role of foreign companies in industry became dominant. Foreign companies employed 47 percent of the workforce in Hungary, and they were responsible for 82 percent of investment, 73 percent of sales, and 89 percent of industrial exports. In the Czech Republic, 27 percent of employment, 53 percent of investment, 42 percent of sales, and 61 percent of exports were attributable to foreign companies at the

[94] Prakash Loungani and Paolo Mauro, "Capital Flight from Russia," *The World Economy*, 24, 5 (2001), 689–706, www.imf.org/external/pubs/ft/seminar/2000/invest/pdf/loung.pdf; A. Abalkin and J. Whalley, "The Problem of Capital Flight from Russia," *The World Economy*, 22, 3 (1999), 421–44.

[95] Ambrose Evans-Pritchard, "Capital Flight Puts Russia on the Ropes," *Telegraph*, April 2, 2008, www.telegraph.co.uk/ . . . Capital-flight-puts-Russia-on-the-ropes.html

end of the century.[96] From the early twenty-first century, European investors began targeting the Balkans, especially the new candidate and then member countries of the European Union, Romania and Bulgaria.[97]

Key investments were made in the most undeveloped infrastructural sphere, especially telecommunications, which have served as the basis for any kind of technological progress to date. Some of the world's telecom leaders began investing and modernizing in a few rapidly changing countries. Direct investments revolutionized Hungarian telecommunications. In 1990, the Hungarian telecommunication system was 45th out of 56 analyzed countries; by the end of the decade, it rose to the top third. The rankings of Russia (43rd to 52nd), Bulgaria (28th to 48th), and Ukraine (50th to 53rd) all declined.

Foreign investors also began creating modern industrial branches and competitive export sectors in the Czech Republic, Estonia, Poland, and Slovenia. In Hungary before the mid-1990s, the proportion of industrial investments was already nearly 80 percent.[98] Consequently, the high- and relatively high-tech branches of industry have gained ground in those countries. During the 1990s, the share of electrical, optical, and transportation equipment in total industrial output increased from nearly 13 percent to more than 25 percent in Hungary, and from 10 percent to more than 22 percent in Slovakia. By creating internationally competitive industrial sectors, multinational companies have started to play an important role in some of the countries of the region. In Hungary – similarly to Ireland – foreign affiliates produce more than two-thirds of industrial output, and they finance roughly 70 percent of the research and development expenditures.[99] The 2008–9 international crisis, however, hit the transforming countries strongly. The boom stopped, and in some of the countries was followed by decline.

[96] "Transition Countries on the Eve of EU Enlargement," *Revue Elargissement*, 43 (April 12, 2003). See ec.europe.eu/enlargement/archives/press . . . /archives_en.htm. In Poland these shares were 29, 63, 49, and 59%, respectively.

[97] Matteo Ferrazzi and Alessia Muzio, "Europe's New Factory Comes Up in the East," *East Europe and Asia* (April 2008), www.eastonline.it/index.php Therefore, by 2008, 43% of total turnover of the economy was made by foreign companies, and they were responsible for 58 and 72% of the imports and exports of Romania, respectively.

[98] Miklós Szanyi, "Experiences with Foreign Direct Investment in Eastern Europe," *Eastern European Economics*, 36, 3 (May–June 1998), 24–48, 35.

[99] OECD, *Measuring Globalization: The Role of Multinationals in OECD Economies* (Paris: OECD, 1999).

The successor states of the Soviet Union, as well as most of the Balkan countries, exhibit very little progress in restructuring. Foreign direct investment has been minimal in this area until the early twenty-first century, and has mostly gone into the extraction of oil, gas, and raw materials. A sort of dual economy has emerged. Only the extractive branches belong to the dynamic export sectors, and they generate one-quarter of the GDP in Russia, while the processing industries produce non-competitive products for the domestic market. As the world's number one total exporter of oil and gas, Russia profited tremendously from the oil price explosion in the early twenty-first century. Economic growth has increased since 1999, and it reached 7 to 8 percent annually after 2002. During the eight years of Vladimir Putin's presidency, Russia's GDP increased by six times, and Russia rose from the twenty-second to the tenth largest economy in the world. However, even in 2005, 40 percent of Russia's GDP was produced by oil, gas, and related industries. The export sector of the country is also based on oil, which accounts for 64 percent of the value of exports, as well as minerals and timber. Together they constitute 80 percent of the country's exports.

High prosperity from oil and raw material exports doubled real income, decreased unemployment from 10 to 6 percent between 2000 and 2006, and strengthened the middle class. Industrial development gained a new impetus to produce for the domestic market, though the generally weak economy is unable to digest the enormous oil income. In the most characteristic sign of this development, a growing part of the increased domestic consumption is covered by imports instead of domestic production. However, Russia's growth rates of 7 to 8 percent annually became one of the highest in the region.

Though it was a powerhouse of mathematics, science, and technology before the collapse, and a country that produced space shuttles and supersonic jets, Russia nevertheless lost its strength and did not gain ground in high-tech sectors. Steven Perlstein of the *Washington Post* summed up the causes in his report: "The technology know-how was trapped in bloated, inefficient state companies and bureaucracies... [They are] slow in adopting the latest information technology... And while Russia excels at the theoretical side of science... they are less skilled... [at] applying their scientific knowledge to practical business application."[100]

---

[100] Steven Perlstein, "As Russia Advances, High Tech Gets Left Behind," *Washington Post*, July 11, 2007.

Several other obstacles blocked the road to structural modernization. One of them was the lack of reliable copyright and patent protection. In a country ruled by persons, and not by law, even existing
laws cannot give protection, because corrupt judges and state connections have much bigger impacts on the course of legal proceedings.
The journalist quoted above speaks about the "curse" of oil because
"as long as huge rewards can be earned buying and selling natural
resource assets, the most skilled and ambitious Russians are probably
not going to opt for the hard work."[101]

The future of structural modernization and the rise of high-tech
industries are in the hands of the government in authoritarian, state-
run Russia. Small and middle-sized private companies are playing a
limited role, producing only 15 percent of the country's GDP, and
the command position of the economy remains in the hands of the
state. Foreign investments also focused on the raw material sector,
and foreign direct investment channeled at other sectors thus declined
between 1999 and 2007 from less than 2 percent to less than 1 percent.
Economic success is thus dependent on political connections and state
decisions. Sergei Ivanov, the deputy prime minister, stated in the fall
of 2007 that, over the next ten years, the government is going to
invest $60 billion from oil income into nuclear technology, aerospace,
electronics, and nanotechnology.[102] Russia's share in the worldwide
high-tech sector stands at a nearly non-existent 0.13 percent, but
they want to increase it to 10 percent. The 2008 financial crisis and
steeply declining oil prices halted the Putin boom and endangered
or postponed the possibility of entering a second and higher stage of
transformation in Russia.

In the Production and Supply Network of the West

The European Union guided and assisted the transformation of
Central Europe and, increasingly, the Balkans, and it integrated the
region into its supply and production networks. This offered special
advantages for the countries of the European Union. The Asian and
North American centers of the globalized world economy enjoyed
organic access to a large and cheap labor force and industrial capacities

---

[101] *Ibid.*
[102] Lybov Pronina, "Russia, a High-Tech Laggard, Aims to Change That," *International Herald Tribune*, November 30, 2007.

Figure 22. The Audi factory in Győr, Hungary, a subsidiary of the Volkswagen empire in Central and Eastern Europe.

in their immediate neighborhood: the Latin American "backyard" of the United States, and the populous Asian countries surrounding Japan. The European center lacked this possibility before 1989. Transformation in Eastern Europe opened the window of opportunity for a regional network in a nearby geographical area, in many cases within a distance of 150–400 kilometers. The main investors in Central and Eastern Europe were the member countries of the European Union: in the case of Hungary, they were responsible for an 80 percent share of foreign investments in the country, while the United States had only a 5 percent share (Figure 22).[103]

German, Austrian, and other West European banks played the leading role in Central and Eastern European banking. In 1990, foreign banks had a minimal share of the region's banking sector – all of 10 percent in three countries. By 2004, however, 80 to 97 percent of the total assets of local banking was in the hands of foreign banks in several countries of the region. The Central and Eastern European region absorbed 24 percent of total international banking investments. Only Latin America had a bigger share (58 percent), while Asia received only 16 percent of it.[104]

---

[103] *Report of the Ministry of Economy and Transportation*, 2006, 6–7.

[104] András Bethlendi, "Foreign Direct Investment in the Banking Sector," *Development and Finance*, 1 (2007), 61–2. The countries with the highest percentage of foreign-owned banking were Bulgaria (80%), Hungary (83%), Czech Republic (96%), Slovakia (96%),

The decisive role of foreign banking seemed to be a great advantage in countries with backward banking systems and a lack of sufficient capital resources. However, the severe international banking crisis in the fall of 2008 radically changed this situation. *The Economist* concluded in October 2008: "The foreign banks are already reining back lending, refusing to issue mortgages . . . The danger is that they may go much further, cutting off new lending or refusing to roll over outstanding loans, even to solid borrowers. That could send bankruptcies and unemployment rocketing."[105]

One of the most important penetrations characterized the *telecommunications* market. The American–German Ameritech–Deutsche Bundespost Telekom consortium made one of the first and biggest investments in the area. At the end of 1993, they bought more than 30 percent of Matáv, the Hungarian state telephone company. In 1995, their share increased to more than 67 percent. Similar investment was channeled into the telecommunications industry in the entire region. In June 1995, five leading telecom companies participated in bidding to buy 27 percent of the Czech telecommunications monopoly, with the possibility to increase this share to 34 percent. The $1 billion deal became one of the biggest transactions in the region.[106] The Baltic countries privatized their telecom systems with leading participation from the merged Swedish and Finnish Nordic Company that controls 49 percent of both the Estonian and Latvian markets, and 60 percent of the Lithuanian market.[107]

The major European retail chains, including the Belgian Delhaize, the German Metro, the British Tesco, and the French Carrefour – indeed, nine of the world's top fifteen retail giants – launched shopping mall and supermarket construction in the Czech Republic. They built nearly 1,000 hypermarkets and cornered 55 percent of retail sales in the country by 2002.[108] In 1992, the multinational PepsiCo announced a $1 billion investment in Central and Eastern Europe

---

and Estonia (97%). The only exception was Slovenia, with a foreign share in the country's banking of only 17%.

[105] "Who is Next?" *The Economist*, October 25–31, 2008, 34.

[106] *Wall Street Journal*, November 7, 1995. Poland sold a huge part of the Polish telecommunications systems to Ameritech-France Telecom; 35% of the Croatian and 51% of the Slovak telecom system were sold to Deutsche Telekom. In 1998, Ameritech Corporation announced its investment campaign of $1–3 billion in Central and Eastern Europe in 1999–2000.

[107] Ian Jeffries, *The Countries of the Former Soviet Union at the Turn of the Twenty-first Century* (London: Routledge, 2004), 171, 211, 246.

[108] Economist Intelligence Unit, *Country Reports* (London: The Economist, 2005), 48.

over the next three years.[109] Philip Morris monopolized 75 percent of the Czech market, and 62 percent of the combined Czech and Slovak markets. The Norwegian Statoil AS opened eighty-five service stations in the Baltic states and other countries. The Swedish IKEA opened seven superstores, and McDonald's established a dense network throughout the region. Trading companies, though market seeking, sometimes also contracted with local companies or established production factories to secure supplies for their shops on the spot. McDonald's has domestic beef suppliers, and IKEA founded a dozen factories in Central and Eastern Europe and the former Soviet Bloc.[110]

Labor seeking investments, which sought to exploit the huge wage differential, primarily in labor-intensive production branches, played a more important role. In the Czech Republic, roughly 70 percent of foreign investment targeted labor-intensive sectors in the first years. Such investment involved contracting and sub-contracting certain phases of production, frequently in the assembly phase. At the beginning of the transformation, Central European wages – counting at exchange rate parity – reached only 7 percent of the Union's level, reaching 15 percent only after more than a decade.[111] At purchasing power parity, however, Central European wages rose to 30 to 35 percent of the EU level.[112] As Miklós Losoncz writes: "The difference between exchange rate parity and purchasing power parity is an important source of the increase of competitiveness... Because of this difference, employers including companies with foreign participation pay employees wages and salaries at exchange rate parity, whereas they get access to goods and services at a higher value at purchasing power parity."[113] By 2008, wage levels doubled on average in most of the Central and Eastern European countries, and they increased three

---

[109] Janet Guyon and Michael J. McCarthy, "Marketing: Coke Wins Early Skirmishes in its Drive to Take Over Eastern Europe from Pepsi," *Wall Street Journal*, June 1, 1992.

[110] Daniel Michaels, "Nordic Interest in Baltic Rim Nations Speeds Ex-Communist States' EU Entry," *Wall Street Journal*, November 7, 1995.

[111] The 2001 average Czech-Polish-Hungarian-Slovak-Slovene monthly wage of €533 was less than one-quarter of the Austrian (€2,205), French (€2,127), German (€2,674), and Danish (€3,047) wages. Romanian and Bulgarian wages were much lower, €136 and €100, respectively.

[112] At purchasing power parity, the Slovene wages were nearly 60% of the Austrian level; Polish wages represented 54%, while the Slovak wages stood at about one-quarter of that.

[113] Miklós Losoncz, *Hungary's Competitiveness in an International Comparison and its Driving Forces* (Budapest: Economic Research Co., 2003), 21.

times in Romania, Serbia, Ukraine, and Russia. Globalization has a huge impact on price and wage leveling, which became a widespread international phenomenon.[114]

It pays to note that wage level differences varied in different branches of industry: while Hungary's average purchasing power parity wage level, i.e., its wage level adjusted to domestic prices, reached 38 percent of the Austrian level in the manufacture of transport equipment, wages were only 19 and 16 percent of Austrian wage levels in the electrical and optical equipment industries.[115] These decreases in the wage gap will continue for decades. Even in 2004, an autoworker in Slovakia got $6 per hour, compared with more than $40 for a similar worker in the German Volkswagen factory. In the Western countries, the average combined wages and benefits for a production worker reached $25–30 per hour in 2005. Reaching that level may take decades in the transforming countries.

Outward processing trade was mostly concentrated on low-value-added activities at the beginning of the transformation in the entire region. Investments involved either contracting or sub-contracting labor-intensive works in textiles, leather, wood, or other so-called light industries. In Poland, clothing and furniture represented less than 7 percent of exports in 1989, but, because of sub-contracting, it increased to 21 percent by 1995. In Hungary, the share of these branches in exports increased from 11 to 18 percent during the first half of the 1990s, and in Czechoslovakia from 6 to 15 percent.

Every second piece of furniture sold in Germany in the mid-1990s was produced by German-owned factories in Poland. The German clothing industry sought to cut production costs by outward processing trade: 60 percent of its output originated from outside the country in 1995. A large share of the capacity of the Central and Eastern European clothing industry, 70 and 50 percent in Romania and Hungary, respectively, worked for Western companies. Between 1988 and 1996, outward processing exports from the East to the European Union increased by 24 percent annually. At the beginning, two-thirds of outward processing exports was clothing, but footwear and furniture

---

[114] *New York Times*, June 18, 2008. China, the most popular target of investors, experienced a nearly 25% annual wage increase in several industries between 2005 and 2007, and investors looked to Vietnam where factory workers earn $50 in a week. Consequently, FDI increased in Vietnam by eight-fold during 2005 to 2007.

[115] Losoncz, *Hungary's Competitiveness*, 14; Tibor Palánkai, *Economics of Enlarging European Union* (Budapest, Akadémiai Kiadó, 2004), 284.

also represented low-skilled, labor-intensive sectors.[116] Romania also
became part of the production networks of the German, French, and
Italian clothing and leather-goods industries.[117]

Low wage levels in the Central and Eastern European countries
were combined with a relatively well-trained and educated workforce. Foreign investors, especially in medium-tech sectors such as the
car industry, prefer this combination. They tend to invest in countries where wages are somewhat higher but the workforce is better
qualified. Consequently, from the later 1990s, Western multinationals turned to more sophisticated industries to establish *complementary
specialization*. Next to China, the world's fastest growing auto-making
center emerged in the Czech Republic, Slovakia, Poland, Hungary,
and Romania. One of the largest investments in the region was the
privatization of the Czech Skoda Company by Volkswagen. As a first
step in 1991, Volkswagen bought 31 percent of the shares. By the early
2000s, Skoda sold 500,000 cars a year. Volkswagen's Bratislava factory
produces 300,000 cars a year and became the most profitable plant of
the company. VW produces its new "Touareg" SUV and Polo small
hatchback, and bodies for its Porsche Cayenne SUV, in this factory.
On a per capita basis, Slovakia became the world's number one car
producer with 800,000 cars per year by 2006.[118] Because of labor cost
differences the company saves $1.8 billion annually in personnel costs.

Since 1995, the leading car-making multinationals invested $24
billion in the region. In 2006, the Czech and Slovak republics, instead
of their 170,000 unit production in 1990, produced 2 million cars. In
2010, these companies are planning to produce 3.8 million cars in the
region, 20 percent of the West European output, mostly for Western
markets. All the leading companies are involved.

In 2000, the ten leading multinationals held an 82 percent share in
Central and Eastern European car production, led by Volkswagen and
Fiat with 22 and 10 percent, respectively. These expanded automotive

---

[116] Constanze Kurz and Volker Wittke, "Using Industrial Capacities as a Way of Integrating
Central and Eastern European Economies," in John Zysman and Andrew Schwartz (eds.),
Enlarging Europe: The Industrial Foundation of a New Political Reality (Berkeley: University of
California Press, 1998), 80; Barry Eichengreen and Richard Kohl, "The External Sector,
the State, and Development in Eastern Europe," in Zysman and Schwartz (eds.), *Enlarging
Europe*, 169–201, 178.

[117] Gábor Hunya, "Restructuring Through FDI in Romanian Manufacturing," *Economic Systems*, 26, 4 (2002), 387–94.

[118] *Automotive News Europe*, 9, 10, 2004, www.highbeam.com/Automotive+News+Europe/
publications.aspx?

industries are playing a leading role in the economic transformation of these countries. The foreign-owned car industry produces 20 percent of the industrial output of the Czech Republic, and Volkswagen is the largest exporter in Slovakia, while its Hungarian engine plant's deliveries represent 7 percent of total Hungarian exports. The Western car industry's drive towards the East is continuing: in the summer of 2008, Daimler AG signed an agreement to establish its first factory of 2,500 workers in the region, in the beautiful Jugendstyl city of Kecskemét, Hungary, to produce the next generation of the compact Mercedes A and B class cars beginning in 2012.[119] The future of the car industry, however, became questionable at the end of 2008. General Motors' factory in Poland that increased sales in 2008 by 10 and 30 percent in Poland and Russia, had a dramatic 57 percent drop in sales in the Baltic countries in the last months of the year. The car industry stopped expanding in the last years of the decade.

The auto supply industry is also shifting towards the East. Volkswagen built a 31-hectare supplier park within 5 kilometers of its Poznań factory in Poland and attracted sixteen international suppliers. One of the leading French supplier companies, Faurecia, built seven plants in Poland.[120] The VW-Skoda company became an outstanding practitioner of domestic participation: in 2003, it bought 70 percent of components and 60 percent of materials from Czech-located producers.[121] Central Europe offers the densest supply network for car factories in Europe.[122]

The development of other modern *high-tech or medium- to high-tech industries* also gained momentum. High-tech sectors, including pharmaceuticals, medical chemicals, computers, TV, communications equipment, medical precision and optical instruments, and aircraft, and high-tech services, especially in telecommunications and research and development, were either missing or technologically backward in state socialist countries. The same can be said about the medium- to high-tech industries, including motor vehicles, locomotives, electrical machinery and equipment, and ship and transport equipment.

---

[119] Investment and Trade Development Agency, Hungary, *Newsletter*, June 25, 2008.

[120] *Automotive News Europe*, 5, 17, 2004.

[121] Michael Steiner, "Restructuring Industrial Areas: Lessons in Support of Regional Convergence in an Enlarging Europe," in Gertrude Tumpel-Gugerell and Peter Mooslechner (eds.), *Economic Convergence and Divergence in Europe* (Cheltenham: Edward Elgar, 2003), 86–107, 93.

[122] "Industry Forecast: The Driving Force," *Business Eastern Europe*, 32, 5 (2003), 6.

After the regime change, important foreign multinational companies invested to create competitive export sectors in some of the countries of the region, mostly in Hungary, the Czech Republic, and Estonia. This phenomenon resembled the Asian development trend, in which Japan outsourced labor-intensive production to Thailand and Malaysia, and high-value-added sectors to Singapore and later China. The development is also reminiscent of the Irish economic restructuring by multinational investments during the 1970s and 1990s. This trend continues.[123]

The spin-off effect of FDI is crucially important for the rise of a modern economy in the transforming countries. In the middle of the first decade of the twenty-first century, during the first years of their Central and Eastern European host countries' EU membership, foreign companies supplied themselves mostly from their other European factories, and much less from domestic companies in those host countries. Foreign owners shipped more than one-third of parts and materials for their Polish and Slovakian subsidiaries from their factories in other countries. This share was much lower in Hungary, only 18 percent. The share of imported supplies for multinational companies reached nearly 70 percent in Slovakia, 58 percent in Slovenia, and 50 percent in Hungary. The role of domestic suppliers is relatively small: in five countries of the region only 34 percent of supplies is produced by domestic companies.

Foreign direct investments generated rapid growth in Central and Eastern Europe, but the integration of local firms into the supply chain remained relatively undeveloped. Only Hungary and the Czech Republic made better progress in this respect among the new EU member countries. As happens worldwide, the less-developed transforming countries are home to the bottom of the product range, and a great number of unskilled or low-skilled laborers are employed in their high-tech sectors. Nevertheless, in certain cases, the whole value chain and even research and development (R&D) capacities are planted in the newly integrated countries. In the first one-and-a-half decades of transformation, however, the spin-off effect from foreign investment was limited, and the role of domestic research and development even

---

[123] Ferrazzi and Muzio, "Europe's New Factory," 48. In 2008, Japanese investors established the most modern factory in Poland to produce, in three years, 80% of the new generation of TV sets for the European markets. Poland also produces 15% of the total number of European air-conditioners, washing machines, and kitchen ovens.

more so. In Central and Eastern Europe, economic growth was not linked to domestic R&D and technology effects. Moreover, expenditures in that area decreased and reached only 0.5 to 1.5 percent of GDP in 2003.

The first chapter of the transformation and adjustment to the market economy, and of integration into the European production network, is thus closed or closing throughout the region. With the assistance of the European Union, the accomplishment is significant, although the transforming countries exhibit varying degrees of success. Furthermore, even the most successful countries of the region are too dependent on foreign banks and multinationals, and they suffer setbacks from time to time. The second chapter of transformation – with further radical social and behavioral changes, as well as the emergence of a domestically based, innovation-driven competitive economy which approaches the West European income level – remains far away even in those countries that have good prospects to achieve it. In others, it may not be achieved at all in the near future. The Western rim of the region has a better opportunity for integration, while two-thirds of the region is lagging far behind in economic modernization. Nevertheless, the consequences of the 2008 international financial crisis have been to slow down significantly and even stop economic development and modernization.

The International Financial Crisis of 2008 – the End of the Neo-liberal Regime?

In the same way as deregulation emerged in and spread from the United States, so did the collapse of the financial market. The downfall began in the housing market and mortgage business, but it extended rapidly to investment banks and other areas of the financial sector.[124] The "bright new financial system failed the test of the marketplace," as Paul Volcker, the former chairman of the United States Federal Reserve, stated. In the globalized world economy, the crisis spread

[124] In Robert Brenner's interpretation, the crisis is the culmination of a long slowing down period. Consecutive bubbles fueled the world's largest market in the United States. The stock exchange and high-tech equity bubbles in the 1990s were followed by the real estate and securitized debt-purchasing bubbles in the first decade of the twenty-first century. All of these bubbles burst and ignited a worldwide deep depression. See Robert Brenner, *The Boom and the Bubble: The US in the World Economy* (London: Verso, 2002).

like wildfire and burned all of Europe. The incredibly inflated credit bubbles suddenly burst, first in mortgages then all the others, and creditors lost a huge part of their investments, among them, West European creditors, most of all Italian, Swedish, and Austrian banks, to Eastern Europe. The scale of the losses is illustrated by the fact that Swedish banks issued loans to the Baltic countries equal to 20 percent of the country's GDP, and Austria's loans to the transforming countries were equal to 70 percent of its GDP. The Eastern European loans from several West European banks became the "equivalent of what subprime mortgages were to American banks."[125] Financial panic exaggerated the domino effect. According to reports in March 2009, worldwide losses are about $50 trillion. Banks reported huge credit-related losses, and various investment banks and hedge funds collapsed. European and American banks will shed about $10 trillion, or 15 percent of their assets. The losses are increasing by days and weeks. For the first time since World War II, according to the forecast of the World Bank, the global economy would decline in 2009, and the euro-zone economy, according to the European Central Bank, would shrink between 2.2 and 3.3 percent in the year. Other estimations spoke of about 2.4 percent decline in the euro-zone, 3.1 percent in Britain, 3.2 percent in Germany, 2.7 percent in Italy, and 2.5 percent in Spain.[126]

Iceland, which emerged as one of the richest countries during the last few decades, based on international banking, collapsed spectacularly. The country's leading banks went bankrupt, and the only way to save them was nationalization. Britain froze Iceland's assets to force repayment. The Geir Haarde government collapsed. The country was saved by a huge, IMF organized rescue package of altogether $10 billion.

The appetite for risk, the prime mover of financial prosperity, disappeared. Credits stopped. Hundreds of banks and companies lost liquidity. The world's bond market in the last three months of 2008 reached $5 billion, down from $50 billion in the second quarter. Foreign direct investments decreased by more than 20 percent in 2008, but foreign investments in Britain, Germany, and Italy dropped by half. Finland and Ireland experienced net capital outflow. Since credits are the fuel of the modern economy, output declined in Britain,

---

[125] Carter Dougherty, "Sweden Aids Bailout of Baltic Nations," *New York Times*, March 13, 2009, B.7.
[126] Economist Intelligence Unit, *The Economist*, March 7, 2009.

France, and Germany. In the last quarter of 2008, German industrial output decreased by nearly 7 percent, while exports, the fuel of the German economy, dropped by 21 percent in January 2009, compared to the previous year. French industrial output decreased by 14 percent in January 2009, and the British output declined by 4.4 percent. Even the latter is more than a 17 percent decline in annualized rate. Ireland, the model country of economic success, fell victim to devastating crises. The country's indebtedness amounted to nine times its GDP. House prices halved and economic growth stopped. At the end of 2008, the IMF forecast for economic growth in 2009 was 2.2 percent in the world economy. After a few months, in the late winter weeks, the forecast was 0.5 percent, and in March 2009 decline became seemingly unavoidable.

In the last weeks of 2008, riots shocked Greece where stagnation and rising poverty ended a long period of gradual improvement. The transforming countries of Central and Eastern Europe suffered even more. Between 2004 and 2008, their high prosperity with sometimes two-digit growth figures was blown away by huge foreign credits. Latvia, one of the envied Baltic tigers, and Bulgaria, a high performer, borrowed from the West the equivalent of 20 percent of their GDP every year. Thirteen successor countries to the Soviet Bloc accumulated $1 trillion in total debts by 2008. Their banking system is mostly Western-owned, and credits dried up. Their currency declined, and their Western markets severely contracted. Russia, an oil and raw material superpower and producer also accumulated an amount of debt impossible to repay. The annual repayment of the Russian banks and corporations in 2009 was $128 billion. According to *Forbes* magazine, the twenty-five richest Russian oligarchs had a combined loss of $230 billion. In January 2009, in an act of desperation, the oligarchs approached President Medvedev and offered to merge their largest mines and factories, the world's largest aluminum and nickel producers, with a state-controlled conglomerate, a reverse of the loan-for-share privatization that had made them multi-billionaires in the 1990s.[127]

The fastest growing, debt-fueled "small Baltic Tigers," Estonia, Latvia, and Lithuania, declined into stagnation and then deep recession. During the first weeks of 2009, riots and street fights flooded the

---

[127] Andrew E. Kramer, "The Last Days of the Oligarchs?" *The New York Times*, March 8, 2009, B.1.

streets of Riga and Vilnius. Tens of thousands of people demonstrated violently, throwing stones and even Molotov-cocktails at government buildings and the parliament. In these former "Baltic tigers" with double-digit economic growth performance, growth was replaced by a 5 percent decrease in GDP, pay cuts of 15 percent and the introduction of austerity measures. In 2009, the income level of the Baltic states was forecast to decline by 6 to 10 percent. The international crisis generated a deep political crisis in these countries where the population's trust in their respective governments "collapsed catastrophically," as President Valdis Zatlers, of Latvia, stated.

Latvia and Lithuania were not alone. Similar events happened in Hungary where the debt crisis exploded somewhat earlier. Mobilized demonstrators had attacked the state television station, destroyed its facilities, and then camped in front of the parliament for weeks in 2006, and violent demonstrations were repeated in 2008. On January 14, 2009, several riots erupted in Sofia because of the dramatically worsening economic situation and the tragic shortage of gas and heating in the middle of an exceptionally cold winter. The Bulgarian rioters demanded the resignation of the government.[128] The international financial crisis suddenly ended economic adjustment and growth in transforming Central and Eastern Europe, which exhibited the extreme vulnerability of the entire transformation process.

Immediate actions were unavoidable throughout the continent, and Europe reacted promptly. The Danish parliament approved a blank guarantee for all bank deposits and other liabilities as early as October 10, 2008, before any other countries in the world. The European Central Bank offered €12 billion credit.[129] Britain took the lead on the world by recapitalizing its banking sector with £37 billion on October 8. The bailout happened in the form of partial nationalization, combined with mandatory crediting of the state money provided to the banks. On October 12, leaders of the euro-zone countries adopted the British method and committed themselves to guarantee debts and recapitalize banks. Germany, France, and the Netherlands established stabilization funds of €500 million, €360 million, and €200 million, respectively. The Swedish government rescued the

---

[128] Ellen Barry, "Lativa is Shaken by Riots Over its Weak Economy," *New York Times*, January 15 and 17, 2009.

[129] Carter Dougherty, "Denmark is Rethinking its Spurning of the Euro," *New York Times*, October 28, 2008, B.10, A.10.

banks with a recapitalization package of $173 billion. The European Central Bank and the Swiss National Bank offered unlimited dollar loans. The governments of the European Union countries spent $380 billion recapitalizing their banking sectors and established a $3.17 trillion guarantee loan to revitalize crediting by March 2009. Actions are being taken to try to save the situation and block the emergence of a new Great Depression. Germany, France, and Britain rushed to assist their economies in 2009–10 by sacrificing 3.5, 1.4, and 1.3 percent of GDP, respectively. The amounts are huge, but probably not enough. The American and Chinese rescue packages are spending 4.8 and 6.0 percent of those countries' respective GDP.

Some of the transforming countries of Central and Eastern Europe are unable to cope with the crisis yet. Without international help, their economies might collapse. The International Monetary Fund started to supply emergency rescue packages from the fall of 2008 and provided a $25.1 billion loan for Hungary, $16.5 billion for Ukraine, a $9.43 billion rescue package for Latvia, and $2.46 and $2.52 billion for Belarus and Serbia, respectively.[130]

The currency of several of these countries is endangered. Sweden rushed to bail out the Baltic countries. As Anders Borg, minister of finance, stated, "they are part of our economic region."[131] At the Paris emergency meeting of the European Union on March 1, 2009, the Hungarian prime minister suggested establishing a $241 billion fund to protect the weakest member countries. According to some calculations, the new member countries of Central Europe needed $380 billion in 2009. The Western leaders, however, rejected the bail out.[132] The meltdown of the Central European currencies since the summer of 2008 is frightening: the Polish zloty declined by 48 percent against the euro, the Hungarian forint by 30 percent and the Czech koruna by 21 percent. Further decline is evident. The crises will get worse before the trend changes and improvement arrives. In 2007, the region's aggregate GDP increased by 5.4 percent, in 2008, by only 3.2 percent, and the forecast for 2009 was 2 to 3 percent decline. Latvia had a 10 percent decline on an annualized basis in early 2009. Although the forecasts for 2010 are signaling some minimal

[130] Reuters Report on IMF emergency rescue actions, March 4, 2009. (www.alertnet.org/thenews/newsdesk/ L4817108.htm-36k)

[131] Carter Dougherty, "Sweden Aids Bailout of Baltic Nations," B.7.

[132] Steven Erlanger and Stephen Castle, "Dire Economy Threatens Idea of One Europe," *New York Times*, March 2, 2009, A.1.

growth, mostly below 1 percent, it will certainly take years before the governments and the European Union can eliminate the credit crisis and its consequences.

What kind of crisis hit the world and the European economy? When it began in late 2008, it looked like a financial crisis. This generated a global trade crisis, and a steep decline of industrial output. This is a new development since neither the Latin American nor the Asian financial crises ignited a worldwide meltdown in the 1990s. In the early spring of 2009, however, serious doubts emerged about the possibility of returning to the pre-crisis situation. Several industries will probably perish and never fully recuperate. Over-investments ballooned several industrial sectors, and the newly emerging countries in Asia and Central and Eastern Europe increased the production of the same products that were produced in the traditionally advanced industrial countries. Did the world enter into a new Kondratiev down cycle twenty-five years after the previous one at the turn of the 1970s to 1980s? Is it a structural crisis, as Joseph Schumpeter interpreted the Kondratiev downturns, when old sectors decline and shrink, and only gradually have been replaced by emerging sectors based on new technologies? Does the slowing down of international trade, capital flow, and labor movements represent a backlash to the previous decades of globalization? Is 2008 a turning point in European economic history? Is it the end of the three decades era of neo-liberalism, and the dominance of a self-regulating market system? Will Europe learn the lessons of the crisis? Will it lead back to the regulated (Keynesian) market system with international, global regulations? There are many more questions than answers in early 2010. This is not too surprising if we consider that a quarter century after the Great Depression John Kenneth Galbraith, in his book on the topic stated that "economics still does not allow final answers" to the causes of the depression.[133] The conservative, laissez-faire-leaning *Economist*, though expressing the hope of a somewhat transitory retreat, gave a brutal answer to the above questions: "The autumn of 2008 marks the end of an era . . . Governments have been forced to step in to rescue banking systems and the markets. In America . . . and in Britain . . . financial firms have had to accept rescue and part-ownership by the state . . . the price will doubtless be stricter

---

[133] John Kenneth Galbraith, *The Great Crash 1929* (Boston: Houghton Mifflin, [1954] 1961), 174.

regulation of the financial industry. To invert Karl Marx, investment bankers may have nothing to gain but their chains."[134]

The neo-liberal concept of the self-regulating market certainly suffered a lethal wound. The most neo-liberal-oriented governments, especially the American one, nationalized part of companies using an unheard-of amount of taxpayers' money. Alan Greenspan, the celebrated financial "maestro" who was appointed by Ronald Reagan to realize his policy at the Federal Reserve, and who served four presidents in a row, had nothing to say but that he was "in a state of shocked disbelief." He admitted that he had put "too much faith in the self-correcting power of the free market and had failed to anticipate the self-destructive power" of reckless financial activities. His "belief in deregulation," he added, "had been shaken."[135]

Some of the European leaders such the French President, Nicolas Sarkozy, stated the end of American-type "robber capitalism." With Gordon Brown and others, they agreed on the need for global regulations and the reestablishment of Bretton Woods. One should not forget that Europe has never totally given up Keynesian state interventionism, and that it has consistently followed a redistributive, high-taxation welfare policy since 1980. The circle is probably closed, and after three decades of market fundamentalism, Europe may return to the regulated market system that worked so well after the war. Not only does the economy have cycles, but economic paradigms as well.

---

[134] "Link by Link,"*The Economist*, October 18–24, 2008, 79. The same journal in "When Fortune Frowned," October 11–17, 2008, 3–16 asks the question: "where – and by how much – financial regulations should be extended . . . Regulatory reforms will, at best, yield only part of the solution," 14.

[135] *The New York Times*, October 24, 2008.

5

Dramatic Demographic Changes, Consumerism, and the Welfare State

Dramatic Demographic Changes

Since 1980, a new chapter opened in the demographic history of Europe. As Massimo Livi-Bacci suggests, five main phenomena deserve special attention: the decline of mortality; the decline of birth rates to below replacement levels; the rapid aging of the population; the end of mass emigration and the beginning of immigration; and last, changes in social rules and behavior (marriage customs, family structures).[1]

Indeed, the *mortality rate declined* to ten deaths per 1,000 at the end of the twentieth century. The decline of infant mortality played an important part in this change. At the turn of the century, only eight to ten infants died per 1,000 live births.

These changes were the culmination of a permanent demographic trend, which gradually accelerated in three distinct, two- to three-decade periods of the twentieth century: the quarter-century interwar period, a quarter-century post–World War II period, and the two to three decades ending at the turn of the twenty-first century. In the end, death rates dropped to one-third and infant mortality to less than one-tenth of the early twentieth-century level. Moreover, the regional differences within Europe, which were significant even in the mid-twentieth century, virtually disappeared.

The new developments were largely the outcome of improvements in health care, the "therapeutic revolution" of the later part of the century. This was also closely connected to the rise of the welfare state in both halves of the continent, which guaranteed full health insurance

[1] Massimo Livi-Bacci, *The Population of Europe: A History* (Oxford: Blackwell, 2000), 166.

for all citizens. Major improvements in consumer goods and housing, long vacations and sick leave, and the much better lifestyle also
played a significant role. Life expectancy at birth increased spectacularly because of declining mortality: in the single decade between
1995 and 2005, life expectancy increased by four years in Europe, and
it reached 81 years by 2005.[2]

Equally surprising was the gradual and then, from 1990, sudden leveling of the demographic gap between the European core and peripheries. By 2005, the Mediterranean countries, which enjoyed only 70
percent of the core countries' life expectancy at the beginning of the
twentieth century, virtually reached Western levels: Spain, Portugal,
Italy, and Greece reached an unweighted average of 79.5 years,
almost the same as in the West. Central and Eastern Europe reached
74.1 years, more than 90 percent of that of the West, by 2005. On the
other hand, the average life expectancy in Russia and Ukraine is still
66.9 years, less than 83 percent of the Western level. Male mortality
rates in Russia reflect the tragic continuation of the health crisis that
emerged during the first years of post-communist transformation. The
main killers are rooted in lifestyle: heavy drinking and self-destructive
behavior. Heart attacks, strokes, suicide, injuries, manslaughter, and
other "external causes" shortened *male* life expectancy to 62 years,
lower than in less developed Bangladesh or Pakistan. The Russian
health crisis is "utterly abnormal for an industrialized society."[3]

The most important demographic novelty, however, was the dramatic *decline in the rate of births*, which surpassed the decrease in mortality around the end of the century. The countries of the European
Union, including the Mediterranean countries, had an average of less
than 12 births per 1,000 in the late twentieth century, less than half of
the world average. It continued declining rapidly, and, by 2005, it was
only 9.7 births per 1,000 inhabitants. After a drastic downward trend,
Central and Eastern Europe and Russia reached the same level as in
the West: 9.6 births per 1,000. The fertility rate, i.e., the average number of children per woman, had dropped by 2005 to 1.5 children in
both Western and Southern Europe. Only the Nordic countries represent an exception, with birth rates around the reproduction level.

---

[2] *OECD in Figures, 2007* (Paris: OECD, 2007), 10–11. It pays to note that life expectancy
was 50 years in 1900, and 67 years in 1950 in Europe.

[3] Nicholas Eberstadt, "Rising Ambitions, Sinking Population," *New York Times*, October 25,
2008.

However, Central and Eastern Europe, including the Balkans and Russia, had a more or less uniform fertility rate of 1.3 children per woman, which was even lower than average. The last time the fertility rate matched the level necessary for population reproduction was during the early 1970s. Since 1980, however, the number of children per woman fell to below 2 in most of Europe.

This was also the outcome of a gradual process. Birth rates have permanently decreased in modern times. In the mid-twentieth century, they reached 15 to 18 per 1,000 in the West, and 22 to 24 in the peripheral countries. In Poland, the Balkans, and the Soviet Union, however, there were still 26 to 30 births per 1,000.[4]

Causes of Population Decrease – Different Trends Among Minorities

Birth rates became lower than death rates, which led to a population decrease. In 2005, the death rate in the European Union (9.9 per 1,000) surpassed the birth rate (9.7 per 1,000). The Eastern half of the continent had an even more negative ratio: in Russia, Ukraine, and the three Baltic countries, which were former Soviet republics, the 9.8 births per 1,000 inhabitants were hugely surpassed by the 14.6 deaths per 1,000. The Balkans was not much better. The Romanian and Bulgarian average was 9.3 births versus 13.6 deaths. The average in the five Central European countries was 9.4 births compared to 10.8 deaths per 1,000 inhabitants.

The sharp decline in birth rates had a whole set of causes. Among the most important was a changing lifestyle and value system, which was associated with a highly urbanized, much more educated European society that enjoyed a much higher standard of living. In addition, women were more liberated, and a great many of them worked outside the family. By the end of the century, women's participation in the workforce nearly equaled their share of the population, reaching 40 to 50 percent of employed people. Their share in Finland, Poland, the Soviet Union, and Yugoslavia reached between 43 and 51 percent. Around the turn of the twenty-first century, nearly 90 percent

---

[4] Brian R. Mitchell, "Statistical Appendix," in Carlo Cipolla (ed.), *The Fontana Economic History of Europe: Contemporary Economies*, Vol. 6 (2) (London: Collins/Fontana Books, 1976), 648–54.

of women between the ages of 20 and 50 were employed in Denmark, more than 70 percent in France, and between two-thirds to three-quarters in Portugal. Female employment was nearly universal in Central and Eastern Europe. These changes during the second half of the century were quite dramatic. Even in 1960, only 20 to 30 percent of married women participated in the labor force, but, by the 1980s, their levels of participation in many countries reached one-half to three-quarters. The Soviet Union had the highest rate (87 percent), while the lowest was in Italy (26 percent).[5]

People also married at a later age, and an increasing number of them did not marry at all. The period of fertility for married couples thus was shortened, and the will to have children partly disappeared. Around the end of the century, the average marriage age for men and women increased to 29.5 and 26.5 in the European Union countries, an increase from 28.5 and 25.3 years, respectively, in 1950. Marriage rates, i.e., marriages per 1,000 people, declined from 6 at the end of the century, to 4.7 by 2005.[6] The share of one-person households increased to roughly one-quarter of all households; in Spain and Portugal they make up only around 10 percent, while in Denmark and Germany, they have reached 30 percent.

A great many couples do not marry, but live together. Their share in Denmark reached 35 percent in the early 2000s, and 30 percent in France. While cohabitation often leads to marriage, it has increasingly become an alternative to marriage. In France and Britain during the last decades of the century, one-quarter of all children were born outside marriage, as were nearly half of the children in Denmark. Childbirth outside marriage remained relatively low, around 10 percent, in several other Western countries. In Germany, only 10 percent of non-married couples have children. Divorce rates increased steeply, and one-quarter to one-third of marriages ended in divorce during the 1980s; in Sweden, more than half of marriages did so.[7] Under these circumstances, family planning became widespread, and was much easier than before, because of developments in the medical field. During the first half of the century, traditional birth control methods dominated, but modern drugs and oral contraceptives have taken

---

[5] ILO, *Year Books of Labour Statistics* (Geneva: ILO, 1980); OECD, *Economic Outlook* (Paris: OECD, 1982).

[6] A drastic decline compared to 1910 when fifteen to sixteen marriages in the West and eighteen to twenty marriages in the East happened per 1,000 people.

[7] *Demographic Yearbook* (New York: United Nations, 1982).

over since the 1960s. Abortion in many countries has been legalized as well.

Leaving aside the peculiarities of the Nordic countries, demographic trends were, in several respects, surprisingly similar in most of Europe, core and peripheral countries alike. However, some *minority populations* experienced different demographic patterns. The most visible difference characterizes the Roma/Gypsy population of Central and Eastern Europe. Their mortality and fertility rates reflect an earlier, or non-European, demographic trend. Mortality rates remained high, especially infant mortality, which reached 40 per 1,000 even in the last decades of the twentieth century. Life expectancy at birth remained low, at 57 years. The fertility rate also remained at traditional levels, even in the 1990s: between 4 and 6 children per Roma woman in Macedonia, Slovakia, Romania, and the Czech Republic. Consequently, Roma population growth has remained very high, from 20 to 27 per 1,000, i.e., about 4.5 times higher than the population growth of the countries in which they live.[8]

Similar differences exist between the North African and Turkish immigrants on the one hand, and the local populations in France, Belgium, the Netherlands, and Germany on the other. While German population growth slowed, and the number of births declined by 50 percent in one decade, births to foreign parents increased by 140 percent. Immigrants' share of total births increased in Germany in the 1980s from roughly 4 percent to more than 17 percent.[9] Although the rapid growth of the Roma, Turkish, and North African minority populations does not change the overall demographic trends, it gradually and consistently increases the minority population in Europe.

Decreasing and Aging Population – Increasing Labor Force

The massive decline of the population, however, did not decrease labor input into the economy. Demographic trends are not the sole determinant of the labor force. The employment level of population

---

[8] Werner Houg, Paul Compton, and Youssef Courbage, *The Demographic Characteristics of National Minorities in Certain European States*, Vol. 1 (Strasbourg: Council of Europe, 1998), 185, 188, 190.

[9] Rogers Brubaker, *Citizenship and Nationhood in France and Germany* (Cambridge, MA: Harvard University Press, 1992), 172.

in active age is another major factor, and it varies country by country. In 2005, twelve countries in Europe had a high employment rate of between 50 and 58 percent, among them Switzerland, the Netherlands, Norway, and Sweden, which is one of the richest countries of the world, but also including some transforming countries such as Russia, Slovenia, and the Czech Republic. Ten other European countries had employment rates between 47 and 50 percent. Some of the South European countries – such as Italy and Greece – and some transforming countries in Central and Eastern Europe – such as Hungary, Croatia, Macedonia, Bulgaria, and Albania – had an especially low employment rate of around 40 to 42 percent of the population. The European Union's Lisbon guidelines of 2000 set the goal of 70 percent employment, a goal yet to be achieved.

In some of the Scandinavian and Nordic countries, the employment of the female population reached almost the maximum level in the early twenty-first century (48 percent of the workforce is female, even among dockworkers in the Malmö-Copenhagen port). In some of the poor transforming countries such as Russia, Ukraine, Moldova, and the three Baltic countries, i.e., in former Soviet republics, 49 to 51 percent of the workforce is female. Although female employment rate is lower than male's in several European countries, and remains far behind the European Union's goal of 60 percent female employment, many more women were working around the turn of the century than in earlier decades, when only one-third of the labor force was female. Guest workers also added 10 to 15 percent additional labor input. Finally, total employment increased by more than 9 percent between 1995 and 2005.

A similarly significant, and in some respects even more dramatic, impact of the drastically changing mortality and fertility rates, was a gradual and significant *aging* of the population. This trend became especially pronounced during the last quarter of the century when the decline of mortality was no longer caused by sharp declines in infant mortality, but instead by declines in elderly mortality. The proportion of young people – those under the age of 15 – gradually but permanently decreased throughout Europe, without major regional differences, from roughly 30 to 24 percent in the first half of the century, to 16 percent in the West by 2005 and slightly more than 15 percent in the East. On the other hand, the elderly population – those above 60 – represented 22 percent of the population in the West and 21 percent in the East by 2005, a dramatic increase from 9 percent at the beginning of the century, and 14 percent at mid-century.[10]

If the trend continues, 29 percent of the population of Western Europe will be older than 65 years by 2050, and the inactive elderly, already 36 percent of the total labor force in 2005, will represent 68 percent of it.[11] Germany may reach that point by 2035, Italy and Austria in the 2040s.

Europe: The Continent of Immigration; Increased Intra-European Migration and Eastern Europe

Against all demographic odds, the population of the major European countries was still increasing around the turn of the century: between 1973 and 2005, the population of France increased by 16 percent, Spain by 12 percent, Italy and Britain each by 6 percent, and Germany by 5 percent.[12] Europe's total population also exhibited a very modest increase, but much slower than the world's total population which increased by 65 percent. Europe's share, therefore, permanently decreased in the world population: it represented 18.4 percent of it in 1973, but only 11.3 percent by 2005 (Table 5.1).

The population of Europe thus has somewhat increased, in spite of higher death than birth rates in almost all of the regions and countries. How did this happen? One may find the key in the 180-degree change of migration trends. The last decades of the twentieth century became the period of worldwide mass migration. According to certain calculations, in the first decade of the twenty-first century, about 200 million people worldwide might be considered stable emigrants. In 1990, 3 percent of the world population was comprised of immigrants, and by 2007, 10 percent. During the first decade of the twenty-first century, migration gained tremendous new speed. Between 2000 and 2005, the number of immigrants increased by

[10] United Nations Economic Commission for Europe, *Aging Populations: Opportunities and Challenges for Europe and North America* (New York: United Nations, 2003); Livi-Bacci, *Population of Europe*, 171; The Economist, *World in Figures, 2008* (London: Profile Books, 2008), 242; Anthony Warnes, "Demographic Aging: Trends and Policy Responses," in Daniel Noin and Robert Woods (eds.), *The Changing Population of Europe* (Oxford: Blackwell, 1993), 82–99, 84–6.

[11] OECD, *Factbook: Economic, Environmental and Social Statistics* (Paris: OECD, 2007), 19.

[12] Based on Angus Maddison, *Monitoring the World Economy 1820–1992* (Paris: OECD, 1995), and *World in Figures, 2008*.

Table 5.1. Population (in 1,000s) 1973–2005[13]

Region	1973	1990	2005
EU–15	346,081	364,133	385,792
Central & Eastern Europe*	108,761	119,980	122,580
Russia & Ukraine	180,931	200,181	189,637
Total Europe	718,628	788,542	728,389
World	3,913,482	5,257,407	6,464,700

* Bulgaria, Czech Republic, Slovakia, Hungary, Poland, Romania, Yugoslavia or successor states.

15 million. Official money transfers by immigrants – an indirect indicator – have increased 90 percent between 2002 and 2005. The numbers are frightening: in 2006, 9.9 million, in 2007, 11.4 million refugees escaped from famine and/or persecution by crossing borders. "We are now faced with a complex mix of global challenges that could threaten even more forced displacement in the future," said the United Nation's High Commissioner for Refugees.[14]

In the world of mass migration, the aging and the declining growth of the European population, in the continent characterized by the "fear of moving" and "fear of people who move," generated a rather different type of population movement than in previous times: *immigration to Europe*. One of the reasons for this reversed migration flow was the spectacular collapse of the colonial system by the 1960s. Millions of people from the former British, French, Dutch, and Portuguese colonies moved to Europe. By the end of the 1960s, roughly 10 million immigrants lived in France, Germany, and Britain, representing 5 to 6 percent of the population.

More importantly, rising standards of living, welfare benefits, and a long-lasting economic boom created a great number of new European jobs, and led to immigration from the poorer European and non-European countries. Additionally, indigenous populations held jobs that were more attractive and were less willing to take positions that required "dirty" or heavy physical labor. Guest workers filled these gaps. Germany signed agreements about guest workers with Italy in 1955, Greece and Spain in 1960, Turkey in 1961, and Portugal in 1964.

---

[13] Based on Angus Maddison, *The World Economy: A Millennial Perspective* (Paris: OECD, 2001), and *World in Figures, 2008*.

[14] Hannah Strange, "UN Warns of Growth in Climate Change Refugees," *New York Times*, June 18, 2008.

Turks, North Africans, Pakistanis, Indians, and Indonesians moved to Britain, France, Spain, Switzerland, the Netherlands, and Germany.

The number of arriving guest workers averaged nearly 220,000 annually during the sixties and seventies, and reached 500,000 during the late eighties. In 1984, net migration was zero, but it turned positive in 1985, and by 1990, reached 2 million. By 1995, 8 to 10 million permanent immigrants lived in Europe. In 2005, 42 million people from the European population were born outside Europe. Until that year, Germany had accepted 700,000 refugees, Britain 294,000, and France 137,000. In 2005, 250,000–300,000 refugees applied for asylum in European countries. In that year, 1.8 million immigrants arrived in Europe. Spain offers a good example: in 2000, 4.6 percent of the country's population was immigrants, but by 2006, this had grown already to 10.8 percent, mostly from North Africa. In eight West European countries, the proportion of immigrants was already in the double digits by 2005, surpassing one-third of the population in the mini-state of Luxembourg, and nearing one-quarter in Switzerland.[15]

Another phenomenon, *intra-European migration*, also became increasingly important. From the mid-1980s onward, growing numbers of ethnic Germans from Russia moved to the West, followed by Russians, Poles, and Romanians. The extreme cases are Albania and Moldova. Though relatively small in absolute numbers, one-quarter of Albania's population emigrated after 1991, and one-quarter of Moldova's workforce has worked abroad since the country became independent in 1991. In both cases, the bulk of the emigrants from these two countries went to Italy. The number of Central and Eastern European emigrants did not surpass 100,000 per year prior to the mid-1980s, but it jumped to 1.2 million in 1989. In 2005, 22,100 Serbs and 21,600 Russians were among those seeking asylum in Europe. During the one-and-half decades after 1989, roughly 10 million European migrants flooded the European Union.

The foreign population of Germany, without German repatriation, amounted to only 0.68 million in 1960. But by the late 1980s that figure neared 5 million, and reached more than 10 million, 13 percent of the population of united Germany, by 2005. A great many

---

[15] *OECD in Figures, 2007*, 6–7. The acceleration of immigration is clearly signaled by the fact that in the decade between 1995 and 2005, the foreign-born population increased from 1.7 to 4.6% in Italy, from 6.9 to 11.0% in Ireland and from 6.9 to 9.7% in Britain.

guest workers settled permanently in Germany. West Berlin became the second largest "Turkish" city. By the late 1980s, 60 percent of foreigners had lived in Germany for more than a decade, 80 percent of them for more than five years, and had residence permits to stay indefinitely. About a million foreigners had already been born in Germany. The naturalization of the former *Gastarbeiter* population began, though little more than two out of every 1,000 who had lived there for more than ten years gained German citizenship during the 1980s. This situation did not change because of the requirement of German blood inheritance (*jus sanguinis*). In 2000, however, the citizenship law changed. The situation was rather similar for the more than 3 million foreigners living in France in the late 1970s. Their number increased to 6.4 million by 2005.[16]

Foreign residents play an important role in the labor force of a country, making up about one-quarter of all workers in Switzerland, 15 percent in Germany and Austria, 13 percent in Spain and Sweden, and more than 10 percent in the Netherlands, Ireland, France, and Britain. Moreover, they represent an increasing part of the population at large: 24 percent in Switzerland and around 10 percent in most of the West European countries.[17] Millions of illegal immigrants moved to Spain, Italy, France, the Netherlands, and Britain. Immigration has become the most important factor in population growth in Europe since the last decades of the century. During the 1990s, 16 million immigrants settled in Europe, and 4 million asylum seekers knocked on the door. The number of foreigners in the advanced Western countries reached nearly 8 million in 1980, and after the sharp increase in the 1990s, about 25 million foreigners lived in Europe in the early 2000s.[18] Because of the demographic trends, associated with a declining and aging native population, according to forecasts, 47 million new immigrants are needed to supply the required workforce for Europe until 2020. That means seven times more immigrants than between 1985 and 1995.[19]

The *Eastern half of the continent* had not been open until 1989–90, and has not been competitively attractive for immigrants since then.

---

[16] Brubaker, *Immigration and the Politics of Citizenship*, 71, 80, 119–20.

[17] *OECD in Figures, 2007*, 6–7.

[18] Based on European Commission, *Eurostat Yearbooks* (Luxembourg: Office for Official Publications, 2000–5).

[19] Leticia Delgado Godoy, "Immigration in Europe: Realities and Policies," 2002, www.iesam.csic.es/doctrab2/dt-0218e.pdf

However, a surprisingly high number of immigrants settled in these countries too after 1990. Russia gained 13 million immigrants, 9 percent of its population. A great many of them, however, are ethnic Russians from neighboring former Soviet republics, such as the three Baltic countries, but also Armenians and Azerbaijani, or Uzbek, citizens from neighboring independent countries. On the other hand, a relatively large immigrant population lives in the Baltic countries, especially in Estonia and Latvia where 15 to 20 percent of the population is considered to be immigrant, mostly Russians who lived in the Baltic countries before they became independent. Serbia had 190,000 immigrants, including uprooted Serbs from neighboring newly independent countries, such as the former Yugoslav republics of Croatia, Bosnia, and Kosovo. From Bosnia and Serbia, 119,000 Croats and 110,000 Bosnians migrated. Hungary also received refugees from Yugoslavia during the years of the Yugoslav civil war; Transylvanian Hungarians permanently moved to Hungary too.

Attractiveness is also relative: working possibilities and living standards in Central and Eastern Europe are not compatible with those in the West, but they are much better than in many other parts of the world and still offer refuge for many. In the first years of transformation, nearly 40,000 Chinese immigrants arrived in Hungary exploiting the lack of visa requirements. Turkish immigrants arrived in Poland. Altogether, 33 million international migrants settled in the transforming countries after 1989, which represents 8.1 percent of the region's population. The ethnic component is rather different from that in the Western half of the continent, but the percentage share of immigrants is very similar.

Integration – Segregation

Permanently settled guest workers, immigrants, and refugees caused fundamental social problems in Europe. What kind of relations emerged between the host majority and the immigrant minorities? "Encounters between groups that perceive themselves as different are potentially difficult... the groups involved may regard their culture as an asset that they wish to preserve. They may therefore want to protect it from mixture with other cultures... [Furthermore] people [may be] wary of entering into detailed relations with others who seem 'different'... [M]embers of [a] majority... may perceive... immigrants, as [an] unnecessary source of competition . . . [especially] in times of important scarcities . . ."[20]

Among the three possible extreme responses to the challenge of the minority question – integration, assimilation, or segregation – the various European countries exhibited different patterns. Their responses strongly depended on their traditional policy and concept of citizenship. The British Empire used the classic rule of the Roman Empire: everybody who was born in the territory of the Empire became a citizen. The *civis romanus sum*, became *civis brittanicus sum*. Until recently, France's immigration policy was dominated by the concept of *jus solis*, the territorial principle, while the *jus sanguinis*, the principle of blood relation, characterized Germany's immigration policy.[21]

Since 1980, however, immigration policy changed in several countries of Europe. High unemployment replaced a labor shortage, and the host population in several countries became less tolerant, even hostile and sometimes violent against immigrant minorities. Under the social pressure of large immigrant communities, both Britain and Germany have changed their attitudes and laws. France, which has traditionally considered people as individuals, and not as members of an ethnic group, continued to try forcing assimilation. The idea of multiculturalism dominated some other countries, but around the turn of the century, it was clear that none of these policies really worked.

Various countries made different efforts and followed different policies regarding the immigrants. Switzerland and Sweden formed the two extremes. Switzerland does not allow permanent immigrants, but instead operates temporary and rotation-based work permits, using fixed annual quotas to keep "Switzerland for the Swiss," as a former referendum slogan phrased it. Sweden, on the other hand, has the most liberal practice. Asylum seekers do not even have to prove that they were persecuted in the country of their origin. Furthermore, Sweden makes the greatest effort to integrate immigrants through organized language courses, job creation programs, and housing assistance.

The integration or assimilation of people coming from rather different cultural environments, and who are mostly uneducated, is considered a hopeless task, or one that takes generations to achieve.

---

[20] Colin Crouch, *Social Change in Western Europe* (New York: Oxford University Press, 1999), 288.

[21] *Ibid.*, 301.

Two-thirds of immigrants in Belgium arrived from Morocco, Algeria, and Turkey. In France, two-thirds originate from North Africa, while nearly half of immigrants in Germany come from Turkey. Most of the immigrants did not even speak the language of the host country. Many of them did not even make an effort to learn it, and remained in ghettoes. People from Muslim countries not only have a different religion, but they also come from societies in which religion plays a central role, in sharp contrast with secular Europe. Most of the immigrant ethnic groups lived at the fringes of society in the European countries. Unemployment, especially young people's unemployment rates, was extremely high among them. In many ways, immigrants are victims of double discrimination: as foreigners who are strongly "other," and as unskilled and unemployed people.[22]

Racist extremists never stop agitating against immigration, and right-wing anti-immigration parties attract a significant fraction of the population in several countries. After September 2001, and especially because of the influence of Islamic fundamentalism among a small layer of the Muslim population of the European Union, revolts, confrontations, and even assassinations became more frequent, and anti-immigration sentiments spread among broad layers of the societies. Segregation has dominated since the 1980s even more strongly than before.

Immigration powerfully influenced the social fabric of Europe and became an essential political question. Strong pressure pushed most governments to strengthen controls on immigration and to curb it. The European Union made a series of efforts to harmonize immigration and asylum policy, and in the spring of 2008, a French–Spanish agreement prepared a common policy recommendation for the Union. In the best case, generational change is needed to approach the goal of integration or assimilation.

Social Fabric: The Rise of the Middle Class and Consumerism in the West

Since 1980, the postwar trends of social transformation, characterized by a substantial decrease in the farmer and blue-collar worker

---

[22] Antonio Ugalde and Gilberto Cárdenas (eds.), *Health and Social Services among International Labor Migrants: A Comparative Perspective* (Austin, TX: CMAS Books, 1997), 124, 128.

population, and the rise of service employment and the middle class, gained new impetus. De-industrialization and the outsourcing of various industrial jobs to low-wage and environmentally less-regulated countries strongly contributed to the progress of this trend.

At the end of the twentieth century, it became impossible and obsolete to describe society based on class categories. Sociologists use various models based on property, authority, and skill, differentiating between nine to eleven social layers. High-grade proprietors, managers, and professionals are on the top, lower-grade proprietors, managers, and professionals follow. Non-manual employees, small proprietors, smallholders, and lower-grade technicians occupy the middle positions of society, while at the bottom of the hierarchy are the skilled manual workers, then semi-skilled and unskilled manual workers, and finally, agricultural workers.[23] However, the available statistics do not use these kinds of categories of social hierarchy; they use a much less sophisticated three- or two-layer model that distinguishes among those in leading positions, middle-rank non-manual employees, and manual workers. Others use the differentiation among service class, intermediate class, and working class.

At the end of the twentieth century, the top managerial and professional layer consisted of 25 to 27 percent of Western Europe's population with quite significant country-by-country differences. The middle-level non-manual working population represented 20 to 25 percent, and the manual working population 30 to 43 percent of the inhabitants of Europe.[24] By 2006, hardly more than 4 percent of the population of the euro-zone of the European Union worked in agriculture, 29 percent worked in industry, and 67 percent in services. Among service employees at the end of the twentieth century, 10 to 15 percent worked in distribution and communication, 3 to 7 percent in business services, 10 to 20 percent in community and social services, and about 4 to 7 percent in personal services. Roughly half of the service employees worked in education, health care, public administration, finances, insurance, and real estate business, areas where service employment provided middle-class status. It is important to realize that the largest group, 35 to 45 percent of the non-dependent population, comprising mostly women, is occupied in the non-paid domestic sector.

[23] John H. Goldthorpe and Keith Hope, *The Social Grading of Occupations: A New Approach and Scale* (Oxford: Clarendon Press, 1974).
[24] Crouch, *Social Change*, 138–9.

It is interesting to analyze the importance of that non-paid "domestic" sector. The more developed a country, the more these household activities became producers of Gross Domestic Product, since in the domestic sector, the households will externalize what were previously household activities.[25] In modern times, especially around the turn of the twenty-first century, when a large service sector served the population, people did not think about the huge value that was still being produced within households. Moreover, according to a calculation based on Belgium, France, and the Netherlands in the 1970s and 1980s, if one adds that non-paid work to what people do outside the household for relatives, friends, or in other informal fashion, including charity and volunteering, it may increase the GDP of a given country by 35 to 50 percent.[26] A new calculation in 2005, based on Hungarian time-keeping statistics, shows that 60 percent of the work of women and 26 percent of men's is non-paid work in the above-mentioned informal area.[27] In other words, the "non-working" housewives, or those who are working, but also doing the household as a "second shift," are producing tremendous value. These activities would increase the contribution of services to GDP by leaps and bounds throughout Europe.

The change of the occupational structure, in connection with the technological, information, and communication revolution, created a *post-industrial* society with a permanently increasing white-collar and middle class. Middle-class self-identification and consciousness characterizes even the lower layers of service employees, those who at least partly perform blue-collar work in the retail trade, hotel, and transportation businesses, and who believe that they are part and parcel of the middle class. It is easy to identify themselves with the middle class, since their home environment and lifestyle eliminated strict social borderlines. Consumerism consumed strict class borders and became a strong equalizer. Family houses and well-equipped households with all the modern household machinery became common. Every family

---

[25] In a traditional society, baking bread, cleaning clothes, making household furniture and tools, teaching skills to the younger generation, etc. were all domestic activities, and were not measured or included in the country's GDP. The same work, if performed outside the household, such as the baker making bread and the dry cleaner replacing the housewife's work, or when kindergartens and schools take over teaching, etc., all these activities became measurable paid-services and contributed to the country's GDP.

[26] Clio Presvelou, "Crises et économie informelle: Acquis et interrogations," *Recherches Sociologiques*, 25, 3 (1994), quoted by Crouch, *Social Change*, 87.

[27] Katalin Koncz, *Nők a munkaerő-piacon* (Budapest: Corvinus Egyetem, 2008).

in the euro-zone countries had a color TV, and most of the people watch similar crime mysteries and football games in the evening. In the first decade of the twenty-first century, every European had a mobile telephone, every second person had a car and a computer, and every second European checked the Internet for information. Winter and summer vacations, partly spent abroad, also became the norm and strengthened middle-class consciousness.

Lifestyle has improved and become more equalized. Shorter working weeks and days played a role in it: in 1973, the average person in twelve West European countries worked 750 hours in a year; in 1990, 701; and only 657 hours at the end of the century. In formerly less-developed countries such as Spain, the decrease was even steeper, from 805 to 648 hours.[28] People spent less for basics: around the turn of the century, only 12 to 20 percent of income was spent on food and clothing. Expenditures that a few decades before were considered to be luxuries, became ordinary and dominant in family budgets. In 2005, the Germans, British, Dutch, French, Italians, Belgians, Spanish, Austrians, Swedes, Swiss, and Norwegians combined spent $278 billion on tourism, an amazing amount that was significantly more than the entire Irish GDP, more than the total Czech and Hungarian GDP combined, and three times more than the GDP of Egypt in that year.[29] Altogether, these wildly spending, well-to-do middle layers represent more than half of the societies in advanced Western countries. Meanwhile societies became more homogenized, income distributions less polarized, and the social safety net prevented poor people from dropping out of society.

Gender and Income Inequality – Minority Underclass

Social homogenization included the deliberate policy of gender equality. From the 1970s on, "state feminism" in the Nordic countries led to striking achievements in this respect. In 1986, Norway made history: the second Gro Harlem Brundtland government appointed eight female ministers into the cabinet of eighteen ministers. Sweden established a special ministry for integration and gender equality. Finland enacted the Equality Act of 1995. Sweden actually realized the equality program: the salary gap between sexes virtually disappeared and

---

[28] Maddison, *The World Economy*, 354.   [29] *World in Figures, 2008*, 77.

female salaries reached 92 percent of male salaries in 2007. Regarding political representation, 47 percent of the members of parliament, 41 percent of politicians of elected local authorities, and 10 out of 22 cabinet ministers are women. In higher education, 60 percent of undergraduates and 44 percent of those who received doctoral degrees are women. In 2003, the United Nations ranked Iceland and Norway number one and two, respectively, in terms of economic and political gender equality.

The European Union considers gender equality to be part of the integration process. Before 1980, statements and political directives required equal employment, wages, and advancement in work. Since 1980, requirements have included equal opportunities in political decision-making. Positive discrimination measures were also broadly used. In February 1986, the Commission worked out its complex strategy for gender equality. Between 1988 and 1995, three action programs helped the realization of those principles. The results were impressive: the share of women among firm directors increased from 5 to 15 percent, and it reached 50 percent at the lower supervisory and managerial level. Since 1999, the European Commission publishes annual reports on gender equality. The Union's Social Agenda 2005–10 also contains targets for gender equality.[30]

Gender policy made impressive progress in Europe, but the targets are far from being realized yet. In the European Union–25 in 2005, the employment rate among people from age 15 to 65 is slightly more than 56 percent for women and 71 percent for men. Regarding part-time employment, women's share is 31 percent versus 8 percent for men. According to the Union's Lisbon agreement, female employment must increase to 60 percent of the female population; while total employment must increase from 64 percent (in 2005) to 70 percent in the EU–25 by 2010. This goal is beyond what is possible. It would require the creation of 22 million new jobs, even though a total of 4 million jobs was created in the member and future member countries of the EU–27 between 2000 and 2006.[31] In 2008–9, the deepening depression in most of the European countries caused huge job losses and unemployment. The goal of the Lisbon agreement was shifted into the future.

Regarding female employment, a huge gap separates the Nordic countries and the Netherlands from the Mediterranean and Central European ones. In 2006, more than 70 percent of women were

[30] Koncz, Nők, 31–9.   [31] Ibid., 69.

employed in Denmark, Sweden, and the Netherlands, while the same figure is around 50 percent in Spain, Italy, Greece, and in most of Central Europe. Women traditionally earn less than men do. The efforts to promote gender equality had a great impact in Europe. In almost all of the countries, the real earnings of women increased more than those of men.[32] Accordingly, the average salary gap between men and women decreased from 16.2 to 14.4 percent in the European Union-15 countries even in the early twenty-first century, though it is still 20 percent in Germany, Britain, and Finland, and 17.5 percent in the new member countries. Women managers earn only 71 percent of what men earn, and in Italy only 65 percent. In professional and technical jobs, they receive 27 percent less.

Political representation is still uneven: in national parliaments, the share of women politicians was 24 percent in 2007, though it increased from 16 percent in 1997. Women in the European Parliament increased their representation from 17 to 31 percent. Spain's socialist Zapatero government made history by organizing the first cabinet with a majority of female cabinet members, while Berlusconi's Italian government has only four female ministers out of twenty-one, and even these have marginal roles. On the corporate level, gender equality is in much worse shape: in 2007, female chairpersons and presidents of executive bodies represented only 1 percent of the total in the EU-15, and 3 percent in EU-27 countries.

The traditional division of labor in the family is still dominant in most European countries: women spend an average of 1.5 hours more per day on domestic work than men. While women in Italy spend five hours per day on domestic work, men spend only twenty minutes. Consequently, men have an average of four hours per day for leisure activities such as watching TV and videos, and for reading.[33]

Gender equality, on the other hand, deteriorated in Central and Eastern Europe during the transformation period. In some of these countries, such as Bulgaria, Estonia, and Slovakia, women's average salary remained 25 to 30 percent behind. Women's political representation hardly existed: in Poland, Lithuania, and Slovakia, respectively, there are only one, two, and three female ministers in the governments.

---

[32] Women's earnings increased 26% versus men's 15% in Belgium, 17% versus 8.4% in the Netherlands, 33% versus 22% in Britain between 1986 and 1995.

[33] European Commission, *Eurostat, The Life of Women and Men in Europe: A Statistical Portrait* (Luxembourg: Office for Official Publications, 2008).

Figure 23. Beggars in Košice, Slovakia. Increased social polarization led to the appearance of beggars and homeless people in the transforming countries of Central and Eastern Europe.

In the Hungarian parliament, only 9 percent of the representatives are women. Domestic traditions are similar to the Italian pattern.

Regarding other inequalities in the European societies, *income inequality* mostly increased, and in spite of impressive material progress, part of the societies remained poor, and a small layer even remained below the poverty line (Figure 23). People who were unable to work, single mother families, the uneducated and unskilled, and the frequently or even permanently unemployed people represented about

10 to 15 percent of the Western societies at the end of the twentieth century. Unemployment has remained high since 1980, when it was a double-digit figure in most of the countries, though it declined to roughly 10 percent in the European Union-15 countries during the 1990s, and from 1997 to 2005, it gradually decreased to 8 percent. A part of the unemployed, however, became jobless on a long-term basis: from the early 1990s to 2005, 40 to 50 percent of the unemployed did not work for at least one year.[34] In 2007, 14 percent of the comparatively rich Irish society lived below the official poverty level. In spite of the generous state assistance in the Nordic and West European countries, 4 and 8 percent of the population, respectively, live in relative poverty, earning less than half of the national average. During the decade between the mid-1980s and 1990s, only four out of eleven European countries experienced faster income increase in the bottom decile of the society than the top one. The poorest 10 percent of full-time workers in Germany earned 60 percent more at the end of the decade, while the top 10 percent increased their income only by 22 percent. In Finland, the equivalent figures were 27 percent versus 19 percent. On the other hand, in Britain wage differences increased; the top 10 percent increased their income by 25 percent, while the bottom 10 percent by only 14 percent. The trend was similar in Italy, Austria, and France.[35] Poor and unemployed people, however, mostly did not drop out from the society because of the social safety net of the welfare states. As *Der Spiegel* reported in the fall of 2006, poor people do not lose their homes; they have food to eat, and some unemployed watch TV half the day.[36]

Although the poor could take advantage of welfare, housing, and health care benefits, a dangerous new phenomenon appeared, a new *underclass*. As a Russian journalist commented on the 2005 French riots: "Benjamin Disraeli described the rich and the poor as two separate nations. Today, this is quite literally true, since the proletariat and the bourgeoisie generally belong to different ethnic groups."[37] Indeed, the non-integrated, ghettoized Roma minorities and the

---

[34] OECD *Factbook* 2007, 137, 141.

[35] OECD, *Employment Outlook* (Paris: OECD, 1997). In Italy the two deciles' income increased by 20 and 7%, in Austria, the top deciles had an 8% increase while the bottom deciles' income stagnated, in France the highest deciles increased their income by 10%, but the bottom deciles' earnings only by 4%.

[36] Conrad Schnibben, "Die Überflüssigen," *Der Spiegel*, October 23, 2006, 28–30.

[37] Boris Kagarlitsky, "The Return of the Proletariat," *Moscow Times*, November 10, 2005.

Figure 24. The Roma, the largest minority in Central and Eastern Europe, are living in deep poverty.

legal and especially illegal immigrants became the reservoir of the new underclass in Western Europe (Figure 24). Their number is significant and increasing. They are much less educated, live in slums in run-down inner city or suburban regions, quite a huge part of them do not speak the language of the host country, have a different religion and culture, different type of family life and gender relations, and most of them remain different in clothing and behavior. They are not integrated into the local society at all, and they are surrounded by suspicion and even hatred.

This is the case with the Roma population, traditionally significant in Spain. Around the turn of the century, their number was officially 600,000, but according to certain evaluations, it probably reaches 800,000 to 1 million. Roma communities are increasing in Western Europe through post-1989 emigration from the East. Germany has developed a Roma community of about 200,000; and about 670,000 illegal, mostly Roma immigrants settled in Italy. Tens of thousands moved to Scandinavia (Figure 25).

In certain Spanish regions where relatively large Roma communities are living, schools became ghettoized: if the number of Roma children

Figure 25. Roma emigrants from Romania in Sweden.

reaches 30 to 40 percent of the student body, in a very short period the school becomes a Roma school with 80 percent or more of Roma children, because the non-Roma parents take their children out of those schools. Roughly half of the Roma people in Spain are unemployed, while the national unemployment rate is 14 percent.

The Roma underclass is especially large in Eastern Europe. Beggars and homeless people, unknown phenomena before 1990, have since flooded the streets of the Eastern European capitals. In Poland, the number of homeless people was estimated at 150,000 to 300,000.[38] A great many of them are Roma. Central and Eastern Europe is the greatest reservoir of the stateless Roma minority. Their exact number is unknown, but it is estimated to be between 4 and 12 million in Europe. According to certain calculations, half or two-thirds of them, and probably as many as 8 million, live in Central and Eastern Europe. Roma communities represent the largest minority in the region, reaching between 7 and 11 percent of the population in several countries. Official and unofficial Roma population figures sometimes reflect a 1:5 ratio of difference. In the case of Romania, the

---

[38] *The Visegrád Yearbook* (Budapest: Central European Partnership Organization, 2003), 291.

official and estimated numbers vary between 400,000 and 2 million, in Slovakia between 92,000 and 550,000, in Serbia between 108,000 and 500,000.

After 1989, part of the Roma population has been in permanent movement. Most of them still preserve nomadic traditions, but some migrated to the West from Romania, Bulgaria, Slovakia, and Ukraine, looking for better welfare possibilities, or trying to escape hatred, violence, and segregation. The large Roma population in the region remained or declined into a classic underclass situation. Deindustrialization and the abolition of the principle of full employment hit the Roma communities hardest. They were the first to be laid off. In countries with about 7 to 10 percent unemployment rates, Roma unemployment reaches a dramatic 50 to 80 percent. According to a UNICEF report of 2005, 84, 88, and 91 percent of the Roma population were below the absolute poverty level in Bulgaria, Romania, and Hungary, respectively. In Serbia, this rate is 60 percent, partly because of a more than 68 percent unemployment rate. In the Belgrade region, less than 8 percent of the Roma population received a regular salary in 2002. Roma children are segregated in schools. As a European Commission report disclosed, 75 percent of Roma children in the Czech Republic are pushed into special schools or classes for the mentally disabled. In Hungary, 700 schools segregated Roma children into separate classes.[39] The education of Roma children is often abandoned: in Serbia, 62 percent of them never finish primary school.

The poverty-ridden, segregated, and discriminated against Roma communities live in slums or special Roma villages. The Council of Europe maintained in a report on Bulgaria in 2003: "Roma districts are turning into ghettos... Most Roma neighborhoods consist of slums, precariously built without planning permission... [and without] basic public services, whether health care, public transport, waste collection or sanitation."[40] Mortality rates among the Roma are much higher than in the surrounding population: in Serbia, they are 50 percent higher than the national average; Roma people have a lifespan that is twelve years shorter than others enjoy. The crime rate is several times higher among Romani than national averages.

---

[39] European Commission, *The Situation of Roma in an Enlarged European Union* (Luxembourg: Office for Official Publications of the European Communities, 2004).

[40] European Commission Against Racism and Intolerance, *The Third Report on Bulgaria*, 2003, www.coe.int/t/e/human_rights/ecri/1-ecri/2-country-by-country_approach/Bulgaria/Bulgaria_CBS_3.asp-182k

The European Union launched the "Decade of Roma Inclusion" project in 2005 and provided $17 billion from its social fund, adding twice as much during 2006 and 2007 from the regional development fund. The Central and Eastern European countries, including new Union members and candidates, agreed to close the gap between Roma and non-Roma populations in employment, housing, education, and health.[41] Except for some isolated actions, such as Bulgaria's spectacular desegregation campaign in schools, very little progress has been made.

The situation is quite similar with the North African immigrants in France. They have a much lower chance of getting a job interview, and 40 percent of them are unemployed. The violent October 2005 riots that erupted in the Paris suburb of Clichy-sous-Bois, and which rapidly spread to 275 cities and led to the introduction of curfews in thirty-one cities, had nothing to do with Islam. It was a typical *sans culottes* uprising. French policy was broadly condemned because it did not recognize diversity in ethnicity, language, customs, and religion and rejected multiculturalism, forcing an artificial unity of French citizens.[42] The traditional French policy that based citizenship on the territorial and not ethnic-blood principle, which had worked for two centuries and hammered out a homogenous French nation, does not work any longer with the new immigrant community. The problem is very complex and strongly connected with a deep cultural divide and even the lack of any attempt to integrate. The situation, however, is not much better in other Western societies that recognize multiculturalism. Significant layers of the immigrant communities, which represent 7 to 10 percent of the population in the Western countries, belong to a segregated underclass.

Social Shock in the East: Harsh Adjustment to New Social Requirements

Turn-of-the-century societies in the Eastern half of the continent have been experiencing a dramatic and painful process of change. In the state socialist countries, which were transforming from poor and strongly egalitarian societies where no one could become rich,

---

[41] "Bottom of the Heap," *The Economist*, June 21–7, 2008, 35–80.

[42] Praful Bidwai, "France Explodes the Uniformity Myth," *Frontline*, November 5, 2005, www.tmi.org/archives/bidwai/myth.htm

but where poverty and the underclass status had been eliminated, a sudden polarization emerged. A significant layer became winners and another, even more significant one, losers. After the economic decline in the early 1990s, these countries did not achieve the pre-1989 living standard – low as it was in comparison with Western Europe – for a whole decade, and not until 2006 in some of the Balkan countries. Using poverty calculations based on expenditures, instead of incomplete "official" income data,[43] poverty in Central and Eastern Europe in the mid-1990s varied from between 7 and 10 percent of the population in Poland and Hungary to 34 and 48 percent in Estonia and Romania, respectively.[44] In the war-ridden western Balkans and in ill-governed Russia, deep poverty remained characteristic for more than half of the population until the turn of the century. The rest of the Eastern European countries, however, mostly halted and even curbed the process of increasing poverty by 1992–3.

Relative poverty measures the layer of the population that earns less than 35 to 45 percent of the country's average wage level. People living below the relative poverty line increased in Czechoslovakia from 4 to 25 percent, and in several countries of the region the relative poverty rate reached 52 to 54 percent.[45] The situation significantly improved from the mid-1990s: around the turn of the century, it reached 20 percent of the population in Macedonia, 17 percent in Poland, and around 13 percent in Romania, Lithuania, Bulgaria, and Latvia. The difference is striking if we compare this to other, more successful and more stable countries of the region, where people in relative poverty represent 8 to 9 percent of the population.[46]

Even at the nadir of the decline in 1992, the so-called Human Suffering Index[47] placed the twelve Central and Eastern European

---

[43] Income data cannot include secondary, illegal, non-reported incomes that represent about 20% of incomes in Central Europe and nearly half of the incomes in Russia around the turn of the century.

[44] Branko Milanović, *Income, Inequality and Poverty During the Transition* (Washington, DC: The World Bank, 1996), 67–8.

[45] In Hungary it increased from 10 to 30%, in Poland from 25 to 44%, in Slovakia from 6 to 34%, in Bulgaria from 14 to 54%, in Romania from 34 to 52% during the first five years of transformation. In Estonia, Lithuania, and Latvia, relative poverty increased from 1% to 37, 30, and 22%, respectively by the mid-1990s.

[46] United Nations, *Economic Survey of Europe* (New York: United Nations, 2000), 170.

[47] A combined index of life expectancy, calorie intake, availability of clean drinking water, immunization of infants, enrollment in secondary education, per capita GDP, inflation rate, civil rights, and the availability of communication technology.

countries among thirty-four countries with "moderate human suffering," with a score between 25 and 47 on a scale of 0 to 100. They were, however, the only European countries placed in this group.

People in the former Soviet Bloc countries suffered a long-lasting *social shock*, and this was not only as a consequence of the decline of their material well-being. Easterners were strongly attracted to the sparkling Western life. They longed for good cars, and to enjoy Western pop culture. From a distance made greater by separation and isolation, most people held and nurtured an idealized picture of the West. In 1989, when the door was opened, imitative development became an official recommendation of the West and a government program in the East. Western institutions and policies were transplanted. Western retail chains and shopping malls set the stage for a new way of living. Although the region remained several decades behind the West in social structure, lifestyle, and behavior, it experienced an agitated rush to catch up and become "Western."

When Easterners took their first steps on the new road, they suddenly experienced the negative features of capitalism, such as unemployment and social polarization, that many did not like. The heroic Polish workers who revolted against the regime and finally forced it onto its knees, as Adam Michnik noted, were "the first to become the victims of the transformation."[48] Peasants, still a significant part of the population, who suffered tremendously during the ruthless collectivization and dreamed about independent farming, gradually adjusted to the situation. Post-1989 de-collectivization proved to be the most difficult experience for many of them. Elderly people were unable to make the transition. Villagers in some places even resisted dissolving the collective farms.

Lukewarm stability disappeared and adjusting to the changes seemed to be impossible for many. New opportunities, as people realized, came bundled with tremendous challenges, most of all lost job security, and the emphasis was now on risk-taking and new life strategies. Sweet daydreams became mixed with confusion and disappointment. The combination of the exhilaration of an open horizon with despair over the distance to reach it became a hallmark of the new life. Social security – one of the advantages of state socialism – disappeared. Macroeconomic stabilization required severe cuts in

---

[48] Adam Michnik, "The Return to History," *Central Europe Review*, 1, 17 (1999), online, http://www.ce-review.org/99/17/michnik17_speech.html

government expenditures. Welfare institutions eroded in a period of rapid inflation when welfare expenditures were not inflation-proof. Personal consumption also deteriorated. The state socialist system was overly egalitarian; now income disparity suddenly increased.

In an essay written in the spring of 1992, "Paradise Lost," the idealist Václav Havel painted a gloomy picture of the rising negative phenomena. "Serious and dangerous symptoms . . . hatred among nationalities, suspicion, racism, even signs of fascism; vicious demagogy . . . a hunger for power . . . fanaticism of every imaginable kind; new and unprecedented varieties of robbery, the rise of different mafias; the general lack of tolerance, understanding, taste, moderation, reason . . . Citizens are becoming more and more clearly disgusted with all these."[49]

Most of the people of the region found themselves bitter and disappointed. They complained about their governments, about the European Union, about prices, and unrealized expectations. Nostalgia for lost security and a more egalitarian society washed over wide swathes of society. Free elections, a dream for decades, were followed soon by huge disappointment. People spoke about "dirty politics and self-serving corrupt politicians." Market transformation strengthened the new individualism and rising apolitical indifference. The "colonization of life by the market"[50] loosened the fabric of society. Disappointment and bitterness, the feeling of being victimized by history is an organic part of the culture of complaint in Central and Eastern Europe. Various peoples of the region traditionally identified themselves in similar ways: "we fought for Europe and were betrayed." The Central and Eastern European culture of complaint and victimization fueled a bitter, nervous, and sometimes even hysterical atmosphere. People nurtured idealistic views about the West. They admired the attractive consumerism, the rich supply of consumer goods, and high living standards, but they neglected to see the price, the work ethic and efficiency, which created it.

Most of all, the transformation, with all of its requirements, collided head on with previously dominant values, cultural habits, and social behavioral patterns. This collision of old internalized values with new requirements played a central role in the social shock that staggered the societies of the region. People had lived under communist rule for two generations by the time the regime collapsed. Whether they liked or

---

[49] Václav Havel, "Paradise Lost," *The New York Review of Books*, April 9, 1992, 6.

[50] José M. Magone, *The Politics of Southern Europe: Integration into the European Union* (Westport, CT: Praeger, 2003), 215.

hated the regime, whether they were interested in politics and ideology or not, all of the people lived in the same social-institutional system, and were educated in its schools. A set of political and ideological values was embedded in the system, and penetrated the society and its institutions. People grew accustomed to living in security and without the need to take risks. They earned little, but could make a living. They knew they would have hospital care when they needed it, and that they would receive cheap or free medication. Their children could go to school and even to university free. Almost everything was guaranteed by the paternalistic state, and hardly anything more was achievable. Risk-taking and entrepreneurial attitudes were kept in check and sometimes even punished. Salaries and incomes were low, but too egalitarian. A modest but stable life did not require much individual initiative. Nobody could be rich, but the social safety net did not allow the bulk of the population to drop out from the society. Unemployment and homelessness were not dangers to worry about. People were used to living in this way and – without even noticing – internalized these values and customs.

Moreover, an anti-entrepreneurial, anti-capitalist attitude had deep historical roots from the nineteenth century on in Central European "noble societies" and communal Balkan peasant societies. They considered capitalism and business to be alien, and left them to non-indigenous elements: Greeks, Germans, and, in many countries, mostly Jews, who were considered non-indigenous despite the fact that they had lived in the countries for generations. In the Balkans, peasant societies where the vast majority of people lived in subsistence peasant-farming households, a capitalist market economy was virtually unknown. The region preserved strong elements of pre-modern society. The most characteristic organizational structure of kinship and networking connections remained an integral part of the social fabric in the region. The traditional paternalistic landlord-peasant and village communities, relationships that survived until the twentieth century, became "institutionalized" as state patronage in state socialist society.

After 1989, the traditional, existing value system was overturned. "Joining Europe," the leading slogan of the time, meant adopting the Western lifestyle, freedom, consumerism, and value system. Risk-taking and entrepreneurship became crucially important, and profitable. The doors were wide open, but most people were frightened to enter into an unknown world. Adam Michnik, one of the founders of post-communist Poland, acknowledged the shock of the emerging new values, and spoke about a "heartless market economy . . . a rat race, [where] money became the only measure of the value ... of life's success."[51] It was difficult to learn the new behavioral patterns. Most of the adult population was unprepared, and became paralyzed and bitter, and a great part of the population of the region looked back to the pre-1989 decades with nostalgia for lost security.

Social shock was not the consequence of economic degradation. The latter hit only certain layers of the society and in many cases only for a few hard years. Social shock was a much more general social phenomenon that characterized a longer period of time in the transforming countries. As Karl Polanyi stated: "Social calamity is primarily a cultural not an economic phenomenon that can be measured by income figures ... Not economic exploitation, as often assumed, but the disintegration of the cultural environment of the victim is then the cause of the degradation ... it lies in the lethal injury to the institutions in which his social existence is embodied ... [It] happen[s] to a people in the midst of violent externally introduced, or at least externally produced change ... though their standard of life ... may have been improved."[52]

Polanyi drew his conclusion from the historical experiences of the British industrial revolution and the impact of colonialism in Africa, when traditional social institutions were equally "disrupted by the very fact that a market economy is foisted upon an entirely differently organized community."[53] A somewhat similar situation emerged in turn-of-the-century Central and Eastern Europe. Absorbing new values and experiencing ugly new phenomena instead of sailing into an imagined paradise contributed to the social shock that these societies experienced. Based on the economic and political transformation, gradual social adjustment will certainly follow, but it may take generations.

The European Social Model: One or Several?
The Union's Policy of "Social Europe"

In 1980, various welfare states still showed signs of their origins in the late nineteenth or earlier twentieth century when they were

---

[51] Adam Michnik, "Confessions of a Converted Dissident: Essay for the Erasmus Prize 2001," Alexandria Biblioteka online, www.alexandria-press.com/online/online20_adam_michnik_confessions.htm-49k-

[52] Karl Polanyi, *The Great Transformation: The Political and Economic Origins of our Time* (Beacon Hills: Beacon Press, [1944] 1957), 157–9.

[53] *Ibid.*, 159.

established. The German, Scandinavian, French, and British welfare states, let alone the poor Eastern European welfare systems, all had different characteristics. Does Europe or the European Union have a "social model"? Most experts answer this question negatively by maintaining that at least three or four different welfare systems exist in Europe: a Scandinavian or social democratic model, a conservative-corporatist model, a Latin or Mediterranean model, and an Anglo-Saxon model.[54] Mark Kleinman, who thoroughly discusses the debates about the topic, concludes: "At present, there is no European welfare state. What do exist are fifteen separate welfare states within the European Union . . . [O]ne cannot speak of a single 'European Social Model' . . . [It] should be considered perhaps as a founding myth which helps to create the concept and reality of 'Europeanism' and a politically integrated Europe."[55] Anthony Giddens also stresses that the European social model "is essentially a contested notion . . . The ESM, it has been said, is not only European, not wholly social and not a model . . . It is not a single model, because there are big divergences between European countries in terms of their welfare systems . . ."[56]

Each of the European welfare states had, indeed, different origins and goals when established, and they exhibit variations and differences from each other. The Central and Eastern European welfare institutions were heavily damaged or even ruined after 1989, but they were genuinely dissimilar from the beginning. Nevertheless, though Europe is not a monolithic block and does not have a uniform European social model, it still provides a model characterized by basic common values such as "universal access to education, accessible and good quality health care, gender equality, solidarity and equity, the recognition of the role of social partners and of social dialogue."[57] Michel Camdessus, managing director of the International Monetary Fund, listed seven main features of the welfare states: free education at

---

[54] Gøsta Esping-Andersen, *The Three Worlds of Welfare Capitalism* (Cambridge: Polity Press, 1990); L. Hantrais, S. Mangen, and M. O'Brian (eds.), *Mixed Economy of Welfare*, Cross-National Research Paper, No. 6 (Loughborough University, 1992); C. Jones (ed.), *New Perspectives on the Welfare State in Europe* (London: Routledge, 1993).

[55] Mark Kleinman, *A European Welfare State? European Union Social Policy in Context* (Houndmills: Palgrave, 2002), 28, 58.

[56] Anthony Giddens, "A Social Model for Europe?" in Anthony Giddens, Patrick Diamond, and Roger Liddle (eds.), *Global Europe, Social Europe* (Cambridge: Polity Press, 2006), 14–36, 14.

[57] Vladimir Špidla, "Some Reflections on the European Social Model," in Detlev Albers, Stephan Haseler, and Henning Meyer (eds.), *Social Europe: A Continent's Answer to Market Fundamentalism* (London Metropolitan University, 2006), 111–17, 112.

all levels; free health care for the population; comprehensive pensions; support for disadvantaged people; compensation for unemployment; subsidies to particular products and activities; and minimum social benefits. He also added: "the term welfare state, has typically been applied to countries in which public spending has risen to very high levels in order to finance social programs."[58]

In spite of various differences, all these characteristics, combined with a uniformly high level of social spending, based on high taxation, are present in the European welfare states. These similarities present a relatively uniform social model for Europe – especially if one compares it to the United States, Asia, or Latin America. Even if some of the non-European countries such as Canada and Australia have similar systems, the welfare state as we know it is closely connected to Europe.

Social policy or the creation of a European social model was not a major consideration in the early development of the integration process. Even the Single European Act signed in 1986 hardly touched this issue. In December 1989, however, the so-called Social Charter was accepted by eleven member states – Britain opted out – on the fundamental social rights of workers, accompanied by a Social Action Program with forty-seven initiatives. In the 1990s, a Social Protocol was attached to the Maastricht Treaty. In 1994, the Commission for the European Union published its White Paper, *European Social Policy: A Way Forward for the Union*. This program set the role of the Union in social policy in a comprehensive way. It maintains that social policy is the responsibility of member states, and the Union does not want total harmonization, but expresses the goal of preserving and assisting and developing the European social model.

It stresses that social standards are not merely costs, but also key elements of competitiveness. Competitiveness and social progress, argues the statement, assist each other: "Progress cannot be founded simply on the basis of the competitiveness of economies, but also on the efficiency of the European society as a whole."[59] The White Paper summarized the shared basic principles of common objectives stressing employment and working condition policies, labor mobility,

---

[58] Michel Camdessus' speech delivered in Paris on October 18, 1998, www.imf.org/external/np/speeches/1998/012198.htm

[59] European Commission, *European Social Policy: A Way Forward for the Union. A White Paper* (Luxembourg: European Commission, 1994), 12.

including integration of immigrants, and gender equality. It reestablished the importance of social protection and inclusion, and the public health system. The European Union gradually developed its social policy agenda in the defense of the welfare state.

This EU document was an implicit response to neo-liberal arguments that set up social security and well-being against the economic requirements of competitiveness. The Union, in contrast, maintained the close interrelations between competitiveness and social well-being. It stressed the importance of combining free market policy with Keynesian interventionism, especially in social affairs. By incorporating principles and social values into the European idea, without attempting central direction, and by maintaining the responsibility of the member states, the social model also became a guideline for social policy for nation-states. The Union's supranational influence may be recognized the most in countries that did not have welfare systems before joining the Union. In Greece, states Ailish Johnson, "supranational governance has been the primary influence in setting new minimum standards for health and safety . . . Greece is modernizing and this is coming from outside."[60] European social policy guidelines influenced advanced welfare states as well. "Even for high-standard Sweden, joining the European Union had transformative effects."[61] In 1988, France also adjusted to the widespread European system by introducing the *Revenue minimum d'insertion*, a guaranteed minimum "integration" income for those who, as President Mitterrand phrased it, "have nothing, can do nothing, are nothing. It is the pre-condition to their social re-insertion."[62]

The Neo-Liberal Attack and the Challenge to the Welfare State

Since 1980, however, the welfare state has been challenged. The unparalleled prosperity of Europe ended in the mid-1970s, and economic growth slowed down significantly. The surplus income that made redistribution easier was lacking, and this forced

---

[60] Ailish Johnson, *European Welfare States and Supranational Governance of Social Policy* (Houndmills: Palgrave Macmillan, 2005), 198–9.

[61] *Ibid.*, 200.

[62] James F. McMillan, *Twentieth-Century France: Politics and Society, 1898–1991* (London: Edward Arnold, 1992), 223.

governments to rationalize and curb expenditures. Globalization sharpened worldwide competition in the spreading international free trade regime. Triumphant neo-liberal economics and neo-conservative ideology claimed that state intervention was the problem, not the solution. Welfare expenditures, they argued, curb competitiveness and are responsible for the slow growth that, in time, undermines social welfare as well. The best welfare policy is, accordingly, to choose efficiency instead of equity, leave the market alone, and let it regulate itself. The market can provide the best social policy.

Neo-conservatives rang the storm-bell and spoke about an "affordability crisis," "accountability crisis," and even a "personal responsibility crisis." The state cannot afford the expenditures, especially because a great part of them are wasted and even undermine social morals by supporting irresponsible individual behavior, and providing a disincentive to work. Its egalitarian tendencies are in sharp contradiction with the basic principle and efficient work of free market capitalism. Opponents used the shortcomings and weaknesses of the welfare institutions against the system. The British Adam Smith Institute's report, "The Omega File: Health Policy" lists "queues for operations" and the bureaucratic character of the system that "serves the administrators rather than patients." The solution for mistakes and shortcomings, it suggests, is privatization.[63]

The welfare systems, without any doubts, had several and sometimes severe shortcomings and negative side effects. The enemies of the systems often used the critical arguments of those who urged the improvement of welfare institutions. Michel Foucault, in an interview in the early 1980s, repeated some of the critical remarks but suggested positive solutions. He maintained that, when the concept of social security emerged, the problem was of "such acuteness and of such immediacy" that other considerations were neglected. From the 1960s and 1970s on, however, "the notion of security has begun to be associated with the question of independence ... [S]ocial security, whatever its positive effects, has also had 'perverse effects' ... [especially] a growth in dependence." Foucault spoke about the "limits" of security, and the need for "individual autonomy," or "optimal social security combined with maximum independence."[64]

---

[63] Ruth Levitas (ed.), *The Ideology of the New Right* (Cambridge: Polity Press, 1986), 13–15.

[64] Michel Foucault, *Politics, Philosophy, Culture. Interviews and Other Writings, 1977–1984* (New York: Routledge, 1988), 160–1.

Stein Kuhnle summarized the main arguments against the welfare state in the following way: "More recently, predictions of crisis and dismantling [of the welfare state] derive from theories that focus on the increasing interdependence . . . or globalization of national economies. The crisis inclined theories now argue that these macro-processes are compelling national welfare states to dismantle their social system radically for reasons of international competitiveness . . . rapidly converging around a lowest common social denominator."[65] Rebecca Blank recalled, "a consensus developed that the cure for Europe's employment problems required . . . a reduction in social protection programs."[66]

Neo-liberal, anti–welfare-state ideas became the newly adopted ideology of the government of the American superpower, the leader of the Western world during the Cold War. The United States has never been a welfare state, but President Franklin D. Roosevelt established major welfare institutions, and the Johnson administration went much further in the same direction. Dean Baker argued: "The election of 1980 was a major turning point for the United States, as the Reagan presidency reversed many of the key trends of the postwar period. Reagan administration policies . . . limited and partially reversed the growth of the welfare state."[67]

The American model, with huge tax cuts and curbed public expenditures, offered better cost-efficiency for the corporate world. The roads of the United States and Western Europe parted ways in this area after 1980. Indeed, Europe has a comparative disadvantage regarding welfare expenditures and tax burdens versus its main rivals, the United States and Japan. Total tax revenue as a percentage of GDP was roughly 26 percent in both the United States and Japan in 2004, compared to an average of 40 percent in the European Union-15. The Nordic countries had the highest taxation level. In spite of significant moderation in the last decades of the twentieth century, it was still 50, 49, 44, and 44 percent of their GDP in Sweden, Denmark, Finland, and Norway, respectively. Taxes on income and profit were only 11 percent in the United States, while they were 30 percent in Denmark, 20 percent in Norway, and 19 percent in Sweden. Similarly, public social expenditures in 2003 amounted to 16 and 18 percent of

---

[65] Stein Kuhnle (ed.), *Survival of the European Welfare State* (London: Routledge, 2000), 160–1, 165.
[66] Rebecca M. Blank (ed.), *Social Protection versus Economic Flexibility: Is there a Trade-off?* (University of Chicago Press, 1994), 21.
[67] Dean Baker, *The United States Since 1980* (Cambridge University Press, 2007), 237.

GDP of the United States and Japan, respectively, but they reached 24 percent in the European Union-15 countries, and 25 percent of GDP in Norway, 28 percent in Denmark, and 31 percent in Sweden.

During the period of postwar prosperity and rapid growth as Rebecca Blank noted: "Social expenditures had grown at a faster rate than real national product... [Prosperity, however,] ended in the early 1970s."[68] Moreover, economic change went hand in hand with the demographic crisis discussed above that itself considerably increased social expenditures, especially pension and health expenses. Mass immigration, also a new factor, brought millions of poor people to Europe to exploit the generous welfare benefits, without proportionately contributing to its funding. Some countries, especially Sweden, did not even differentiate between citizens and other people located in the country.

The OECD published its report in 1981 with the dramatic title, *The Welfare State in Crisis*.[69] Hundreds of studies and public discussions suggested that the welfare state was in crisis. In a speech in 1998, titled "Worldwide Crisis in the Welfare State: What Next in the Context of Globalization?" Michel Camdessus, managing director of the IMF, stated: "Welfare systems, based on the best possible motivation of... improving human welfare, have come to represent an enormous drain on the resources and the efficiency of many of the so called welfare states."[70]

Camdessus argued in the usual way: the welfare state has an enormous cost in two senses. The social expenditure is a too-heavy burden, but the more challenging cost is the loss of efficiency. Competitiveness is undermined in the globalized world economy because of too-high labor costs and high taxation, which become unbearable in the worldwide "tax competition." Moreover, generous unemployment benefits contribute to high unemployment because they kill the incentive to work. The managing director of the IMF did not recommend the abolition of the welfare state, but suggested radical reforms to reduce "unproductive spending" and to "improve" the tax system. Since he compared the European and American taxation levels, his reform suggestion — based on American welfare expenditures and taxation system — would implicitly eliminate the comprehensive welfare state in Europe as we know it.

---

[68] Blank, *Social Protection*, 44.

[69] OECD, *The Welfare State in Crisis: An Account of the Conference on Social Policies in the 1980s* (Paris: OECD, 1981).

[70] Camdessus, Paris speech, 1998, www.imf.org/external/np/speeches/1998/012198.htm

The main neo-liberal and neo-conservative arguments suggest the need for large-scale deregulation and privatization, including of social security and pensions, and the reinvention of the welfare state as a *security state* that provides assistance only for the very poor on social minimum level. In the Netherlands, for example, two sets of Memoranda on the Reconsideration of Public Expenditures were sent to parliament with a comprehensive privatization agenda in 1981–2.[71]

The situation of the welfare regimes definitely changed, but the European countries seemed to be resistant to change for a while. It was partly against the solidarity principles they had learned during the war and had preached for half a century. Furthermore, the welfare state was extremely popular. According to various polls, two-thirds of European citizens want to maintain social protection, even at the cost of higher taxes. The majority of the population – measured in seven West European countries – accepts the need for higher taxes and believes in paying a fair share. "Core services of the welfare state – health, education, housing, and provision for old age, illness, and unemployment – are regarded as a government responsibility by more than 90 percent of the public."[72] Cutting benefits and changing major elements of the system generated militant popular opposition and endangered the possibility of remaining in power for governments where there was a system of regular elections. Nevertheless, most European countries were unable to keep their welfare policy unchanged.

Pension Crisis and Reforms

The pension system became the most vulnerable welfare institution. A rapidly aging population generated a major crisis in the pension sector of the system. In 1980, Europe had a widespread state-run and guaranteed pension system. Although payments into the pension funds were accumulating in all of the European states, in reality, the life-long depositing of the retirees did not cover pension expenditures. Almost all of Europe based the pension systems on the "Pay-As-You-Go" principle, meaning that present payments of the active population are the source of current pension disbursements. Similarly, pensions provided 70 percent (in Sweden) to 90 percent (in Italy) of previous

---

[71] Rob Kroes (ed.), *Neo-conservatism: Its Emergence in the USA and Europe* (Amsterdam: VU Uitgeverij, 1983), 39–41, 45.
[72] Kleinman, *A European Welfare State?*, 18–19.

income level, and required – varying in different countries – between thirty to fifty years of active working. Pension contributions to the companies' pension funds significantly increased labor costs, which was a burden for European companies in the context of global competition, because the United States and Japan had much lower social benefit burdens on companies.

Pension expenses caused a less and less bearable load on society and business. In France, in 1960, four active workers financed each pensioner. By 2000, because of the demographic trend discussed above, only two active workers supported each pensioner. If the trend continues, by 2020, the ratio between active and retired employees will be even. Ireland has the lowest ratio of elderly population among the OECD countries, but it is also inching towards crisis: those 65 years old or older currently account for 21 percent of the population, but by 2025 it will be 29 percent and by 2050, 56 percent.

On the other hand, if pension systems remained unchanged, the growing layers of the elderly population would double the pension expenditures in advanced countries in twenty years. Consequently, either pensions will decline by 50 percent, or pension contributions will double. Actions were definitely needed in the present, but they were painful and sometimes violated rights guaranteed by constitutions. Strong resistance by the population was widespread and in some countries violent. Several governments, however, have introduced, or tried introducing, pension reform schemes.

Nevertheless, state-guaranteed pension systems were replaced around the turn of the century with mixed two- and three-pillar systems in Switzerland, Britain, Germany, France, Finland, Sweden, Italy, and in almost all of the Central and Eastern European countries. The retirement age increased and several privileges were abolished, which eased about three-quarters of the demographic and other pressures on the pension systems.

Switzerland pioneered a new pension model in the 1980s. An obligatory state insurance scheme, including for the self-employed and unemployed, was introduced in 1948, as was done on most of the continent in the postwar years. Wage earners contributed 8 and then 10 percent of their income. It was generous: everybody was eligible if they contributed at least for a full year and reached the age of 64 and 65 for women and men, respectively.

In 1985, Switzerland introduced a "second pillar" of the pension system, mandatory pension insurance with employees contributing

7 to 18 percent. The first and second pillars provided about 60 percent of the previous income as pension. It was soon completed by the introduction of the "third pillar," a voluntary personal pension insurance scheme encouraged by tax incentives. By 2003, half of the employed population participated.

The World Bank in its "Averting the Old Age Crisis" report of 1994 recommended the introduction of three-pillar pension systems. The non-contributory first pillar, the basic pension, was a flat-rate, anti-poverty guarantee of a minimum income; the second pillar was forced savings; while the third was voluntary savings (sometimes with tax concessions). A "fourth pillar" initiative recommends the extension of work years by part-time work in the early retirement age.

From the 1990s on, accumulating deficits forced pension reforms throughout Europe. In Sweden, the more than 4 percent surplus in the public budget in 1990 was replaced by a more than 12 percent deficit by 1993. France and Austria had more than 6 percent and 5 percent deficits by the mid-1990s, respectively. Sweden transformed its universal basic pension into a guaranteed minimum, and it meanwhile introduced individual pension accounts in 1999. Ireland also introduced a flat-rate minimum pension in 2002 and pushed the population towards private schemes. Germany and Italy launched individual pension schemes in 2001 and 2008, respectively.

The Central and Eastern European countries were unable to keep state socialist state-financed pension schemes. Economic and fiscal pressure from a declined national income, high unemployment rates, and the extremely low retirement age of 55 and 60 for women and men, respectively, cried out for change. Mass early retirements in the very first years of transformation increased the percentage of pensioners among the employed from 46 to 75 percent (!) in Hungary. The transforming countries became pioneers for introducing three-pillar pension systems. The situation was somewhat similar in the South European countries that began adjusting to Europe during the 1980s: Spain introduced the three-pillar system in the 1980s, though the voluntary pension insurance assisted by tax exemptions was introduced only in 1995. The three-pillar system was introduced in Hungary in 1998, Poland in 1999, Bulgaria in 2002, and Romania in 2006. Sudden change was, of course, impossible and some transition years were needed. In Hungary, for example, the new system became compulsory for those who enrolled in the workforce after the summer of 1998, but remained optional for others.

Russia moved slowly and introduced the three-pillar system beginning in January 2002. The pressure became overwhelming. Traditional
state-guaranteed pensions were only periodically indexed, and so they
lost their values and became equal to about 20 percent of average
salaries. The deep demographic crisis decreased the employed to pensioner ratio from 5.6:1 to 1.6:1. Additionally, Russia did not change
the retirement age of 55 and 60 for women and men, respectively. The
three-pillar system, based on the Swedish model, guarantees a state
pension based on social security contribution to every citizen, but
the amount is only $100 per month. The second pillar based on social
security contributions that are transferable to private funds, has been
introduced, but it is hardly working yet. Only 4 percent of people
transferred their money to private funds because of the lack of trust
in private insurers. However, this method may lead to a monthly
$300 pension in the next decade. The third pillar, the entirely private
insurance, needs much more time to be effective.

Curbing generous benefits, increasing pension contributions and
retirement age, and cutting special privileges for certain layers of
employees became general practice around the turn of the century.
The retirement age was increased to 65 in Ireland, and compulsory
retirement was abolished in 2003. State pensioners in Italy had the
privilege to retire at the age of 57; this was increased to 60 in 2005.
In France, state employees had to accumulate 37.5 years for a full
pension, and this was modified to 40 years. In state socialist countries,
the retirement age gradually increased from 55 for women and 60 for
men to 62 for both sexes, and is gradually increasing; in the Czech
Republic it became 65 by 2009. Germany introduced benefits due to
increased life expectancy, and replaced the "best three years" or "last
three years" principle in calculating pensions with one based on an
individual's average lifelong income.

In several European countries, early retirements were encouraged
by various concessions. These were all eliminated. In some countries,
public sector workers enjoyed several privileges. It became a major
problem in France where one-quarter of the workforce – teachers,
nurses, police officers, public transportation employees, and utility
workers – all belonged to that category. They enjoyed the privilege of
earlier retirement at the age of 55, and even 50 in certain categories,
as well as bonuses, such as adding an additional 19 and 35 percent
to the pensions of police officers and overseas employees, respectively. After 2003, governments tried to eliminate these privileges.

This generated militant reactions and mass strikes in 2003, 2007, and 2008 that sometimes crippled the country and forced the government to withdraw. French Prime Minister Alain Juppé lost the subsequent elections because of his attempt at radical reforms. In May 2008, strikes swept 153 cities and involved 700,000 workers.

Health Care Systems and Reforms

The well-established European health care systems required reforms and rationalization from 1980 on. The new demographic trends, economic troubles and slowing down, pushed health care expenditures up and state income down. Aging, with higher than average disabilities and chronic diseases, exponentially increase expenditures from the age of 60. An ever-increasing group of elderly population, and a period of about twenty years when medical problems become dominant, steeply increase expenditures. A calculation based on Britain's demographic trends concluded that health expenditures would increase by more than 8 percent during the two decades between 1994 and 2014.[73]

Another important factor in the increase of expenditures is the impressive progress of medical technology, the introduction, among other things, of scanners, MRI, and lithotripters. Pharmaceutical research produced new, sometimes very expensive, but life-saving drugs that help the treatment of previously incurable diseases. Investment and operating costs, however, have increased health expenditures. Besides, medical inflation was more excessive than consumer price increase in general during the entire period. This situation pushed European governments to cut expenditures and introduce cost containment measures. These goals have been at the center of health care reforms from the 1980s. These unavoidable reforms started in the Netherlands, Britain, and Sweden in 1988, and since that time, there has been a constant wave of rationalizing reforms within Europe.

The task, however, was extremely delicate. Health care systems have deep roots in Europe going back to the late nineteenth century in Germany and, in the most "recent" cases, to the end of World War II. One cannot speak about a uniform system in the continent since some of the health care regimes are covered by general taxation,

[73] Elias Mossialos and Julian Le Grand (eds.), *Health Care and Cost Containment in the European Union* (Aldershot: Ashgate, 1999), 55.

others by health insurance. Centralized national systems exist in some cases, while locally managed in others.

However, similarities are more important. All of the systems are state run and offer universal coverage. All citizens have to participate in funding, either by tax payment or by mandatory social–health insurance. In 1996, guaranteed health care covered more than 99 percent of the entire population in thirteen out of fifteen West European countries, and only two countries, Germany and Greece, had 92 and 74 percent coverage, respectively.[74] Europe considers health care a social good, not a market product for profit. It carries basic social values, as the title of the European Community's health ministers' statement of 2003 expressed: "Health, Dignity, and Human Rights." A health service has to provide social cohesion and solidarity.

Regarding the quality of the European health care system, Western Europe was the healthiest region of the world in 2002, as a survey of 175 countries proved. Based on various parameters, nine of the world's ten healthiest countries – Belgium, Iceland, the Netherlands, France, Switzerland, Austria, Sweden, Italy, and Norway – are European, and Germany, Denmark, and Australia share tenth place. It is extremely paradoxical that the United States, which spends the most on health (13 percent of its GDP, or $4,180 per person in a year) is only seventeenth on the list. Belgium, internationally the first in terms of the health of its population, spends only 9 percent of its GDP, i.e. $2,179 per person, hardly more than half of the American total.[75] Analysts maintained in 2007: "West Europe's aging population is exceptionally healthy. As a result, western Europeans are more capable of remaining productive."[76]

The West European countries sought both to reform the system and to preserve its major achievements. How can one cut expenditures, and still keep the basic characteristics of the European health care systems? The European Parliament's session on health care reform summed up the main principles of the reforms in September 2003, and while it stressed the importance of cost containment, it clearly reaffirmed the principle of state-regulated health care systems, as well as the importance of monitoring the potential danger of reducing access to health care. While recommending the introduction of

---

[74] OECD, *Health Data* (Paris: OECD, 1997).

[75] articles.mercola.com/sites/articles/archive/2002/ou/10/health.aspx-48k-

[76] Nicholas Eberstadt and Hans Groth, "Healthy Old Europe," *Foreign Affairs* (May/June, 2007), www.foreignaffairs.com . . . eberstadt-and . . . groth/healthy-old-europe

co-payments to doctors or for hospital visits, it also warned of the danger that higher patient co-payments, or an increase in private insurance schemes, may reduce accessibility to general health coverage.

These guiding principles clearly express that the European Union wants to preserve its social system and does not recommend reforms in the direction of the privatization and marketization of the health service. Instead, they aim at cost containment, micro-level efficiency, better management, competition between state-owned institutions reorganized as independent public firms, and the combination of public and private provider systems. Nevertheless, marketization efforts and elements of privatization appeared in the reform process. Margaret Thatcher argued for marketization in 1988, maintaining that the National Health Service had become a "bottomless pit." The outcome in 1989, the policy document "Working for Patients," introduced only "quasi-market" reforms. People are able to choose doctors, and buy health service outside the national system. The Labour government did not change this system in its 1997 White Paper, or in its 2000 plan.[77] The role of the private sector was re-emphasized, and it became a co-provider of health services. About 15 percent of health service is privately funded. In the hospitals of the National Health Service, 1,400 pay-beds are available for private patients, in surgical hospitals nearly 11,000, and in non–National Health Service institutions nearly 1,700. Although one-third of them are funded by religious and charitable organizations, profit-making organizations run the bulk of them. Nevertheless, the National Health Service, established in 1948 to provide a free service for everybody, remained state-owned and publicly funded. The NHS provides 85 percent of the health services financed from public and collective sources. The central government remained the decision-maker, and public health expenditures significantly increased from 4 to nearly 6 percent of GDP between 1973 and 1993.[78]

In the Netherlands, the Dekker Committee in 1988 recommended the unification of funding sources, and heated debates over a turn towards a market-oriented health care system accompanied the reform process. At the end of the century, compulsory schemes covered

---

[77] Ian Greener, "Consumerism in Health Policy: Where Did it Come from and How Can it Work?," in Alison Hann (ed.), *Health Policy and Politics* (Aldershot: Ashgate, 2007), 59–74, 62–3.

[78] Giovanni Fattore, "Cost Containment and Health Care Reform in the British NHS," in Mossialos and Le Grand (eds.), *Health Care*, 733–81, 739, 768–9, 775.

60 percent of the population, and the remaining 40 percent, above a certain income level, were encouraged to join the voluntary health insurance schemes of various private insurance institutions. Long-term care schemes, however, cover the entire population in a compulsory, state-directed way.[79] On the other hand, voluntary health insurance in the European Union countries is not very widespread, and in most cases, it does not substitute for, but rather supplements public insurance. In France, 85 percent of the population has such additional insurance, but in Sweden, less than 1 percent joined.

The number of private hospital beds is insignificant in the Nordic countries, less than 10 percent, while in France, Spain, Greece, and Ireland only slightly more than half of the hospital beds are publicly owned. In Belgium, the Netherlands, and Luxembourg, most of the acute hospitals are private. In Germany, half are publicly owned, and the other half belong to non-profit institutions.[80] The state, nevertheless, strictly regulates and monitors private health institutions and hospitals throughout Europe.

In spite of the introduction of some market elements and private initiatives in European health care systems after 1980, the systems remained strictly state-run and publicly financed. In 1971, public sources covered two-thirds of the health expenditures in the European Union countries. By 1981, it increased to 80 percent, and in the later 1990s, it remained 78 percent. Public health expenditures consumed an increasing part of GDP in the Union member countries: only 3.5 percent in 1971, but 5.7 percent in 1980, and 6.1 percent in 1996.[81] According to forecast calculations, health spending in Western Europe will increase from $9.6 billion in 2007 to $12 billion by 2011, partly because of the planned improvement of the system's information and communication technology.

Cost containment and various measures to increase efficiency were at the center of rationalization and reform. One of these measures was to cut the length of hospital stays. In Germany, for example, the average length of a hospital stay decreased from fourteen to nine days, still more than 50 percent longer than the American five to six days

---

[79] Mirjam van het Loo, James P. Kahan, and Kieke G. H. Okma, "Developments on Health Care Cost Containment in the Netherlands," in Mossialos and Le Grand (eds.), *Health Care*, 573–603, 578, 600.

[80] Mossialos and Le Grand (eds.), *Health Care*, 14.

[81] *Ibid.*, 48. This work is the basis of the narrative in the next two pages.

average. Ireland decreased the average length of stay in hospitals by 19 percent and hospital bed-days by 25 percent. These steps decreased the expenditure on hospital services by 15 percent.

Medical technology, arthroscopic and laser surgeries offered another major possibility for cost decrease: several surgical interventions became possible without hospitalization. The ten most frequent day-case (without hospitalization) surgical procedures, e.g., hernia, meniscus repair, certain vein surgery, cataract removal, etc., account for half of the total. (Cataract surgery using traditional methods required six to ten days hospitalization in several European countries.) In Britain in the early 1990s, nearly one-third of surgery occurred without hospitalization. In Mediterranean countries, however, these procedures are only slowly gaining ground. Rationalization allowed a decrease in the number of expensive hospital beds. Between 1980 and 1995, the number of beds per 1,000 inhabitants decreased by 58 percent in Sweden, 47 percent in Ireland, 42 percent in Britain, and 40 percent in Finland and Denmark. In most of the other countries, the decrease was 15 to 20 percent.

Most of the countries also introduced deductibles and moderate co-payments, partly to decrease public expenditures, but mostly to decrease the number of visits. In Germany, when the system was introduced in 1997, the number of visits declined by 15 percent. France introduced a Health Care Card in 1996 to monitor the visits, and, on the other hand, established the Couverture Maladie Universelle in 2000 for the underprivileged. Patient co-payment, except in Germany and France, remained marginal, contributing 1 to 3 percent of financing, compared to nearly 8 percent in America. In Ireland, 36 percent of the population does not have to pay; in France, health services are completely free for 10 percent of the population. Germany introduced a ceiling, equal to 2 to 4 percent of a family's income. Sweden's maximum co-payment may not surpass €300 per year, and people of low income and with chronic diseases are exempt from paying.

Home care and nursing services are very developed and publicly financed in several Scandinavian countries: users pay only 5 to 10 percent in Denmark, and between 10 and 35 percent of the cost in Finland. In Italy, they pay nothing at all for such services, but the system is non-existent in the other Mediterranean countries. In six Union member countries, co-payment for home service does not exist.

Most of the countries introduced price control for pharmaceutical products and bind local price levels to a combination of other European countries' levels. User contribution is common, but low-income people and those with chronic diseases get full or 50 percent reimbursement. In Italy, for example, users paid only 16 percent of pharmaceutical expenditures, while public sources covered 84 percent.

Several other measures were taken, including budget fixing and rearrangement of the traditionally fragmented organization. Norway transferred all public hospitals from the county to the national government level, and then transformed them into quasi-independent public firms. In 1989, Spain changed its system from a social insurance-funded model, to a tax-funded national health service. Organizational changes also served efficiency and cost containment.

Transforming Central and Eastern Europe faced a rather different situation. These countries inherited a poor, but working nationwide health care system. The *Economic Survey of Europe* evaluated in 2004: "Under the socialist system, access to health care was not an issue, with universal entitlement to [a] comprehensive and free, but inefficient . . . [and poorly equipped] system. Indicators of population health were good by international standards. Tragically, the decade after the regime change has seen [a] major reversal in both health and health care."[82] In the region, cost containment was not a solution.

Macroeconomic stabilization and debt repayment required severe cuts in state expenditures. This had a deadly effect on the entirely state-financed health system. Cutting health care expenditures was strongly "advised" by international financial institutions, and pushed by pressing budgetary deficits. Sickness benefits dropped in the Czech Republic by 16 and 33 percent in 1995 and 1999, respectively.[83] Subsidies for drugs virtually ended, and elderly and retired people could not buy even prescription drugs.

This went hand in hand with the beginning of the privatization of health care services. The process was very slow and controversial and met with agitated resistance. Demonstrations and referenda blocked the way to closing hospitals and introducing co-payments. To avoid a

[82] United Nations, *Economic Survey of Europe* (New York and Geneva: United Nations, 2004), 170.
[83] Władisław Adamski, Pavel Machonin, and Wolfgang Zampf (eds.), *Structural Change and Modernization in Post-Socialist Societies* (Hamburg: Reinhold Krämer, 2002), 42.

major health crisis, the state still covers the deficits of the system and provides insurance for roughly 90 percent of the population.

A report in 2002 describes a steeply deteriorating health care situation: "Hospitals and other facilities are left to rot for lack of maintenance or shut down altogether . . . Medicines and other substances . . . are no longer affordable."[84] The United Nations International Labour Organization (ILO) warned in its 2001 press release: "The economic and social situation in several East European countries has resulted in the near collapse of some health care systems."[85] The People's Security Survey of the ILO reported that most Hungarian families claimed to be unable to afford even basic care. Hungary announced the closing of forty hospitals in the spring of 2006. Poland closed one in every twenty hospitals between 1998 and 2001.

The average number of hospital beds in eleven countries of the region dropped from 942 to 719 per 100,000 inhabitants, and it nearly halved in Estonia in the decade between 1993 and 2003. The rationalization of hospital services was unavoidable: the inefficient socialist health regime used expensive hospital beds as nursing home places, and even as shelters for the homeless. In 1993, the ratio of hospital beds to the population was one-third higher than in the European Union countries, and even after the reduction, it remained 18 percent higher by 2003. The process is not yet complete.

Difficulties, however, are mounting. The decline in the level of health in some of the countries of the region reached tragic proportions: by the end of the 1990s, tuberculosis reemerged in some countries: Latvia and Lithuania saw 80 cases per 1,000 people, a higher incidence than in the Third World (68.6 per 1,000). In Romania, this ratio exceeds that of sub-Saharan Africa.[86] Sickness and health care benefits, which reached an average €1,900 per person in the EU-15 countries, reached only €400 in Poland, and around €300 in Latvia and Lithuania.[87]

---

[84] Sam Vaknin, "World in Conflict and Economies in Transition," United Press International, May 9, 2002, www.samvak.tripod.com/briefs/html-22k

[85] International Labour Organization, "East European Healthcare in Crisis," Geneva, ILO/01/53, ILO, Press release, December 10, 2001.

[86] World Bank Report, October 12, 2005 (Washington, DC: World Bank, 2005); Sam Vaknin, "The Dying Breed: Healthcare in Eastern Europe," 2006, http://samvak.tripod.com/pp143.html, 1–9; Eurostat, 2005 on-line.

[87] Eurostat, 2005 online. Benefits were higher in Slovenia and the Czech Republic, €1,300 and €1,000, respectively, and €800 in Hungary.

Educational Systems and Reform; Higher Education and the Tuition Fee

European educational systems, though well developed, required further major reforms to be able to respond to the new requirements of a knowledge-based economy, global competition, and European integration from 1980 on. The new age required increased enrollment, especially in higher education, and the modernization of training at all levels. The decline of blue-collar jobs and the rising service revolution made it vital to learn new skills. Rapid technological changes often made old skills obsolete and workers required retraining, even lifelong training.

The integration made it necessary to harmonize education and to assist the development of a common European identity with convertible qualifications that would be accepted throughout Europe. It also forced new strategies in language education and exchange programs. Budgetary strains and the need for cutting public expenditures, including educational expenses, accompanied towering new challenges. West European countries faced the multiple tasks of modernizing, maintaining, and further developing the achievements of the educational systems, while at the same time rationalizing expenditures. The West focused strongly on education and prepared new legislation to increase the length and improve the structure and level of training. The Treaty of Rome in 1957 did not include the problems of education, and the Maastricht Treaty of 1992 was the first that introduced education into Union treaties.[88]

Extended education, as a new trend around the turn of the twenty-first century, meant not only post-elementary training, but *pre-school training* as well. The recognition of the importance of early schooling was not new; attention had already been drawn to it by Jean-Jacques Rousseau. The institution, though not compulsory everywhere, became widespread during the last decades of the century. Enrollment, on average, included more than 87 percent of children between the ages of 3 and 5 in the European Union-25 countries.

The countries of the Union also extended compulsory education to 9 or 10 year olds. For the first time in history, part of secondary education became compulsory, common to nearly all children. Various measures were taken to create a more democratic and comprehensive educational system. All of the countries postponed specialization to

[88] *Ibid.*, 96.

strengthen basic, general education. Spain abolished specialization before the age of 16 in 1990, and Finland delayed it until the end of compulsory education. Some countries, again a novelty in European education, introduced a unified, single-stream school curriculum at the secondary level from the 1970s to 1980s on. Norway, Sweden (with their nine-year common school), Italy (*scuola media*), and France (*collèges d'enseignement secondaire*) introduced a single-stream comprehensive curriculum at least for the lower secondary levels.

In most cases, however, as in Germany, Austria, and Switzerland, parallel streams of extended primary school, "short" or upper-primary, and "long" or pre-university schools preserved a dual system. "In most of Europe," stated an OECD report, "the selective nature of general education at secondary level and the great differences in content of general and vocational courses are outstanding features."[89] In one way or another, vocational training, which was not a part of institutionalized education and followed only a modernized version of a guild-type apprenticeship, training on the job, now became an organic part of secondary education and a mass training ground for those between the ages of 15 and 18.

Enrollments in secondary schools started to balloon in the 1970s, and during the 1980s the percentage of enrolled students increased to two-thirds of the age group. In several West European countries, this share reached 75 to 90 percent. As a new achievement, 80 to 90 percent of students in upper secondary education graduated in 2004.[90] This made higher education accessible for huge masses.

Belgium offers one of the best examples of the turn-of-the-century educational revolution. In the 1980s, pre-schooling became virtually the norm: 90, 97, and 100 percent of the 3-, 4-, and 5-year-olds, respectively, attended pre-schools. In a pioneering move, and the first in the continent, a law of June 1983 introduced twelve years of compulsory education, from 6 to 18 years of age. The huge educational budgets made the schools well equipped and efficient. The student–teacher ratio was 20:1. Secondary education offered general, technical, and vocational training.[91]

[89] OECD, *Structural Adjustment and Economic Performances* (Paris: OECD, 1987), 72.
[90] *OECD in Figures*, 2007, 52–3. In Belgium, Sweden, Switzerland, and Austria, between 80 and 90% of the generation enrolled in secondary education. Around three-quarters of the age group enrolled in France, Denmark, and Norway, and nearly as much in Italy.
[91] European Commission, *Educational Structures in the Member States of the European Communities* (Brussels: European Commission, 1987).

An important new feature of post–1980 educational progress was the catching up of previously peripheral Mediterranean countries with backward educational systems. The new member countries of the European Union during the 1980s followed in the footsteps of the old West European member countries and modernized their educational systems accordingly. Spain, for example, gradually began to catch up with Western Europe, and introduced the *jardin de infancia* for 2- and 3-year-old children and *escuela de párvulos* for 4- and 5-year-olds. More than 90 percent of the relevant age group was enrolled in the second type of pre-school in the mid-1980s. This was followed by the compulsory eight years of basic education. At the secondary level, the Integrated Secondary Education system that prepares students for universities and vocational training remained separated into different institutions.

The Eastern half of the continent had a well-advanced educational system in the 1980s. Kindergartens and pre-school systems – state, community, and enterprise institutions – were established throughout the Soviet Bloc. These institutions absorbed more than 90 percent of children between the ages of 3 and 5 years. Basic general school education lasted from eight to ten years. For the first time in the region's history, almost the entire 14 to 18 age group enrolled in secondary education during the 1980s. However, this new mass education was over-specialized at all levels. At the secondary level, three types of schools were available. One was the German-type "gymnasium" (grammar schools) with a strong general education. Another was the so-called "technicum" with limited general education combined with specialized skills. The third type was a vocational training institution combined with some elements of basic general education. Such education was targeted to provide immediately usable practical skills, instead of strong basic education that could offer further and even lifelong training and retraining. Most of the secondary school children enrolled in vocationally oriented studies. In Czechoslovakia in 1990, 61 percent of the age group studied in vocational schools, 20 percent in technical schools, and only 15 percent in gymnasiums.

Higher education became a mass phenomenon in postwar Europe and included one-fifth to one-quarter of the age group between 18 and 24 in the Western half of the continent. In some countries, e.g., Britain, this percentage neared one-third of the generation, and in some countries, like Sweden, it was even higher.[92] The average years of education for the adult population increased dramatically during the 1980s: from twelve to sixteen years in France, from ten to thirteen years in the Netherlands, and from twelve to fourteen years in Britain.[93] By 2004, the average number of years in school reached seventeen years in some European countries such as Finland and Norway.

As a striking sign of the growing importance of higher education, 75 percent of the newly created jobs in Western Europe during the second half of the 1990s occurred in high-education sectors, i.e., knowledge-based economic branches where more than 40 percent of workers had tertiary education. In 2005, the employment rate for highly skilled people reached 83 percent, while only 46 percent for the low skilled. The high-educational sectors represented about one-quarter of the total labor force.[94]

Higher education in Eastern Europe also became a mass phenomenon: 10 to 15 percent of 18- to 24-year-olds enrolled in some form of higher training during the 1980s, including evening and part-time training. Central and Eastern Europe, for the first time in its history, began catching up with the rest of the continent in terms of the numbers of young people enrolled in higher education. However, similarly to secondary education, tertiary training was also over-specialized and strongly practical, which did not provide a good enough foundation for retraining and flexibility in further education. Half of the students in higher education studied in various *Hochschule*-type institutions that prepared them for agriculture, foreign trade, the hotel and restaurant business, construction work, etc. At certain periods, students in economics received thirty-six different types of diplomas in Hungary. After the collapse of communism in 1989, enrollment in higher education significantly increased and reached the West European level.[95]

---

[92] During the 1980s, adult enrollment of people above 25 and even 30 also became significant. Their percentage at higher educational institutions surpassed one-third (Switzerland, Holland, France), or reached one-half (Germany, Finland, Denmark) of the enrolled.

[93] Maddison, *Monitoring*, 37. To give an international comparison, students spend 9 years in school in Asia and 7.6 years in Africa.

[94] European Commission, *European Economy* (Brussels: European Commission, 2000), 37; *OECD in Figures, 2007*, 52–3.

[95] In Poland, the rate rose from less than 10% to nearly 16%, in several other countries of the region from 10–15 to 20–25% by 2004. In Russia, enrollment exploded and reached more than 56% of the age group between 25 and 34.

In a painful change, the welfare states, which previously offered education at all levels free of charge, gradually introduced *tuition fees* for higher education. Britain initiated this trend in 1998, which then spread throughout the continent. The Netherlands, Austria, Italy, Spain, and Portugal all followed the British example, but Scandinavia remained an exception. As *The Guardian* reported in October 2003, "With German universities in crisis, and no help forthcoming from the government, vice-chancellors in Germany are now contemplating the previously unthinkable: tuition fees."[96] Seven *Ländern* in Germany introduced tuition fees in 2005 and 2006, and they were met with major student demonstrations in Hamburg and other parts of the country. Demonstrations spread throughout the continent. In Greece, where the constitution guaranteed free education, students demonstrating against tuition fees occupied 400 universities in July 2006. Compared to American universities, tuition fees are moderate in Europe. The highest British fees vary between £1,025 and £3,000 per year. The second highest fee in the Netherlands is €1,445 (less than £1,000). In most of the countries, it varies between €600 and €1,450.

The introduction of tuition fees has already been supported by the European Commission, as its February 20, 2008 report illustrates. The income from tuition fees moderately contributes to higher educational expenses, but it also assists rationalization. The free educational system caused huge amounts of waste in several countries because of postponed graduation. At Italian universities, 70 percent of the students are not graduating on time but "parking" at the universities for years. "Long-term students" are present everywhere, though the Guinness world record was certainly kept by the Freie Universität Berlin, where one of the students studied for ninety-two semesters, i.e., for forty-six years. In Germany, tuition fees reduced the number of enrolled students by 15 percent. Reducing the numbers is especially important in Central and Eastern Europe where an overblown student body and the lack of appropriate financing led to a major decline in the quality of education.

Although the Nordic countries, Sweden, Denmark, and Finland, kept free higher education, several other countries also tried to counterbalance the introduction of tuition fees. The Netherlands,

---

[96] Luke Harding, "Tuition Fees Gain Allure in Cash Hit European Campuses," *The Guardian*, October 13, 2003, 15.

for example, introduced a loan system. Every student is eligible to receive a loan of €2,640 per year, which becomes a grant if the student meets certain academic criteria. Hungary offers another example: they kept a tuition-free system, but limited the number of tuition-free university places during the second half of the 1990s to those students who achieved the best results, while other candidates were also accepted and enrolled, but had to pay for tuition. By 2006, 40 percent of university students paid tuition fees. The number of tuition-free places was later further limited by an additional 10 percent in 2006. From 2007, the government announced the cautious adaptation of the Australian system: after graduation, students must repay part of their educational costs. State loans, however, do not accrue interest, and the annual repayment schedule is capped at 6 percent of a graduate's income. Below a certain income level, repayment is waived.

European countries spent a significant part of their GDP on education in 2003, most of them between 5 and 6 percent. The level, however, was not even: Iceland and Denmark spent 8 and 7 percent, respectively, while Greece spent only slightly more than 4 percent, and the Czech Republic and Spain spent nearly 5 percent each. Between 1995 and 2003, educational expenditures increased by from 10 to 30 percent in most of the European countries, and in Ireland as much as 65 percent. Spending is rather uneven and differs vastly among the European regions. The South and East spend much less than the West and Scandinavia, but Europe as a whole spends half as much as the United States.[97]

In the Central and Eastern European countries, the ballooning number of students in tertiary education was not accompanied by increased spending: while the number of students increased by 86 percent, expenditure per student only increased by 39 percent in the Czech Republic between 1995 and 2003, thus expenditure per student

---

[97] OECD, *Factbook*, 2007, 183, 185; *OECD in Figures*, 2007, 50–1. In 2003, the average spending on education per student at the primary level – using purchasing power parity dollars – was $6,000–$7,000 in Western Europe, and $3,000–$4,000 in Southern and Eastern Europe. At the secondary level, spending was $7,000–$8,000 in the West, and $3,000–$4,000 in the East, while at the tertiary levels the West spent $10,000–$12,000, and the East $5,000–$8,000. The United States spent roughly twice as much: $8,305, $9,590, and $24,074 at the three levels, respectively. Expenditure for students in tertiary education exhibits major differences among the European countries: the highest level characterizes Switzerland ($25,900 per student) and Sweden ($16,073), the other Nordic countries have spent $12,000–$14,000; Belgium, France, and Germany more than $10,000; but Greece, Poland, and Slovakia only roughly $4,000, and Russia $2,400.

dropped to 74 percent of the 1995 level. In Poland, this decline was even sharper: expenditures reached only 63 percent of the 1995 level in 2003.

As in health care, however, spending does not determine the quality and success of education. The OECD's Programme for International Student Assessment (PISA) reflects that, at the age of 15, the mean score in reading in 2003 was higher than the OECD average in six European countries, and in science, it was higher in nine countries. In spite of much lower spending, the scores in the Czech Republic and Hungary were higher than in Germany or in the United States. While Finland had the highest literacy score and the lowest under-achievement rate (10 percent), the United States – spending twice as much as the European countries – had the lowest mean literacy and by far the highest under-achievement rates (60 percent). On the other hand, higher education is better in the United States than in Europe: in 2005 there were seventeen American universities among the world's top twenty universities, and only two European ones (Cambridge and Oxford).[98] Regarding the use of modern technology in education, 90 percent of Finnish primary school students used computers, while this figure is only 25 percent in Italy. One-half of students in the Nordic countries, and one-third of them in most Western and some of the Southern and Central European countries, have used computers for more than five years by the age of 15. These percentages were significantly lower in Greece, Slovakia, Italy, and Poland (between 14 and 20 percent).[99]

Although schooling provides the most important basis of knowl-edge, it was certainly not the only one at the turn of the century. The European Union declared 1996 the "Year of Lifelong Education." By means of various courses, training and skill-retraining became widespread in Europe: 40 percent of Irish workers, 30 percent of Dan-ish, French, and British workers, and 20 percent of Italian, Greek, and Portuguese workers participate in continuing vocational training. This form of training is sometimes also internationalized and offers training abroad, and is combined with language education. Online degrees and other sources help lifelong learning even without formal schooling.

---

[98] Joseph Zajda (ed.), *International Handbook on Globalization, Education and Policy Research* (Dordrecht: Springer, 2005). In 2009, there were thirteen American universities in the top twenty.

[99] OECD, *Factbook*, 2007, 177.

"Europeanization" of the Educational Systems

Around the turn of the century, a *major wave of reforms* changed the
European educational systems. One of them was the European Union's
initiative to give a "European dimension" to education. Education is
the responsibility of national authorities, but the Union initiated several programs to influence it and promote European cooperation, in
a slow and gradual development towards a Europeanized educational
system. One of the most important initiatives towards this goal was the
introduction of the *Socrates* program in 1995. Its main actions aimed at
European cooperation and exchange at the various levels of education.
It included the *Comenius* program from pre-schools to secondary level;
the *Erasmus* program for tertiary levels, and the *Grundtvig* program for
adult education. In 1994, the European Council also introduced the
Leonardo da Vinci program for implementing a common vocational
training. In connection with that, the *Europass* training in 1999 introduced work-linked training and apprenticeship in another European
Union country. In connection with all the educational programs, the
Socrates *Lingua* program assisted extensive language studies at all levels, with a target of teaching at least two or even three languages
during studies throughout the Union. The *Minerva* program made
new incentives for use of information and communication technology in education.

The program had immense success and established a broad network of cooperation. Partnership cooperation already involved 10,000
schools from the existing 340,000 European schools in the first
five years. Textbook revisions and changes aimed at the avoidance
of national (nationalist) stereotypes and the strengthening of a pan-
European identity. In 1997, a new initiative advocated uniform subjects throughout the Union, "to introduce . . . in all EU schools a
specific academic subject . . . taught to all EU children and its content
would be the same across the Union."[100] The Union-wide subjects
would serve the development of common knowledge on Europe and
the development of a European identity. Teachers and future teachers
gained grants to spend time and take courses in other countries. Language teaching gained a new incentive from primary schools onward
and through the exchange of students.

---

[100] European Commission, *Education – Training – Research: The Obstacles to Transnational Mobility*
(Brussels: Economic and Social Committee of the European Communities, 1997).

On the higher educational level, with the involvement of virtually all of the European universities, the Union initiated the successful Erasmus exchange program (in 1987, actually before the Socrates program). In 2002, it celebrated the one-millionth participant. By 2010, the Union's plan is to treble the number of participants. In the exchange program, students studied at universities of another country for a period of three to twelve months, financed by Union grants. Grants also financed language studies for students before they traveled abroad. Countries with fewer spoken languages began internationalizing their university education: Amsterdam University teaches one-quarter of its courses in English to make exchange easier. Teacher exchange and cross-teaching, preparation of joint courses, and intensive summer sessions all promote close cooperation and the Europeanization of higher education.

In 2000, the second phase of the Socrates program aimed to enlarge the number of participating institutions and students. Recruited from thirty-one countries, students also participate from non-member, or not even candidate, countries of the European Union. During the seven years between 2000 and 2006, the Union's budget spent €1.9 billion on these educational programs. Most of the Union's programs and financing, however, aimed to generate appropriate local educational programs and cooperative arrangements, initiated by EU pilot programs and seed money.[101]

The single market project and the requirement for the free movement of labor required the harmonization of the structure of higher education. This requirement led to the initiative of Italy, France, Germany, and Britain in 1998 to "harmonize the architecture of the European higher education system." The next year, twenty-nine countries signed the Bologna Declaration. It is not a European Union agreement, though all of the member countries participated, and the Union's Commission plays an important role in the organization. According to the Bologna process, the member countries of the "European higher educational area" – in 2008, already forty-nine countries – will reorganize their university systems to make them compatible and comparable by 2010. Based on the American three-cycle structure, separated, but also closely connected BA, MA,

---

[101] European Commission, *Gateway to Education. Socrates: European Community Action Programme in the Field of Education (2000–06)* (Luxembourg: Office for Official Publications of the European Communities, 2000); Council of the European Union, *Statements on Education, Training and Young People, 1998–2001* (Luxembourg: Office for Official Publications of the European Communities, 2002).

and PhD cycles follow each other. Italy and Hungary, among other countries, have already introduced this system with a three- to four-year Bachelor, and two-year Masters cycle. For those who go on to an academic career, a three-year PhD follows.

To be comparable and compatible, the European system introduced qualification norms and quality assurance. Since the diplomas are recognized throughout Europe, a peer review system and accreditation bodies control and compare quality requirements. The European Credit Transfer System (ECTS) harmonized the credit systems and degrees that make it possible to study for a certain period at another country's university. The European university degree system will be uniform on the continent.[102]

The State of the Welfare State

The welfare institutions have definitely been weakened since 1980: the pension system has been transformed, citizens' participation in financing pensions increased dramatically, as well as increasing somewhat in both health care and education. All of the countries also reformed and rationalized several other elements of the welfare system. Unemployment compensation that had more than doubled between the mid-1980s and 2000 was reformed by eliminating its "work disincentives" character. Compulsory programs were introduced, retraining courses, participation in some form of work, lowering payments – in Spain it was half to two-thirds of the minimal wage – and penalizing the rejection of reasonable job offers aimed at the reactivation of the unemployed. The countries of Europe combined welfare and "workfare" policies.

Home care services, provided for elderly people in their own homes, a general policy of several West European countries, involved private providers, though they were state financed. In Sweden, it became restricted to those who are in need, but it was no longer a routine service provided for everyone. Paid parental leave is still rather generous in the Nordic countries. In Norway, it was extended to forty-two weeks on full pay, or fifty-two weeks with 80 percent of the salary.

---

[102] Council of Europe, *Strategies for Educational Reform: From Concept to Realization* (Strasbourg: Council of Europe Publishing, 2000); *Standards and Guidelines for Quality Assurance in the European Higher Education Area* (Helsinki: European Association for Quality Assurance in Higher Education, 2005).

Sweden made it possible to take off a whole year with 80 percent of the previous salary. In several European Union member countries parental leave has been extended to thirty-six paid weeks, while in Britain it is limited to twenty-six weeks, and the extension of such leave, though possible, becomes unpaid. The European Union's 1992, and then 1998, directives recommended a three months' parental leave policy that influenced member countries to issue new parental leave policies. Every country introduced paternity leave to stress gender equality. Austria offers three parental leave years if the father takes off the last six months. Denmark, Norway, and Sweden offer one additional paternal leave on a "use it or lose it" basis.[103]

Altogether, Europe preserved the welfare state. They combined flexibility with security, or introduced, as the euro-jargon calls it, "*flexicurity*." The essence of reform, as Poul Rasmussen, former socialist Danish prime minister phrased it, is renewing, not rolling back, social Europe.[104]

Moreover, the European Community initiated *new programs* to strengthen its social model and welfare institutions around the turn of the century. The Irish initiated the Action Program to combat "chronic poverty" and to help the "neglected minority of chronically poor, such as the 'unemployables' and their families; families on exceptionally low incomes, or fatherless families."[105] The cohesion policy and Community interventions also gained impetus from the 1980s to counterbalance the negative impact of free market forces for less developed areas, and regions of high unemployment. "The Act established a Community policy of economic and social cohesion to counterbalance the effects of the competition of the internal market on the less developed Member States and to reduce development discrepancies between the regions."[106] Social policy has to shape the impact of globalization and counterbalance its negative social consequences.

---

[103] Although there are significant differences in parental leave policy among the member countries of the Union, these are insignificant compared to that between the EU countries and the United States, where the 1993 law introduced twelve weeks unpaid, job-protected maternity leave.

[104] Poul N. Rasmussen, "Renewing not Rolling Back Social Europe," in Detlev Albers, Stephen Haseler, and Henning Meyer (eds.), *Social Europe: A Continent's Answer to Market Fundamentalism* (London Metropolitan University, 2006), 117–24, 117.

[105] Jane Dennett, Edward James, Graham Room, and Philippa Watson, *Europe Against Poverty: The European Poverty Programme 1975–80* (London: Bedford Square Press, 1982), 3–5, 210.

[106] Activities of the European Union: Surveys of Legislation, europa.eu/scadplus/treaties/singleact_eu.htm-31k-

One of the best parameters by which to evaluate the state of social policy practice in Europe is the *social expenditure* that, in spite of some restrictions, continued to rise. Social transfer, as an average, was only 6 to 10 percent of GDP in 1950, and it rose to 15 to 20 percent by the mid-1970s. After 1980, it continued to grow: between 1990 and 2003, social expenditures increased by more than 9 percent and reached roughly 22 to 24 percent of the GDP in the various EU-15 countries.

The Mediterranean countries, in connection with their acceptance by the European Community in the 1980s, followed in the footsteps of the old member countries of Western Europe and built up similar welfare systems. Spain increased social expenditures from 15 to 22 percent of its GDP during the 1980s, and Portugal gradually elevated its expenditures to a similar level that represented a more than 70 percent increase in social expenditures between 1990 and 2003. At the same time, Greece's social expenditures also increased faster than the EU average by nearly 15 percent and reached the Western level.

In spite of the often-discussed "crisis" and ideological attacks against the welfare state, Europe continues to spend more on modifying the social consequences of market forces than before. The ideas of Thomas Humphrey Marshall, elaborated in his Cambridge University lectures in 1949 about *social citizenship*, basically remained in force in turn-of-the-century Europe. According to Marshall, in contrast to neo-liberal views, market capitalism is not almighty and cannot solve social problems. Markets genuinely generate inequalities. To avoid reproducing social exclusion, corrective forces are needed to establish a social right to live the life of a civilized being according to the standards prevailing in the society, as part of citizenship rights.[107]

The state continued to play a redistributive role via taxation. Budgetary expenditures are financing about one-fifth to one-quarter of private consumption in most European countries. As one analyst, Peter Lindert, summed up: "This quarter-century has seen a wave of enthusiasm for cutting taxes and transfers [tax based government spending], privatizing state industries and trimming union power . . . [However] the welfare state is not an endangered species among the industrialized OECD countries. While its growth clearly slackened after 1980,

---

[107] Thomas H. Marshall, *Citizenship and Social Class and Other Essays* (Cambridge University Press, 1950); Amartya Sen, *Inequality Reexamined* (Oxford: Clarendon Press, 1992).

social transfers continue to take a slowly rising share of GDP . . . There is no sign of a global 'race to the bottom,' either in the 1980s or since 1990. There is nothing that even faintly suggests that countries are scrambling to reduce the tax rates implied by their social budget, to compete for mobile factors of production."[108]

In the Eastern half of the continent, however, the post-communist transformation endangered the poor but universal welfare systems. The paternalistic state rapidly withered away, and social security payments by the state – in constant prices – fell. Full employment was replaced by high unemployment. Child benefits decreased to less than 43 percent of the 1989 level by 1995, and to less than 33 percent by 1999. Family allowances decreased from 3 percent of the GDP in 1989 to less than 1 percent by 2002 in Hungary.

Reform and rationalization were really needed as well as better health and children's services. This double task, however, was beyond the capabilities of the transforming countries in the first two decades after regime change. Governments were in a difficult situation. Eliminating welfare institutions is a risky task. The Czech government wanted a new law introducing tuition fees at the universities in the mid-1990s but it failed in the parliament. They also had to postpone the planned privatization of hospitals. The Constitutional Court of the country rejected the co-payment scheme for certain services as being unconstitutional.[109] Co-payment, however, was introduced in 2008. In 1998, the populist Hungarian Fidesz party reintroduced while in government several state subsidies, which had been eliminated by its predecessor socialist government. Austerity measures to reestablish a balanced budget ignited violent riots and atrocities in the fall of 2006 and the spring of 2007. Co-payments for visits and hospital days were voted down by a referendum organized by Fidesz. Gradually limiting social and welfare benefits, however, gained ground. In the mid-1990s, the Hungarian government tried to introduce tuition fees at universities, but had to withdraw them. Subsequently, however, tuition fees have been introduced in a gradual fashion.

---

[108] Peter H. Lindert, "What is Happening to the Welfare State?" in Paul W. Rhode and Gianni Toniolo (eds.), *The Global Economy in the 1990s: A Long-Run Perspective* (Cambridge University Press, 2006), 234–62, 234, 261.

[109] František Turnovec, "Political Economy of Social Welfare Reform: The Parliamentary Elections of 1996 in the Czech Republic," in Irwin Collier, Herwig Roggemann, Oliver Scholz, and Horst Tomann (eds.), *Welfare States in Transition* (Houndmills: Palgrave Macmillan, 1999), 114–36, 115.

In the first period of transformation, on the other hand, the Central and Eastern European countries, at least temporarily, had to introduce various kinds of new social assistance schemes. Among others, families below the poverty threshold became eligible for social assistance benefits in cash or in kind.[110] The increased poverty of the elderly led to the introduction of home care services, including professional nursing services in Hungary in 1977. To counter the dramatic decline in the birth rate, Lithuania introduced 126 days of paid parental leave in 1996. Estonia and Latvia offered 112 days of leave, paying 60 to 70 percent of the mother's previous earnings, in 2004 and 2005, respectively. Latvia and Estonia also reintroduced universal child allowances, but the amount is not greater than about 5 percent of the parents' average earnings.[111]

Altogether, welfare institutions are declining. However, they are still comprehensive but too expensive for the Eastern countries. Total expenditures on social protection absorb 20 to 25 percent of GDP in Slovenia, Poland, Hungary, and the Czech Republic, and 13 to 14 percent in the Baltic states. This share is much higher than in Latin America (10 percent), which has a somewhat similar income level. The redistribution rate of GDP, i.e., the percentage of direct and indirect taxes, and the social security contribution, is still very high in Central Europe: roughly 39 percent of GDP around the turn of the century. Although this percentage is somewhat lower than in the European Union, it is much higher than in the United States and Japan. In the given situation, it represents a heavy burden on the budget and the economy.

Nevertheless, the relative and absolute level of welfare expenditures in Central and Eastern Europe is far below the average of the EU-15. In 2003, the latter spent nearly €7,000 for social protection expenditures per head, while the most generous Central and Eastern European countries, Slovenia, the Czech Republic, and Hungary, spent roughly €3,000, €1,600, and €1,600, respectively. Poland allocated only €1,100 in expenditures per person, Estonia €800, and Latvia and Lithuania €600.

[110] Alfio Cerami, *Social Policy in Central and Eastern Europe: The Emergence of a New European Model of Solidarity*, Third Annual ESPAnet Conference, September 2–24, University of Fribourg, Switzerland, 2005.

[111] Dorothee Bohle and Béla Greskovits, "Neoliberalism, Embedded Neoliberalism and Neo-corporatism: Towards Transnational Capitalism in Central and Eastern Europe," *West European Politics*, 30, 3 (May 1, 2007), 443–66.

Moderate Inequality in Welfare States

Because of state redistribution, income disparities decreased throughout the continent. This had already begun during the postwar decades,
compared to prewar years. In Sweden, the income share of the top
5 percent of the population declined from 28 to 18 percent and in
Britain from 30 to 19 percent. Meanwhile, the bottom 60 percent's
share increased from 23 to 33 percent in Sweden and from 33 to 37
percent in Britain.[112] Comparing the top 10 percent to the remaining 90 percent of wages, average wage inequality in Western Europe
in 1980–4 was 2.3-times, i.e., the top 10 percent earned more than
twice as much as the remaining 90 percent. By 1995–9, wage disparities somewhat increased to 2.7-times, but still remained far below the
American level of 4.6-times.[113]

At the beginning of the twenty-first century, state safety net benefits via redistribution radically curbed the layer of relative poverty,
i.e., those who earned less than half or 40 percent of the average
income of the country. In the Nordic countries, their share decreased
from nearly 14 percent to 4 percent of the population, in five West
European countries from 19 percent to less than 8 percent.[114] The
most widespread method to measure income disparity is the *Gini coefficient* that categorizes countries on a scale of 0 to 100, where 0 means
absolute equality of income of all citizens, and 100 means that one
person receives the entire income of the country. According to the
World Bank's *World Development Indicators* of 2007, the countries of
Europe, with very few exceptions, have the most moderate income
disparities in the world. The lowest disparity characterizes the Nordic
countries with an average Gini coefficient of 25 to 26, joined by
Germany and Austria with coefficients below 30. Most of the West
European countries have a coefficient of 32 to 34, while only three
countries, Britain, Italy, and Portugal have 36 to 38. Disparity, in spite
of the sharp increase of income differentiation during the transformation decades, still remained on the low side in most of the Central

---

[112] Franz Kraus, "Economic Equality: The Distribution of Incomes," in Peter Flora and
   Arnold J. Heidenheimer (eds.), *The Development of Welfare States in Europe and America*
   (New Brunswick: Transaction Books, 1981), 187–238, 217–18.
[113] OECD, *Employment Outlook* (Paris: OECD, 2004).
[114] D. Bradley, E. Huber, S. Moller, F. Nielsen, and J. D. Stephens, "Determinants of Relative
   Poverty in Advanced Capitalist Democracies," *American Sociological Review*, 68, 1 (2003),
   22–51.

European countries: similarly to the Nordic countries, the coefficient is 25 to 26 in the Czech Republic, Hungary, and Slovakia, and it is still below 30 in Slovenia, Croatia, Bosnia, Bulgaria, and the Ukraine. The Baltic countries as well as most of the former Soviet republics are 35 to 37, and Russia, in a dramatically speedy change, reached 41.

To interpret these figures, it pays to compare them to other countries and regions. Among the advanced countries, the United States has the sharpest income disparities, expressed by its 40.8 Gini coefficient. Interestingly enough, Japan, which lacks a developed welfare system and is in many ways similar to the United States in taxation and social expenditures, has a much more egalitarian income distribution, which is on about the North European level (24.9). Canada's level is equal with the West European one (32). Except for the American income disparity, extreme income disparities of 50 to 60 are mostly characteristic for the less-developed countries of Latin America and Africa.[115]

The comparison of income disparity figures and economic growth rates clearly documents that state redistribution, based on higher taxes, and social expenditures that create more moderate income disparities, are not blocking the road of economic growth. In most cases, just the opposite is true. Great income disparities weaken the domestic market, and a more equal income system creates a healthier and better-educated population, and strong domestic consumption, the engines of growth. Finland, with a high degree of redistribution had a higher growth rate (3.5 percent per annum) than the United States (3.4 percent) in the age of global competition between 1995 and 2005. Countries with high taxation and public social expenditures, such as the Nordic countries, have an average 2.7 percent annual growth rate that surpasses the average euro-zone growth rate (2.1 percent), and strongly surpasses the Italian economic growth of 1.3 percent per annum, despite Italy having one of the highest income disparities in Western Europe. Western Europe in general, with its much higher taxation and social spending, far surpassed Japan's economic growth (1.3 percent), even though the latter had much lower "social burdens."

Several factors influenced growth results, but one may safely state that the welfare system and the redistributive role of the state do not

---

[115] World Bank, *World Development Indicators 2007* (Washington, DC: World Bank). See Africa (Sierra Leone 62.9, Zambia 50.8, Niger 50.5, Zimbabwe 50.1) and Latin America (Bolivia 60.1, Haiti 59.2, Colombia 58.6, Brazil 57.0, Chile 54.9, Argentina 51.3, Mexico 46.1).

slow down economic growth. Similarly, the lack of welfare institutions and a high income disparity are not sources of rapid economic growth either. One analyst looked back in 2001 at the OECD report from twenty years earlier and concluded: "Contrary to the general recipe proposed by the OECD crisis report of 1981, i.e. stimulate non-state [private] welfare provisions, Scandinavian countries have consolidated a state welfare solution . . . and the four countries have all entered a new period of steady economic growth . . . [H]istory has proven the OECD 1981 diagnosis to have been ideologically motivated . . . [and] welfare state growth and economic growth can still go hand in hand in 'advanced' welfare states."[116]

What happened in the later 1990s has continued during the first decade of the new century. In September 2006, the conservative *Economist* stated, "In recent years defenders of the European social model – capitalism tempered by a generous and interventionist welfare state – have taken to praising Scandinavia to the skies. The Nordic region, to go a bit wider, has the world's highest taxes and most generous welfare benefits. And yet, Sweden, Finland and Denmark . . . have delivered strong growth and low unemployment, and rank among the world's most competitive economies . . . Their health-care and educational systems are much admired. And, unlike other European countries, most Nordic states run healthy budget and current-account surpluses . . ."[117]

At this point, one has to consider that, as Nicholas Barr convincingly proved, the welfare state is not primarily a "Robin Hood" state providing poverty relief using tax money from the rich, but most of all a "Piggy Bank," that "provides insurance and offers a mechanism for redistribution over the life cycle." Barr argues that because information is limited for a given individual, the uncertainty and risk is too high for them to be amenable to any insurance scheme except one that is publicly organized. If such insurance is a private responsibility, a great many people will exclude themselves from society, but their decision will not only be a private matter. Society will ultimately be responsible for those who remain uninsured, such as sick children of failed uninsured families, or will have to intervene to eliminate the

---

[116] Stein Kuhnle, "The Nordic Welfare State in a European Context: Dealing with New Economic and Ideological Challenges in the 1990s," in Stephan Leibfried (ed.), *Welfare State Futures* (Cambridge University Press, 2001).

[117] "Admire the Best, Forget the Rest," *The Economist*, September 9–15, 2006, 27.

socially dangerous health hazard represented by the non-insured.[118] Calculations for Britain illustrate that one-quarter to two-thirds of welfare spending is life-cycle redistribution, and only one-quarter to one-third of spending is "Robin Hood" action.[119]

The European social model remained unique and effective for improving the quality of life in modern society. According to the United Nations Development Programme's Human Development Index,[120] eighteen countries out of the top twenty-one in the world (with scores higher than 93 on a scale from 0 to 100) are West European countries, and seven of them scored better than, or equal to, the United States, the richest country in the world, in 2004. Among the top forty-five countries with the best human development index (with a score higher than 84), nine Central and Eastern European countries are also listed.[121] Europe is still combining economic and social values and correcting the social outcome of market forces. The European "social market," to use the German terminology, is still at work.

---

[118] Nicholas Barr, *The Welfare State as Piggy Bank: Information, Risk, Uncertainty, and the Role of the State* (Oxford University Press, 2001), 1, 6, 7, 42.

[119] Jane Falkingham and John Hills, *The Dynamic of Welfare: The Welfare State and the Life Cycle* (Hemel Hempstead: Prentice Hall, 1995).

[120] This index combines per capita GDP, life expectancy, adult literacy, and average years in school, i.e. economic, health, and educational factors.

[121] *World in Figures, 2008*, 30.

Epilogue: *Quo Vadis Europa?*

Black Prophecies – or the Rise of a European Superpower?

World War II destroyed and weakened most of Europe, and the Cold War soon divided the continent into two separate and hostile halves. The West needed American financial and military assistance to rebuild its economy and to secure itself from outside dangers. A third of a century later, however, Western Europe rose as an economic superpower and the cradle of the welfare state. Besides postwar prosperity and its successful adjustment to globalization after the shock of the 1970s, the most important factor of Europe's rise was its rapid integration process, the foundation and enlargement of the European Union.

However, frightening negative demographic trends accompanied and counterbalanced the main positive trends. Europe's population is decreasing and aging and the ratio of active to inactive people will be 50:50 in a few decades. Rapidly increasing immigrant labor is replacing the inadequate domestic labor force. Immigrant minorities, mostly from non-European Muslim cultures, are rapidly increasing. Integration or assimilation is painfully slow, or non-existent. A part of the immigrant population, especially the illegal ones, form a new underclass. Anti-immigrant hostility and intolerance are fueling extreme right-wing political trends. The minority question became a source of explosive tension on the continent. *Quo vadis Europa* in the twenty-first century? What will take over and dominate, positive or negative tendencies?

The answers to these questions exhibit an extreme variety of views. The most pessimistic prophecies are based on the emerging challenge from within Europe. Walter Laqueur, the well-known historian, gives an unambiguous prediction – unlike the classic Delphic oracle – in his book with the frightening title *Last Days of Europe: Epitaph for an Old Continent* (2007). Laqueur does not say anything new, but he interprets the known facts in a cruelly blunt and "politically incorrect" way. According to his diagnosis-and-prophecy, three main internal challenges are undermining Europe. The first of these is the demographic decline that will decrease the continent's population by 130 million people by 2050 and require 700 million immigrants to do the work for the aging population. Immigration is the second major threat, especially because Europe, burdened with the shame of its colonial past, "surrendered" to multiculturalism and will not be able to integrate the minorities that are gradually emerging as the majority. The "clash of civilizations" is inevitable within Europe. Finally, the immune system of the continent is weakened by "welfare state mentality," a state of comfortable decadence. Is Europe in a process of decline and disappearance? Probably not, but Europe's dominant role in the world is "a thing of the past." Europe, as Laqueur states, is "bound to change, probably out of recognition."[1] He is not alone with his gloomy forecast. Several others have joined him. Bruce Thornton's vision anticipates an Islamized Europe under *Sharia* law and speaks of the "Decline and Fall: Europe's Slow Motion Suicide."[2]

One may not exclude the possibility of strengthening negative tendencies. However, the situation is pregnant with very different possibilities as well. Immigration will definitely change the continent and, moreover, the entire "Western world." In the middle of the century, immigrants may become the majority in the United States. Similarly, the immigrant population will represent an increasing part of the European population. Is this the end of Europe? The Hungarian writer Péter Zilahy has an opposite vision, based on history: "Barbarians," he said, often attacked and even occupied Europe or parts of it, but "all once feared enemies turned European . . . Europe was always conquering her conquerors . . . and [was] regularly reborn at the hands of Barbarians."[3] One may add that peoples outside the Western world are already partly assimilated to Western civilization,

---

[1] Walter Laqueur, *Last Days of Europe: Epitaph for an Old Continent* (New York: Thomas Dunne Books, 2007).

[2] Bruce Thornton, *Decline and Fall: Europe's Slow Motion Suicide* (New York: Encounter Books, 2007).

[3] Péter Zilahy, "How European," in Guido Snel (ed.), *Alter Ego: Twenty Confronting Views on the European Experience* (Amsterdam University Press, 2004), 129–39, 131.

to the industrial-urban culture that was born in Europe. Intolerant religions may certainly be "domesticated" and religious nations secularized during the modernization process. After all, Europe and Christianity were equally intolerant a few centuries ago. Visions and prophecies are like a house of cards.

Moreover, instead of decline and "slow motion suicide," the possibility of coping with the various challenges and of the rise of Europe to a new superpower status is also a probable scenario. The integrating and enlarging European Union has already emerged as an economic superpower. In 2005, the European Union had a Gross Domestic Product of $14,300 billion, somewhat more than the United States' $13,185 billion. The population of the European Union surpassed 500 million by 2008, compared to the United States' 300 million. The European Union became the most important player in the global economy. The value of European exports of goods and services – only $0.14 trillion in 1950, and $0.90 trillion by 1973 – surpassed $4.1 trillion by 2005, compared to the USA's $1.3 trillion. Exports played an ever-increasing role in the economic performance of Europe, reaching 36 percent of the aggregate GDP at the end of the century, twice as high as the world average and by far the highest level when compared to all other countries or regions of the world.

Europe became the number one capital investor in the world. America dominated the world's financial markets and foreign direct investments (FDI) after World War II: in 1973, American investments abroad represented nearly half of the world's total, while continental Western Europe accounted for only 25 percent. By the end of the century, Europe's 39 percent share in the world's stock of FDI far surpassed the United States' 21 percent.[4] In another decade, outward direct investment stocks, the accumulated amount of European foreign investments, reached $4,930,228 million. This amount is twice as much as the United States' $2,399,224 million.

FDI stocks reflect the aggregate sum of investments, accumulated until a certain year. They reflect the past. Regarding the present, the annual average outflow of direct investments is more expressive. The latter measure became more European than American much earlier: during the first half of the 1980s, Europe's share of annual average outflow of FDI reached 41 percent of the world's total, while the

---

[4] Angus Maddison, *The World Economy: A Millennial Perspective* (Paris: OECD, 2001), 147.

United States had only 31 percent.[5] By 2005, Europe's dominance was even more impressive, when the amount of FDI outflow, a figure that characterizes the present activity, reached $427,329 million, while the United States' investments abroad reached only $109,754 million.[6]

Besides quantitative developments, Europe adjusted the most successfully to the emerging new type of division of labor that characterized the decades of globalization. The geographical destination of Germany's foreign direct investments reflects a radical change: in 1961, Germany channeled 46 percent of its investments abroad into developing or less developed regions, and only 14 percent into other European Community countries. By 1990, less than 20 percent of investments went to developing countries, and 41 percent went to other advanced European countries. In 1990, Germany directed only 2 percent of its FDI into mining industries, while nearly 40 percent went to trade, banking, and insurance business, and another one-third to chemical, electrical, machine building, and the car industries. Swedish multinationals established subsidiaries in eighty-three other advanced countries, but in only seventeen Latin American, Asian, and African developing countries.

Contrary to the postwar situation, transatlantic investments became a two-way street. By the mid-1990s, European multinationals owned nearly 60 percent of total foreign direct investments in the United States, while the United States held less than half of the total FDI inflow to Europe. American subsidiaries in Europe produce one-third of European imports from the United States, but European subsidiaries in the United States are responsible for 38 percent of American imports from Europe.[7]

Europe without Peripheries?

Europe's future rise as a superpower has gained new momentum through its role and impact on eliminating peripheral backwardness in former low-income regions of the continent. Europe, during its entire modern history, has been a continent of sharp disparities that

---

[5] Geoffrey Jones and Harm G. Schröter (eds.), *The Rise of Multinationals in Continental Europe* (Aldershot: Edward Elgar, 1993), 4, 10.

[6] OECD, *Factbook, Economic, Environmental and Social Statistics* (Paris: OECD, 2007), 61, 65, 69, 77–9.

[7] Mark A. Pollack and Gregory G. Shaffer (eds.), *Transatlantic Governance in the Global Economy* (Lanham: Rowman and Littlefield Press, 2001), 12–14.

have weakened it. Around the turn of the twenty-first century, however, the trend of catching up with the Western core became dominant
in Ireland and the former Mediterranean peripheries. The common
market and the deliberate cohesion policy of the Union assisted backward regions and elevated several countries to the core's level. The
catching-up process also appeared in some of the lately joined Central
and Eastern European countries. As a surprising result, the cohesion
policy significantly equalized disparities among member states, while
regional disparities increased. That was the consequence of special
centralization, the formation of urban agglomeration economies to
exploit the advantage of proximity of production and service industries. This phenomenon, characteristic of modern technology-based
industries and the globalization process, creates advantage for certain regions and leaves behind others. The traditional peripheries of
Europe, however, have already been shrinking significantly and will
probably melt away in the coming twenty to thirty years. Europe without peripheries is certainly not a real possibility during the lifetime
of the next generation, but the further enlargement of the European
core is an ongoing process.

In its entire modern history, Europe's economic development
has been very uneven. From early modern times, Western Europe
emerged as the core of the world system, but the Nordic countries,
Mediterranean Europe, and Central and Eastern Europe became its
peripheries, producing food and raw materials for the core, and reaching about half to 60 percent of its income level. The Scandinavian
countries, which used to be grain, fish, wood, and iron ore producing
and exporting countries, with 70 percent of the population employed
in agriculture and primary producing sectors in 1870, began a rapid
catching-up process from that time on. They too became industrialized, and in less than half a century they neared the per capita GDP
level of the Western core, from being at roughly 60 to 76 percent
of the core level before World War I. By 1950, the Scandinavian per
capita GDP level surpassed the West European's by 7 percent, and
the region became an organic part of the core. Finland, somewhat
later, repeated the Scandinavian success: in 1950, its per capita income
level reached 64 percent of the total per capita income of six traditional West European economic leaders, but by 2005, it surpassed it by
16 percent.

The historical legacy of the peripheral countries of the Mediterranean and Central and Eastern European regions, however, remained

unchanged for more than one-and-half centuries. They started changing after World War II, and most significantly after 1980. Europe gradually formed a single market and accepted the formerly less-developed
Ireland and three of the Mediterranean countries from the 1970s and
1980s, and it introduced a deliberate cohesion policy to assist backward
regions and countries through the central redistribution of income
from the budget of the Community. Ireland, Greece, Spain, and Portugal all became eligible. The Community directed massive assistance
to these countries. Probably more important was the economic integration of these countries into the European economy, and the huge
amount of foreign direct investments from American and Japanese
companies that used the new candidate countries as a springboard to
the European markets.

All these factors contributed to an exceptional GDP growth rate in
the newly accepted countries: between the late 1980s and mid-1990s,
Ireland, Portugal, and Spain achieved two to four times faster growth
than the eight developed member countries.[8] Joining the European
Union successfully assisted the catching-up process and helped elevate
Ireland and the Mediterranean countries near or even beyond the level
of the core during the last quarter of the twentieth century. Ireland
reached only 57 percent of the West European income level in 1973,
but in 2005, Ireland had a 15 percent higher income level per capita
than the twelve traditionally richest West and North European countries. Spain, Portugal, Ireland, and Greece together reached only 49
percent of the per capita GDP of Western Europe in 1950, but that figure rose to 63 percent by 1973, and 93 percent by 2005.[9] After joining
the European Union, the Irish and Mediterranean peripheries became
part of the European core around the turn of the century. The 2008–9
economic crises, however, exposed the still existing weaknesses of
these regions and stopped their steep elevation.

Is catching up also the future of the new Central and Eastern European member countries? That region, in spite of quite a few attempts,
was unable to break out from its distinctive backwardness and, at the
beginning of the twenty-first century, remained the only relatively
backward periphery of the continent. The *longue durée* of nearly two
centuries reflects a surprising continuity of relative backwardness. In

---

[8] Lisbet Hooghe (ed.), *Cohesion Policy and European Integration: Building Multi-Level Governance* (Oxford University Press, 1996).

[9] Based on Maddison, *World Economy*; OECD, *Factbook*.

1820, Central and Eastern Europe's per capita income level reached 59 percent of that of the West, by 1913, 46 percent, in 1950, 51 percent, and by 1989, 40 percent.[10]

The countries' postwar drive for industrialization and modernization became a detour from the periphery back to the periphery. The Balkans and the successor states of the former Soviet Union declined into backwardness of tragic proportions during the 1990s. At the nadir of decline in 1998, the per capita income of Russia, the Ukraine, and Belarus reached only 22 percent of the West European level, and other former Soviet republics reached only 14 to 18 percent. The gap – or, better still, the abyss – has never been so wide as at the end of the twentieth century. Most of the Balkan countries and the successor states of the Soviet Union became more peripheral than ever.

Recovery followed during the first decade of the twenty-first century, especially in the Russian Federation, which achieved an annual 7 to 8 percent economic growth by profiting tremendously from the new oil price explosion. By 2008, however, little has happened in structural and technological modernization. In the case of Russia, 80 percent of the exports are energy and raw materials, and in the former Soviet, now independent republics, cheap low-technology products represent the bulk of the exports. The 2008 financial crisis and declining oil prices may close, or at least temporarily halt, the short period of Russian prosperity.

In 2004, when the Central European countries joined the EU, the average income in the eight most advanced countries of the region was only 45 percent that of the fifteen countries already in the Union. The miraculous economic performance of Ireland and Spain in the last third of the century offers a comparison and hope for the possibility of a spectacular catching-up by the Central European transforming countries. If one speaks about catching up, it always means a process stretching over one or two generations. In other words: the Central European countries, in the best case, may reach or approach the European Union's average income level of 2005 around 2025–30. To accomplish this miracle, these countries must achieve roughly two to three times higher economic growth than the old member countries of the Union.

It is a statistical commonplace that the rate of growth strongly depends on the level of the base, or starting, year or period. From

---

[10] Angus Maddison, *Monitoring the World Economy 1820–1992* (Paris: OECD, 1995), 228.

a lower income level, it is easier to achieve a higher growth rate. The Harvard economic historian, Alexander Gerschenkron, spoke about the "advantage of backwardness," i.e., the possibility of adopting technology and management from advanced countries and, as a consequence, achieving faster growth. This assertion is true regarding a certain medium level of backwardness, but not when backwardness eliminates the social capability to absorb modern technology and knowledge. Most of the Central European countries are above that threshold. In theory, catching up is indeed possible.

Reaching the Western level strongly depends on future capital inflow to the region. The European Union and its assistance may play an important further role. On December 17, 2005, the Union approved its budget for the seven-year period of 2007–13. Nearly 36 percent of the budget, about $337 billion, finances the Union's cohesion fund to subsidize the less developed regions. The new member countries will receive $140 billion (or €100 billion). The Union also distributes another $60 billion among the Union's partner countries in the Balkans. The region will also profit from the Union's agricultural subsidies.

Altogether, Central and Eastern Europe will receive more from the European Union during the 2007–13 budget period than the West received from the legendary Marshall Plan after the war. This aid, together with foreign direct investments that have determined the region's development since 1989, might help the new countries to achieve a growth rate higher than the EU average, thus contributing to the catching-up process with the West. The present and future growth of the "old" European Union strongly influences the process of convergence. Catching up is extremely difficult if the target countries are running fast. What is the possible rate of growth for the former European Union-15? Between 1950 and 1973, Western Europe reached its fastest-ever economic growth rate of 4.08 percent per year. Between 1973 and 1998, however, the average annual growth of the region declined to 1.78 percent. Between 1993 and 2003, the so-called euro-zone had a 2.1 percent annual growth. In 2005, the rate was only 1.6 percent. Catching up with Western Europe would be hopeless if the region regained its postwar quarter of a century speed of around 4 percent per annum. If it continues, however, at the slower 2 percent annual growth rate, reaching a rate in Central and Eastern Europe that is two or two-and-half-times faster is possible.

The first years of the twenty-first century already offer a solid comparison between the old and new (and candidate) countries of the Union. The average annual growth of the countries that joined the Union from the region reached 4.3 percent between 2000 and 2006, with significant national differences. During the first half decade of the twenty-first century, productivity in manufacturing (GDP per hour) increased 2.5 times faster in the transition countries than in Germany, France, and Austria. Increasing productivity may still be combined with relatively low wages in Central and Eastern Europe for quite a while, and attract foreign investors. According to the UNCTAD forecast, by 2020 the eight transition countries' average wages will reach 39 percent of the "old" Union members' average wage level.[11]

If the growth trend in both the West and the East continues after the trauma of the 2008–9 crisis, and the slowdown and decline that followed, Slovenia may near the Western level within a decade, while the Czech Republic, Hungary, Slovakia, Poland, and Estonia need twenty to thirty-five years to catch up with the European Union average. Latvia, Bulgaria, and Romania may achieve the same progress in forty to forty-three years. Lithuania, however, will need seventy years.[12] The catching-up with the West has actually begun. Hungary, Poland, Slovakia, Slovenia, and the Czech Republic's per capita purchasing power parity GDP has increased from 55 to 63 percent between 2000 and 2005.[13] Based on the assumption that the European Union will reach 2 percent and the Central and Eastern European countries 4 percent annual GDP growth in the coming decade, the level of GDP per capita in purchasing power parity may reach an average of three-quarters of the EU level in the most successful Central European countries of the region. The Balkans will still remain just above one-third of the EU level by 2015.[14] All of these kinds of forecasts, however, became questionable in 2008–9.

Forecasts are always just extending existing trends. That may have little to do with future reality. During the transition period between

[11] UNCTAD, *United Nations Conference on Trade and Development: Handbook of Statistics*. Online, 2005, www.thefreelibrary.com/UNCTAD+handbook+of+statistics+2005

[12] Mihály Simai, "The World Economy and Europe at the Beginning of the 21st Century," *Development and Finance*, 1 (2006), 3–11.

[13] Based on European Commission, *Eurostat Yearbooks* (Luxembourg: Office for Official Publications, 2000–5).

[14] Based on Ivan Teodorović, Željko Lovrinčević, Davor Mikulić, Mustafa Nušinović, and Stjepan Zdunić (eds.), *The Croatian Economic Development: Transition Towards the Market Economy* (Zagreb: Institute of Economics, 2005), 326.

1989 and 2007, the basis of economic growth was the recovery from disruptions generated by the deep crisis and the collapse of state socialism and the steep decline that followed. During the transformation period, under-employed rural labor and superfluous (over-employed) industrial labor were rationalized, and the economies and employment restructured. The most important growth factors, nevertheless, were the inflow of foreign capital, advanced technology, and managerial skills. The first signs that foreign direct capital investment was shifting farther towards the East appeared already in the early twenty-first century. In the coming decades, a radical shift from an extensive development model towards an intensive, knowledge- and innovation-based development model is needed to perpetuate rapid economic growth in Central and Eastern Europe. Continuous rapid growth performance also requires speeding up spin-off effects, integrating local industry and services into the multinational supplier chain.

Growth rates, however, slowed down significantly between 2006 and 2008: Hungary's growth rate halved. Latvia's growth rate dropped to one-third, and its industrial output declined by more than 6 percent. Estonia's growth rate slowed down from 11 to 2.3 percent. Both countries accumulated huge current-account deficits and had 17 percent inflation. In 2009, economic decline hit some of the transforming countries hard. These may be transitory phenomena. In some of the new member countries, instead of catching up with the EU-15, a dual economy may emerge. This is even more likely in the case of the candidate countries of the Balkans. In such a scenario, their level of development would improve after joining, but remain stuck behind the Western level. Multinational companies would constitute the advanced sector of the economy, while an adequate national innovation system would not develop, and local companies would remain in a backward situation. In this case, multinational companies may form isolated enclaves in the national economy, while the host countries remain on the periphery of Europe, with an institutionalized division of labor that separates the advanced countries from the laggards.

In other words, some of the countries of the region with a resource-driven specialization and/or as providers of cheap labor in low-tech sectors for advanced partners could remain behind and profit less from globalization. A much lower living standard than in the core would result. Instead of calculating the years and decades of catching up, one has to consider markedly different outcomes of the ongoing transformation, which would result from the failure to catch up in some countries or in sub-regions of Central and Eastern Europe. A periphery-less Europe is not on the horizon yet, but Central Europe may return to its pre-2008–9 tendency of moving gradually towards the European core.

The most important question for the future of Europe, however, is the further development of integration: Can Europe – besides being an economic powerhouse – emerge as a political and military super-power?

Federal Europe of the European Nation – or Disintegrating Alliance?

In an earlier stage of development, the founding fathers of the European Community considered economic integration to be a road towards political integration and the federalization of Europe. This idea was not on the agenda during the sixties, but it was never dropped. Several major architects of the European Union systematically worked on the gradual realization of this concept by building more and more supranational elements and institutions into the integration process. John Pinder of the Policy Studies Institute in London argued in 1986 for paving the way towards federal rearrangement exactly in this grad-ual and sometimes indirect way: federalization is "not a single act, but also an evolutionary development." He differentiated between a "federalizing process" and the "federal end." Pinder maintained that smaller states "harbor few illusions about the reality of national independence," while others are worrying "about the challenge from America and Japan... Economic and political systems and culture are... sufficiently similar among West European countries to facili-tate a substantial degree of integration." Pinder refers to a study that concludes that if "India is seen as a nation, then Europe may well be described as an emerging nation."[15]

The architects of integration are still working on the "federalizing process" when redesigning textbooks to eliminate hostile national-ist concepts and regulating appropriate language instruction so as to

---

[15] John Pinder, "European Community and Nation-State: A Case for a Neo-federalism?" *International Affairs*, 62, 1(January 1986), reprinted in Brent F. Nelsen and Alexander Stubb (eds.), *The European Union: Readings on the Theory and Practice of European Integration* (Boulder, CO: Lynne Rienner, 1998), 189–94, 190, 192.

develop some *lingua francas*[16] – perhaps two or three – over time. They initiated some harmonization of higher education and degrees, as well as an extensive student exchange program at all levels of education within the framework of the "Socrates" project. The Single Market Act swept away several obstacles to the free movement of labor. Returning guest workers and former exiles became the "bridgehead of mutual understanding," and free movement of labor created the "breeding ground of a European consciousness."[17] The European Union is trying to educate a new generation of Europeans. The Union gradually increased the role of the European Parliament from being a talking shop for delegated parliamentarians, to being a directly elected body with the authority to make budgetary decisions and to be a co-legislator with the European Council, the representatives of the member countries' governments. The first tentative steps were also taken to form European political parties by creating "party families" from among the various national social democratic, conservative, green, and populist parties in the member countries.

More importantly, Hartmut Kaelble argues, a "civil society is in the process of emerging on the European level." Spontaneous "European movements" arose after the war, and then various all-European organizations such as the European Trade Union Confederation, Amnesty International, the Rotary Club, Lions Club as well as various transnational church, sports, and cultural organizations. The networks of civil organizations continued to develop. At the end of the twentieth century, the number of intermediary groups with offices in Brussels reached 3,500.[18]

When thinking about the future of an "ever closer union" of Europe, it is natural to begin thinking about the possibility of creating a "European nation." Those who argue along this line rightly maintain that national consciousness and self-identification were also "artificially" created, and the national community – as the title of Benedict Anderson's book expresses – is only ever an "imagined community."[19]

---

[16] Two special forms of the "common language" are "Kanak sprak," the mixed Turkish-German, and "Denglish," the mixed German-English.

[17] Karen Schönwälder, "Integration from Below? Migration and European Contemporary History," in Konrad H. Jarausch and Thomas Lindenberger (eds.), *Conflicted Memories: Europeanizing Contemporary Histories* (New York: Berghahn Books, 2007), 154–63, 156.

[18] Hartmut Kaelble, "A European Civil Society?" in Jarausch and Lindenberger (eds.), *Conflicted Memories*, 209–22, 212–15.

[19] Benedict Anderson, *Imagined Communities: Reflections on the Origin and Spread of Nationalism* (London: Verso, 1983).

America emerged as a nation-state from various immigrant nation-als. The countries of Europe have sufficient historical and cultural similarities to build upon and to gradually develop a European iden-tity. Around the turn of the century, the new features of European development were strengthening these similarities. Hartmut Kaelble convincingly documents the rise of a European model of consumer society with strongly standardized consumer goods and consump-tion practices. One may speak of an increasing standardization of the European way of life.[20] Consumption eliminates many of the national differences and contributes to the forging of a European convergence. "It is better to think of Europe as a conflictual space of existence rather than as a chosen place of belonging. And yet, this Europe is also a place in which no part can leave the others alone, because each part depends . . . on the others. Europe is constituted historically and in the present inasmuch as . . . it has been able to make this competitive interdependence its common project."[21]

Although this is a historically well-based set of arguments, it is also questionable. Several newly founded states in the twentieth century attempted to repeat the nineteenth-century creation of "artificial" national consciousness and community. They all failed. Newly created Czechoslovakia and Yugoslavia tried to homogenize their different ethnicities and forge Czechoslovak and Yugoslav nations after World War I. It seemed to be logical and natural since they were all Slavic peoples who spoke the same or closely related languages. Some of the architects of those states themselves had mixed ethnic backgrounds, like Tomáš Masarýk in Czechoslovakia or Josip Broz Tito later in Yugoslavia. Their nation-building efforts, however, failed. National conflicts shocked the newly created countries from the late 1920s on, and they erupted during World War II. Although both multinational countries were reestablished after the war, both were rearranged as federal states, and they exploded and terminally separated again after more than sixty years of existence. The Soviet Union also nurtured the ambitious dream to create a "Soviet nation," but it failed as well, and the traditionally multi-ethnic country disintegrated in 1991. For

---

[20] Hartmut Kaelble, Jürgen Kocka, and Hannes Siegrist (eds.), *Europäische Konsumgeschichte: Zur Gesellschafts- und Kulturgeschichte des Konsumes (18. bis 20. Jahrhundert)* (Frankfurt: Cam-pus Verlag, 1997); Hartmut Kaelble (ed.), *The European Way: European Societies during the Nineteenth and Twentieth Centuries* (New York: Berghahn Books, 2004), 304.

[21] Michael Geyer, "The Subject(s) of Europe," in Jarausch and Lindenberger (eds.), *Conflicted Memories*, 254–80, 274.

the advocates of an "Arab nation," the founding in 1958 of a United Arab Republic, with a federal constitution and the participation of Egypt and Syria, was supposed to begin to unify the Arab people. Iraq was on the verge of joining in the early 1960s, but the enterprise had already collapsed miserably by 1961, without reaching the initial stage of nation-building.

In other words, nineteenth-century nation-building was never successfully repeated in the twentieth century. In interwar Europe, national self-identification and nationalism became the political and ideological mainstream that mobilized even small ethnic communities to fight for independence. In a paradoxical way, European unification also generated movements of national minorities to gain autonomy or independence. Historical trends do not encourage a belief in the possibility of a pan-European nation.

Similarly, the dream of a United States of Europe is also fading away. It had a stronger attraction and larger basis after the war than at the turn of the century. The six founding members of the European Union shared this idea as a long-term goal and possibility. Though the (over)enlarged European Union of twenty-seven countries has made impressive progress in integration and in creating supranational institutions, the member countries exhibit a broad diversity and a much stronger will to preserve national sovereignty (whatever they take that to mean). The British, Swedish, and Danish decision to remain outside the euro-zone, the French and Dutch "no" votes on the planned constitution, and the first Irish "no" on the Lisbon Treaty that sought to realize the main elements of the failed constitution for further political integration, clearly signal the difficulties, although a second Irish vote in October 2009 opened the road to further integration. Most strikingly, some of the new member countries such as the Czech Republic and Poland, which dreamed and longed for membership until a few years ago, have now joined the camp of "euro-skeptics." The further the enlargement of the Union advances, the weaker the possibility that it will realize the genuine federal idea of the six founding members.

An attempt to "round up" twenty-seven member nations towards a common goal will always carry within itself the seeds of conflicts and backlashes. Further enlargement may generate resistance on the part of some old member countries, and they may even decide to split. Some national leaders riding on populist-nationalist waves may advocate in favor of national interest against the Union, threatening it with disintegration. Similar phenomena have already caused some crises and cannot be excluded from future scenarios.

On the other hand, the half-century history of European integration offers the lesson of a path paved with conflicts and solutions, ideal goals and pragmatic compromises, a stop-and-go process with periods of stagnation and sudden breakthroughs. The basic interest in joining and being a member of the Union has always defeated the doubts and reservations. Integration was and is an elemental interest of the European countries. It was the central security interest during the Cold War, and it became a basic economic interest in the age of globalization with its cutthroat worldwide competition.

Europe's Future Place in the World

Although the continuation of the above-described positive development trends is a realistic possibility, no one can deny the *relative* decline of the European continent, compared to rising Asia, especially China, which is regaining its ancient leading position. Europe is gradually losing its position in the world. In 1900, at the end of its glorious century, Europe represented more than 26 percent of the world population and produced 45 percent of the world's total GDP. In 1950, Europe's share of the world population had declined to less than 23 percent, and it accounted for 39 percent of the world's GDP. At the end of the twentieth century, Europe's share was only 13.5 percent of the world population and 26 percent of total GDP. If current trends in population growth continue, Europe will represent only 4 percent of the world population by 2050, less than the lifetime of two generations. Individually, the middle-sized and small countries of the continent become less and less able to remain main players of the world system.

The United States itself is losing ground in the international arena. The world's society, economy, and politics are gradually being restructured. New rising superpowers, China, India, and gradually Brazil, have appeared on the horizon. China and India, according to the IMF's calculations in 2007, represent nearly 16 percent of the world's aggregate GDP (in parity purchasing power, i.e., on a market exchange rate basis). Based on expanded growth trends, in the single decade between 2005 and 2015, both China and India will more than double their GDP. If the international financial crisis of 2008–9 does not change the trend, China will grow from $8,092 billion to $17,533 billion and surpass the United States as the number one economy in the world. India's economy will grow from $3,603 billion to $7,015 billion and rise to third place in the world, while Brazil's income will increase from $1,553 billion to $2,252 billion, reaching seventh place in the world, which it will share with Britain.[22]

Since 1980, the catching-up process of China and India has been dramatic; in gross GDP, China surpassed France in 1984, Russia in 1985, Germany in 1987, and Japan in 1995 – and will probably surpass the United States by 2015. India surpassed Italy and France in 1985, Russia in 1992, and Germany in 1997. The World Bank's forecasts in 1997 were not exaggerated: "The world economy will change fundamentally over the next 25 years as Brazil, China, India, Indonesia, and Russia assume a more central role in the global market place." The "big five," according to the World Bank's calculations, may reach an annual 5 to 6 percent growth and double their output and exports. "This challenge would be unprecedented in both its size and speed."[23]

Losing ground to outside competitors looks to be an evident trend in the coming decades of the twenty-first century if "normalcy" returns after the 2008–9 crisis. Is it the end of Europe? The nineteenth century was a British century, shared with a few other European nations. The twentieth century became an American century, but Europe became more prosperous than ever. The twenty-first century might be a Chinese century, shared with other Asian nations. Europe certainly will lose its dominant position in the world, though it may still play an important role more closely tailored to its real shape in terms of area and number of population. Integration is in the basic national interest of the advanced European countries because a modern division of labor is happening among highly industrialized countries and among, and between, industries. It is in their interest because it offers the possibility of building up supply and production networks in neighboring low-wage countries with a well-educated labor force. But it is also advantageous for the less-developed European countries because of substantial direct investments and European aid, and imports of the most modern technology and business culture.

---

[22] Consensus Economics, *Consensus Forecast*, April, 2005.
[23] World Bank, *Global Economic Prospects and Developing Countries* (Washington, DC: World Bank, 1997).

The caravan of Europe sometimes stops for a while, but in the long-run it is in continuous movement towards deeper integration. Economic cooperation has already been elevated to a strikingly high level. Further political integration is also on the agenda, as failed attempts illustrate. Over-enlargement caused major trouble during the 2008–9 crisis and threatened to break up the Union. Failures, however, have always generated new attempts and have not stopped the progress of integration. The failed constitution generated a new version of its essence in the form of the Lisbon Treaty of 2007, and the failed Lisbon Treaty generated new attempts, new versions, and new referendum to go ahead towards the goal. Federal Europe may be replaced by a European confederation, or a "two-tier" Europe with a faster-moving and further integrated core, and a slower-moving, less integrated outer ring, as has already been recommended several times, but always rejected. This solution, however, may return. New and as yet invisible solutions may drive the Union forward. The national interest in integration and outside challenges are the strongest glue to keep the Union together and drive it towards higher levels of unification.

Quo vadis Europa? There are several options and alternatives as well as frightening possibilities. Historical forecast, however, is not a genre of historiography. Anticipating the future based on the present is more than questionable. History is a complex fabric of thousands of threads, and an unpredictable mixture of continuity and change. Existing trends have always been changing, and major turning points have often generated international conflicts and opened new ways. Asking the question, *Quo vadis Europa?* generates various kinds of answers. Optimistic forecasts may strengthen belief in the future and increase efforts to achieve the goals of the Union. Pessimistic answers may call attention to real dangers to be avoided if these goals are to be realised.

Bibliography

Abalkin, A. and J. Whalley, "The Problem of Capital Flight from Russia," *The World Economy*, 22, 3, 1999, 421–44.

Adamski, Władisław, Pavel Machonin, and Wolfgang Zampf (eds.), *Structural Change and Modernization in Post-Socialist Societies*, Hamburg: Reinhold Krämer, 2002.

Ágh, Attila, "Hungarian Politics in the Early 21st Century: Reforms and Post-EU Accession Crisis," *Südosteuropa Mitteilungen*, 48, 2, 2008, 68–81.

Albers, Detlev, Stephen Haseler, and Henning Meyer (eds.), *Social Europe: A Continent's Answer to Market Fundamentalism*, London Metropolitan University, 2006.

Anderson, Benedict, *Imagined Communities: Reflections on the Origin and Spread of Nationalism*, London: Verso, 1983.

Appleby, Joyce, Lynn Hunt, and Margaret Jacob, *Telling the Truth about History*, New York: Norton, 1995.

articles.mercola.com/sites/articles/archive/2002/ou/10/health.aspx-48k-

Aust, Stefan, "Terrorism in Germany: The Baader-Meinhof Phenomenon," *Bulletin of the German Historical Institute*, Fall, 43, 2008, 45–57.

Automotive News Europe, 5, 17, 2004.
    9, 10, 2004.

Az MSzMP KB állásfoglalása, *Népszabadság*, July 14, 1987.

Bailey, Joe (ed.), *Social Europe*, Second edition, London: Longman, 1998.

Baker, Dean, *The United States Since 1980*, Cambridge University Press, 2007.

Baker, James, in National Security Archive, Cold War Interviews, 1992, www.gwu.edu/~nsarchiv/coldwar/interviews/episode-23/baker3.html

Ball, Terence and Richard Bellamy (eds.), *The Cambridge History of Twentieth-Century Political Thought*, Cambridge University Press, 2003.

Barr, Nicholas, *The Welfare State as Piggy Bank: Information, Risk, Uncertainty, and the Role of the State*, Oxford University Press, 2001.

Bataković, Dušan T., *Kosovo i Metohia, istorija i ideologija*, Belgrade: Hriscanska Misao, 1998.

Baun, Michael J., *A Wider Europe: The Process and Politics of European Enlargement*, Lanham: Rowman and Littlefield, 2000.

Bell, David S. and Christopher Lord (eds.), *Transnational Parties in the European Union*, Aldershot: Ashgate, 1998.

Berend, Ivan T., *Central and Eastern Europe 1944–1993: Detour from the Periphery to the Periphery*, Cambridge University Press, 1996.

Berend, Ivan T. *et al.*, "Történelmi utunk. A Munkabizottság állasfoglalása," *Társadalmi Szemle*, Special issue, 44, March, 1989.

Bethlendi, András, "Foreign Direct Investment in the Banking Sector," *Development and Finance*, 1, 2007, 61–2.

Bettin Lattes, Gianfranco and Ettore Recchi (eds.), *Comparing European Societies*, Bologna: Monduzzi Editore, 2005.

Betz, Hans-Georg, *Radical Right-Wing Populism in Western Europe*, Houndmills: Palgrave Macmillan, 1994.

Bidwai, Praful, "France Explodes the Uniformity Myth," *Frontline*, November 5, 2005, www.tmi.org/archives/bidwai/myth.htm

Bjelajac, Mile, "Migrations of Ethnic Albanians in Kosovo 1938–1950," *Balcanica*, 38, 2007, 219–30.

Blanck, Dag, "Television, Education, and the Vietnam War: Sweden and the United States During the Postwar Era," in Alexander Stephan (ed.), *The Americanization of Europe: Culture, Diplomacy, and Anti-Americanism after 1945*, New York: Berghahn Books, 2006, 91–114.

Blank, Rebecca M. (ed.), *Social Protection versus Economic Flexibility: Is There a Trade-off?* University of Chicago Press, 1994.

Bobbio, Norberto, "L'Utopia Capovolta," *La Stampa*, June 9, 1989.

  Left and Right: The Significance of a Political Distinction, University of Chicago Press, 1996.

Bohle, Dorothee and Béla Greskovits, "Neoliberalism, Embedded Neoliberalism and Neocorporatism: Towards Transnational Capitalism in Central and Eastern Europe," *West European Politics*, 30, 3, May 1, 2007, 443–66.

Boltho, Andrea, *The European Economy: Growth and Crisis*, Oxford University Press, 1982.

Borradori, Giovanna, *Philosophy in a Time of Terror: Dialogues with Jürgen Habermas and Jacques Derrida*, University of Chicago Press, 2003.

Botsiou, Konstantina E., "The Interface Between Politics and Culture in Greece," in Alexander Stephan (ed.), *The Americanization of Europe: Culture, Diplomacy, and Anti-Americanism after 1945*, New York: Berghahn Books, 2006, 277–306.

Bozo, Frédéric, "The Failure of a Grand Design: Mitterrand's European Confederation, 1989–1991," *Contemporary European History*, Special Issue, 17, 3, August 2008, 319–412.

Bradley, D., E. Huber, S. Moller, F. Nielsen, and J. D. Stephens, "Determinants of Relative Poverty in Advanced Capitalist Democracies," *American Sociological Review*, 68, 1, 2003, 22–51.

Brandt, Loren and Thomas G. Rawski (eds.), *China's Great Economic Transformation*, Cambridge University Press, 2008.

Brenner, Robert, "Uneven Development and the Long Downturn: Advanced Capitalist Economies from Boom to Stagnation, 1950–1988," *New Left Review*, Special issue, May–June, 1998.

  The Boom and the Bubble: The US in the World Economy, London: Verso, 2002.

Brubaker, Rogers, *Immigration and the Politics of Citizenship in Europe and North America*, Lanham: University Press of America, 1989.

Citizenship and Nationhood in France and Germany, Cambridge, MA: Harvard University Press, 1992.

Buchanan, Tom, *Europe's Troubled Peace, 1945–2000*, Oxford: Blackwell, 2006.

Burcin, Boris and Tomáš Kučera, "Socio-Demographic Consequences of the Renewal of Prague's Historical Center," in György Enyedi and Zoltán Kovács (eds.), *Social Changes and Social Sustainability in Historical Urban Centers: The Case of Central Europe*, Pécs: Center for Regional Studies, 2006, 174–88.

Bush, George H. W., Presidential Library and Museum, "Address Before a Joint Session of the Congress on the Cessation of the Persian Gulf Conflict," Bushlibrary.tamu.edu/research/public_papers.php 1991-03-06

Business Eastern Europe, 1/27, 32, 5, 2003.

Butler, Lawrence, "Peace Implementation in Bosnia and Herzegovina: Challenges and Results," *Südosteuropa Mitteilungen*, 4–5, 2005, 73–7.

Camdessus, Michel, Speech delivered in Paris on October 18, 1998, www.imf.org/external/np/speeches/1998/012198.htm

Caron, François, *An Economic History of Modern France*, New York: Columbia University Press, 1979.

Cerami, Alfio, *Social Policy in Central and Eastern Europe: The Emergence of a New European Model of Solidarity*, Third Annual ESPAnet Conference, September 2–24, University of Fribourg, Switzerland, 2005.

Chandler, Alfred, *The Visible Hand: The Mangerial Revolution in American Business*, Cambridge, MA: The Belknap Press, 1977.

Scale and Scope: The Dynamics of Industrial Capitalism, Cambridge, MA: Harvard University Press, 1990.

Chandler, Alfred, Franco Amatori, and Takashi Hikino (eds.), *Big Business and the Wealth of Nations*, Cambridge University Press, [1997] 1999.

Churchill, Winston, "The Tragedy of Europe," [1946] in *His Complete Speeches, 1897–1963*, Vol. 7, in Brent F. Nelsen and Alexander C.-G. Stubb (eds.), *The European Union, Readings on the Theory and Practice of European Integration*, Boulder: CO: Lynne Rienner, 1998, 7–11.

Clark, Ian, *The Post-Cold War Order: The Spoils of Peace*, Oxford University Press, 2001.

Collier, Irwin, Herwig Roggemann, Oliver Scholz, and Horst Tomann (eds.), *Welfare States in Transition*, Houndmills: Palgrave Macmillan, 1999.

Consensus Economics, *Consensus Forecast*, April, 2005, www.consensuseconomics.com/-11k

Convention between Belgium, Germany, Spain, France, Luxembourg, the Netherlands and Austria in Stepping Up of Cross-border Cooperation Particularly in Combating Terrorism, Cross-border Crime and Illegal Migration, Brussels: Council Secretariat, July 7, 2005, 10900/05.

Crawford, Beverly, "Explaining Defection from International Cooperation: Germany's Unilateral Recognition of Croatia," *World Politics*, 48, 4, 1996, 482–521.

Crouch, Colin, *Social Change in Western Europe*, New York: Oxford University Press, 1999.

Cullen, L. M., *An Economic History of Ireland Since 1960*, London: Batsford, 1987.

Delgado Godoy, Leticia, "Immigration in Europe: Realities and Policies," www.iesam.csic.es/doctrab2/dt-0218e.pdf 2008.

Delors, Jacques, "Address by Mr. Jacques Delors, Bruges, 17 October 1989," in Brent F. Nelsen and Alexander C.-G. Stubb (eds.), *The European Union: Readings on the Theory and Practice of European Integration*, Boulder, CO: Lynne Rienner, 1998, 55–68.

Demographic Yearbook, New York: United Nations, 1982.

Dennett, Jane, Edward James, Graham Room, and Philippa Watson, *Europe Against Poverty: The European Poverty Programme 1975–80*, London: Bedford Square Press, 1982.

Derrida, Jacques, *Writing and Difference*, University of Chicago Press, [1967] 1978.

Dinan, Desmond, *Ever Closer Union?* Boulder, CO: Lynne Rienner, 1994.

Djilas, Milovan, "Hungary and Yugoslavia," in Béla Király *et al.* (eds.), *The First War Between Socialist States: The Hungarian Revolution of 1956 and Its Impact*, New York: Brooklyn College Press, [1957] 1984, 91–4.

Dulles, Allen, *The Marshall Plan*, Houndmills: Palgrave Macmillan, 1948.

Eberstadt, Nicholas and Hans Groth, "Healthy Old Europe," *Foreign Affairs*, May/June 2007, www.foreignaffairs.com/ . . . eberstadt-and . . . groth/healthy-old-europe

The Economist, September 9–15, 2006.
    January 6–11, 2007.
    March 24–31, 2007.
    July 7–13, 2007.
    June 21–7, 2008.
    October 11–17, 2008.
    October 18–24, 2008.
    October 25–31, 2008.
    March 7–13, 2009.
    May 2–8, 2009.
    May 9–15, 2009.

The Economist, *World in Figures, 2007*, London: Profile Books, 2007.

World in Figures, 2008, London: Profile Books, 2008.

Economist Intelligence Unit, *Country Reports*, London: The Economist, 2005.

Eichengreen, Barry, "Institutions and Economic Growth: Europe after World War II," in Nicholas Crafts and Gianni Toniolo (eds.), *Economic Growth in Europe Since 1945*, Cambridge University Press, 1996.

The European Economy Since 1945: Coordinated Capitalism and Beyond, Princeton University Press, 2007.

Eichengreen, Barry and Richard Kohl, "The External Sector, the State, and Development in Eastern Europe," in John Zysman and Andrew Schwartz (eds.), *Enlarging Europe: The Industrial Foundation of a New Political Reality*, Berkeley: University of California Press, 1998, 169–201.

El-Agraa, Ali, *The European Union: Economics and Politics*, Harlow: Prentice Hall, 2004.

Emmerij, Louis (ed.), *Economic and Social Development into the XXI Century*, Washington, DC: Inter-American Development Bank, 1977.

Enyedi, György, *Városi világ – városfejlődés a globalizáció korában*, Pécs: Pécsi Tudományegyetem Közgazdaság-tudományi Kara, 2003.

(ed.), *Social Change and Urban Restructuring in Central Europe*, Budapest: Akadémiai Kiadó, 1998.

Enyedi, György and Zoltán Koràcs (eds.), *Social Changes and Social Sustainability in Historical Urban Centers: The Case of Central Europe*, Pécs: Center for Regional Studies, 2006, 174–88.

Enyedi, Zsolt, "The Social and Attitudinal Basis of Political Parties: Cleavage Politics Revised," *European Review*, 16, 3, July, 2008, 287–304.

Esping-Andersen, Gøsta, *The Three Worlds of Welfare Capitalism*, Cambridge: Polity Press, 1990.

European Bank for Reconstruction and Development, *Transition Report Update*, London: EBRD, 1999.

Transition Report 2000: Employment, Skills and Transition, London: EBRD, 2000.

Transition Report 2001: Energy in Transition, London: EBRD, 2001.

Transition Report Update 2005, London: EBRD, 2005.

European Commission, *Basic Statistics of the Community*, Brussels: Statistical Office of the European Community, 1977.

Communication to the Council and to the European Parliament on the Establishment of a New Financial Perspective for the Period 2000–2006, Luxembourg: Office for Official Publications of the European Communities, 1998.

Education – Training – Research: The Obstacles to Transnational Mobility, Brussels: EcoSoc, 1997.

Educational Structures in the Member States of the European Communities, Brussels: European Commission, 1987.

Europe Agreements and Beyond: A Strategy to Prepare the Countries of Central and Eastern Europe for Accession, Brussels: Communication from the Commission to the Council, 1994.

European Economy, Brussels: European Commission, 2000.

European Social Policy: A Way Forward for the Union. A White Paper, Luxembourg: European Commission, 1994.

Eurostat, online, 2005.

Eurostat, The Life of Women and Men in Europe: A Statistical Portrait, Luxembourg: Office for Official Publications of the European Communities, 2008.

Eurostat, Regions: Statistical Yearbook 2005, Luxembourg: Office for Publications of the European Communities, 2005.

Eurostat Yearbook, Luxembourg: European Commission, 1998–99.

Gateway to Education: Socrates: European Community Action Programme in the Field of Education (2000–2006), Brussels: European Commission.

Regional Cooperation in South-east Europe: "Enlargement Package," ec.europa.eu/ enlargement/press_corner/key-documents/reports_nov_2007_en.htm-61k-

The Situation of Roma in an Enlarged European Union, Luxembourg: Office for Official Publications of the European Communities, 2004.

The Stabilization and Accession Process for South East Europe, First Annual Report, Brussels: European Commission, 2002.

The Third Report on Bulgaria, European Commission Against Racism and Intolerance, 2003, www.coe.int/t/e/human_rights/ecri/1-ecri/2-country-by-country_approach/Bulgaria/Bulgaria_CBS_3.asp-182k

Towards a European Research Area: Science, Technology and Innovation, Key Figures, Luxembourg: Office for Official Publications of the European Community, 2002, www.dft.gov.uk/stellent/groups/dft_about/documents/pdf/dft_about_pdf_503849.pdf-12k

Urban Sprawl in Europe: The Ignored Challenge, European Environmental Agency Report No. 10, Luxembourg: Office for Official Publications of the European Community, 2006.

European Council, *European Council in Copenhagen 21–23 June 1993*, Brussels: European Commission, 1995.

Presidency Conclusions of the Lisbon European Council on 24 March, Brussels: European Commission, 2000.

Statements on Education, Training and Young People 1998–2001, Luxembourg: Office for Official Publications of the European Community, 2002.

Strategies for Educational Reform: From Concept to Realization, Strasbourg: Council of Europe Publishing, 2000.

European Union, Maastricht Treaty, www.eurotreaties.com/maastrichttext.html-18k-

Activities of the European Union: Summaries of Legislation, europa.eu/scadplus/treaties/singleact_eu.htm-31k-

Evans-Pritchard, Ambrose, "Capital Flight Puts Russia on the Ropes," *Telegraph*, April 2, 2008.

Falkingham, Jane and John Hills, *The Dynamic of Welfare: The Welfare State and the Life Cycle*, Hemel Hempstead: Prentice Hall, 1995.

Fattore, Giovanni, "Cost Containment and Health Care Reform in the British NHS," in Elias Mossialos and Julian Le Grand (eds.), *Health Care and Cost Containment in the European Union*, Aldershot: Ashgate, 1999, 733–81.

Ferrazzi, Matteo and Alessia Muzio, "Europe's New Factory Comes Up in the East," *East Europe and Asia*, April, 2008, www.eastonline.it/index.php

Fine, Ben, Costas Lapavitsas, and Jonathan Pincus (eds.), *Development Policy in the Twenty-first Century: Beyond the Post-Washington Consensus*, London: Routledge, 2001.

Fischer, Wolfram, Jan A. van Houtte, and Herman Kellenbenz, *Handbuch der Europäische Wirtschafts- und Sozialgeschichte vom Ersten Weltkrieg bis zum Gegenwart*, Vol. 6, Stuttgart: Franz Steiner, 1987.

Flora, Peter and Arnold J. Heidenheimer (eds.), *The Development of Welfare States in Europe and America*, New Brunswick: Transaction Books, 1981.

Fortune magazine, July 25, 1994, money.cnn.com/magazines/fortune . . . /1994/ . . . 25 . . . index.htm

Foucault, Michel, *Madness and Civilization: A History of Insanity in the Age of Reason*, New York: Pantheon Books, [1961] 1965.

Politics, Philosophy, Culture: Interviews and other Writings, 1977–1984, New York: Routledge, 1988.

Friedman, Milton, *The Program for Monetary Stability*, New York: Fordham University Press, 1959.

Inflation: Causes and Consequences, New York: Asia Publishing House, 1963.

The Optimum Quantity of Money and Other Essays, Chicago: Aldine Publishing Co., 1969.

The Tax Limitation, Inflation and the Role of Governments, Dallas: Fisher Institute, 1978.

Fukuyama, Francis, "The End of History?" *The National Interest*, Summer, August 27, 1989, 27–46.

The End of History and the Last Man, Harmondsworth: Penguin, 1992.

Furet, François, *Interpreting the French Revolution*, Cambridge University Press, [1978] 1981.

G-24, *Coordinated Economic Assistance*, Brussels, June 13, 1991.

Gabanyi, Anneli Ute, "Rumänien: Populismus als Instrument der Machtsicherung," *Südosteuropa Mitteilungen*, 48, 2, 2008, 56–67.

Galbraith, John Kenneth, *The Great Crash 1929*, Boston, Hawghton Mifflin, [1954] 1961.

Garavini, Giuliano, "The Colonies Strike Back: The Impact of the Third World on Western Europe, 1968–1975," *Contemporary European History*, 16, 3, August, 2007, 141–59.

Garton Ash, Timothy, *The Polish Revolution: Solidarity*, New York: Vintage Books, 1985.

"Europe's Endangered Liberal Order," *Foreign Affairs*, 77, 2, March/April, 1988, 51–65.

Geyer, Michael, "The Subject(s) of Europe," in Konrad H. Jarausch, and Thomas Lindenberger (eds.), *Conflicted Memories: Europeanizing Contemporary Histories*, New York: Berghahn Books, 2007, 254–80.

Giddens, Anthony, "A Social Model for Europe?" in Anthony Giddens, Patrick Diamond, and Roger Liddle (eds.), *Global Europe, Social Europe*, Cambridge: Polity Press, 2006, 14–36.

Giddens, Anthony, Patrick Diamond, and Roger Liddle (eds.), *Global Europe, Social Europe*, Cambridge: Polity Press, 2006.

Global Power Europe, www.globalpowereurope.eu/2007/10/european-military-spending-must-be-more.html.126k-

Global Research, "Kosovo Independence: End of Europe: Top Political Analysts on Russian Foreign Minister Lavrov's Kosovo Warning," February 16, 2008, www.globalresearch.ca

Goldthorpe, John H. and Keith Hope, *The Social Grading of Occupations: A New Approach and Scale*, Oxford: Clarendon Press, 1974.

Golsan, Richard J., "From French Anti-Americanism and Americanization to the 'American Enemy'?" in Alexander Stephan (ed.), *The Americanization of Europe: Culture, Diplomacy, and Anti-Americanism after 1945*, New York: Berghahn Books, 2006, 44–68.

Gower, Jackie and John Redmond (eds.), *Enlarging the European Union: The Way Forward*, Aldershot: Ashgate, 2000.

Grazia, Victoria de, *Irresistible Empire: America's Advance Through Twentieth-Century Europe*, Cambridge, MA: The Belknap Press, 2005.

Greener, Ian, "Consumerism in Health Policy: Where Did it Come from and How Can it Work?" in Alison Hann (ed.), *Health Policy and Politics*, Aldershot: Ashgate, 2007, 59–74.

Habermas, Jürgen, "Modern and Postmodern Architecture," in Jürgen Habermas, *The New Conservatism: Cultural Criticism and the Historians' Debate*, ed. Shierry Weber Nicholsen, Cambridge, MA: MIT Press, 1989, 13–21.

"Neoconservative Cultural Criticism in the United States and West Germany," in Habermas, *The New Conservatism*, ed. Shierry Weber Nicholsen, Cambridge, MA: MIT Press, 1989, 22–47.

The New Conservatism: Cultural Criticism and the Historians' Debate, ed. Shierry Weber Nicholsen, Cambridge, MA: MIT Press, 1989.

"Taking Aim at the Heart of the Present: On Foucault's Lecture on Kant's What is Enlightenment?" in Habermas, *The New Conservatism*, ed. Shierry Weber Nicholsen, Cambridge, MA: MIT Press, 1989, 173–9.

"What Europe Needs Now," www.signandsight.com/features/1265.html

Hantrais, L., S. Mangen, and M. O'Brian (eds.), *Mixed Economy of Welfare*, Cross-National Research Paper, No. 6, Loughborough University, 1992.

Harding, Luke, "Tuition Fees Gain Allure in Cash Hit European Campuses," *The Guardian*, October 13, 2003.

Harrison, Joseph, *The Spanish Economy in the Twentieth Century*, London: Croom Helm, 1985.

Havel, Václav, "Paradise Lost," *The New York Review of Books*, April 9, 1992.

Hillgruber, Andreas, *Zweierlei Untergang: Die Zerschlagung des Deutschen Reichs und das Ende des europäischen Judentums*, Berlin: Siedler, 1986.

Hobsbawm, Eric, *On the Edge of the New Century* (conversation with Antonio Polito), New York: The New Press, 2000.

Hoffman, George W., *Europe in the 1990s. A Geographic Analysis*. Sixth edition, New York: John Wiley & Sons, 1990.

Hollander, Paul, *Anti-Americanism: Critiques at Home and Abroad, 1965–1990*, New York: Oxford University Press, 1992.

Hooghe, Lisbet (ed.), *Cohesion Policy and European Integration: Building Multi-Level Governance*, Oxford University Press, 1996.

Houg, Werner, Paul Compton, and Youssef Courbage, *The Demographic Characteristics of National Minorities in Certain European States*, Vol. 1, Strasbourg: Council of Europe, 1998.

Huntington, Samuel P., *The Third Wave: Democratization in the Late Twentieth Century*, Norman: University of Oklahoma Press, 1991.

Hunya, Gábor, "Restructuring Through FDI in Romanian Manufacturing," *Economic Systems*, 26, 4, 2002, 387–94.

Inklaar, Robert, Mary O'Mahony, and Marcel Timmer, *ICT and Europe's Productivity Performance*, Research Memorandum GD-68, Groningen: Groningen Growth and Development Center, December, 2003.

International Herald Tribune, May 4, 1996.

May 2, 2006.

November 30, 2007.

August 29, 2008.

International Labour Organization, *Year Books of Labour Statistics*, Geneva: ILO, 1980. "East European Healthcare in Crisis," Geneva, ILO/01/53, Press release, December 10, 2001.

Investment and Trade Development Agency, Hungary, *Newsletter*, June 25, 2008.

Iványi, Gábor, *Hajléktalanok*, Budapest: Sík Kiadó, 1997.

Jarausch, Konrad H. and Thomas Lindenberger (eds.), *Conflicted Memories: Europeanizing Contemporary Histories*, New York: Berghahn Books, 2007.

Jeffries, Ian, *The Countries of the Former Soviet Union at the Turn of the Twenty-first Century*, London: Routledge, 2004.

Johnson, Ailish, *European Welfare States and Supranational Governance of Social Policy*, Houndmills: Palgrave Macmillan, 2005.

Jones, C. (ed.), *New Perspectives on the Welfare State in Europe*, London: Routledge, 1993.

Jones, Geoffrey and Harm G. Schröter (eds.), *The Rise of Multinationals in Continental Europe*, Aldershot: Edward Elgar, 1993.

Judt, Tony, *A Grand Illusion? An Essay on Europe*, New York: Hill and Wang, 1996.

    Reappraisals: Reflections on the Forgotten Twentieth Century, New York: Penguin Press, 2008.

Kaelble, Hartmut, "Social Peculiarities of Nineteenth and Twentieth Century Europe," in Hartmut Kaelble (ed.), *The European Way: European Societies during the Nineteenth and Twentieth Centuries*, New York: Berghahn Books, 2004, 276–317.

    "A European Civil Society?" in Konrad H. Jarausch and Thomas Lindenberger (eds.), *Conflicted Memories: Europeanizing Contemporary Histories*, New York: Berghahn Books, 2007, 209–22.

    (ed.), *The European Way: European Societies during the Nineteenth and Twentieth Centuries*, New York: Berghahn Books, 2004.

Kaelble, Hartmut, Jürgen Kocka, and Hannes Siegrist (eds.), *Europäische Konsumgeschichte: Zur Gesellschafts- und Kulturgeschichte des Konsumes (18. bis 20. Jahrhundert)*, Frankfurt: Campus Verlag, 1997.

Kagarlitsky, Boris, "The Return of the Proletariat," *Moscow Times*, November 10, 2005.

Kezán, András, "E-kereskedelem az Európai Unióban," *Európai Tükör*, 13, 4, April 12–14, 2008.

Kleinman, Mark, *A European Welfare State? European Union Social Policy in Context*, Houndmills: Palgrave, 2002.

Koncz, Katalin, *Nők a munkaerő-piacon*, Budapest: Corvinus Egyetem, 2008.

Kraus, Franz, "Economic Equality: The Distribution of Incomes," in Peter Flora and Arnold J. Heidenheimer (eds.), *The Development of Welfare States in Europe and America*, New Brunswick: Transaction Books, 1981, 187–238.

Kroes, Rob, "Imaginary Americas in Europe's Public Space," in Alexander Stephan (ed.), *The Americanization of Europe. Culture, Diplomacy, and Anti-Americanism after 1945*, New York: Berghahn Books, 2006, 337–60.

    (ed.), *Neo-conservativism: Its Emergence in the USA and Europe*, Amsterdam: VU Uitgeverij, 1983.

Krugman, Paul, *The Return of Depression Economics and the Crisis of 2008*, London: Penguin, 2008.

Kuhnle, Stein, "The Nordic Welfare State in a European Context: Dealing with New Economic and Ideological Challenges in the 1990s," in Stephan Leibfried (ed.), *Welfare State Futures*, Cambridge University Press, 2001, 103–22.

(ed.), *Survival of the European Welfare State*, London: Routledge, 2000.

Kurz, Constanze and Volker Wittke, "Using Industrial Capacities as a Way of Integrating Central and Eastern European Economies," in John Zysman and Andrew Schwartz (eds.), *Enlarging Europe: The Industrial Foundation of a New Political Reality*, Berkeley: University of California Press, 1998, 63–95.

Ladányi, János and Iván Szelényi, "Class, Ethnicity and Urban Restructuring in Postcommunist Hungary," in György Enyedi (ed.), *Social Change and Urban Restructuring in Central Europe*, Budapest: Akadémiai Kiadó, 1998, 67–86.

Laqueur, Walter, *Last Days of Europe: Epitaph for an Old Continent*, New York: Thomas Dunne Books, 2007.

Larres, Klaus, "Margaret Thatcher, the British Foreign Office, and German Unification," *Cercles: Revue Pluridisciplinaire du Monde Anglophone*, 5, 2002, 165–73.

Leerkes, Arjen, Godfried Engbersen, and Marion Van San, "Shadow Places: Patterns of Spatial Concentration and Incorporation of Irregular Immigrants in the Netherlands," *Urban Studies*, 44, 8, 2007, 1491–516.

Leibfried, Stephan (ed.), *Welfare State Futures*, Cambridge University Press, 2001.

Leisner, Walter, *Demokratie: Selbstzerstörung einer Staatsform*, Berlin: Duncker und Humblot, 1979 quoted by Iring Fetscher (ed.), *Neokonservative und "Neue Rechte": Der Angriff gegen Sozialstaat und liberale Demokratie in den Vereinigten Staaten, Westeuropa und der Budesrepublik*, Munich: Verlag C. H. Beck, 1983.

Levitas, Ruth (ed.), *The Ideology of the New Right*, Cambridge: Polity Press, 1986.

Lindert, Peter H., "What is Happening to the Welfare State?" in Paul W. Rhode and Gianni Toniolo (eds.), *The Global Economy in the 1990s: A Long-Run Perspective*, Cambridge University Press, 2006, 234–62.

Livi-Bacci, Massimo, *The Population of Europe: A History*, Oxford: Blackwell, 2000.

Losoncz, Miklós, *Hungary's Competitiveness in International Comparison and its Driving Forces*, Budapest: Economic Research Co., 2003.

Loungani, Prakash and Paolo Mauro, "Capital Flight from Russia," *The World Economy*, 24, 5, 2001, 689–706. www.imf.org/external/pubs/ft/seminar/2000/invest/pdf/loung.pdf.

Ludlow, Piers N. (ed.), *European Integration and the Cold War: Ostpolitik–Westpolitik, 1965–1973*, London: Routledge, 2007.

Lyotard, Jean-François, *The Postmodern Condition: A Report on Knowledge*, Manchester University Press, [1979] 1984.

Maclennan, Robert, "Foreword," in Guido Snel (ed.), *Alter Ego: Twenty Confronting Views on the European Experience*, Amsterdam University Press, 2004.

Maddison, Angus, *Explaining the Economic Performance of Nations*, Aldershot: Edward Elgar, 1995.

Monitoring the World Economy 1820–1992, Paris: OECD, 1995.

Two Crises: Latin America and Asia 1929–38 and 1973–83, Paris: OECD, 1985.

The World Economy: A Millennial Perspective, Paris: OECD, 2001.

The World Economy in the 20th Century, Paris: OECD, 1989.

Magone, José M., *The Politics of Southern Europe: Integration into the European Union*, Westport, CT: Praeger, 2003.

Marcuse, Herbert, *One Dimensional Man*, London: Routledge, 1964.

Marshall, Thomas H., *Citizenship and Social Class and Other Essays*, Cambridge University Press, 1950.

Mastanduno, Michael, *Economic Containment: CoCom and the Politics of East-West Trade*, Ithaca: Cornell University Press, 1992.

McCullagh, C. Behan, *The Logic of History: Putting Postmodernism in Perspective*, London: Routledge, 2004.

McMillan, James Edward F., *Twentieth-Century France: Politics and Society, 1898–1991*, London: Arnold, 1992.

Meinecke, Friedrich, *Weltbürgertum und Nationalstaat: Studien zur Genesis des deutschen Nationalstaates*, Munich: R. Oldenbourg, 1908.

Michnik, Adam, "Confessions of a Converted Dissident: Essay for the Erasmus Prize," 2002, Alexandria Biblioteka online www.alexandria-press.com/online/online20_adam_michnik_ confessions.htm-49k-

"The Return to History," *Central Europe Review*, 1, 17, 1999. Online: www.ce-review.org/99/17/michnik17_speech.html

Takie czasy – rzecz o kompromisie, London: Aneks, 1985.

Milanovič, Branko, *Income, Inequality and Poverty During the Transition*, Washington, DC: The World Bank, 1996.

Mitchell, Brian R., *International Historical Statistics: Europe 1750–1993*, fourth edition, London: Macmillan, 1998.

"Statistical Appendix," in Carlo Cipolla (ed.), *The Fontana Economic History of Europe: Contemporary Economies*, Vol. 6 (2), London: Collins/Fontana Books, 1976.

Mitterauer, Michael, "A 'European Family' in the Nineteenth and Twentieth Centuries?" in Hartmut Kaelble (ed.), *The European Way: European Societies during the Nineteenth and Twentieth Centuries*, New York: Berghahn Books, 2004, 140–60.

Mitterauer, Michael and Reinhard Sieder, *The European Family: Patriarchy to Partnership from the Middle Ages to the Present*, Oxford: Blackwell, 1982.

Morrison, Rodney J., *Portugal: Revolutionary Change in an Open Economy*, Boston: Auburn House, 1981.

Mossialos, Elias and Julian Le Grand (eds.), *Health Care and Cost Containment in the European Union*, Aldershot: Ashgate, 1999.

Mount, Ferdinand, *The Subversive Family: An Alternative History of Love and Marriage*, London: Jonathan Cape, 1982.

Muço, Marta and Luljeta Minxhozi, "Albania: An Overview Ten Years After," in Domenico Nuti and Milicia Uvalic (eds.), *Post-Communist Transition to a Market Economy: Lessons and Challenges*, Ravenna: Longo Editore, 2003, 181–202.

Nelsen, Brent F. and Alexander C.-G. Stubb (eds.), *The European Union: Readings on the Theory and Practice of European Integration*, Boulder, CO: Lynne Rienner, 1998.

Ners, Krzysztof J. and Ingrid Buxell, *Assistance to Transition Survey 1995*, Warsaw: PECAT, 1995.

New York Times, June 18, 2008.

October 24, 2008.

October 25, 2008.

October 28, 2008.

January 12, 2009.

January 15, 2009.

January 17, 2009.

March 2, 2009.

March 8, 2009.

March 13, 2009.

Noin, Daniel and Robert Woods (eds.), *The Changing Population of Europe*, Oxford: Blackwell, 1993.

Nolte, Ernst, "Die Vergangenheit, die nicht vergehen will," *Frankfurter Allgemeine Zeitung*, June 6, 1986.

Norpoth, Helmuth, "Guns and Butter and Government Popularity in Britain," *The American Political Science Review*, 81, 3, September, 1987, 949–59.

Nove, Alec, *The Soviet Economy*, New York: F. A. Praeger, 1966.

OECD, *Economic Outlook*, No. 15, Paris: OECD, 1974.

   Economic Outlook, Paris: OECD, 1982.

   Employment Outlook, Paris: OECD, 1997.

   Employment Outlook, Paris: OECD, 2004.

   Factbook, Paris: OECD, 2008.

   Factbook: Economic, Environmental and Social Statistics, Paris: OECD, 2007.

   Health Data, Paris: OECD, 1997.

   Measuring Globalization: The Role of Multinationals in OECD Economies, Paris: OECD, 1999.

   OECD in Figures, 2007, Paris: OECD, 2007.

   Science, Technology and Industry Outlook, Paris: OECD, 2000.

   Structural Adjustment and Economic Performance, Paris: OECD, 1987.

   The Welfare State in Crisis: An Account of the Conference on Social Policies in the 1980s, Paris: OECD, 1981.

Palánkai, Tibor, *Economics of Enlarging European Union*, Budapest: Akadémiai Kiadó, 2004.

Palomba, Rossella, "Value Preferences and Attitudes on Population," in Rossella Palomba and Hein Moors (eds.), *Population, Family, and Welfare: A Comparative Survey of European Attitudes*, Vol. 2, Oxford: Clarendon Press, 1998, 51–71.

Palomba, Rossella and Hein Moors, "The Image of the Family," in Rossella Palomba and Hein Moors (eds.), *Population, Family, and Welfare: A Comparative Study of European Attitudes*, Vol. 2, Oxford: Clarendon Press, 1998, 72–93.

Palomba, Rossella and Hein Moors (eds.), *Population, Family, and Welfare: A Comparative Survey of European Attitudes*, Vol. 2, Oxford: Clarendon Press, 1998.

Pelikan, Jiři, *The Secret Vysocany Congress: Proceedings and Documents of the Extraordinary Fourteenth Congress of the Communist Party of Czechoslovakia, 22 August, 1968*, London: Allen Lane, 1971.

Perlstein, Steven, "As Russia Advances, High Tech Gets Left Behind," *Washington Post*, July 11, 2007.

Pinder, John, "European Community and Nation-State: A Case for a Neofederalism?" *International Affairs*, 62, 1, January 1986, reprinted in Brent F. Nelsen and Alexander C.-G. Stubb (eds.), *The European Union: Readings on the Theory and Practice of European Integration*, Boulder, CO: Lynne Rienner, 1998, 189–94.

Piore, Michael J. and Charles F. Sabel, *The Second Industrial Divide: Possibilities for Prosperity*, New York: Basic Books, 1984.

Polanyi, Karl, *The Great Transformation: The Political and Economic Origins of our Time*, Beacon Hills: Beacon Press, [1944] 1957.

Pollack, Mark A. and Gregory G. Shaffer (eds.), *Transatlantic Governance in the Global Economy*, Lanham: Rowman and Littlefield Press, 2001.

Presvelou, Clio, "Crises et économie informelle: Acquis et interrogations," *Recherches Sociologiques*, 25, 3, 1994, quoted by Colin Crouch, *Social Change in Western Europe*, New York: Oxford University Press, 1999.

Prizel, Ilya, "The First Decade After the Collapse of Communism: Why Did Some Nations Succeed in their Political and Economic Transformation, While Others Failed?" *SAIS Review*, 19, 2, 1999, 1–15.

Rasmussen, Poul N., "Renewing not Rolling Back Social Europe," in Detlev Albers, Stephen Haseler, and Henning Meyer (eds.), *Social Europe: A Continent's Answer to Market Fundamentalism*, London Metropolitan University, 2006, 117–24.

Reinhard, Wolfgang, *Lebensformen Europas: Eine historische Kulturanthropologie*, Munich: C. H. Beck, 2004.

Report of the Ministry of Economy and Transportation, Budapest: Hungarian Ministry of Economy, July 12, 2006.

Reuters Report on IMF emergency rescue actions, March 4, 2009, www.alertnet.org/thenews/newsdesk/L4817108.htm-.36k

Revue Elargissement, 43, April 12, 2003.

Rhode, Paul W. and Gianni Toniolo (eds.), *The Global Economy in the 1990s: A Long-Run Perspective*, Cambridge University Press, 2006.

Santini, J.-J. (ed.), *Les privatisations à l'éntranger: Royaume-Uni, RFA, Italie, Espagne, Japon*, Paris: La Documentation Française, 1986.

Sassen, Saskia, *The Global City: New York*, Princeton University Press, 1991.

Sassoon, Donald, *The Culture of the Europeans from 1800 to the Present*, London: HarperCollins, 2006.

Saward, Michael, "Making Representation: Modes and Strategies of Political Parties," *European Review*, 16, 3, July, 2008, 271–86.

Schönwälder, Karen, "Integration from Below? Migration and European Contemporary History," in Konrad H. Jarausch and Thomas Lindenberger (eds.), *Conflicted Memories: Europeanizing Contemporary Histories*, New York: Berghahn Books, 2007, 154–63.

Schüler, Sonja, "Zur politischern Kultur im heutigen Bulgarien," *Südosteuropa Mitteilungen*, 48, 2, 2008, 38–55.

Schumpeter, Joseph, *Capitalism, Socialism and Democracy*, London: Allen and Unwin, 1976.

Scoreboard of Assistance Commitments to the CEEC 1990–1994, Brussels, February 8, 1995.

Scruton, Roger, *The Meaning of Conservativism*, London: Penguin, 1980.

Sen, Amartya, *Inequality Reexamined*, Oxford: Clarendon Press, 1992.

Simai, Mihály, "The World Economy and Europe at the Beginning of the 21st Century," *Development and Finance*, 1, 2006, 3–11.

Singer, Edward N., *20th Century Revolution in Technology*, Commack, NY: Nova Science Publisher, 1998.

SIPRI Yearbook 2008: Armaments, Disarmament and International Security, Stockholm International Peace Research Institute, 2008.

Snel, Guido (ed.), *Alter Ego: Twenty Confronting Views on the European Experience*, Amsterdam University Press, 2004.

Soros, George, *The Crisis of Global Capitalism: Open Society Endangered*, New York: PublicAffairs, 1998.

 Bulletin of the European Union, "Special Berlin Council 24–25 March, Conclusion of the Presidency," 3, 1999.

Špidla, Vladimir, "Some Reflections on the European Social Model," in Detlev Albers, Stephen Haseler, and Henning Meyer (eds.), *Social Europe: A Continent's Answer to Market Fundamentalism*, London Metropolitan University, 2006, 111–17.

Der Spiegel, October 23, 2006.

Standards and Guidelines for Quality Assurance in the European Higher Education Area, Helsinki: European Association for Quality Assurance in Higher Education, 2005.

Steiner, Michael, "Restructuring Industrial Areas: Lessons in Support of Regional Convergence in an Enlarging Europe," in Gertrude Tumpel-Gugerell and Peter Mooslechner (eds.), *Economic Convergence and Divergence in Europe*, Cheltenham: Edward Elgar, 2003, 86–107.

Stephan, Alexander, *The Americanization of Europe: Culture, Diplomacy, and Anti-Americanism after 1945*, New York: Berghahn Books, 2006.

 "Cold War Alliances and the Emergence of Transatlantic Competition: An Introduction," in Alexander Stephan (ed.), *The Americanization of Europe: Culture, Diplomacy, and Anti-Americanism after 1945*, New York: Berghahn Books, 2006, 1–22.

Stiglitz, Joseph, "The EU's Global Mission," April 22, 2007, in *Project Syndicate*, www.project-syndicate.org/commentary/stiglitz85

Stonor Saunders, Frances, *The Cultural Cold War: The CIA and the World of Art and Letters*, New York: New Press, 2000.

Swyngedouw, Erik, Frank Moulaert, and Arantxa Rodriguez, *The Global Restructuring and Social Polarization in European Cities*, Oxford University Press, 2003.

Sýkora, Luděk, "Commercial Property Development in Budapest, Prague and Warsaw," in György Enyedi (ed.), *Social Change and Urban Restructuring in Central Europe*, Budapest: Akadémiai Kiadó, 1998, 109–36.

Szanyi, Miklós, "Experiences with Foreign Direct Investment in Eastern Europe," *Eastern European Economics*, 36, 3, May–June, 1998, 24–48.

Tableau de bord des aides d'état, Commission of the European Union, Brussels: European Commission, 2002.

Teodorović, Ivan, Željko Lovrinčević, Davor Mikulić, Mustafa Nušinović, and Stjepan Zdunić (eds.), *The Croatian Economic Development: Transition Towards the Market Economy*, Zagreb: Institute of Economics, 2005.

Thatcher, Margaret, Speech at the College of Europe in Bruges, September 20, 1988, reprinted as "A Family of Nations," in Brent F. Nelsen and Alexander C.-G. Stubb (eds.), *The European Union: Readings on the Theory and Practice of European Integration*, Boulder, CO: Lynne Rienner, 1998.

Thomas, Martin, Bob Moore, and L. J. Butler, *Crisis of Empire: Decolonization and Europe's Imperial States, 1918–1975*, New York: Oxford University Press, 2008.

Thornton, Bruce, *Decline and Fall: Europe's Slow Motion Suicide*, New York: Encounter Books, 2007.

The Times, March 10, 2007.

Tocqueville, Alexis de, *The Old Regime and the French Revolution*. Gloucester: Peter Smith, 1978.

Tokes, Rudolf L. (ed.), *Eurocommunism and Détente*, New York University Press, 1978.

Transparency International, Worldwide Corruption Perception Index, www. transparency.org/policy.research/surveys_indices/cpi-19k-

Tumpel-Gugerell, Gertrude and Peter Mooslechner (eds.), *Economic Convergence and Divergence in Europe*, Cheltenham: Edward Elgar, 2003.

Tupy, Marian L., "The Rise of Populist Parties in Central Europe: Big Government, Corruption, and the Threat of Liberalism," Washington: CATO Institute, November 8, 2006, www.cfr.org/publication/11847/cato_institute.html

Turnovec, František, "Political Economy of Social Welfare Reform: The Parliamentary Elections of 1996 in the Czech Republic," in Irwin Collier, Herwig Roggemann, Oliver Scholz, and Horst Tomann (eds.), *Welfare States in Transition*, Houndmills: Palgrave Macmillan, 1999, 144–36.

Ugalde, Antonio and Gilberto Cárdenas, *Health and Social Services among International Labor Migrants: A Comparative Perspective*, Austin, TX: CMAS Books, 1997.

UNCTAD, *World Investment Report*, New York: United Nations, 2006.

UNICEF, *Central and Eastern Europe in Transition: Public Policy and Social Conditions: Crisis in Mortality, Health and Nutrition*, Economies in Transition Studies, Regional Monitoring Report, No. 2, Florence: UNICEF Regional Office, August 1994.

Social Monitor 2003, Florence: Innocenti Research Centre, 2003.

United Nations, *Economic Survey of Europe*, New York: UN, 1991.

Economic Survey of Europe, New York: UN, 1998.

Economic Survey of Europe, New York: UN, 2000.

Economic Survey of Europe, New York: UN, 2004.

Economic Commission for Europe, *Aging Populations: Opportunities and Challenges for Europe and North America*, New York: United Nations, 2003.

United Nations Conference on Trade and Development: Handbook of Statistics, Online.

USA Today, February 18, 2008.

Vaknin, Sam, "The Dying Breed: Healthcare in Eastern Europe," 2006, www.samvak.tripod.com/pp143.html

"World in Conflict and Economies in Transition," United Press International, May 9, 2002, www.samvak.tripod.com/briefs/html-22k

Van Ark, Bart, Robert Inklaar, and Robert H. Guckin, "ICT and Productivity in Europe and the United States: Where do the Differences Come From?" *CESifo Economic Studies*, 49, 3, 2003, 295–318.

Van der Wee, Herman, *Prosperity and Upheaval: The World Economy 1945–1980*, Berkeley: University of California Press, 1986.

Van het Loo, Mirjam, James P. Kahan, and Kieke G. H. Okma, "Developments on Health Care Cost Containment in the Netherlands," in Elias Mossialos and Julian Le Grand (eds.), *Health Care and Cost Containment in the European Union*, Aldershot: Ashgate, 1999, 573–603.

Van Kempen, Ronald, Marcel Vermeulen, and Ad Baan, *Urban Issues and Urban Policies in the New EU Countries*, Aldershot: Ashgate, 2005.

The Visegrád Yearbook, Budapest: Central European Partnership Organization, 2003.

Wall Street Journal, June 1, 1992.

November 7, 1995.

March 30, 1998.

Warnes, Anthony, "Demographic Ageing: Trends and Policy Responses," in Daniel Noin and Robert Woods (eds.), *The Changing Population of Europe*, Oxford: Blackwell, 1993, 82–99.

Weimer, Wolfram, *Deutsche Wirtschafts-geschichte: Von der Währungsreform bis zum Euro*, Hamburg: Hoffman und Campe, 1998.

Williamson, John, "The Washington Consensus Revisited," in Louis Emmerij (ed.), *Economic and Social Development into the XXI Century*, Washington, DC: Inter-American Development Bank, 1997, 48–61.

Wittgenstein, Ludwig, *Philosophical Investigations*, Oxford: Blackwell, 1953.

Wolin, Richard, "Introduction," in Jürgen Habermas, *The New Conservatism: Cultural Criticism and the Historians' Debate*, ed. Shierry Weber Nicholsen, Cambridge, MA: MIT Press, 1989.

World Bank, *Global Economic Prospects and Developing Countries*, Washington, DC: World Bank, 1997.

World Bank Report, Washington, DC: World Bank, October 12, 2005.

World Development Indicators, Washington, DC: World Bank, 2007.

World Tables 1984–90, Washington, DC: World Bank, 1990.

World Tourism Organization, *Tourism 2020 Vision*, Madrid: World Tourism Organization, 2001.

Young, Hugo, *This Blessed Plot: Britain and Europe from Churchill to Blair*, London: Macmillan, 1998.

Zajda, Joseph (ed.), *International Handbook on Globalization, Education and Policy Research*, Dordrecht: Springer, 2005.

Zaslove, Andrej, "Here to Stay? Populism as a New Party Type," *European Review*, 16, 3, July, 2008, 318–32.

Zilahy, Péter, "How European," in Guido Snel (ed.), *Alter Ego: Twenty Confronting Views on the European Experience*, Amsterdam University Press, 2004, 129–39.

Zysman, John and Andrew Schwartz (eds.), *Enlarging Europe: The Industrial Foundation of a New Political Reality*, Berkeley: University of California Press, 1998.

Index